Reviews:

"In Douglas Boggs' book *"Quantum of Justice"* we see a first-hand account of the breakdown and failures of the US banking industry and the jurisprudence system that we all thought was designed to protect consumers from abuse. While introducing readers to technical concepts that the average layperson is unaware of, such as non-judicial foreclosures, he takes us through a very human story to give a palpable context and insight into the damage that these technicalities can cause. This book serves as both a cautionary tale of the dangers of playing in a world with an inherent unfair playing field, as well as, a glimpse of just how hard a determined man is willing to work."

Paul F Bohan, Vice-Chairman Hyperledger Fabric SIC, CEO and Chairman, Lenderblocks, Inc.; former Board Member, Mortgage Bankers Assoc. of America's Secondary Market and Capital Markets Committees; Founder, CEO and Chairman of The Bohan Group, Inc.

. . . .

"In *Quantum of Justice,* Douglas J. Boggs documents the same injustice resulting from fraud in our courts that I have observed as a lawyer fighting foreclosures in Washington state for over a decade. The fraud which I believe routinely occurs in this area of law because, as Boggs explains in his book, our judges too often allow our courts to be used to process foreclosures in order to transfer the Peoples' wealth to money lenders, debt buyers and their government supporters, which include the judges themselves. Boggs makes this point over and over again in many different ways. Perhaps best by attempting to square the kangaroo court proceedings he found himself in with those concepts of justice and law which have traditionally been applied to litigants by judges over the centuries.

Quantum of Justice is well worth a read because it demonstrates to all – lawyers, non-lawyers, and citizens alike – the modern judiciary's brazen indifference to those ideals which our ancestors determined were necessary for the legitimate exercise of judicial power by governments."

Scott Stafne – (Stafne Law) permitted to practice before the United States Supreme Court, the Ninth Circuit Court of Appeals, and the United States District Courts for the Eastern and Western Districts of Washington; Washington Supreme Court justice candidate; Washington Congressional candidate

. . . .

"I thought I understood a lot, but my good friend and inspiration, Douglas Boggs, demonstrated to me what a warrior for truth and justice actually constitutes. Boggs painstakingly deconstructs and demonstrates exactly how the world's largest conspiracy played out in the courts that destroyed tens of millions of lives. To say what Doug accomplished is beyond believable might barely

scratch the surface of the insane amount of work he had to foster through his own effort that would turn the entire fraud inside out and answer questions about the court system that is nothing short of monumental.

Every single person who lost their home to foreclosure must read this to come to understand the mechanics of how it all works and to what end. The determination to lay it out on a silver platter is like nothing I have ever experienced. I think *"Quantum of Justice"* should be read by every person in this country as a cold bucket of water to the face about how power in this country truly works and towards what ends. If I didn't live through it myself, I wouldn't believe it. Trust me, you have to read this book to understand what happened to you and all of us. It's an accomplishment that defies reason."

Producer of the acclaimed films THE CON and "Waking Up the American Dream"; and Podcast "The New Untouchables" "The New Untouchables" Patrick S. Lovell

....

I truly believe that your book fully encompasses EVERY single aspect of fraudulent real estate transactions which are supposed to be a system that has the interest of the "homeowner" in mind but of course, that would be further from her "truth." This book is directly helping me in staying in my home and to be able to fight back against these real estate tyrants. This is a great book for ALL those who are going to be purchasing their first home or want to learn more in detail of the real estate transaction process, this will cover it all. I hope to meet you one day Mr. Boggs, as I cannot fully describe to you what an astronomical help you have given me and my future family ... thank you for going through the wringer and coming out with a great message.

Alex Keleman

....

When Truth is all that will do ... I am the co-host of the podcasts *The New Untouchables* and the host of *Macro n Cheese* and founder of the nonprofits *Real Progressives and Real Progress in Action*. I work with the whistleblowers and modern untouchables who know this game inside and out.

Doug is a well-researched writer who has documented fraud that he experienced and had the smarts to fight back. This book is a must read for anyone interested in seeing how deep the rabbit hole of corruption goes. Be careful. Be warned. You will not be the same after reading this masterpiece.

Steven D. Grumbine, MBA –Founder of RealProgressives.org and Real Progress in Action; Modern Monetary Theory expert and Founder/CEO of Real Progressives.org

. . . .

I received my *Quantum of Justice* book today around 12:30 this afternoon and I can't put it down. I've already learned something new on pick-a-pay-loans. This is the loan with Wells Fargo that landed me a wrongful foreclosure and illegal eviction causing me to lose everything I owned and my home. To the author, Douglas Boggs, thank you for sharing your story and for all your hard work. You are a warrior! If you're reading my review and you're in foreclosure, buy this book. You won't be sorry.

Wendy Cottrell

. . . .

I read this book to try to understand how so many foreclosures happened in California. Having lived through the torture of foreclosure himself, Douglas undertook a massive feat in writing at a level equal to a master of an unjust real estate market unknown to the common person. His research is astounding in scope, and he was able to explain it in a way that a layperson could mostly understand. It is a difficult read for a person unfamiliar with foreclosure but is a very important book that shows how rampant the fraud is, and how easily it is perpetrated by large real estate investors, banks, and judges. [This is true] Even as he worked tirelessly for years to save his house. A must read for anyone looking at foreclosure.

Denise Cook

. . . .

Doug Boggs bravely puts the truth to paper for all to know what our criminal system is doing to its citizens every day. It is authentic. It is heartfelt. It is heroic. I appreciate being able to recommend my friend's book to my homeowners for some comfort. To let them know they are not alone. White-collar crime is not victimless. This Mafia crime headed by Wall Street, our government, enforced by our legal system and law enforcement, is responsible for PTSD on a massive national level, illness, divorces, domestic abuse & violence, homelessness, and countless suicides (which I like to label manslaughter).

Nationally recognized paralegal; as seen in the film "THE CON"
Paris Dube

QUANTUM

OF

JUSTICE

**THE FRAUD OF FORECLOSURE AND THE ILLEGAL
SECURITIZATION OF NOTES BY WALL STREET**

"... the true David and Goliath story of one man against the system"

Douglas J Boggs

Copyright ©2021 by Douglas J Boggs. All rights reserved.

No part of this publication may be reproduced, stored in a retrieval system, or transmitted in any form or by any means, electronic, mechanical, photocopying, recording, scanning, or otherwise, without either the prior written permission of the publisher. For information address the Permissions Dept., Olive Publishing, LLC, 30 N Gould St., Suite 4000, Sheridan, WY 82801

Limit of Liability/Legal Disclaimer: While the publisher and author have used their best efforts in preparing this book, they make no legal representations and any information contained in this book is not intended to constitute legal advice. Readers should not act upon any information within this book without seeking professional legal counsel. The advice and strategies contained herein may not be suitable for your situation. Neither the publisher nor author shall be liable for any loss of profit or any other commercial damages, including but not limited to special, incidental, consequential, or other damages.

Every reasonable attempt has been made to trace copyright holders of material reproduced in this book, but if any have been inadvertently overlooked the publishers would be glad to hear from them.

Edited by Kat of Genesis Design and Editing, LLC; Cover Art by Ola Betiku; Cover layout by Ruth Adedeji

Library of Congress Cataloging-to-Publication Data:

Boggs, Douglas J - Quantum of Justice – The Fraud of Foreclosure and the Illegal Securitization of Notes by Wall Street /

Douglas j Boggs - "An Olive Publishing, LLC book"   First U.S. Edition 2021

includes exhibits and references

1. Fraud 2. Foreclosure 3. Truth 4. Justice 5. Securitization 6. Deed of Trust 7. Wells Fargo Bank 8. Title 9. Douglas J Boggs

ISBN(s) - 978-1-7364715-4-8 hardcover; 978-1-7364715-0-0 softcover; 978-1-7364715-3-1 audiobook; 978-1-7364715-2-4 Ebook

https://quantumofjustice.com - book website
10 9 8 7 6 5 4 3 2 1

Table of Contents

Acknowledgements	3
Foreword	7
From the Author	11
The Beginning	21
Part One	21
Part Two	31
Part Three	49
Paralegal	69
Trustee	79
Deed of Trust	97
Bona Fide Purchaser	119
Presumption of Correctness	125
The Law	129
Corruption	141
Fraud (18 U.S.C. 47 § 1001)	151
World Savings	185
Unlawful Detainer	189
Objection to Summary Judgement	227
The Making of Senate Bill 1638 to Amend CA Civil Code 2934a	303
Securitization	331
New Legal Actions for Standing	401
The Final Stand on Standing	405
A Call to Action	417
Postscript	419
Exhibits	423

Acknowledgements

A project like this cannot be completed alone. It takes a village. It takes people filled with interest and compassion to work through it to the end result. I want to take this opportunity to acknowledge the efforts of those who without their inclusion in the creation of this book, and their participation in my life, it would have never come to pass.

A very special thank you goes out to Michelle Moquin. Without our life and work together we would have never been able to complete the arduous process of such a major legal endeavor of suing one of the largest corporations in the country. We would have never been able to uncover the systemic atrocities and expose them. We scaled and moved mountains. Your tireless and attentive work helped us both navigate the legal world and the ways of jurisprudence. We went into the trenches together and twenty-five years later we both came out changed forever.

A special thank you goes to Bill, my friend to the end. You have led me through the darkness to help me open my mind to see that which normally remains unseen. You have shown me and exposed me to things that man has yet to learn and I am forever in your debt. Your guidance and encouragement were paramount in helping me through this entire process. My life here is forever changed because you are in it. You will forever be my Yoda.

To Joan Ivazes, for being by my side through so much. For hearing me tell these stories over and over again and always being there feigning a continued interest. I appreciate those endless conversations where you would get me to continue to clarify things so that it would finally end up being understood. When I would see your eyes gloss over, I knew where I needed to rewrite. For your support and confidence that I would be able to finally pull this project off. I can only hope that your love, kindness, assistance and participation in this project and in my life has not left you lingering and loitering for too long in the darkness.

To Maria Hollowell-Fuentes, for all of your help with the hundreds of documents that I wrote up that needed proper Service of Process. You were always there to make sure that the documents were served.

To Leah Ahn for working on your case in the San Francisco Law Library, it was nice to bounce ideas off of each other.

To the University of CA Berkeley Law Library, the Hastings Law Library, the San Francisco Law Library, and the Alameda County Law Library for all of your assistance in helping find the necessary volumes of Bender books and such in order to complete my lawsuit effectively.

To Marv Hippen, my high school creative writing instructor, you allowed me the freedom to begin my writing adventure. When you gave me an A++ for my 108 page "short story" assignment, you gave me the confidence to not let go of my desire to become a writer. It took a little while, but here we are! I also wish to express my gratitude to Don Swenson. You pulled me out of high school study hall and into your office to teach me the art of meditation, manifestation and Buddhism. You have no idea how much that action affected my life, and I am forever grateful for your insight, empathy and compassion.

To my editor Kat of Genesis Design and Editing, LLC, for taking over where Debs Arden left off. You coached me and guided me through the post-production and editing process. I appreciate you for allowing me to go through the editing process together in which for me was a very unconventional way to, what I thought was, the usual book writing process. You have taught me invaluable information as I move forward for my next writing project. You came into my project at just the right time and were able to be those final eyes of detail that caught all of the nuances that were glossed over. I cannot thank you enough for your diligence and thoroughness making the final manuscript worthy of the expectations that I was looking for.

To Bonnie Coren, for your extra set of eyes and your attention to detail. I appreciate your putting yourself out there to help me with beta-reads and other extra editing issues. You have heard me talk about this project since the day we met, and it has finally come to pass! Your excitement while reading gave me peace in knowing I was successful in trying to create a page turner.

To Krista Taylor, for being there at just the right time. I appreciate your ears for listening to me read, your interest and creativity for helping me reach my final cover concept, and for your business acumen to help me traverse some of the tasks necessary to complete such a project. I am grateful for your heart for holding space and allowing me and my project the room necessary to expand and become the flower that I have always wanted to see bloom. I am grateful for you to help the light shine brightly so my dream could have the energy needed to become what I was wanting it to be. I look forward to so much more as this is just the beginning.

To Ola Betiku for my cover art. To Ruth Adedeji for completing the cover design. You both delivered on my idea in such a professional manner. Your talents are comforting in knowing my project was in the right hands. I look forward to doing more work with you.

To Patrick Lovell, for your keen intelligence and our endless conversations on topics that most people find difficult to hold with cognitive dissonance. We have both pulled back the curtain, taken a peek behind and have been exposed to the nasty parts of our world. We have been through the ringer of emotional content in order to bring our individual messages to the public in order to inform the readers and viewers of a truth that is staring us all in the face, but most people refuse to allow themselves to see. I can only hope that through my book, and your film series, "The Con", will we be able to shed the necessary light on such powerful information that becomes palatable enough to the masses in order to help facilitate the changes that are necessary to a broken and corrupt system.

To all at Olive Publishing, LLC, for coming forward to publish this "pain in my ass". All of your efforts and tireless work to get this out and into the public will never go unappreciated. A very special Thank You to your staff for always being there to coach me through the stages of creating this book. You all have helped me continue to see the light at the end of the tunnel, all the while helping me see the forest through the trees. You have held the torch for me when I have stumbled, and you have carried me when I could no longer move forward.

To my family for being there when I was broken so that I could learn to pick up the pieces again. A special Thank You to you, Mom. Without your encouragement and support, our lengthy discussions, and without your unending faith in me, I would have never been able to make it to the end of this process. I wish I could have finished this before Dad left this realm. You both taught me to stand up to what is wrong no matter if you are the only one standing. Your faith in me during this process helped me hold my head high knowing that I had more than only a quantum of justice with the system but was backed by truth.

Foreword

Life is really a ridiculous juggernaut of survival meets the enlightened capacity to ensure survival. As Americans, we're all taught from an early age the entire point of our country is the equality and integrity of the rule of law. Presumably, this meant that no one is above the law and everyone is accountable to it. Given the revelations of the recent past, most of us have come to the conclusion that this assumption is unfortunately the presumption of making an ass out of you and me. We all know the system is rigged. We all know the system is corrupt. But few of us know how.

It's the embodiment of this massive perversion that led me on my journey. I am the filmmaker of a 5-part docu-series, entitled The Con, that painstakingly deconstructs the largest engineered financial crime and cover up in history.

Like millions of others, I lost my home to foreclosure. The process that got me to that point never made any sense and always seemed to create a mountain of questions against what the mainstream media was reporting at that time versus what I was experiencing. One thing led to another, and I found the opportunity to try and untangle this madness and eventually me and my team did, to a point. However, as most of us have learned that have gone the distance in this madness, one can never fully understand every aspect of this massive, massive, criminal enterprise because it never ends. However, my friend and author of Quantum of Justice did exactly that.

It's difficult to quantify the effort Doug went through against all odds to pull this mammoth revelation together, but suffice to say, he did so with a heroic and herculean effort, and I'm befuddled how he did it.

Let me first say that I think this effort is worthy of every American who cares about the importance of the system of justice in our country. However, I recommend this as a necessary read for anyone who went through the foreclosure crisis of the 09-12 vintage and of course all who are going through it today, because surprise folks, nothing has changed.

Doug masterfully deconstructs the largest engineered crime and cover up in history as it literally unwinds in the courts. To fully understand how the system gets away with it, you have to understand how the system is set up, and how it's supposed to function and that's how you uncover how it's anything but the way it's designed to be.

Doug Boggs was an all-around renaissance man before the collapse of 2008. He worked in the music industry in the San Francisco bay area with some of the biggest acts in rock & roll history and he was the CEO of a real estate investment group and designer/builder of significant accomplishment. For anyone who understands those professions, you would know how incredibly capable and detailed one has to be to flourish in both respected enterprises. Doug's experience evolves harmonically in his seemingly effortless approach to the literary translation of legalism hell.

What I found incredible was this unbelievably honest portrayal of his perspective of the world he thought he actually lived in with the tumultuous world he discovered in the aftermath of the '08 colossal wreckage.

For those of you who lived through the madness and continue to do so, you'll come to discover your story embedded in Doug's revelations. You'll come to remember, and possibly re-experience, the trauma of dealing with the run around of servicers and supposed modification policies that never added up.

Most of us gave up early. Most of us just threw in the cards because we thought we failed and did what the media said we did, which was to bite off more than we could chew. Most of us had no idea we were set up in the largest heist in the history of the world and many of us actually owned our homes outright before we got hooked into the conveyor belt of disaster, otherwise known as the securitization process.

Look, there's a lot of elements to this. There's a lot of nuances baked in from state to state depending on the judicial/non-judicial status and everything that tends toward, however, it's all the same story. The 2008 housing collapse and foreclosure crime literally impacted tens of millions of people if not hundreds of millions. It wasn't a natural disaster. The whole thing was designed.

I knew I was being played 12 years ago and that's how it led to my odyssey. I've crisscrossed the nation 12x's picking up different pieces of the puzzle and quite frankly I thought I knew a lot. But in comparison to Doug, I didn't know the details in a way I do now having read his masterpiece.

When I was a kid growing up in the 70's, I loved the Steven Spielberg movie called, "Close Encounters of the Third Kind". I literally became Richard Dreyfuss' character building the Devil's Tower in my kitchen by the time I first started piecing my story together. And I know millions of you feel the same way. When I went on my journey of discovery, I came to understand millions of us were discovering the same thing. When the mainstream media and government shut us down, we found each other. And from that growth came even more discovery.

My team and I were so incredibly lucky to put our movie, The Con, out there for the world to see. But I'm here to tell you, the genuine masterpiece is what Doug Boggs has managed to put on paper. It's like the ABCs of the largest criminal enterprise in history and what he discovers is what we all know intuitively. That the judicial system played accomplice to the financial mob scheme that rules this country. When you find out how, first your head will explode, and then you'll want to get it together and join Doug's just war against corruption.

There is only one pathway forward and that's the truth. Doug has served it up to us on a silver platter. All you have to do is educate yourself through his work. Quantum of Justice is a game changer if millions of us get on board.

Patrick S. Lovell

~ Producer of the acclaimed films "THE CON" and "Waking Up the American Dream"; and Podcast "The New Untouchables".

From the Author

Either write something worth reading or do something worth writing.

~ Benjamin Franklin ~

Writing this book has been the most challenging experience that I've ever had in my life. I must have started over at least ten times. It has been a project that I have worked on, or thought about in some capacity, every day for the past ten years. I thought that suing Wells Fargo Bank, one of the nation's largest corporations, while I was acting as my own attorney was hard, and it certainly was by all accounts. However, trying to put this information together in book form, so that other people would be able to understand it, and possibly be entertained sufficiently to stay interested and learn from my experiences, is another mountain to climb entirely. Well, all of that was a task at a level of difficulty that I didn't fully comprehend when I set out on this journey. It's hard enough to deliver the facts to people who understand the ins and outs of real estate, contracts and their intricate laws and procedures. But I've come to find that, sometimes, we know things to a point where we become too close to the information and can't see the forest for the trees.

I invite you to read this book from the beginning through to the end, in its entirety, first. This book is designed so that you, the reader, can take yourself through all the text, including the detailed legal documents that have been inserted to help lay out the legal premise and theories involved so you are able to learn the information in the way it unfolded to the author. Through the text and the legal documents, the truth and the legal story will unfold in a way that I hope will convey clear and meaningful information that you can take with you and understand those things that pertain to your own life situation. There are sections in the book where I revert back in time, and it seems confusing. Like taking one step forward and two steps back. This was intentional for the reader to feel slightly confused while learning such detailed and delicate information just as it was when I learned it. I want the mind of the reader to be malleable and open to learn within the confusion.

There were times when I'd look back while I was writing this and think, "Why couldn't I have just moved on and restarted my life? Why did I feel the need to put myself through this legal nightmare?" In addition to that, after the legal action, I asked myself, "Why do I continue with this and feel the need to write a book?" My conscience just wouldn't let me move on without addressing the problem. What problem? Well, where shall I begin?

We will have a detailed look at the current state of affairs, however, here's a bit of background. Let us go back to June 6, 1933, when President Roosevelt signed into law a bill written by congressional sponsors, Senator Carter Glass and Representative Henry B. Steagall. This legislation described four basic provisions of what became known as the United States Banking Act of 1933. Their bill was designed to separate commercial and investment banking to help stave off another Wall Street collapse similar to the Great Depression of 1929. At the time, the country was still feeling the depths of its destruction. The sponsors of the bill were both Southern Democrats. Senator Carter Class of Virginia, who in 1932 had been in the House, Secretary of the Treasury, or in the Senate for the preceding thirty years, and Representative Henry B. Steagall of Alabama who had been in the House of Representatives for the preceding seventeen years.

The idea was to separate commercial and investment banking to prevent securities firms and investment banks from taking deposits, and commercial Federal Reserve member banks from:

1. dealing in non-governmental securities for customers,

2. investing in non-investment grade securities for themselves,

3. underwriting or distributing non-governmental securities,

4. affiliating (or sharing employees) with companies involved in such activities.

Interpretations of the Act, beginning in the 1960s by federal banking regulators, allowed a wider interpretation of the Act to be permitted to commercial banks, and especially commercial bank affiliates, to engage in an expanding list and volume of securities activities. There were congressional efforts to repeal the Glass-Steagall Act, referring to those four specific provisions. Even more specifically, there were only two provisions that restricted affiliations between commercial banks and securities firms. The fight against the Act finally culminated during the Clinton Administration in 1999 with the passing of the Gramm-Leach-Bliley Act. This Act repealed the two provisions, restricting affiliations between banks and securities firms.

By that time, there were many commentators who argued that Glass-Steagall was already "dead". One most notable action was an interpretation under the Federal Reserve Board of the 1998 affiliation between Citibank and Solomon Smith Barney, one of the largest U.S. securities firms at the time. The board's interpretation and permission to allow these two companies to do business together made President Clinton publicly declare "the Glass-Steagall Act of 1933" was no longer appropriate.

Some commentators have stated that the Gramm-Leach-Bliley Act and its repeal of the affiliation restriction of the Glass-Steagall

Act was an important cause of the financial crisis of 2008. Joseph Stiglitz, the noted Nobel Prize winning economist laureate, argued that the effect of the repeal was "indirect", stating, "when repeal of Glass-Steagall brought investment and commercial banks together, the investment-bank culture came out on top." However, economists at the Federal Reserve, such as Chairman Ben Bernanke, argued that the activities linked to the financial crisis weren't prohibited (or in most cases, even regulated) by the Glass-Steagall Act.

Ben Bernanke attended Harvard University in 1971, where he lived in Winthrop House, along with the future CEO of Goldman Sachs, Lloyd Blankfein. He was named chairman of President George W. Bush's Council of Economic Advisers in 2005. This council was largely viewed as a test run to the president's choice to succeed Greenspan as Federal Reserve chairman the following year on February 1, 2006. By virtue of his chairmanship position, he also sat on the Financial Stability Oversight Board, which oversaw the Troubled Asset Relief Program (TARP) or the socialist bailout for the "too big to fail" corporations that created the economic collapse of 2008. After the public watched the multi-trillion-dollar bailout of Wall Street and the financial system juggernauts by President Bush and also President Barack Obama, who referred to Bernanke as "the epitome of calm", he was confirmed for a second term on January 28, 2010.

Now, I'm just trying to get some clarity here. Bernanke argues that the activities linked to the financial crisis were not prohibited and/or even linked to the financial crisis of 2008 by the Glass-Steagall Act. But wouldn't it seem logical that because of the actions created by the 1933 legislation, and the fact that there hasn't been any catastrophic collapse since then, it could be argued that it was largely due to the regulations associated with the Act? And if the deregulation of the Glass-Steagall Act in 1999 — through the Gramm-Lean-Bliley Act — took away those regulations, and subsequently only a handful of years followed before there was a global economic crisis, one could also easily argue that those regulations, and similar ones, are deemed necessary to maintain a more regulated Wall Street. It has been exposed and proven countless times since 2008 that Wall Street and the financial institutions that helped perpetuate the 2008 economic disaster each received hundreds of billions of dollars in government assistance. Yet we, the taxpayers, have found little to no help through any restitution, litigation, or legislation.

It is certainly clear that it doesn't matter which party is in the White House. Since the Great Recession of 2008, Republican President George W. Bush has spent over $700B in bailout loans to Wall Street and other financial institutions. Following this was Democratic President Barack Obama handing over more than $1T in additional government payments — funded by us, the people, through taxes — socialist assistance to the corporations, leaving the people in its wake.

There have been no new regulations signed since then that changed any of the behavioral patterns, which helped the financial institutions destroy the global economy. In fact, during the Trump Administration, we found that we had a president who was widely known as someone who had made much of his money purchasing foreclosed properties, creating even less oversight of Wall Street. In fact, he even wrote a book on the subject titled *Art of the Deal*. Also, he named Steve Mnuchin as his Secretary of the Treasury. Mnuchin is also widely known as a foreclosure king who, as a board member, oversaw the bankruptcy and liquidation of retail giants Sears and K-Mart before buying the failed residential lender IndyMac during the 2008 financial breakdown. Which when all is said and done, he purchased without having to use his own money. In fact, the government paid him to take over the firm.

In addition to this, during the Obama administration, Mitch McConnell, the Kentucky Senator who held the Senate leadership position, blocked hundreds of Federal bench seats from ever bringing any Obama administration nominations to the floor for a vote. Now, while the Trump administration was in the White House, McConnell opened the floodgates and over 25% of all Federal judge seats have been filled with Republican nominees, many of whom have no legal background, whatsoever.

Make no mistake, I enjoy a good pot of stew. However, the ingredients are not looking too healthy, and things seem as if the pot is about to boil over once again.

It looks like the emperor has a new coat.

* * *

In early 2014, when arguing our fourth amended complaint in court, I finally asked the judge, "Your honor, with all the evidence that we've presented here in your court over the past three and a half years of this litigation, and the 114 different motions and responses in this case that have been submitted, I ask Wells Fargo Bank to answer this one detailed question. If they can simply answer it and tell me that I am wrong, I'll stop the litigation and leave. And the question is this, your honor:
"Isn't it true that a financial institution knows that a trustee in a Deed of Trust contract has absolutely no power to police a beneficiary's actions in a power of sale clause in such a contract due to SB1638(1996), which beginning on Jan. 1, 1998 changed the wording to California Civil Code section 2934(a) therein giving the power to the beneficiary to substitute the trustee at their will, thereby eliminating any independence that the trustee is supposed to possess,

as originally intended by the State Supreme Court in 1978 through the Garfinkle v Contra Costa County case?

As a lender knows this and can subsequently choose the trustee who will do the bank's bidding for them, they can therefore submit fraudulent documents at any time to the county office and illegally begin the foreclosure procedure against any borrower and steal their home whether they are current on their mortgage or not. Isn't this prima facie evidence that there is no independence of the trustee in a Deed of Trust?

And if the trustee doesn't hold any power to police the actions of the beneficiary in a Deed of Trust agreement, doesn't that make the deed of trust agreement void on its face? And if the banks know this and fail to inform the borrower of this fact, doesn't it then mean that this is actionable fraud based on the withholding of vital information that would be pivotal to the borrower's final decision-making process before entering into the contractual agreement? And through the deceptive acts of the lender in the real estate transaction by withholding information from the borrower, doesn't this simply mean that there is not a true meeting of the minds due to the contract's concealment of information by the bank from the borrower? And if there were no true meeting of the minds, which is a cornerstone of contract law and the definition of a legal, binding agreement based on the statute of frauds (1677), does not this mean the contract is then indeed void?

And if the Deed of Trust agreement is void, does it not mean that the beneficiary can be held liable for all the funds they received from the borrower throughout the duration of the contract agreement, including penalties? And wouldn't it also mean that they deceived the court by stating that they have any standing or jurisdiction to argue a contract that is void on its face due to the fraud they perpetrated against the borrower now here in the court?

And wouldn't they also be liable to the borrower for all profits made by their manipulation of the borrower's contract through the securitization of that note on Wall Street. And would the beneficiary also be liable to the borrower for committing mail fraud for every document sent to the borrower during the duration of the contract, thereby acting on behalf of a fraudulent contract agreement to entice and coerce to incite any payments or penalties accrued from the borrower based on the fraudulent Deed of Trust contract agreement?

And wouldn't that also mean the security with which that contract was pooled into each tranche of an investment vehicle, such as a mortgage-backed security, then indeed, be based on fraud, making that investment vehicle void? And wouldn't the beneficiary also be liable to the court for knowingly deceiving and committing fraud against the court for every Deed of Trust and foreclosure document filed into the court system?"

The judge sat quiet and motionless. One could hear a pin drop in the capacity filled courtroom of Alameda County, CA. You could see the wheels of jurisprudence weighing heavily behind the eyes of the electable caped adjudicator.

"Can they show me that I am wrong?" I added as the string of lawyers from Wells Fargo Bank sat silently with no response.

They couldn't show the court that I was wrong then and are unable to still today.

But let's not get ahead of ourselves. Let's go back to the beginning.

Full disclosure: *I have read the book, written by the former reality TV star and doubly impeached former President of the*

United States, Donald Trump's, Art of the Deal. I have purchased foreclosed properties, and I have also had to deal with the litigation of foreclosure. Over the years, I've supported Republican, Democrat, and Independent politicians. I have been the CEO of companies in various states and have never declared bankruptcy.

Science and real-life experience have shown us that humans have extreme difficulty self-regulating as a species.

The Beginning

Part One

Okay, if you are a bank, you are in the lending business. If you are a bank that lends money to borrowers to buy real estate, then you are also in the foreclosure business. You see, if you are a bank that lends money to borrowers to buy real estate, then the chances are extremely high that you've foreclosed on a borrower. If you are a bank, then it is your obligation — according to the Universal Commercial Codes (UCC) — to know the rule of law and the ethics of doing commerce as it applies to you and your business. If you lend money, it is your obligation to know the rule of laws that pertain to lending money. If you lend money for real property transactions, it is your business obligation to know the rule of law pertaining to real estate transactions. If you lend money for real property and have foreclosed on a borrower, then it is your obligation as a business to know and follow the rule of laws regarding foreclosure as they pertain to each state.

If you are a borrower, your sole obligation is to pay your mortgage. If you do that, you are supposed to be able to say that eventually you will own your home. But what if none of this were true?

Let's say you want to buy a home, but you might need $500,000 that you don't have. You will need to borrow the money if you want to buy that home. Our society has developed a structure for this kind of transaction. In fact, it is something that happens across the world, day in and day out. But what if the system that we've all come to take for granted as being lawful, fair, and balanced was all just smoke and mirrors? Millions of people have entered into debt by borrowing money for a home, their business, a new car, or college. Hundreds of millions of people put their trust in the systemic façade with their life savings. Most people have entered the world of debt in one shape or another. But for right now, we are going to deal with real estate.

Now, to borrow the money to buy that house, there is a high chance that you will be dealing with a Deed of Trust real estate contract. In a Deed of Trust contract, it is the trustee who is part of the transaction to make sure that both the borrower and the lender act in accordance with the rules of law throughout the duration of the real estate contract. They are acting on behalf of the courts and the legal system through the Deed of Trust agreement. But what do you do when you find out that a trustee holds absolutely no power to protect your title from the bank from any wrongdoing? What do you do when you find out that the banks know that the trustee holds no power to protect your title from any harm or fraudulent acts, yet will offer the borrower a Deed of Trust contract to buy that house?

The borrower places a certain amount of trust in the system, believing that they are not being defrauded or swindled by the financial institution as there are rules and laws in place to monitor the actions of the lending institution. This trust comes from the design of the system that has placed a third party into the transaction to act on behalf of the courts to make sure the rules of law are followed by both parties. Sort of like the hall monitor. Simple, right? In fact, California's Supreme Court explicitly stated in Garfinkle v. Superior Court of Contra Costa County (1978) that "... the trustee in the transaction is to be an independent third party and held at arm's length ...." The trustee is the party tasked to watch over the borrower and the lender in the contract to oversee and administer the rules of the contract for both parties fairly, and act upon that information in proxy for the court system. But something happened on the way to the forum.

I never had reason to know or even doubt any of this prior to buying any property. But sometimes life throws you into an abyss that you are then supposed to find your way out of. So, as the mouth of the abyss opened and I began to fall into a foreclosure process of my own, I began to ask different questions that revealed information to me in a different light. I read a lot. I asked questions that lawyers do not find any reason to ask. However, when I discovered another party can take your home from you even if you are current on your mortgage or paid cash and had never used a bank, this was information that I just couldn't let go of. As I learned the details about this, I felt that I wanted people to understand how fraudulent and corrupt our systems had become. I couldn't simply walk away from someone who was stealing and pilfering everything I had spent the past decades working for from under me and in such a fraudulent and illegal manner. Grand theft. And not only me, but it was also happening to millions across the nation.

I needed to confront them and try to stop them. I realized during the process that this wasn't only about trying to save my home from being foreclosed on illegally. It was also about trying to put a stop to how this could happen to anyone, anytime, anywhere. I wanted to try to put a stop to the corruption happening daily across the country and fix the system that had become so broken. It might have been admirable, or maybe just stupid. Either way, I ultimately came to understand that I was naïve. I was hoping to fix a proverbial hole in the proverbial boat. When I tried the legal avenues, I saw firsthand how corrupt things had become. It was now a two headed monster that was much more than I could handle alone. However, I believe that by writing this book, I might plant seeds in others, so that, in their own way, they could take up the torch to help move things forward and create reparations and a means of change for the future.

Most people don't have the capacity to fight the financial institutions while going through such a personal nightmare as a foreclosure, whether they use an attorney or not. And that's okay. Most people lose their homes by acquiescence and try to move on with their lives. And that's okay, too. Most tend to shy away from the world of law due to its confusing processes and hard to understand rules and language. And that is okay, too. We must maintain our own levels of sanity and know our own capabilities when we're dealing with such a difficult situation. But I hope that upon completion of reading this book, you will understand your place in your struggle and find a new strength to perhaps take up the task to confront the atrocities that happened to you. I hope that you can begin to find answers to your situation that will help shed light, so you have a clearer understanding of what has happened to you.

Those people who have or are stepping up and fighting the system against their foreclosure, should understand that you are a rare breed. If you are doing so as your own attorney, even more kudos are saved for you.

We are told that some of the most stressful events that people have in their lives are divorce, moving, job loss, losing their home, and major injury to name a few. Due to the nature of the repercussions of the 2008 economic collapse, I know I and millions of others had to deal with many of those issues all at the same time. While coping with those most stressful life events simultaneously, I also had to learn the world of law. It became imperative that I understand the ways of writing legal documents, so that I could submit different motions and responses in our legal case effectively. I had to learn how to publicly argue my case file in the court of law in front of a judge. I had to understand how to deal with the different types of courts and their various rules in CA Superior, Appellate, State Supreme, Federal District court, Unlawful Detainer court, and IRS court. In my case, I was juggling numerous courts and cases all at the same time. Learning how to put my emotions in check to accomplish the legal processes in front of me was paramount. I had to learn all of this while going through the most challenging and emotional time of my life.

* * *

I grew up in the quaint, Midwest town of Mount Vernon, Iowa. It is a historic, small college town in the eastern part of the state, where the corn and soybeans grow tall, and everyone knows everybody else and their business. The beautiful tree lined streets, with one traffic light and barely 2000 people, is an idyllic place for a family to grow. My parents worked hard trying to make an all-American family. We would pack all five of us into the small, baby-blue Ford Pinto station wagon and go on a vacation every year. Despite the high interest rates or gas rations of the 1970s, my parents would find a way for us to venture around the United States to grow and learn.

We would go camping in Minnesota in the summer or skiing in Colorado in the winter. My father once put together a caravan of people and we headed to an Indian reservation in Washington State with some of the church congregation to help rebuild the Native American community. There was a college football Rose Bowl in California or Sugar Bowl in New Orleans. Dad was able to get tickets from his college coaching friends around the nation, who he knew through his part-time college football coaching and various refereeing positions.

Sometimes, on trips, we would walk through our country's history in Gettysburg or Monticello because of some James Joyce books that my parents had recently read. They worked hard to give us a life they never had and made it seem that everything would always be okay. Perhaps this came from their strong religious faith that they tried to pass on to their children. My father was hard working, and strong on common sense. He was a blue collar, self-educated and self-employed businessman for most of his life. My mother was an intelligent, hardworking elementary school teacher. They were vocal members and leaders of their respective unions throughout their lives. They fought hard in their careers for better pay and protection for their pensions. They took truth to task.

I believe I received my inquisitive nature from my parents. Although I didn't know it at the time, upon reflection and writing this book, I realized that this was where I got the strength to fight against Wells Fargo Bank. As a child, I was taught to try to right wrongs in a constructive way, and that truth was the better part of valor. Also, respect and common decency were the cornerstones of becoming a decent human being. I learned to take a stand against those who wronged me and to hold firm and oppose the injustices against our fellow human beings. I didn't know it then, and they certainly didn't either, but my parents had prepared me for this moment in time.

By the time Wall Street imploded on itself in 2008, I had become a professional real estate investor/developer and builder. I owned or was a partner in twenty different front doors across the country. Those front doors were on condos, apartments, and single-family homes, all of which were being rented. Frequently, I traveled to Florida, Nevada, Arizona, New Mexico, and Texas from my home base in California to deal with various property, sales, purchases or tenant issues. I was also heavily involved in the development and building of eighteen new homes I had designed for a new golf course community east of Dallas, Texas, when August 2008 happened. At that time, I was employing nearly thirty people in Texas and had another fifteen employees for projects being handled by my construction company in California. Then, overnight, it all just stopped; the economy shut down and it all came to a screeching halt.

When Wall Street collapsed, President George W. Bush was dealing with the fallout and constructing the bailout packages for the same companies that had created the debacle. There were certain sectors of work across the nation that hadn't just tapered off but stopped. Those main sectors of industry were real estate and construction. Both of which had become my means of livelihood for well over the past decade. By the time I had to deal with my foreclosure situation, I had been out of work for almost two years. I was running out of savings which left me no money for an attorney. So, I had to act as my own. But I was current on my mortgage.

I'm no rocket scientist, or brain surgeon, and certainly not an attorney. However, someone told me once that an attorney is simply someone who knows sufficient material well enough on a particular day to be able to answer enough questions to pass a test. That is all.

Over time, they become experienced and experts at a certain point in their craft, but we must remember that they are human just like everyone else. They have their points of personal contention, their own bills to pay, and their place of personal growth just like everyone else.

My background in real estate or contracts is nothing special outside of simply doing the processes that I had learned for my building and real estate businesses over the previous decades. However, circumstances put me in a situation where I had to be my own attorney. I subsequently began looking at the foreclosure and judicial processes through a non-attorney's eyes. By doing this, I was able to see things others missed that didn't seem right. They did not follow the rules of law or logic. Not being an attorney allowed me to see legal issues that just didn't make any sense. It let me see things that an attorney wouldn't notice because they couldn't see the forest for the trees.

* * *TEXAS* * *

The tiny, pink bloom sat alone under the hot sun among the dry grasses behind the new home. In the back patio area of no man's land, the lone flower danced and swayed in the breeze. It was the part of the construction site where materials had normally been piled. Only, at this point of the building project, the home was nearly complete. Some of the landscaping was being put in, but everything was going slow and had nearly come to a stop. There was no more money left. As the developer, I felt as though I had failed.

Feeling as alone as the flower, I was by myself that day, trying to complete the punch list of finish work for the final details of the home I had designed and built. I was hoping to do so without having a complete nervous breakdown but couldn't understand what had happened. I thought I had thought of everything. However, I hadn't planned on an entire global economic collapse. Over the years, I had learned to diversify my real estate investment portfolio by purchasing properties throughout the United States. So, I wasn't solely invested in one property or region. But this was something of a different circumstance altogether.

Chase bank was the construction lender on my home I was building, and they decided to stop paying the declared construction payments due on each home that my company was trying to complete, despite the approved independent inspections and signoffs clearing the funds for release. The economic collapse of August 2008 happened just six months earlier. But the world was still turning, and we were now sitting in deep doo-doo. Wall Street and the "too big to fail" financial institutions had already received their multi-billion-dollar bailout packages. However, the banks had stopped creating any new lending, making the real estate and construction industries come to a complete halt. Now, it seemed that they had also decided to stop honoring their previous construction lending contracts, leaving me and my firm out to dry for well over $500,000.

Mine was a small firm, and this was killing me. My employees and various subcontractors had been working on the first four homes that I had going up. But now, there I was, alone in Texas and some 2000 miles away from my home in California, still trying to finish the homes using funds out of my own pocket. I was trying to do right and finish so that the investors and I might be able to sell the homes and recoup some of our investment. It was, indeed, a losing battle. Being bled dry, I came to the realization that things weren't going to turn around any time soon. Things were dire and I was done.

Deciding to try to clear my head again, my emotions came and went in waves. Some days I could last for a few hours, but this day seemed to be catching up with me. After working for about twenty minutes, the anguish would become completely overwhelming. It reached the point where all I could do was sit in the corner with my head in my hands, sobbing, and watching from the outside as the world I had designed and created simply imploded. There seemed to be nothing I could do about it.

I went outside to the back of the house. The home sat with a southwest twist, so the patio area faced the lake and looked over the

13th fairway. As I closed the sliding glass door, the sound of classical music from the radio began to fade into the background of the gentle wind. I had spent many days in a haze as millions of thoughts and doubts crowded my sanity. Meandering aimlessly, I sat down in the grass that was only eking out its existence in the dry ground located just thirty minutes east of Dallas, TX.

Until the moment that I sat cross-legged, my hands in my lap, I hadn't noticed it. Taking a deep breath, I saw the small, delicate flower sitting all alone right in front of me. I reached down and gave it a gentle caress. It caught me for that moment. I was impressed and taken aback how such a fragile, yet beautiful plant managed to find its way in such a place. There were no other flowers around as far as I could see. Just groomed dry grass and weeds in the "out of bounds." However, this one bloom struggled triumphantly to keep its existence through the dried-out, clay soil.

That flower saved my life that day. It showed me that, despite the odds, you can still come out of some of the harshest situations and flourish. I heard its swan song screaming at me, telling me to keep my chin up and my head in the game. Sometimes, life isn't easy and can get really messed up. But on that day, this flower shouted out to me that no matter how stark things might seem, you can make it through. Sitting there with the lone flower, feeling the breeze caress my skin and the Texas midday sun quickly heating us both, I took a sip from my bottle of water. I gave the last few sips of water to the flower, thanked it, got up and went back inside to see about getting more work done.

* * *OAKLAND, CA* * *

The envelope was postmarked Dec. 31, 2010. Nothing could have prepared me for what I found inside when I opened it. I don't think anyone ever really could be. It is powerful just how much weight one single sheet of 20lb paper, with the words **"Notice of Default"** printed across it can make you feel. (See Exhibit 1a-c) It began with my legs becoming weak, followed by a shortness of breath. A slight fog began to cloud my vision as the blood drained from my head. The sounds became muffled and quieter, as if large, cotton wool balls were slowly being slipped into my ears. My heart was beating more erratically, and I could hear it getting louder as the noises outside my head were snuffed out by those imagined cotton wool balls. Let us just say that it can make someone feel as if they are carrying the weight of the world on their shoulders.

I needed to sit down on our 1950s retro, orange sectional sofa from Sears. I stared across the living room, looking deep into the colorfully stained tree stump chair that we spotted while on a vacation a few years before and had shipped home. It was created by a Balinese artist who had carved a fish scene into the wood and accentuated it with a beautiful, hand-rubbed stain. I was looking right through it simply trying to figure things out that I didn't understand.

The air was stiff and confining. I felt its syrupy heaviness as I inhaled. The act of breathing had become substantially more difficult. I felt as if the living room's golden, sponge painted walls were closing in on me. For me, it is a day that will live in infamy. It became one of those defining moments that I knew would remain embedded deep within my psyche for the rest of my life.

Maybe if I breathe into a bag.

Foreclosure? Why? What in the hell is going on?

I mean, we were current on our mortgage payments.

Part Two

The Hebrew word for pillar refers to a garrison or a deputy, or something that is set to watch over something else to help protect it. Due to the de-regulation of the financial industry by President Bill Clinton in 1999, there was no longer anyone left watching over the pillars of Wall Street. It had all become the financial wild, wild west.

With the derailing of the financial regulations, Wall Street firms eventually began paying off, or shall I say, illegally bribing the credit rating agencies, such as Moody's, Standard and Poor's, and Fitch. To get their flawed securities, Wall Street peddled a more favorable investment rating than they deserved. The payback for these payoffs were a AAA credit worthiness rating of funds, mortgages, corporations, mortgage-backed securities, and other financial instruments. They needed these ill-gotten ratings to sell the underperforming mortgage-backed securities into packages for hedge funds at a premium. These false AAA securities would eventually crumble as they were based on the houses of cards that were already tumbling. The pillars of Wall Street had eroded and there was no one watching over and protecting the public anymore. It has been proven time and again that absolute power corrupts absolutely, and due to this, as a species, we are incapable of policing ourselves against the demon called greed. However, Wall Street remained unregulated, unhinged, and paid out billions of dollars of bonus packages to their employees for doing fraudulent acts against the public.

It was in 2005 when Wall Street began the process of creating an investment instrument allowing investors to bet against the real estate market. It began with Goldman Sachs through what became known as credit default swaps (CDS) against vulnerable, subprime mortgages and mortgage-backed securities (MBS).

There were others who saw the writing on Wall Street. Those who created the global economic collapse knew. The participants who relished profits over ethics knew. So, they came to the trough of excess to feed and engorge themselves to the detriment of the rest of society. It was they who committed rampant and systemic fraud. It was "they" who created it. But who is the proverbial "they"? Wall Street is the "they". How can I state that "they" knew it and created it? Let us pull back the curtain to see who the "they" are. According to the book, *Too Big to Fail (2009)*, by Andrew Ross Sorkin, a special meeting was held by:

1. The presiding Secretary of the Treasury Hank Paulson

(July 2006 – Jan 2009)

2. The Chairman of the Federal Reserve Ben Bernanke

(Feb 2006 – Jan 2014)

3. New York Federal Reserve Chairman Timothy Geithner

(Nov 2003 – Jan 2009 Taking over Secretary of the Treasury after Paulson)

4. FDIC Chairman Sheila Bair

(Jun 2006 – July 2011)

They attended this secret meeting on October 13, 2008, at which a plan was presented to the CEOs of nine major banks. The now infamous meeting of thirteen high-ranking, financial juggernauts met privately in a room to discuss the government giving hundreds of billions of dollars to the financial institutions to bail them out, to keep them from failing due to the massive losses they had created by not being fiscally responsible and regulating themselves. The financial losses were rampant and overextended their balance sheets by well over 1000%, in many cases through fraud and misappropriation. The government thought these corporations needed to be rescued from their impending bankruptcies, which they had created themselves.

These unregulated financial institutions knew of the imminent economic collapse, because it has since become evident that they were betting against the securities they were selling in order to manage the downside risk of those securities. They began putting huge investments into insuring the mortgage-backed securities they were selling. They knew those securities were bad performers, which is why they paid off the credit agencies for the high AAA ratings. They bought insurance policies against possible failure of those securities. The Wall Street firms knew because they spent billions insuring themselves against the upcoming "theoretically possible" heavy financial losses. It was unclear how far things would collapse, but as time and the economy played itself out from 2008 until today, we have found that those firms not only bought insurance against their investments, but they also advised their clients to buy the investments that they knew to be worthless, in order to create commissions for the firm. The Wall Street firms knew they would profit either way as they were covered by their insurance premiums when things went south.

Despite Wall Street making these bets, the reaction from them was that there were tens of millions of families who had seemingly "got themselves into the same situation" as the corporate mass media began putting it. Millions mysteriously seemed to have suddenly reached a point where they were unable to pay their mortgages. Ironically, it seemed as if, according to the government and the media, for some reason, tens of millions of American families had all purchased loans that they couldn't afford. Wall Street was shifting the blame and collecting the money. The word on the street would always be that tens of millions of Americans all made the same wrong decision. It was being reported to us that a large percentage of the American people were deadbeats trying to cheat the system. The counter statements were that the small cadre of large financial institutions, which no longer had oversight or regulations, was in the "right". So, the banks received trillions of dollars from the government. Now, remember, the word government here simply means the American people, through taxes. First, through a generous bailout from the Bush administration, then another from the Obama administration. This was paid for with the tax dollars of the same people whom the banks were stealing homes from. The global economy had crashed in 2008, and the American economy was now going into its third year of serious job loss, long-term unemployment, and economic instability. But it still seemed to be the fault of the tens of millions of deadbeat borrowers. It just didn't make sense to me.

By the beginning of 2008, the insanity of it all was that the Wall Street trading houses had been using fraudulent payoffs and reinsurance strategies for over a decade or more. At that point, this was no in-house secret. But bear in mind, no one knew the extent of what was going to happen when the dominoes began falling. Outside of that small investment world, the rest of the planet was shocked when the entire house of cards came tumbling down so quickly. It surprised everyone because it had become such a convoluted process of shuffling assets, corrupt rating practices, bogus accounting practices, and simply blatant lies and fraud. This was so much so, that there were very few people who could even understand what Wall Street was doing. However, doing it they were. Even Wall Street didn't know what was going on. They could only see the profits that were being generated but hadn't looked into the extent of the repercussions of their asset base.

> *I hope we shall take warning from the example and crush in its birth the aristocracy of our monied corporations, which dare already to challenge our government to a trial of strength, and to bid defiance to the laws of their country.*
>
> ~ *Thomas Jefferson*   ~

As they sift through the remnants of our current society, will the archaeologists and psychologists of the future find us to be intelligent and sentient beings who eventually found the capacity to rise above our greed, selfish desires, and pleasures to become a more elevated species due to our communal efforts for all? The protection of the hive is for all as a collective, not only for the elite 1% of those who control the man-made ideology and paradigm such as money, fiat debt, and capitalism. It is widely known that capitalism is a paradigm that has no protections to its environment, wildlife, or human beings, whatsoever. The corporation lives but only for a corporate profit to the detriment of anything left in its wake. Its sole means of existence is for profit. This is the base definition of a corporation.

Since the economic collapse of 2008, there has been a growing, worldwide grassroots movement generically given the title of "the 99%". The mass media has done well to eliminate this from the public discourse. But there are groups, large and small, that have sprung up throughout the world with people inquiring more into the socioeconomic paradigm that we all have been participating in. The 99% are asking deep and more thought-provoking questions based on new experience and information. This is new evidence, and conditions, that millions and millions of people have begun to participate as a collective. Some of these new social constructs that are being questioned are the unchecked power of governments, the elevated international effects of the power of international corporations, the fragility of unregulated systems, and the freedoms given to the global, international banking cartels. The seven deadly sins of Wall Street consist of pride, greed, lust, envy, wrath, gluttony, and sloth. Have we collectively allowed the creation of the modern Sodom and Gomorrah? Was all this destined to collapse? Can history teach us anything?

The story of Sodom and Gomorrah can be found in both the Hebrew and Christian Bibles, as well as the Quran. In the book of Genesis 13:10, it is through the gates to the city of Sodom where financial and judicial transactions took place. Sodom was one of the five "cities of the plain" located by the Jordan River in the Canaan Valley at the south of the Dead Sea. Archaeologists claim it could be compared to "the Garden of Eden". That part of the valley, at that time, was extremely green and fertile. The valley was well-watered, and lands were filled with green grasses for grazing.

The story tells us of two angels who entered the city of Sodom. Lot, who was the nephew of Abraham, saw them and invited them to stay with him and his family in their home. They informed Lot that Sodom was going to be destroyed by the hand of God, due to their excess, depravity, and greed. The angels told Lot and his family that they needed to leave the city immediately to be saved. They were instructed that when the destruction began, they had to leave and not look back. If they looked back, they would be turned into a pillar of salt.

Wall Street had certainly become akin to the excesses of Sodom. Their extravagances gave them the sole feeling of the safety experienced in the Garden of Eden. It seemed nothing could touch them. Traders and Wall Street executives were living in paradise and not looking back. The economic growth beginning from the mid-1990s can be traced back to Democratic President Bill Clinton and his removal of the regulations that the financial industry had been working under since the Great Depression. With these systemic feelings of paradise came the "irrational exuberance", a phrase coined by Federal Reserve Board chairman, Alan Greenspan, in a speech given at the American Enterprise Institute during the dot-com bubble on Dec. 5, 1996. It was a free for all for the financial industry. Their profits during this time became that of legend. However, the true, unchecked profits were yet to come and were just around the corner.

The financial city of the time, Sodom, and its neighboring city, Gomorrah, were near the Dead Sea, which is known for its high saline content, making it one of the world's saltiest bodies of water. Because of the salt content, there is little life that exists in the Dead Sea. Wall Street had become the Dead Sea of investments with no life left in the financial institutions' portfolios. The bonds and securities were barely existing on life support. The smoke was clearing, and the mirrors were breaking. Greed and corruption would soon destroy the public's faith in the system. However, the system would quickly plow forward, leaving the public in its wake and caught in the rubble, most of them lost and gasping for air. Having lost their homes and pensions, they looked back as there was nothing left to look forward to. Subsequently, the public too became frozen like pillars of salt destined to watch the collapse in front of their eyes. The same devils, feeding at the trough and carrying on with no justice, rubbed salt into the wound.

Salt can be a contradiction. On one hand, all life on Earth has evolved to depend on its existence to survive. Humans have used the compound salt for thousands of years for the preservation of food, which was a foundation to the development of human civilization.

Hippocrates, known as the father of medicine, encouraged his fellow healers to use salt water to heal various ailments by immersing the patient in sea water. We have come to learn about the electrolytes. Being able to preserve salt made it possible for humans to transport food over much greater distances. It eliminated the dependence of humans to only eat seasonal food. Mankind depends on the processing of salt in our bodies for our nervous system, our blood and digestion. Beginning in the early recorded years around 6000 BC, at the time of the human evolutionary process, salt was difficult to obtain. It was a highly valued item and even considered by many as a form of currency. For thousands of years, salt was a representation of wealth. Kings and governments paid for their wars by taxing salt and paid the soldiers and workers with salt. The word "salary" comes from the Latin word for salt.

On the other hand, if there is too much salt, nothing can survive. The Dead Sea, where little life exists, has more than 30% salinity, while the oceans contain 3.5%. In the Nevada salt flats, located in the western United States, one can look across the miles of desolate emptiness of the ancient, salt lake beds that have dried out, leaving large swaths of dead zones bereft of most life.

In 2008, behind the pillars of Wall Street, too much salt was what took place. There became a groundswell of foreclosures across the country. The salt of the earth, the common homeowner, was going under. There was too much salt in the wounds of too many job losses, too many defaults. The people were caught looking back, trying to figure things out and unknowingly turning to salt. Eventually, they were left with little, or no economic value and their financial states were considered dead zones to the economy.

***

In early September 2008, I remember having lunch with a banker friend of mine who had just finished a long conference call with his upper management. It seemed that, as the news media had finally been predicting, the economic collapse that had begun to take place was in full force now. Bear Stearns was going to go under. It appeared that the government was willing to save Lehman Bros., but not Bear Stearns. At one point in the lunch, he looked around suspiciously and leaned over the table. He whispered that his college roommate who worked in Washington had told him that Lehman was the investment house that all the Washington politicians used to funnel money to their offshore accounts. Continuing, he explained that if Lehman went bankrupt, then the "off the books" books might become an open platform and there would be a media frenzy. If this were true, the public would be exposed to the financial information of many past, as well as current, prominent politicians. So, the decision within the next few days was to keep Lehman, but Bear Stearns was long done. As the days moved on, the government proceeded to bail out Wall Street.

In 2010, the documentary *Inside Job* was released. It would later win an Oscar. The public was becoming more informed that not all the ducks were lining up to explain how this house of cards had fallen. Wall Street firms that had created the mess were the same group of banks that had been bailed out. The foreclosures were running rampant throughout the country, and nothing was being done about it. There had been no convictions for any wrongdoing, and no new legislation had been put in place to change anything. The line from the corporate media remained the same, "It is a case of the deadbeat homeowner." It was as if the party line of those in power was that "it isn't real. If we don't shed light on it, it won't be real. Just tell them that it is deadbeat homeowners and eventually it will all go away."

It wasn't going to go away. How could we have reached the point of being foreclosed on? I mean, we were current on our mortgage despite the difficulty after the 2008 economic collapse. The thought of having my home taken from me was enough to stop me in my tracks. As a repercussion of the downturn in the economy, I was hoping that all of this wouldn't take me down farther into the abyss. I felt as if my life was now moving aimlessly from pillar to post, and I was entering one bad situation right after another. There I stood, fighting to understand, yet determined to be like Lot and move forward and not become frozen like his wife. The bank sent us the Notice of Default (See Exhibit 1a-c) in the first week of the New Year, in 2011. It seemed that the foreclosure was imminent. Or was it? It hit hard at the foundation of the very fabric of what we had been taught for the past hundred years by the government propaganda machine regarding what it is to be an American. We have all been told that home ownership is the centerpiece of the "American Dream". That we all deserve that white picket fence. As Americans, we have been continuously urged to go out and invest in a piece of the American Dream... a home.

It's true, the economic collapse of 2008 had devastated my business and financial life, but we were still making ends meet. However, I had reached the point where I felt helpless and defeated. My real estate investments were imploding. My development project in Texas had come to an end. Chase Bank, the bank acting as the primary construction lender on the homes I was building in Texas, slowed and eventually stopped their progress payments for work completed. The red tape that Chase instituted internally made it impossible to continue to receive progress payments. I remember one day when I was on the phone with Chase to discuss an invoice and a $57,000 payment request that was still outstanding on four different requests. I was transferred, put on hold, transferred again, put on hold, to later be told that they would send a partial payment. It was then that I knew things were over and the nation's economy was coming to a screeching halt. So, I had to close my business in Texas, leaving dozens of people out of work and suppliers that had to be paid out of my own pocket.

I stopped receiving the progress payments from Chase in August of 2008. It was in October and November that we first missed our HELOC (Line of Credit), or our second Deed of Trust payments. We were able to get back on track, but it was an exceedingly difficult time. We had previously contacted the bank, Wachovia Mortgage, immediately after I knew I wasn't going to get any more money from the construction lenders, to let Wachovia know that we were anticipating difficulties in the very near future with meeting the current payment amount, because of unemployment. We tried extremely hard to continue to make payments with Wachovia, despite various part-time work that was interspersed with multiple durations of unemployment for myself. In July of 2009, we sent a hardship letter to Wachovia stating that we anticipated by the year's end we would no longer be able to afford the payments at the current levels and applied for the loan modification process. In August of 2009, we sent a letter to our state Senator, Barbara Boxer, detailing the situation and asking for assistance. Also, in August of 2009, we sent a letter to John Sumpf, the CEO of Wells Fargo Bank, explaining that we had been in discussions with Wachovia for loan modification and needed assistance because those discussions weren't getting us anywhere.

It was then, in December of 2009, when we reached an official point of being unable to continue to make the payments at their current levels. We were placed into yet another loan modification program, which took us to late February 2010, when we were once again declined a loan modification. Then, in March of 2010, we sent another letter to Senator Barbara Boxer, further detailing our fight for our home. Also, in March of 2010, we were placed into another modification program called MAP, and worked with a representative named Zenon Cantu. Only one month later, we were denied. In June of 2010, we sent another letter informing Senator Barbara Boxer of our continued struggle and modification nightmare with Wachovia. Four days later, Zenon Cantu informed us that there was a new program available called MAP II. Throughout the month of July, we made multiple attempts to reach Zenon Cantu to apply. Then, in August of 2010, Zenon Cantu informed us that he couldn't help us and gave us a new name and phone numbers of where to apply. So, we contacted the new representative to help us, Kodi Schaffer.

In August 2010, we wrote another letter to Barbara Boxer explaining the repetitive runaround we had been receiving from the banks as we tried to modify our loan. Also, in the month of August, we sent another hardship letter to Wachovia asking for more help to modify our loan. Bear in mind, we were still current on the mortgage. We were simply trying to work with Wachovia for solutions to a financial result we could see approaching on the horizon. Shortly thereafter, we received another notice of denial for modification. So, in September and November of 2010, we sent Senator Barbara Boxer letters keeping her informed of the failure of the practices and processes that the bank continued to put borrowers through to no avail.

Also, in September of 2010, Kodi informed us that loan modification was difficult to impossible, based on the parameters of the government programs for mortgage assistance. We didn't qualify for any mortgage assistance since we were current on our mortgage payments. Again, we explained that, for nearly two years, we had been trying to discuss with someone the problem we might come up against due to the nature of the economy and my long-term unemployment. We were simply trying to be proactive to our situation. It was then that he informed us that it would be much better for us if we were to stop our payments. If we stopped our mortgage payments and were behind, we might then qualify for government mortgage assistance. So, we followed the advice of the representative of Wells Fargo Bank that, to qualify for the HAMP program, we stopped paying the mortgage. This advice was against everything we believed in. It was against everything we were doing. We had been paying our mortgage. We were simply trying to discuss with the lender the possibility of a time when we might NOT be able to pay the mortgage, which I knew wasn't too far down the road.

So, in the month of November, we stopped paying the mortgage, based on the advice from the representative of the financial institution we were supposed to pay. They acted quickly because it was only the next month that all hell broke loose.

On December 28, 2010, Wells Fargo Bank filed a Notice of Default against our property for breach of contract for non-payment. They did this and filed the paperwork to begin the foreclosure process. At the same time, they acknowledged that we were still in negotiations with Wachovia Mortgage, through the representative, Kodi Schaffer, for loan modification at the time of Wells Fargo filing the Notice of Default.

In late March of 2011, we applied for loan modification again through a program called HAMP. Once more, we were represented by Kodi Schaffer. Then, the first week of April of 2011, we wrote another hardship letter to Wachovia regarding our financial situation and the need for modification assistance. We could see that the modification process wasn't working, and the banks had no intention of using the process as a tool for solutions for us as the borrower. So, we decided that the only resource available to us to save our property was to file a lawsuit against Wells Fargo Bank. We were subsequently denied a loan modification since we had filed a lawsuit to stop the illegal foreclosure.

It is always easy to point fingers and heal once you start peeling things apart and understanding with hindsight. However, this is where the danger is for the homeowner who is being foreclosed on without 20/20 hindsight. Those people need to know that the system is rigged and filled with fraud. Knowing this can help you navigate through the corruption of a foreclosure procedure and not have your family or yourself ripped apart.

Acknowledging this was my first step in understanding that the foreclosure wasn't our fault. We were trapped in a shell game created by the financial institutions and the judicial system. The fraudulent actions of Wall Street created a chain reaction that decimated the real estate and construction sectors, leaving myself and millions of others unemployed in its fallout. As the stock market fell, retirement accounts across the globe were hammered, stripping people of their life savings. Corporations large and small began to collapse in the aftermath of the greed and corruption of the behemoth financial institutions.

***

I finally stood again after sitting on the sofa. I was curious as to why there were so many errors in the information on the document. How could this be so incorrect? With these paperwork errors, we were heading toward losing our home. I didn't know what to do, but I did know this was something I was going to have to fight for. I mean, if I didn't, I would lose my home.

In the Notice of Default documents, (See Exhibit 1a-c) Wells Fargo Bank checked a box claiming they had complied with CA Civ Code 2923.5(g). At that time, the code stated that the beneficiary must make every attempt to contact the borrower in an effort for both parties to try to rectify the issue. Those efforts should include mail, phone, or any other electronic means available. There is a timeline associated with these attempts. If the bank makes all the attempts and doesn't receive a response within the appropriate timeline, they can then check this box truthfully, making the claim that they obliged the necessary tasks in order to comply with that code. So, they checked this box, claiming they had made every attempt to contact the borrower but were unable to connect with them to discuss ways for the borrower to rectify the issue. The truth of the matter is that they didn't comply with that rule. However, they filed the documents incorrectly claiming that they did comply with that rule, which allowed them to quickly foreclose on us.

In CA, there is a ninety-day timeline in the foreclosure process to allow both parties to act and possibly rectify the issue. The checked box meant that they were stating that they had complied with this issue and made every attempt to contact us to resolve the issue but were unable to communicate with us in order to rectify the situation, this was a blatant lie. This action circumvented our rights that allowed us to rectify the situation before the foreclosure process went into effect. Through filing these misrepresentations, it meant that they had committed perjury and fraud against the court by incorrectly claiming they had done so and filing that information with the court.

We sat on the edge of the sofa, motionless and quiet, as though we were in a state of shock, reviewing the notice sent by Wells Fargo Bank to explain that they were considering commencing the process of foreclosure.

My wife at the time, Michelle, was frustrated, since this was going against everything she had been discussing on the phone with the bank regarding the possibilities of modification. Despite our previous efforts to inform and work with Wachovia Mortgage and Wells Fargo Bank, regarding our financial situation, it now seemed they were moving forward with filing the Notice of Default. It made no sense since we had been current on our payments until their advice to stop making the payments.

Eventually, we were dealing with Wells Fargo Bank and their Home Loan Modification Programs on a near daily basis for almost two years. Though we were still paying our mortgage on time, we could see the writing on the wall. We were planning and beginning our own economic strategies to maintain our monthly payment. We were being proactive and had been in negotiations with the bank for nearly two years, knowing these harder times would come. It was they who had told us to stop making payments. Then, only thirty days later, we began receiving our first foreclosure documents. What about the hundreds of times we spoke with them on the phone? What about the ninety-day timeline before those documents are to be distributed? They submitted those documents fraudulently, thereby dismissing our opportunity to rectify the issue and bring the note back to current. They took away our right to rectify any discrepancies and to make things right.

I had now been out of work for nearly two years. During this entire time, Michelle had spent hundreds of hours trying to negotiate with the banks to modify our loan. We knew the day might come when we were no longer able to make payments. Now that day was looming sooner rather than later. We had reached a point where we had depleted our savings and borrowed from relatives to keep up. The situation had begun to look pretty dire, and things had become very difficult given the state of the economy. The banks had created a complete paradigm shift throughout the economy. They were no longer in the lending business. They were now in the foreclosure business.

We received the documents that stated the bank could not reach the borrower in order to rectify the situation and claimed they had made the required attempts to contact us but were unable to reach us. They stated this for them to seem that they were qualifying the necessary requirements of Civil Code 2923.5(g) of the non-judicial Foreclosure procedure, all the while we had been instigating discussions with them about modifying our loan. Michelle had been working tirelessly with the dozens of modification representatives who were shuffled in and out of our account and within the multiple programs that we would get bounced in and out of, whether from the government, or directly working within the financial institution's modification departments. We had dealt with every entity such as MAP I & II, HAMP, and NEVO. Honestly, it was extremely exhausting and to no avail.

She would be on the phone with someone from Wachovia talking, emailing, and faxing various documents. The bank would constantly misplace, lose, or simply request the documents only to ask that they be sent to them again. Then, the assistant she had been working with consistently for months, would suddenly disappear as if they had quit or been fired. Subsequently, a new assistant would take over our file and communications would commence once more, beginning with a request that all the documents that had been submitted over the previous six months be filed again. She would reach a point where they said that we would qualify for a program and would be moving forward with a modification, only to receive an email a few days later stating that the program we qualified for had ended. This was so frustrating to her that she would reach the point of crying after many of these phone calls because of the negligence and incompetence of the bank, or the unempathetic and uncompassionate people used by the financial institutions as their customer assistance professionals.

So, at one point, one of the customer service reps told her that it would be best if we stopped paying our mortgage so that the bank would see things as more dire and aid in the facilitation for modification. The agent assured us that due to the nature of the programs available, we needed to be behind in our payments to qualify. We had been discussing our financial hardship with Wells Fargo. The only advanced advice that we ever received was to stop paying to qualify for a mortgage assistance program.

This treadmill of "working with" financial institutions for assistance is simply as ironic as a screen door on a submarine, or the words "jumbo shrimp". The word that continually comes to mind for me is "useless". The bank's repeated incompetence through the modification programs helped shed light on the fact that they held no intentions to assist their "failed" borrowers. The various programs held no incentive for the financial corporations to do so after the United States government had bailed them out and then set up programs that were counterintuitive for any type of successful assistance or modifications. The government programs were paying the financial institutions large sums of money for open accounts they had in the modification process. So, for Wall Street and financial institutions it was profitable to have customers in the modification pipelines because they received a government sponsored financial incentive to be "attempting" to help customers rectify their loans. They were not paid these incentives based on actually helping the customers, but to have on record the accounts showing their attempts to rectify. The government funded program was designed for failure.

Part Three

Justice is the idea of being seen and heard by one's peers, allowing an agreed upon community ideal to give subsistence to society at large, and for the betterment of all as a collective. It is what separates us from the apes. So, is truth and justice an inherent part of the continued quest of the human experience? After all the generations stemming from the courts and tribunals of early man, including the Sumerians, Genghis Khan, the Greeks, and the Romans, evolving into the modern-day international organizations and governments throughout the world, why then is it something that continues to elude us today? Corruption, racism, classism, and sexism all have a stranglehold on justice. There is no true justice for all.

To solve this dilemma, we must delve much deeper into facts, and how that affects human behavior, in order to shine the light on truth and justice. However, despite having all the facts, would we ever be able to grasp the truth behind what eludes us? I mean, the facts don't change minds. Minds tend to be far more receptive to facts given to them if they are more comfortable and confirm what the mind insists on believing, despite the evidence to the contrary that might be right in front of us. The effects of global warming are a perfect example. The Trump administration defied all scientific evidence that supports the fact that global warming exists. Regardless of how and why it exists, there was simple disregard of facts. That leaves us on a path that is far more fragile than we would ever like to believe is real, and on top of this, we bring with us a group of adversaries such as social, economic, and racial biases. Despite all evidence, there are those skeptics who know that *"fill in the blank"* cannot be true. And we must also include the most elusive of all our enemies, our collective conscience. The group-think and mass acceptance to what we all feel is comfortable as a collective—I recommend reading *Mobs, Messiahs, and Markets* by Bill Bonner and Lila Rajiva.

I have found through my own personal litigation experience that one can never actually win an argument. In life's bigger picture, it isn't possible to, based on the benefit or detriment to all within the moral grounds of humanity. You see, if you lose, then you lose, and if you were to win, you will also lose. Because, in the fall out, while you might feel fine and proud of your victory, what about your adversary? Despite what you may feel about them or know about their indiscretions, you have now insulted their judgment, intelligence, self-respect, and pride. This is not very constructive overall to a society at large. But this is the current world we live in, and every year more and more lawyers enter our society.

How can we have an equal, true, and just judicial system that is able to deny evidence necessary in order to reveal the truth? The reason that facts are secondary to us as a collective to becoming a better species, and to experience truth and justice for all beings, is that our monetary, legislative, and judicial systems are all run and overseen by individuals who have a stake in what they do, and that stake includes pride, intelligence, judgment, profit and self-respect.

In David Ehrenfeld's essay, *The Coming Collapse of the Age of Technology*, he notes, "One of the most serious challenges to our prevailing system is our catastrophic loss of ability to use self-criticism and feedback to correct our actions when they place us in danger or give bad results. We seem unable to look objectively at our own failures and to adjust the behavior that caused them."

I used to wonder why most people tend to hold so tightly to their ideas, even though they are faced against such irrefutable evidence to the contrary of those ideas. This psychological phenomenon is known as cognitive dissonance. In order to understand what this means, we should break it down to the term's cognition and dissonance. The word cognition is the mental action or process of acquiring knowledge and understanding through thought, experience, and the senses. This differs from dissonance which is a tension or clash resulting from the combination of two disharmonious or unsuitable elements. Therefore, cognitive dissonance refers to the state of having inconsistent thoughts, beliefs, or attitudes, especially those relating to behavioral decisions and attitude change. This state will create feelings of disharmony, aggravation, and discomfort. The human mind will intrinsically look to maintain and restore harmony and to create comfort again to quell what is known as a fight or flight mechanism that lies deep within our DNA. The mind looks to change attitudes and beliefs, or perhaps, even reject outright the conflicting information.

Sometimes, people don't want to hear the truth because they don't want their illusions destroyed.

~ Friedrich Nietzsche ~

For us as a society, either locally or globally, to create change to this paradigm, we must stop refusing to see what is right in front of us. We must allow ourselves to see the writing on the wall. We must create and adhere to systems of transparency that hold us accountable to the collective. As a collective, we must also begin to muster the energy to then act on and make definitive and decisive actions against those who have broken these systems against the collective.

I believe that to have a true democracy based on the rule of law, the law must be fair and impartial. Is this too much to ask? Otherwise, what is law in a "democratic" society to be? If law is to be just, then there is no other way than to have justice that is equal to all. Without this, it is impossible to have a democracy based on the rule of law when there are clear advantages to one party over another. However, we don't live in a democracy. Our legal system isn't designed for this to be the case, but it is, and we all know that it is. We know and most of us turn away from the fact that it is clearly an unjust and corrupt judicial system. Most people don't know how to fix it, and if they are not affected by the injustice, it is easy to let it remain out of mind. This defeats the entire paradigm of fair and just. The thought that if I could negotiate the rules needed to present my case, and then be able to do so to an unbiased judge and have my day in court to be heard by a jury of my peers ... nothing could be more ridiculous.

So, to learn and change things we must understand how we got to be in such a place to begin with. We must be able to assess where we are within the framework of the rule of law. The law must have transparency to be fair. Law is to be followed by all people and no one should be above the law, including lawyers, judges, CEOs, and politicians. We must hold people accountable for their actions. We must stand as a society and hold the truth to be self-evident for every person to be able to have the same access to life, liberty, and the pursuit of happiness.

We were told to take out a loan and buy ourselves a dream home. So, as with millions of other Americans, we did just that. We followed the rules of the game and joined in the "American Dream". We bought our first home.

We had been renting in San Francisco for years, but eventually decided that we were priced out of homeownership there. Because of the dot-com industry, the San Francisco home pricing had begun to soar through the roof. We found we could get a better bang for our buck if we crossed the Bay bridge to the east bay of Oakland. It was a small, hundred-year-old bungalow style home that needed serious TLC. The realtors use the acronym TLC for tender loving care. That can be translated as meaning that the home will need major repairs. It would be something that we could sink our teeth into and create more value by remodeling the entire home. We scraped and borrowed to make our "American Dream" come true.

It was a profound and prophetic experience to participate in and feel my life's dreams, and all the work, begin to disappear in front of my own eyes. I sat in the living room reflecting over the past ten years that we had owned and lived in our house.

As soon as the escrow closed and the keys were in our hands, we immediately went to work. I went on to remodel our home from the foundation to the roof with my own hands. It became a bonding experience for me and some of my family. My father, and my father-in-law, came to help me pour my foundation and do some of the plumbing and rewiring of the house. I made beautiful, concrete kitchen countertops, a two-headed, white concrete shower, and a terra cotta colored concrete sink for the master bath. On the ground floor level were beautifully stained and polished concrete floors. I painted and even re-roofed the whole house. The roof project gave me two sprained ankles...

There is pride in the feeling of homeownership. There is a distinct feeling between the idea of paying rent and paying a mortgage. The amount could even be the same, but to have the feeling that it is yours is amazing. Then, slowly, yet methodically, over the following eight years, we began to witness our dreams quickly rise, and then even faster, unravel right before our own eyes until it was as if the world had taken a massive rug and pulled it straight out from under us. We felt quite alone, although we knew there were millions of others going through the same thing, not only those in our neighborhood, but throughout the nation.

The reasons why so many millions of people had reached the point of no longer being able to afford their mortgage varied widely. Besides the job loss or long-term unemployment, some people had health related problems, some people had children with children's issues, or perhaps, some had aged parents or relatives who were staying with them. Despite any stories one's life might be involved in, once they began the nightmare of the foreclosure process on their home, they would eventually all be left feeling alone, confused, and beaten.

It was July of 2009, after losing my businesses and what seemed to me as everything, when I had reached the emptiness of life. There on the table was *The Oprah Magazine*, with its caption "Jumpstart your Dreams". Michelle looked at me and asked, "What do you think we should do?"

My response was immediate, "Honestly? I want to take the last bit of money we have, buy an RV, pack it up and head out across the country and begin producing a documentary on the failed American Dream."

The phone rang. The last thing I wanted to do at this point was to talk to anyone. Well, we all seem to have one person who can pierce that veil. That's what friends are for. He always seemed to know when it was a good time to call. This was one of those times.

I went into the kitchen to grab the phone. "Hello." I said, mustering enough strength to say a word.

"How are you?" Bill asked. He was already privy to the fact that we were having financial troubles and were attempting to work with the banks to modify our loan.

"Well, all of that modification headache of the past year and a half or so seems to have come to an end. We got a Notice of Default from Wells Fargo Bank. It now seems they want to foreclose," I said flatly.

"Ah, I see. They're going to try to take your home?"

"It seems so."

"So, are you going to lose your home?"

"Well, we don't have the money anymore."

"I asked if you were going to lose your home."

"I don't know. I'm running out of ideas."

"Maybe, maybe not. You won't know the answer to that unless you act upon it and take action to try to stop the foreclosure," Bill replied.

"That's all well and good, but we can't afford any lawyers."

"But you're a sharp and intelligent guy. You can move your way around the internet. You can read between the lines, the bullshit, the lies, and find truths that many people don't see. You know you can represent yourself for free, while the banks are paying at least $500/hr. for each of their lawyers. This was the backbone of America in its early days."

"Mm, hm ..." I mumbled as I listened. I felt numb. Whatever I had as a basis of reality was foggy at best. My mind was in a continuous blur with the economic pressures. Only a year prior to this point, I was giving lectures on real estate investing at many of the bay area real estate investment groups. And I had been interviewed on CNBC for my real estate experience. I thought that things were moving in the right direction. But it is easy to lose track when things are flowing. Now, it was all coming from a much different vantage point. I didn't feel as if I had any control over anything anymore. I possessed a constant feeling of uneasiness, and my confidence was waning. Now, I was being advised to file a lawsuit and litigate that lawsuit against one of the nation's largest financial institutions, Wells Fargo Bank.

"Yeah, this was how things got done back when this country was beginning. It was primarily a bunch of farmers, a few shopkeepers, and a few lawyers. It seemed that most lawyers became politicians. It used to be that the common man would argue his own case, since most people didn't have the money for an attorney. Or perhaps, they might be able to trade a cow or goat for some lawyer's services. The legal process still makes it available for one to argue their own case.

"I don't know if I can do that," I said doubtingly, as the little bit of self-confidence I had left sat warily on my back.

"You didn't listen to the first thing I said." Bill said sternly.

"What's that?"

"You can do this. I said you're sharp. I mean, what else have you got to do? You haven't really had much work in over two years, so you have time."

"Yeah, rub my unemployment into my open wounds," I replied smartly.

"What I mean is that you have time. You don't have kids. Your health is good. I mean, you have what is necessary to take this on with the least number of roadblocks, outside of a pretty harsh learning curve. But, again, you are an intelligent guy."

"I don't know." I was feeling beaten.

"I know things are hard but look at what has come out in the papers, all the corruption, the fraud. Chances are, it has happened to you, but you just don't know it yet. Let me put it to you this way," he continued, "What would you do if you were leaving the gym and you had a million dollars in your gym bag? Everything you had to your name is in that bag. Then, a person named Wells Fargo Bank comes walking down the street behind you and snatches the bag from you and takes off. I mean, think about it, would you go after them?"

I nodded, understanding the metaphor, although my legs still felt weak thinking about the undertaking. I could barely stand up, let alone chase after Wells Fargo down the street.

"If you don't try to fight them, they will take your home. If you do try to fight them, they might not take your home. They still might succeed, and right now they are running down the street with your bag of money. The question is can you catch up with them? Do it and see what happens. You have nothing left to lose at this point. You're still young, and there are plenty of years to rebuild your life."

I hung up and pondered this for a few days. I knew it wouldn't be easy. I had no idea what I was doing or even where to start. But I had never liked banks. When I was a young boy, I had a bank savings account to hold my newspaper route earnings. I remember one day going to the bank and owing the bank money. I couldn't figure out why that would be. But it seemed that their fees had made me overdrawn. I was a kid and to me the bank stole my money. Since then, I have always perceived them as a legal mafia, and now I was pissed off, tired, and broken. Never underestimate the man who is at the bottom of his abyss. This brings to mind the lyrics of songwriter Bob Dylan, "When you ain't got nothing, you got nothing to lose," from his legendary song "Like a Rolling Stone", from the Highway 61 Revisited album.

I had seen the bottom, which wasn't something I would ever wish on anyone. I had recently returned from the trip where I found myself in the field alone with the only flower in sight. Now, home again in CA, I had lost what it felt like to be a provider. I had lost all confidence and was left without direction, had few opportunities, and I had not experienced a positive outlook for some time. I was in a very dark place and feeling extremely alone.

It was a beautiful, bay area, clear blue-sky morning in July. There are many of those days that can be foggy from the Golden Gate during this time of the year, but today was amazing. Despite the beautiful weather, I was having a difficult time breathing. My focus was lost. At this point, I was depressed while I was awake, and this morning was not getting any better. I was tired. I felt like a burden to my family and friends.

I sat on the bench at the end of the bed, across from the opened door that led to the garden from the bedroom. I could hear the birds dancing in between the grape vine and the apple tree, singing their songs. They had no idea of the economic collapse that was taking place. I had been in my office the night before going over finances and things realizing that I was worth more dead than alive. I felt very much like the character, George Bailey, played by Jimmy Stewart, in the classic film *It's a Wonderful Life*. Because of my life insurance, I was worth more dead than alive. As I sat on the bench, listening to the birds in the garden, I gently held on to the cold steel of the 9mm semi-automatic pistol.

Life is simply a collection of small moments. What we do and how we act in each of those small moments will dictate our lives. In this small moment, I was holding a revolver, while in an emotional and depressed state. I felt myself shifting between dark and light, caring and not caring, thinking, and not thinking. The tears rolled down my face as I pleaded to myself inside my head, trying to talk some sense into this guy who was sitting on the edge. I stared out into the garden thinking of how much I enjoyed gardening. I find it to be a very meditative experience for me. Such an irony, I thought, sitting on a bench in my bedroom with a loaded pistol looking out onto my garden, reflecting on how much I enjoy gardening and it being a meditative experience. I shook my head to stop the saline streams, to shake the guilt, humiliation, and shame from my shoulders. It was time for me to decide what was to happen at this moment.

My hands were sweating and shaking as I set the gun down and slowly got up from the bench. I stood there in between my meditative garden calling me to come out and play, and the cold, black steel instrument of death. With one foot in front of the other, I slowly made my way across the room and stood in the doorway. I turned back to my pistol as if it had called to me, begging me not to go. I knew then that if I didn't go out to the garden, I would never get out alive. Taking a deep breath, I turned my back to my pistol, saying to myself that I needed to get that out of my life. I would find a way to release it from my life.

I walked out into the garden and grabbed the hose. This was a trigger that I felt much more comfortable pulling. As my hand tightened, a light mist began to emerge. I guided the mist over the artichoke plants that sat near the base of the grapes. The grapes stretched across in both directions along the fence, giving the perception of a living fence. The artichokes lay positioned in between the grape vine and the Meyer lemon tree. While I stood there holding the flexible tube, the water, along with the morning sunlight, created a wonderful rainbow. I watched the colors of the rainbow breathe as a light wind moved in and out of the mist. It was then that the large, beautiful butterfly appeared in the middle of the rainbow. The water spread over the tiny, colorful, iridescent wings, keeping it floating stationary about a foot in front of my face. We were looking into each other's eyes, neither of us moving, except for the wings of the sweet little creature.

In the Old World, the connotation was negative. The butterfly was thought to be the spirit of the dead. Over time, this view changed as we began to understand the metamorphosis that a butterfly goes through in their short lives. The butterfly is a symbol of a spirit animal as a totem, representing personal transformation. They guide you to be sensitive to your personal life cycles of growth and expansion. They also represent the beauty of life's continuing unfolding. One of the messages carried by the spirit of the butterfly is about the ability to go through important changes with grace and lightness. It represents transformation because of its impressive process of metamorphosis.

It changes from an egg, to larvae, better known as the caterpillar. Then it changes again to a pupa, which is also referred to as the chrysalis or cocoon. Then, from out of the confines of the cocoon a butterfly emerges in all her unfurling glory. She challenges us to accept the changes in our lives as elegantly and casually as she does. She embraces the changes of her body and her environment. She beckons us to keep our faith as we undergo transitions in our lives. She is there to remind us that despite all our anger and anxiousness, or any toiling and fretting, they are meaningless against the continuous turning tides of nature. We look to the eloquence and grace and come to understand that the only guarantee is the journey itself. It is our responsibility to make our way, accepting the changes that come, and emerge through to the other side of our transitions as brilliantly as the butterfly.

The tears continued to fill my eyes, creating a wash of my ocular senses. The colors of the garden began to blend into each other. Within a few seconds, everything began to blur into each other. I felt as if my feet had left the ground and I was there floating in the mist with the butterfly. I was lost in the moment. This went on for a short while. The colors of life spiraled around my head, leaving me dazed. After a time, the swirling color began to slow, the garden began to reappear and to take shape again as my feet felt as if they sat back onto the grass.

I glanced into the misty rainbow again and watched the butterfly give me one last look just before she flew out of the mist and away from my garden. I could feel the message and the power within that moment.

The Butterfly Effect

The Universe and mind meld through lucid purity.

The ground swirled like that of an Edvard Munch painting.

Pondering the circle of life while watering the yellow squash,

the butterfly dances to the glances of the eyes through the mist.

The quail cooed in the orange glow of the lingering sunset over the bamboo.

Softly blowing in the wind, painting a small rainbow that floats in the garden.

Grounded in the unity as my feet lose touch with the grass,

I enjoy the moment of oneness without purpose, accepting the sign.

Sensation of clarity if only for a moment

albeit a moment is but a part of time, which

is yesterday's then, and the morrow's morrow.

In the yearbook of my senior year in high school, I received the notation of being the class clown and the class optimist. I had never really put much thought into that section of any previous year's release of the yearbook. Prior to the release, I hadn't heard that I would be honored with such accolades. Others were voted most likely to succeed, class king, class queen, most likely to become a politician, most likely to do whatever. But I had never thought that I would be someone voted class optimist. But there I was, nonetheless, the class clown and class optimist. Okay, so what does that mean to be voted class optimist? I had no idea what the future had in store for me as I headed out into the big, cruel world.

As Descartes once most notably stated, "I think, therefore I am." I thought that common sense and decency were more prevalent in the judicial system than I have now come to find out through experience and must now accept. I have come face to face with the ugliness and extremity of greed and corruption at all levels of the capitalist charade.

"Recession, my ass!" I would yell at the newscaster. "I don't care what anyone says, it is a depression, and it doesn't seem to be over just yet, either."

Recession was the code word for the media in hopes that the people wouldn't revolt. Make it seem less destructive than the first depression by giving it a more colorful name. Something that might have a little optimism to it ....

Between multiple lengthy bouts of unemployment and the ever-present overhead I had accumulated while running a business and investing what I could, primarily in real estate, I began to watch everything I had been working for quickly wither away. It was quite interesting once I learned to detach myself from the situation. Of course, this was done only for sanity's sake. There was nothing I could do any longer. Literally, there was no money coming in and it had been that way for a very long time. The economic valve had been shut, with no drips of anything to pacify the need to pay the bills. And it seemed to simply spiral down farther without an end in sight.

Despite all the work, all the dreams, all the sweat, the birthdays, holidays, parties with friends and everything we, as a society, tend to feel is what makes a home a home, it's far from the truth and must be understood by those who are dealing with foreclosure. The property where all those memories took place is simply a building. Whether it is made of wood, concrete, glass, or whatever building material, it is simply a building. Through this process, I learned that a home is not the structure. The home is the memory of the work, the dreams, the sweat, the birthdays, the holidays, the family, and the friends who participated with you in building your life. The home had nothing to do with the building itself. That was just wood and plaster.

One of the first things I did when we began to find ourselves in the unenviable, yet very real position of being foreclosed on, was to learn to begin to detach from the place we had called home for so long. That is not to say that we lost or denied any emotional meaning that had become numerous memories for us within those blessed walls, but to understand that a home is not a structure or a building. It is the emotions and the myriad of people who commiserate and celebrate life within the walls of that building. It takes a lot of courage to step out of your comfort zone and the ideal of the structure that holds you and your family safe, and into your fear. You have to detach yourself from the situation and understand that you and your family and friends are still good, healthy, and will make it through this. This was the first stage to being able to make a positive step in the right direction. That gave us the strength we needed to pick ourselves up and begin to develop the energy necessary to take on the big, scary financial institution called Wells Fargo Bank and to file a lawsuit to help us stop them from illegally foreclosing on us.

As we were getting deeper and deeper into researching for a lawsuit, and as new evidence began to blossom out of the documents and multiple think tank sessions we would have, the ironies became so much more visible. We would watch and listen to the news in awe, while the global foreclosure crisis widened. We were dumbfounded by how the media ran with stories that would deviate from the true evidence that would get someone to the essence of the root of the evil. "You cannot fix a leaking boat with a Band-Aid," I would yell at the television. The water will still get in and sink the boat. One needs to find the holes and fix them. Permanently. So that is precisely what I ended up setting out to do. It took some insight from my friend to help us eventually make the decision to take on the fight. After a week or so of inquiry and deep reflection, I finally reached that point of acquiescence.

"Why not?" one night out of the blue, I said aloud to the television while watching the news in the living room.

"Why not what?" Michelle asked loudly from the other room.

"Fuck it, let's sue the shit out of them!" It was time to dig in. I can say, although it wasn't easy, we weren't in denial about the situation. In this place of denial or fear of the unknown, most people freeze or don't allow themselves to be calm enough to think straight, due to the stresses that come with this situation. It took a lot of strength for us to put ourselves into a non-emotional place to make the correct decisions to address the specific notice or document that might be on the table at that time.

We weren't in denial because we had been conscious and proactive in the situation as much as we could, and when we then detached ourselves from the property itself, we were able to step up to the challenge at hand. Although, in no way does that mean we had the strength to take on the big banks at that time. However, as you take steps to protect you, your family, and your biggest asset that the bank is trying to take away from you, you begin to build confidence. That confidence began to grow exponentially as I traversed through our legal process and learned to empower myself with knowledge. I found myself heading off in the mornings to spend the day studying at the University of Berkeley Law Library or to downtown Oakland to the Alameda County Law Library. Or I would head into San Francisco to study at the Hastings College of Law, University of California San Francisco Law Library, or the San Francisco Law Library.

I began to understand just what we were going to be up against. I was constantly watching the news to keep up with the most current stories of the day. I could hear what was happening to millions of others, but due to what I was learning about how Wells Fargo was breaking the laws, I felt we would be able to make something happen. We might be able to fix the situation with the bank. The more I learned, the more I hoped the nightmare wouldn't come to find us. I listened to various cable news sources, as well as numerous online outlets, to try to make sense of this senseless situation. We understood the hurdles and the repercussions if things didn't play out as we hoped, but it can never really sink in unless you are actually in the trench.

I came to learn it is good to try to continue to breathe through the foreclosure process so you can stay alert and pay attention. The breathing helped keep a steady flow of oxygen heading into my brain. Being conscious of how I was breathing helped me stay calmer, so that I could comprehend all the new information I was absorbing.

These feelings we were experiencing as we looked at the Notice of Default, (See Exhibit 1a-c) and other subsequent documents that were being filed, were not new, as they continued to seemingly be the focus of our existence for some time. It was just that this document, the first one that began to create the difficult financial struggles that we had been enduring, was now put into words. Those words were being transcribed by someone with no emotional attachment whatsoever. We had gone through the gauntlet of all the emotions over the past few years, which brought us to this moment. The feeling of helplessness, loneliness, failure, guilt, was all very real and coming steadily to the forefront of my core. I felt that I had let everyone in my life down. The confident decisions to buy the property at the time now seemed like such a lost and distant thought. One must understand that it is not your fault. Once you begin to get involved with your papers, you will probably find that the financial institutions and the companies that are helping them with the foreclosure do not know what they are doing either.

The first thing I needed to do was review all the documents being sent for the foreclosure. I looked over every date, every name, every amount, every number. One of the things I needed to understand was that just because the bank was filing these papers with the court, it didn't mean any of the information should be considered to be correct.

Paralegal

I knew next to nothing of the rules or the process of foreclosure in the state of California. What I did know was that there was a rather short timeline that we were now up against, and that was about it. I didn't know who to contact about this because I didn't have the money to talk with an attorney. Even if we had the money for an attorney, it would be unlikely that any attorney would ever take the case on because they knew the cards were stacked against them, and they don't like to lose. However, there are those attorneys who will take on your case simply to move you forward into the process by advising you or pushing some paper around. But they won't actually get right into the basics of filing a lawsuit. Most attorneys know it is an extreme uphill battle to win against the big financial institutions, even more so for someone representing themselves.

Where did that leave us? We had to begin to find information that could help us steer through the maze of legal rules and jargon to make sense of the information we were receiving. The hard part was finding the answers to the questions that we didn't even know to ask. How could I begin to learn the basics of law without missing a step? There aren't a whole lot of avenues for this when you are simply a normal person who has to go against the system. The financial institutions know this and expect the difficulty on your end of the legal process to eventually bog you down so much that you will either quit their lawsuit or make a mistake that they can capitalize on.

With everything that was going on, and the pressure that was mounting on our shoulders, it was easy for our emotions to overtake any efforts to think rationally. We were losing our home and it would seem only natural that our emotions were running rampant. I needed to find a place within myself, breathe and relax. This needed to be our priority despite our "American Dream" deteriorating in front of our eyes. This was our first home and one we spent years and tens of thousands of dollars and thousands of hours of time remodeling. We were deeply invested in our home and now someone was simply trying to take it away. It is very difficult to think rationally when one is in this state. But we had to plod on. So, we made some phone calls.

I can assure you that if you were to ever find yourself in this situation, you won't be in the kind of mindset to go and tell all your friends and family that your financial lives have failed and that you are about to lose your home. For many, the pride and ego get in the way of looking to their immediate circle of influence in order to find assistance or resolution. But *non tantum hominum*—we are only human.

One day, I needed to switch my mindset, so I took myself out for a bit for a change of pace. I was sitting alone having some risotto and found myself next to a few lawyers who were out eating their lunch. Sparking up a conversation, we spoke about the economy and our individual views as to what we each thought were the reasons why things had crashed so profoundly. I discussed some of my story and what was going on, and at one point, one of the lawyers advised me to find a paralegal who might be able to help me. She thought, since I had no money for attorney's fees, this might be the next best thing.

I began making calls to dozens of paralegals. I was informed in numerous discussions that the state of California had made it difficult for a paralegal to do any work outside of assisting an attorney of record. A paralegal is supposed to work under the wing of an attorney. So, where does this leave someone who is deciding to litigate an issue themselves? This rule makes it difficult for someone if they don't have the money for an attorney and need to use a paralegal instead, as the state makes you go through an attorney to get to the paralegal. It defeats the purpose of options and strips away the opportunity for the "little guy" to receive legal advice and fairness in the justice system. From the responses I was getting, it seemed that the paralegals were all saying they had to work for attorneys due to this rule. However, I was persistent and kept calling around.

It took the better part of three days of phone calls and hearing, "No, I'm sorry, I can't help you without you talking with one of our attorneys." It was difficult going through the confidence roller coaster of feeling that this wasn't going anywhere while still trying to hold on to the optimism. I finally reached someone who was open to helping us wrap our minds around what the legal papers were telling us, so we sat down to discuss our options.

It was a nondescript office building located in the industrial/warehouse district of Oakland, CA. From the parking lot, one could see the stadium where the Oakland A's and Oakland Raiders play. I stood there staring at the stadium thinking how significant that was. I was never really a competitive person, but there I stood near a major sports facility about ready to head into an office to discuss a situation that would place me in an extremely competitive battle with one of the largest corporations in not only the country, but the world.

After I pushed the intercom button, she answered it almost immediately. In this neighborhood, security is a must. The area tends to get a bit rough at times.

"It's Doug Boggs. You gave me the address, but I don't know the code to get in," I stated.

"I'll buzz you in. Then take the elevator up to five. Go right, then another right, and down the hall. My door is on the right," She replied.

"Hello!" I said as I reached the office, knocking lightly on the door, which was slightly ajar.

Across the hall was a man reclining in his leather office chair with his door open. His shoes were off, and his feet were up on the desk. He looked up and smiled, then went back to typing on his Bluetooth keyboard laying in his lap as his eyes searched deeply into his computer screen.

"Come on in," her voice announced from the antechamber. "There's some coffee and tea there, go ahead and help yourself if you wish. I'll be right with you."

I slowly entered the room. There were scores of legal books filling the three cases that lined the wall behind the empty desk where a receptionist might normally be seated. The old, stained, leather couch had various daily newspapers strewn across. There were broken frames that held the art precariously on the walls. They reminded me of items that must have been purchased at some hotel auction.

She was vibrant, gregarious, and to the point. I sat across from her at a table in her office and we began to get to know each other. I went through our story to give her a background of what was going on and how we got to be in the position we were in. She asked some questions and said not to leave anything out. The two hours went by quickly, but we had already begun formulating a couple of causes of action that we could start with. I went home with a plan of action, a spring in my step, and a new person on the team who understood what was going on and how we could move forward legally.

By this time, I was reading anything and everything I could get my hands on to help my mind get into the world of law. This was when I started to frequent the numerous law libraries I had available within a half hour drive from me. I would sit in the libraries for hours on end and read through the dozens of thick legal volumes from Bender to West and everything in between.

I slowly started to open up a bit and talk with people who would study at the library, discussing similar issues, approaches, results, legal precedents, and civil codes and procedures that I was going to have to become intimately acquainted with. I fervently began to search out and acquire my own copies of *Black's Law Dictionary; California Pre-Trial Civil Procedure (Lexus/Nexus); California Civil Practice Statutes and Rules; Tort Law and Alternatives; Equitable Remedies, Restitution, and Damages; Sales and Secured Transactions; California Rules of Court; Federal Rules of Court;* and more.

I would search everything from garage sales to Craigslist, to friends, and even a book collector's convention that I attended. I didn't really find anything relevant there for me at the book show, but I did find a handwritten diary of legal thoughts from Thomas Jefferson. It was such a breath of fresh air to read some of his thoughts and to know that there were times when even he felt defeated. However, Thomas Jefferson had a knack to put the right words together to help him see through his hurdles and give himself a boost of energy to continue. I would have loved to buy the book, but I just didn't have $40,000 at the time.

I met with the paralegal a couple of days a week. We would sit together and hash out what was going on. She would keep things on track, yet she also took the time to help me to understand this new world of thinking: this world of law and the language that goes with it. She would remind me that we would have to understand the legal process of the case and be able to tell the story in a way that we could argue it in a courtroom. To do that, we not only needed to know the story inside out, but to tell it in a way that used the legal system and its rules and codes and language in the proper fashion within the confines of the courtroom.

We were told that we had ninety days from when we received the Notice of Default. At the end of that ninety-day period, the new timeline of when the house would go on the auction block at the county courthouse steps would begin. After the auction we would then receive a 3-Day Notice to Quit. This would be sent to us by the new owner. If we didn't leave within the three days, they would file what is called an Unlawful Detainer. That is when the previous owners refuse to leave the premises and an Unlawful Detainer is filed by the new owner from the auction to get the previous owner out of the house. After the end of the Unlawful Detainer action, the sheriff would issue an order to vacate. There will be a date that the sheriff comes to the property to make sure the foreclosed homeowner has vacated the premises, or they will then proceed and arrest the homeowner and remove all the contents from the home.

Or, we were told, we could file for bankruptcy. We were also informed that we could file a document that is called a Lis Pendens. This document is filed when the homeowner files a lawsuit against the bank for the wrongful foreclosure of the property and is then filed with the county recorder to be placed in the public documents pertaining to the property.

So, my question then was, "How do we go about filing a lawsuit?"

I talked for some time with the paralegal about our Deed of Trust, and how to find any improprieties within the documents filed by the bank that might allow an avenue to construct a lawsuit. You cannot file a Lis Pendens unless you file a lawsuit, since a Lis Pendens is basically the document that is filed at the County Recorder's Office to let the public know that there is litigation pending on the property. (See Exhibit 2 a-c)

The paralegal informed me that we couldn't simply file a lawsuit with the court. We had to detach ourselves from the situation enough to review the documents and find something that was questionable under the rule of law. Filing a frivolous lawsuit could cost us a lot more money and even land one in jail.

So, we then began to review all the documents that were being sent by the bank and all the documents that dealt with our Deed of Trust and any pre-loan documents that were part of the loan.

When filing a lawsuit, you must find a cause of action. This is what the paralegal meant by finding something that is questionable under the rule of law. Then you must learn the procedures of filing a lawsuit in the specific court where you will be filing.

There is a State Court and there is a Federal Court. Each court has a different set of rules and procedures as to how to file, what information the documents are to contain, and how they are to be structured.

Another thing is the jurisdiction of the parties involved. Where did the crime or illegality take place? Were the parties involved both from the same state? Or if one was not, such as a corporation, were they licensed to do business in that state? Little did I know then how important that question really is. It seemed trivial at the time because what bank would issue contracts and lend hundreds of thousands of dollars if they weren't legally able to do so? That would just seem so blatantly illegal.

For the State Superior Court in the state of California, there are documents that are to be filed with the cause of action, or your lawsuit. These documents are like cover pages, and must be contained within the documents filed, or the court will not accept your lawsuit paperwork.

1. When filing in the California Superior Court you must have a minimum of two copies of the documents you are submitting.

2. The original document with the original signatures must be two-hole punched at the top of the document and the other copies not.

3. The clerk will take the original and place it into the judge's personal docket file for the case.

4. The copies will be returned to you for your records and to use to serve to the other party by the deadline of the document.

5. The clerk of the court will review and accept the documents or perhaps explain what changes might need to be made for their acceptance.

6. The clerk is not able to answer legal questions. However, procedural questions regarding the paperwork can be assisted with.

7. When you file a lawsuit, you must also serve a summons to all the parties involved in the suit.

8. If it is a corporation, you must find the address to serve legal documents to the corporation and appropriately serve them at that address.

9. When the summons or subsequent lawsuit documents are served to the opposing parties, you must also submit a Certification of Service.

10. Once the lawsuit and summons are served properly, the opposing party has twenty-one days in which to respond to the legal allegations against them.

11. After the opposing party responds in this timeline, you then have fourteen days to respond to their response.

12. The opposing party is given one more opportunity to respond to your response and has seven days to do so. After this, there are no more opportunities to address any issues pertaining to any of the documents that have been filed.

13. The court will read through these documents and find room for cause. At this time, a schedule of events will begin with the court regarding having a case management conference.

The list of things to learn, tasks to do, timelines to adhere to, and legal pages to research and write seemed daunting. But like Thomas Jefferson said in his diary, "This is not for another man, but for me to task." Our meetings with the paralegal became much more intense. We read through countless legal cases, codes, procedures, and precedents as we began to prepare our lawsuit. We spent days putting together the cause of action documents and writing a Lis Pendens to file when we filed the lawsuit.

The first thing we had to learn about was the simple question as to what constitutes a contract. What is a deed of trust? There are rules and regulations the state has that helps answer these questions. We needed to learn those rules and then cross-reference that with what we had and see if everything was done correctly and by the rule of law.

To understand what a deed of trust contract is it is important to understand what a trustee is. Without the knowledge of what a trustee is, you will not be able to understand what a deed of trust is. So, we started there.

Trustee

On December 28, 2010, the trustee acting on behalf of Wells Fargo Bank filed the Notice of Default documents (See Exhibit 1a-c) stating they pertained to the Cal. Civ. Code 2924. This rule outlines the process and procedures that the financial institution is to follow to properly begin the Non-Judicial Foreclosure process in the state of California. This process had to be followed by Wells Fargo Bank due to the wording in the Deed of Trust contract. The wording of the contract states that the bank must follow the power of sale clause in the event of the need to foreclose. It is the power of sale clause that is defined in Cal. Civ. Code 2924.

The documents included a declaration from Wells Fargo (See Exhibit 1a). In this declaration, they marked a box that stated that they complied with the Cal. Civ. Code 2923.5(g) to make every attempt to contact us to discuss the defaulted loan in order to find resolution in an alternate means, and the Notice of Default. The Notice of Default is also outlined in the Civil Code regarding the information that is to be included within the Notice.

Declaration of non-monetary status in a legal dispute is the idea of eliminating a defendant based on their lack of legal and monetary interests in the case. This was the claim the defendant and original trustee, Golden West, was attempting to push through the court system. They claimed their innocence and therefore non-monetary status of their position of trustee.

How could this be so far from the truth? The trustee is an integral part of a non-judicial foreclosure procedure. It is their job to keep both parties at arm's length and make sure that both parties follow the civil procedural rules that govern the non-judicial foreclosure process. There are strict guidelines, dates, signatures, notices, and filings that must be adhered to in order to perfect the non-judicial foreclosure process. It is the job of the trustee to make sure that the paperwork being filed with the county recorder is correct and within the guidelines of the power of sale clause. This is the civil code that dictates the rules of the power of sale clause in California, known as Cal. Civ. Code § 2924.

There are tasks that are to be completed by a beneficiary prior to acting on Cal. Civ. Code § 2924. These rules were set up by the state to make sure that the borrower would be informed, or that the beneficiary be able to document that every step is being taken to inform the borrower against the impending foreclosure process.

There are rules set up whereby the beneficiary is to make every attempt possible to get in touch with the borrower to discuss options to rectify the debt and to make steps to bring things current in the possibility to avoid the foreclosure.

In our case, we had been in contact with Wells Fargo on a weekly basis via phone, email, or fax for well over a year and a half as we had been discussing our financial difficulties with them. This process is known in the industry as a modification. We went through every attempt and every program available, but they continued to turn us down for one reason or another. There were times when we would be waiting for a decision and the bank would respond by saying that they were missing some documents. So, once again we would send out documents to fulfill their request, only to be turned down. This happened repeatedly. They would lose documents, misfile paperwork, claim they never received papers, finally get the package of correct papers, and quickly deny the modification. This meant we would have to find a new program that might be available and begin the entire process all over again.

Despite all of the mishandling of our files and private information on a continual basis by Wachovia, if we could modify things, we wouldn't have to find ourselves in the position of dealing with a foreclosure. So, we finally took Wachovia's advice and stopped paying the mortgage as they had instructed us. We felt assured that by doing so we would be in a better position for them to grant us a modification based on new rules or new programs.

Modification was not their plan at all. Again, a misrepresentation of facts as they immediately filed a Notice of Default, defying all California non-judicial foreclosure rules.

As we reviewed the Declaration document, I found a good legal website that I felt comfortable with and trusted where I could look up this kind of information. I was soon reading through the California Civil Code rule 2923.5, which they referred to in their Declaration, and you will find below. I read through all the other codes referenced within Cal. Civ. Code 2923.5. Using all the codes referenced I began piecing the puzzle together, but things weren't making sense. It wasn't easy to read through these codes and understand them. It took numerous reads, besides time to step back and try to digest all the legalese stated. It isn't easy for a beginner, at all. I spent hours poring over this document alone and going through legal websites, legal definitions, codes, etc. Until then, I was looking over things and thinking that even on the first document things weren't adding up.

If we had been in contact with Wachovia Mortgage, on a near daily basis during the past eighteen odd months discussing loan modification, then their use of section CCP 2923.5(g) was incorrect. (NOTE: You will find that it now pertains to section (e) in the current code shown below.) Therefore, filing this document with incorrect information is a fraud against, not only us, but also the court. They were denying us our legal right to remedy the situation.

Only as things progressed did I realize how much fraud is done against borrowers and the court by all the lenders in the non-judicial foreclosure process, in the state of CA. When they file their documents, the lender is given the presumption of correctness as there is an independent party named as trustee who is entrusted to review all the information on the documents to be true and correct, so there is plenty of room for corruption and fraud to take place. But I digress.

This section where it states, "Wells Fargo Bank, N.A., has tried with due diligence, as prescribed by California Civil Code Section 2923.5(g), to contact the borrower," which they checked on their document, pertains to the section of the code that discusses all the ways in which the lender must attempt to contact the defaulted borrower. My initial question was why would they check this box stating that they had tried everything to contact the borrower but to no avail? In fact, we had been in contact with them frequently regarding loan modification for nearly two years. It didn't make sense.

You will find their reference to section (g) is now section (e) in the more current code, shown below. Notice all the requirements that are necessary to claim this section. They must have completed ALL the points listed in the section, not some of them, but ALL of them to legally check that box.

At this point, this might seem trivial to you, as it did to us. We didn't know at the time that EVERY point must be addressed to the court. EVERY false claim, every name, position, date, signature, everything becomes ammunition for a cause of action. Here we were on the very first page, just beginning this process and finding fraud. Little did we know how deep this went. Over time, researching and learning more about the process of a non-judicial foreclosure and the part that the trustee plays in the transaction, I kept coming back to the point that the trustee allowed a blatantly false document to be filed with the court and submitted to the County Recorder's Office, allowing the lender to begin their non-judicial foreclosure against us.

As I learned more about the process and read California Civil Code 2924, I kept thinking, "How could this happen if the trustee is independent?"

California Civil Code 2923.5

1) A mortgage servicer, mortgagee, trustee, beneficiary, or authorized agent may not record a notice of default pursuant to Section 2924 until both of the following:
    a) Either 30 days after initial contact is made as required by paragraph (2) or 30 days after satisfying the due diligence requirements as described in subdivision (e).
    b) The mortgage servicer complies with paragraph (1) of subdivision (a) of Section 2924.18, if the borrower has provided a complete application as defined in subdivision (d) of Section 2924.18.
2) A mortgage servicer shall contact the borrower in person or by telephone to assess the borrower's financial situation and explore options for the borrower to avoid foreclosure. During the initial contact, the mortgage servicer shall advise the borrower that he or she has the right to request a subsequent meeting and, if requested, the mortgage servicer shall schedule the meeting to occur within 14 days. The assessment of the borrower's financial situation and discussion of options may occur during the first contact, or at the subsequent meeting scheduled for that purpose. In either case, the borrower shall be provided the toll-free telephone number made available by the United States Department of Housing and Urban Development (HUD) to find a HUD-certified housing counseling agency. Any meeting may occur telephonically.
    a) A notice of default recorded pursuant to Section 2924 shall include a declaration that the mortgage servicer has contacted the borrower, has tried with due diligence to contact the borrower as required by this section, or that no contact was required because the individual did not meet the definition of "borrower" pursuant to subdivision (c) of Section 2920.5.

b) A mortgage servicer's loss mitigation personnel may participate by telephone during any contact required by this section.

c) A borrower may designate, with consent given in writing, a HUD-certified housing counseling agency, attorney, or other advisor to discuss with the mortgage servicer, on the borrower's behalf, the borrower's financial situation and options for the borrower to avoid foreclosure. That contact made at the direction of the borrower shall satisfy the contact requirements of paragraph (2) of subdivision (a). Any loan modification or workout plan offered at the meeting by the mortgage servicer is subject to approval by the borrower.

d) A notice of default may be recorded pursuant to Section 2924 when a mortgage servicer has not contacted a borrower as required by paragraph (2) of subdivision (a) provided that the failure to contact the borrower occurred despite the due diligence of the mortgage servicer. For purposes of this section, "due diligence" shall require and mean all of the following:

    (1) A mortgage servicer shall first attempt to contact a borrower by sending a first-class letter that includes the toll-free telephone number made available by HUD to find a HUD-certified housing counseling agency.

    (2) After the letter has been sent, the mortgage servicer shall attempt to contact the borrower by telephone at least three times at different hours and on different days. Telephone calls shall be made to the primary telephone number on file.

e) A mortgage servicer may attempt to contact a borrower using an automated system to dial borrowers, provided that, if the telephone call is answered, the call is connected to a live representative of the mortgage servicer.

f) A mortgage servicer satisfies the telephone contact requirements of this paragraph if it determines, after attempting contact pursuant to this paragraph that the borrower's primary telephone number and secondary telephone number or numbers on file, if any, have been disconnected.

3) If the borrower does not respond within two weeks after the telephone call requirements of paragraph (2) have been satisfied, the mortgage servicer shall then send a certified letter, with return receipt requested.

4) The mortgage servicer shall provide a means for the borrower to contact it in a timely manner, including a toll-free telephone number that will provide access to a live representative during business hours.

5) The mortgage servicer has posted a prominent link on the homepage of its Internet Web site, if any, to the following information:

a) Options that may be available to borrowers who are unable to afford their mortgage payments and who wish to avoid foreclosure, and instructions to borrowers advising them on steps to take to explore those options.
b) A list of financial documents borrowers should collect and be prepared to present to the mortgage servicer when discussing options for avoiding foreclosure.
c) A toll-free telephone number for borrowers who wish to discuss options for avoiding foreclosure with their mortgage servicer.
d) The toll-free telephone number made available by HUD to find a HUD-certified housing counseling agency.
e) This section shall apply only to mortgages or deeds of trust described in Section 2924.15.
f) This section shall apply only to entities described in subdivision (b) of Section 2924.18.
g) This section shall remain in effect only until January 1, 2018, and as of that date is repealed, unless a later enacted statute that is enacted before January 1, 2018, deletes, or extends that date. 2923.5. (a) (1) A mortgage servicer, mortgagee, trustee, beneficiary, or authorized agent may not record a notice of default pursuant to Section 2924 until both of the following:

6) Either 30 days after initial contact is made as required by paragraph (2) or 30 days after satisfying the due diligence requirements as described in subdivision (e).
7) The mortgage servicer complies with subdivision (a) of Section 2924.11, if the borrower has provided a complete application as defined in subdivision (f) of Section 2924.11.
   a) A mortgage servicer shall contact the borrower in person or by telephone to assess the borrower's financial situation and explore options for the borrower to avoid foreclosure. During the initial contact, the mortgage servicer shall advise the borrower that he or she has the right to request a subsequent meeting and, if requested, the mortgage servicer shall schedule the meeting to occur within 14 days. The assessment of the borrower's financial situation and discussion of options may occur during the first contact, or at the subsequent meeting scheduled for that purpose. In either case, the borrower shall be provided the toll-free telephone number made available by the United States Department of Housing and Urban Development (HUD) to find a HUD-certified housing counseling agency. Any meeting may occur telephonically.
   b) A notice of default recorded pursuant to Section 2924 shall include a declaration that the mortgage servicer has contacted the borrower, has

tried with due diligence to contact the borrower as required by this section, or that no contact was required because the individual did not meet the definition of "borrower" pursuant to subdivision (c) of Section 2920.5.

c) A mortgage servicer's loss mitigation personnel may participate by telephone during any contact required by this section.

d) A borrower may designate, with consent given in writing, a HUD-certified housing counseling agency, attorney, or other adviser to discuss with the mortgage servicer, on the borrower's behalf, the borrower's financial situation and options for the borrower to avoid foreclosure. That contact made at the direction of the borrower shall satisfy the contact requirements of paragraph (2) of subdivision (a). Any loan modification or workout plan offered at the meeting by the mortgage servicer is subject to approval by the borrower.

e) A notice of default may be recorded pursuant to Section 2924 when a mortgage servicer has not contacted a borrower as required by paragraph (2) of subdivision (a) provided that the failure to contact the borrower occurred despite the due diligence of the mortgage servicer. For purposes of this section, "due diligence" shall require and mean all of the following:

  (1) A mortgage servicer shall first attempt to contact a borrower by sending a first-class letter that includes the toll-free telephone number made available by HUD to find a HUD-certified housing counseling agency.

  (2) After the letter has been sent, the mortgage servicer shall attempt to contact the borrower by telephone at least three times at different hours and on different days. Telephone calls shall be made to the primary telephone number on file.

8) A mortgage servicer may attempt to contact a borrower using an automated system to dial borrowers, provided that, if the telephone call is answered, the call is connected to a live representative of the mortgage servicer.

9) A mortgage servicer satisfies the telephone contact requirements of this paragraph if it determines, after attempting contact pursuant to this paragraph that the borrower's primary telephone number and secondary telephone number or numbers on file, if any, have been disconnected.

  (1) If the borrower does not respond within two weeks after the telephone call requirements of paragraph (2) have been satisfied, the mortgage servicer shall then send a certified letter, with return receipt requested.

(2) The mortgage servicer shall provide a means for the borrower to contact it in a timely manner, including a toll-free telephone number that will provide access to a live representative during business hours.

(3) The mortgage servicer has posted a prominent link on the homepage of its Internet Web site, if any, to the following information:

10) Options that may be available to borrowers who are unable to afford their mortgage payments and who wish to avoid foreclosure, and instructions to borrowers advising them on steps to take to explore those options.
11) A list of financial documents borrowers should collect and be prepared to present to the mortgage servicer when discussing options for avoiding foreclosure.
12) A toll-free telephone number for borrowers who wish to discuss options for avoiding foreclosure with their mortgage servicer.
13) The toll-free telephone number made available by HUD to find a HUD-certified housing counseling agency.
    a) This section shall apply only to mortgages or deeds of trust described in Section 2924.15.
    b) This section shall become operative on January 1, 2018.

I removed this document, one of three pages that were in the #10 envelope and began to look things over. Remember, at this time in the process we didn't know what we were doing. We didn't understand what we were looking for. Because of this, all we could do was panic. We were numb and sitting on the couch trying to stay calm. Basically, we were getting documents stating that we will be losing our home. The hardest part for us to understand was that we were told by the lender to stop paying our mortgage so that we would qualify for a modification and within a month of that we had received these papers beginning the non-judicial foreclosure procedure on our home.

One thing we noticed was the amount, which seemed arbitrary as we weren't behind by that amount, so this was the first item we had questions about. The second thing was that there was a party on the document who had nothing to do with our mortgage whatsoever. NDEx West, LLC was a party we had no knowledge of or what they were doing participating in this process. You see, the trustee in our original note was not NDEx West, LLC. So, we had questions about that as well. We made a note of the trustee sale number and put this all in the folder we were beginning to put together for our case that wasn't even an idea yet...

I became antsy and had an idea, so I decided to head downtown to the County Recorder's Office to see what had been recorded against our property. I really needed a chance to get out of the house and clear my head. Things were spinning around faster than I was able to maintain. I needed some air and something else to think about for a little while.

Without any concept at the onset, this ended up becoming a good idea. What I learned from this was where the building was, how to access the computers at the County Recorder's Office and how to get information on either a property or a person. I found out where to park and learned the office assistants' names. I didn't realize how important all this was and how it would come in handy as we moved forward. You see, by understanding my way around this office and its practices, as soon as things got filed and we eventually began our court case, we were able to get things handled quickly and efficiently. Sometimes, when you are really under a court deadline to file a document or research information, it is good to get some of the basics out of the way.

So, we kept reviewing it repeatedly, taking notes on anything else we found suspicious or that didn't seem clear to us. We did all this while reviewing the civil code that these documents were related to. That was California Civil Code 2924.

California Civil Code 2924

1) Every transfer of an interest in property, other than in trust, made only as a security for the performance of another act, is to be deemed a mortgage, except when in the case of personal property, it is accompanied by actual change of possession, in which case it is to be deemed a pledge. Where, by a mortgage created after July 27, 1917, of any estate in real property, other than an estate at will or for years, less than two, or in any transfer in trust made after July 27, 1917, of a like estate to secure the performance of an obligation, a power of sale is conferred upon the mortgagee, trustee, or any other person, to be exercised after a breach of the obligation for which that mortgage or transfer is a security, the power shall not be exercised except where the mortgage or transfer is made pursuant to an order, judgment, or decree of a court of record, or to secure the payment of bonds or other evidences of indebtedness authorized or permitted to be issued by the Commissioner of Corporations, or is made by a public utility subject to the provisions of the Public Utilities Act, until all of the following apply:
2) The trustee, mortgagee, or beneficiary, or any of their authorized agents shall first file for record, in the office of the recorder of each county wherein the mortgaged or trust property or some part or parcel thereof is situated, a notice of default. That notice of default shall include all the following:
    a) A statement identifying the mortgage or deed of trust by stating the name or names of the trustor or trustors and giving the book and page, or instrument number, if applicable, where the mortgage or deed of trust is recorded or a description of the mortgaged or trust property.
    b) A statement that a breach of the obligation for which the mortgage or transfer in trust is security has occurred.
    c) A statement setting forth the nature of each breach known to the beneficiary and of his or her election to sell or cause to be sold the property to satisfy that obligation and any other obligation secured by the deed of trust or mortgage that is in default.
    d) If the default is curable pursuant to Section 2924c, the statement specified in paragraph (1) of subdivision (b) of Section 2924c.
3) Not less than three months shall elapse from the filing of the notice of default.
4) Except as provided in paragraph (4), after the lapse of the three months described in paragraph (2), the mortgagee, trustee, or other person authorized to take the sale shall give notice of sale, stating the time and place thereof, in the manner and for a time not less than that set forth in Section 2924f.
5) Notwithstanding paragraph (3), the mortgagee, trustee, or other person authorized to take sale may record a notice of sale pursuant to Section 2924f

up to five days before the lapse of the three-month period described in paragraph (2), provided that the date of sale is no earlier than three months and 20 days after the recording of the notice of default.

6) Until January 1, 2018, whenever a sale is postponed for a period of at least 10 business days pursuant to Section 2924g, a mortgagee, beneficiary, or authorized agent shall provide written notice to a borrower regarding the new sale date and time, within five business days following the postponement. Information provided pursuant to this paragraph shall not constitute the public declaration required by subdivision (d) of Section 2924g. Failure to comply with this paragraph shall not invalidate any sale that would otherwise be valid under Section 2924f. This paragraph shall be inoperative on January 1, 2018.

7) No entity shall record or cause a notice of default to be recorded or otherwise initiate the foreclosure process unless it is the holder of the beneficial interest under the mortgage or deed of trust, the original trustee, or the substituted trustee under the deed of trust, or the designated agent of the holder of the beneficial interest. No agent of the holder of the beneficial interest under the mortgage or deed of trust, original trustee, or substituted trustee under the deed of trust may record a notice of default or otherwise commence the foreclosure process except when acting within the scope of the beneficial interest.

    (a) In performing acts required by this article, the trustee shall incur no liability for any good faith error resulting from reliance on information provided in good faith by the beneficiary regarding the nature and the amount of the default under the secured obligation, deed of trust, or mortgage. In performing the acts required by this article, a trustee shall not be subject to Title1.6c (commencing with Section 1788) of Part 4.

    (b) A recital in the deed executed pursuant to the power of sale of compliance with all requirements of law regarding the mailing of copies of notices or the publication of a copy of the notice of default or the personal delivery of the copy of the notice of default or the posting of copies of the notice of sale or the publication of a copy thereof shall constitute prima facie evidence of compliance with these requirements and conclusive evidence thereof in favor of bona fide purchasers and encumbrancers for value and without notice.

    (c) All of the following shall constitute privileged communications pursuant to Section 47:

8) The mailing, publication, and delivery of notices as required by this section.

9) Performance of the procedures set forth in this article.
10) Performance of the functions and procedures set forth in this article if those functions and procedures are necessary to carry out the duties described in Sections 729.040, 729.050, and 729.080 of the Code of Civil Procedure.

    (a) There is a rebuttable presumption that the beneficiary knew of all unpaid loan payments on the obligation owed to the beneficiary and secured by the deed of trust or mortgage subject to the notice of default. However, the failure to include a known default shall not invalidate the notice of sale and the beneficiary shall not be precluded from asserting a claim to this omitted default or defaults in a separate notice of default. (f) With respect to residential real property containing no more than four dwelling units, a separate document containing a summary of the notice of default information in English and the languages described in Section 1632 shall be attached to the notice of default provided to the mortgagor or trustor pursuant to Section 2923.3.

***

Through our continual efforts of locating, faxing, emailing documents, and making phone calls—only to be put on hold for over an hour in a queue that eventually hangs up—we were seemingly ending one phase of the façade and entering a new one of litigation. Judging by the date on the document, attached here below, there wasn't much time in between our modification counselor's advice to stop paying the mortgage and the initiation of the foreclosure process. It made me go hmmm.

I began reading as much as I could find about how to file a lawsuit without an attorney. There wasn't much out there about this that I found very helpful. There was a lot of information, but there seemed to be little that was focused on the individual in this specific situation. One thing we began to learn while researching was that the state of CA is a Deed of Trust state. This means that the loan is attached to a Deed of Trust, a document that uses the borrower's property as security for the loan. To facilitate this process and contract agreement, the state included an independent third party, called a trustee, to be in the middle of the transaction in order to facilitate a reconveyance or foreclosure, and to protect both parties from being in possession of the title while the mortgage contract is in effect. The powers of the trustee come from a part within a Deed of Trust contract called the power of sale clause. The power of sale clause is written in the California Civil Code under section 2924. The Deed of Trust outlines the position of the trustee stating that its powers within the contract are derived from this code.

The trustee's position is to protect the borrower's title from the lender having any control of the title throughout the life of the contract, and to then give the title back to the borrower upon a reconveyance of the mortgage. This means that after the borrower pays off that loan, the trustee is then instructed to give the title back to the borrower. The trustee is also part of the transaction to protect the lender in the event of a default by the borrower, at which time, the trustee is then given strict rules to follow from code 2924 that must be adhered to for the lender to commence a non-judicial foreclosure action properly and legally.

We also found that the homeowner must file a lawsuit against the bank in a foreclosure action because the state is a non-judicial foreclosure state. In other words, the legal system in the state of California has entrusted the "too big to fail" financial institutions with the presumption of correctness in the documents that they must file to the County Recorder's Office to substantiate and initiate a foreclosure. Because the trustee is charged with making sure that all documents to be filed by the foreclosing party are true and correct and that all actions according to those documents have been verified, it is assumed that is indeed the case. In theory, a non-judicial foreclosure process is designed for mitigation of the litigation in the courts. This presumption of correctness is due to the check and balance structure via the trustee that was designed to alleviate taking all the foreclosures into the courtrooms. The only recourse a borrower might have when they find that the foreclosing party is wrongly foreclosing on them is to file a lawsuit against them for wrongful foreclosure, fraud, or other complaints.

Therefore, we began thinking, how could this document be filed by the trustee if the statements made within the document are incorrect? What I found interesting in this document was that the bank was declaring that it complied with California Civil Code section 2923.5 to fulfil the bank's obligations with the rules of a non-judicial foreclosure. The funny thing that struck me was that they checked the box that stated they complied with code section 2923.5(g).

The trustee is there, as an independent party within the transaction, to oversee the non-judicial foreclosure process and verify the accuracy of documents and actions that are to be followed by the lender in order to foreclose on a defaulted borrower properly and legally. The trustee is then responsible to affirm the accuracy of the documents to be submitted by the lender. The trustee then gives those approved documents to a title company to file on behalf of the lender as true and correct. Then, the title company files those documents with the County Recorder's Office. In theory, this check and balance process is designed to keep all this cumbersome paperwork out of the courts.

One thing I had read when I began doing my initial research was to review every word and to tear apart every sentence. If the document said that the bank did something, make sure they did what they said they stated.

As I stated previously, the Notice of Default ("NOD") had three pages (See Exhibit 1a-c). As we researched the rules about this CCP 2923.5 that was mentioned in the declaration, and associated rules CCP 2924 that was mentioned within 2923.5 and others we investigated, we wanted to make sure that the paperwork complied with the rules. We were so new at this we didn't quite know what we were looking for. Remember, this was January 2011. There had been a lot of news about corruption at this point, however, the courts were siding with the banks, and the press was claiming that the problems with the economy were based on homeowners failing and trying to cheat the system. The system was winning.

We scoured the Notice of Default. It now seemed to be naming all the players, although, when we got out our Deed of Trust and cross-referenced the information, we found some names we didn't recognize. There was a firm called NDEx West, LLC, and a title company named LSI Title that we had no reference to in the original Deed of Trust (See Exhibit 3). We began making notes and writing these bits of information down. No matter how confusing, ridiculous, or minute the information was, we wanted to make sure we had referenced every detail in order to look things up later.

I also found that they were referring to our second note, or the line of credit that we had taken out against the home for repairs and renovation. The amount of that note was $100,000. However, it was noted in this document that the delinquency was due against the senior lien. It also stated the date of delinquency was 02/15/2011 on this note. That seemed odd, since we were current until the bank recently told us to stop paying in order for modification. So, the note didn't correspond, the amount due on that note didn't correspond, the dates didn't correspond, and some of the players in this charade didn't correspond. The timing seemed off due to the nature of our modification process that we had been going through, as it was so soon after we were told by the bank to stop paying our mortgage to comply with the needs of the modification process. We wrote down the numbers on the pages, the names on the pages, the Civil Codes referenced within the documents, the dates, the signatures… everything started to become part of our notes. Now, we needed to figure out what to do with that information.

Deed of Trust

None of it made any sense.

Increasingly, over time, it all began to play itself out in front of me, as I peeled through the layers of the legal volumes of Matthew Bender or West Publishing. The walls continued to close in on me with every breath and turn of a page. Generally, I am a conspiracy person. But as my friends would attest, I say, "I only believe in the conspiracies that are true." I have learned to question everything.

Everything I was learning from the research I was doing was meant to give me answers to the questions I was asking but instead was simply creating more questions. Sometimes, it felt as if I were spinning around on a carousel in my mind while playing musical chairs listening to repeats of the old 70s television game show, *The Gong Show*. Only what I was finding was that the "American Dream" was going to be gonged right out of existence.

If what I thought was going on were true, the fallout would be unparalleled. If it were true, it would mean a measure of fraud and corruption at such a scale that no one could seem to fathom. In fact, I had yet to fully comprehend the extent of what I was about to find.

Could it have all been orchestrated? Could it be a multi-decade long master plan from the global elite and Wall Street? Or was it simply the continued unfolding of the quiet, yet seemingly inevitable demise of the human spirit through a failing capitalistic paradigm? We were experiencing the disappearance of the heralded ideal that is known throughout the world as the "American Dream".

1. Breakdown of the backs of the pillar of the American society known as the middle-class.

2. The continued collapse of the celebrated mighty dollar. The currency of choice throughout the world, the dollar, has seen its value drop 90% in four short decades.

3. The legal tender note used for nearly all debts, public and private that is backed by the full trust and faith in the stability of the United States government who—through the quiet and calculated efforts that span both sides of the political isles over decades of policy decisions by mostly aged, white, millionaire men traversing the sidewalks of K, H, and G streets, and Pennsylvania Avenue in the nation's capital—have left a wake of ignoring our social infrastructure and created destruction from deregulation and failed economic policy decisions.

What I needed to do was find a real Deed of Trust that had been filed and constructed correctly as per the rule of law. I wanted to find a few that I could then use as exhibits to show the court what a true and correct Deed of Trust looks like because my Deed of Trust was not making any sense as to what I was understanding the rules of civil procedure in the state of California to be. Things weren't clear and there seemed to be too many loose ends. There seemed to be too many mistakes that were being made and showing up in the documents being filed with the County Recorder's Office about the impending foreclosure happening against my personal property.

What I decided to do was to go through computer files at the County Recorder's Office and see how far back I would have to go to find a Deed of Trust document that had been recorded and was true and correct. By that, I mean as per the rules of law in the state of California and which contained the legal structure and wording as per the California Code of Civil Procedure, which dictate what makes up a correct Deed of Trust mortgage contract in a real estate transaction.

Why did I feel there were some issues with my Deed of Trust and why was I suspicious about it being true and correct? What was it that I found that sparked my curiosity as to the legitimacy of my Deed of Trust?

To answer these questions, we must start at the beginning. We need to review the first documents I received that began my non-judicial foreclosure fraud. We will take apart each document that began to open my eyes to the fraud that was being perpetrated as I did.

I learned and soaked up as much information as I could while I had the paralegal working with me. I found that in law you must question everything, and every word is specific and necessary. So, the first thing I wanted to do was to find out what a contract was.

A contract is an agreement between two or more persons that creates an obligation to do or not to do a particular thing. Its essentials are competent parties, subject matter, a legal consideration, mutuality of agreement and mutuality of obligation. Lamoureux v Burrillville Racing Ass'n. 91 R.I. 94, 161 A.2d 213, 215 *Black's Law Dictionary 5th Edition 1979* (c) West Publishing. In other words, a contract is an agreement between two or more people. This agreement is based on those people involved and something specific that is outlined in the contract to do. So, the parts of the contract would contain the names of the people who are involved in the agreement about what the specific task or obligation is, a detailed description of what that task or obligation is exactly, descriptions and details of any legal rules and regulations that must be followed by either party involved in the agreement, and the mutual consent of agreement of both parties involved in the contract and each party's obligation.

Now, Real Contracts are those in which it is necessary that there should be something more than mere consent, such as a loan of money, deposit, or pledge, which from their nature, require a delivery of the thing (*res*). In common law, a contract respecting real property — such as a lease of land for years — is called a "real" contract. *Black's Law Dictionary 5th Edition 1979* (c) West Publishing. So, a real contract is when real property is involved in the transaction, and when a promise is included with a transfer of money.

For any contract to be legitimate, there must be a meeting of the minds. This goes to the part of the description that states a "mutuality of agreement and obligation." A meeting of the minds is when two parties to an agreement (contract) both have the same understanding of the terms of the agreement. Such mutual comprehension is essential to a valid contract. It is provable by the express provisions of a written contract, without reference to any statements or hidden thoughts outside the writing. There would not be a meeting of the minds if Bill Buyer said, "I'll buy all your stock," and he meant shares in a corporation, and Sam Seller said, "I'll sell all my stock to you," and meant his cattle. *The Free Dictionary©1981-2005* by Gerald N. Hill and Kathleen T. Hill. All Right reserved.

Now, in the United States, there are two different types of mortgage agreements. As of this writing, there are thirty-two states that deal with a Deed of Trust mortgage. The other states deal with a standard mortgage agreement, although many states continue to create Deed of Trust state legislation to further add to that growing list. Let us begin with a mortgage. What is a mortgage? A mortgage, or a mortgage loan, is used by a party who is purchasing real property and needs to borrow the funds necessary to buy the real estate. It is also used when an existing property owner might want to raise money for their child's college, or perhaps for retirement, or a vacation whereby a lien would be placed on the property to "secure" the loan. This simply means that a legal mechanism, a lien, is filed in the County Recorder's Office to put in place a document that allows the lender to take possession and sell the property that is secured by the lien, in order to pay off the loan in the event that the borrower defaults on the loan agreement or fails to abide by the terms as they are detailed in the contract. So, a mortgage is described as "a borrower giving consideration, or the property in the form of collateral for a benefit, or for the use of the loan proceeds to the borrower."

Mortgage borrowers can be either individuals borrowing for their residential property, or for a business for their commercial property — for example owning their own business premises or owning a residential property that is leased to tenants or used in an investment portfolio.

The lender will typically be some sort of financial institution, such as a bank or credit union. The loan arrangements can be made directly between the lender and the borrower, but they can also include third parties to act as intermediaries. Some of the features that a mortgage loan has are the size of the loan, the duration or maturity of the loan, the interest rate on the amount borrowed, and the method of repaying the loan. There are also other characteristics that can vary considerably.

The lender's rights over the secured property take priority over the borrower's other creditors, which means that, if the borrower were to ever become bankrupt, or insolvent, the other creditors will only be repaid for their debts owed them after the mortgage lender has been repaid in full using the proceeds from the sale of the property.

To be clear, all states allow a mortgage agreement. However, if the mortgage is being created in a Deed of Trust state and it is done using a federally insured lending institution, then the contract that the financial institution lending the money to the borrower would use is a Deed of Trust contract. This contract is fairly standard and is distributed to the lending institutions through the organization known as Fannie Mae, or Freddie Mac.

Fannie Mae, as it is more commonly known, is the Federal National Mortgage Association. It was founded in 1938 during the Great Depression that came out of what was known as the New Deal. It is a government sponsored enterprise and has been publicly traded since 1968, whose purpose primarily is to expand the secondary mortgage market by securitizing mortgages in the form of what has now become commonly known as a mortgage-backed security (MBS). This allows lenders to reinvest their assets into more lending and thereby increase the number of lenders in the mortgage markets by reducing the reliance solely on local community banks and savings and loans.

The reason that so many states have turned away from the standard mortgage agreement and switched over to the Deed of Trust mortgage agreement is to help reduce the overloaded court system. This was to be accomplished in part because of the premise of the Deed of Trust. So, rather than the lender needing to sue the borrower who may have defaulted on the loan in order to be repaid for the outstanding balance due from the money borrowed, a Deed of Trust is designed to have an independent third party involved in the agreement whose sole purpose is to make sure that both parties in the transaction abide by the rules set forth in the contract and handle the foreclosure outside of the courts, thereby reducing the burden of the courts to settle the agreement. The idea that the trustee is an independent third party to the transaction allows a non-judicial foreclosure process, as it is known in the state of CA.

In a non-judicial foreclosure proceeding, the lender doesn't have to go to court in order to foreclose on the property. The financial institutions enjoy this feature as it means that the foreclosure can proceed quicker. Due to the costs of litigation and the overburdened court system, it saves the states money if they bypass the court system.

If the property is in a Deed of Trust state, the borrower would likely sign the main documents in order to buy or refinance a property. There is a Promissory Note and a Deed of Trust. The Deed of Trust (DOT) is used to turn the Promissory Note into a debt that is secured by a lien, or encumbrance or legal claim on the property. The DOT gives authorization to the lender to foreclose on the property if the borrower were to default. The DOT gives strict guidelines that are to be administered in accordance with the rules of law and codes of civil procedure and allows the foreclosure to proceed out of the courthouse, and under the state law.

Each state's law sets out the ways and means of the foreclosure procedure. Some of these rules would include how much notice a borrower would get, how the property will be sold, and what rights the borrower might have to have the loan reinstated before the foreclosure date, or how to recover the title of the property after it had been sold at an auction, for example.

The timeline to the foreclosure process is drastically reduced in a non-judicial state. This means the borrower must act and act quickly to stop and rectify the process to save the property. This is because the borrower will receive little notice of a foreclosure sale. In the state of CA, this process from the beginning of a foreclosure to the date of sale can be as little as ninety days. So, if a borrower is in the foreclosure proceeding in a non-judicial state, they don't have much time to learn about and act on their behalf to stop the foreclosure and find a means to rectify the situation.

<u>Notice of trustee sale.</u> In some states, your first notice of the proceeding will be the notice of sale. Depending on the state, this notice will be either served on you personally, published in the local newspaper, posted in the courthouse and on the property itself, or by some combination of the above.

<u>Notice of default and notice of trustee sale.</u> Some states provide you with two notices—a formal written notice that you are in default (usually about thirty days, but sometimes more and sometimes less) and another formal notice that your house will be sold at auction (again, usually about a month). (See Exhibit 4)

<u>Right to reinstate.</u> Between the notice of default and notice of sale, you can typically reinstate the mortgage by paying off what you owe, plus fees and costs (which can be very high). With a couple of exceptions, however, once the sale occurs, your house is gone.

<u>The auction is held.</u> If you don't reinstate the mortgage, the home will be sold at auction. As with judicial foreclosures, if no one meets the minimum bid, the property goes to the lender.

<u>Right to redeem.</u> A few states give you some time after the foreclosure auction to redeem the property (to recover ownership of the property by paying off the successful bidder).

You can challenge a non-judicial foreclosure in court. However, you don't have the opportunity to raise a defense in the case of a non-judicial foreclosure. If you wish to contest the foreclosure, you will have to file a lawsuit yourself. When you do this, you ask the court to temporarily stop the foreclosure so that you can resolve the legal issues in court (and possibly at trial). Once you are in court, you can raise the same defense you would have raised in a judicial foreclosure proceeding.

In these lawsuits, you typically ask the court for three things, in the following order:

1. A temporary restraining order, which lasts about ten days.

2. A preliminary injunction, which in foreclosure actions will last until the court decides the case.

3. A permanent injunction, which will be issued if the judge decides in your favor.

So, let's break this down a little further and find out what a deed of trust is.

Deed

A conveyance of realty; a writing signed by grantor, whereby title to realty is transferred from one to another. National Fire Ins. Co. v Patterson, 170 Okl., 593, 41 P.2d 645, 647. A written instrument, signed, and delivered by which one person conveys land, tenements, or hereditaments to another. *Black's Law Dictionary 5th Edition 1979* (c) West Publishing.

A Deed of Trust is an instrument in use in some states, taking the place and serving the uses of a mortgage, by which the legal title to a real property is placed in one or more trustees, to secure the repayment of a sum of money or the performance of other conditions. Though differing in form from mortgage, it is essentially a security. In re Title Guaranty Trust Co., Mo. App., 113 S. E.2d 1053, 1057.

The term security is usually applied to a deposit, lien, or mortgage voluntarily given by a debtor to a creditor to guarantee payment of a debt. Security furnishes the creditor with a resource to be sold or possessed in case of the debtor's failure to meet his financial obligation. In addition, a person who becomes a surety for another is sometimes referred to as a "security".

Among millions, they did this by filing fraudulent documents into the County Recorder's Office to quickly foreclose on the property. I proved this fact in court to a corrupt judge, who stated in court that he totally understands that it is the job of the trustee, as it is laid out by the CA Supreme Court, that the trustee is to be at arm's length from all parties in the transaction and to be independent. This was the intention of the legislation when they created the non-judicial foreclosure process used as a means to reduce the burden on the courts from the court required mortgage agreement process needed to settle a default in a real estate transaction. The trustee is in place to make sure that both parties perform their tasks as outlined in the contract agreement.

Even though he stated in court that he understands this issue, immediately, he then dismissed the case and silenced the paperwork. Paid off? Perhaps. Justice served? Not a chance. Have there been any changes done to stop the fact that anyone acting as a bank or a trustee can file fraudulent paperwork into the court and illegally foreclose on anyone at any time because the trustee holds NO power at all to stop the action from taking place? No.

The trustee is not independent, as the ruling of the Supreme Court of CA has stated the case to be. The banks know this yet issue a Deed of Trust agreement to a borrower knowing full well that the trustee in the agreement holds no power to protect the borrower's position in the agreement whatsoever. The banks skirt around the rule of Cal. Civ. Code 2924 in their ability to name a new trustee at will. How could this be independent?

My question is: If a trustee is to be an independent third party to a Deed of Trust agreement in order to protect both parties from any harm from either party, but they are allowed by the courts to file fraudulent paperwork on behalf of the banks during the foreclosure process, how then is it NOT fraud if the banks know this, yet still offer borrowers a Deed of Trust document knowing that the trustee is NOT independent and file fraudulent paperwork on behalf of the banks, when it is the job of the trustee to make sure BOTH parties are acting in accordance with the rules of law regarding the contract agreement?

The complicit nature of the courts allowing the banks to file fraudulent paperwork also allows banks to foreclose on someone who doesn't even have a loan with any lender. As soon as I showed this information to the court, the judge dismissed my case. Despite other corruption I experienced in the courts, this was the biggest. This action allows the banks to illegally foreclose on anyone, anytime, anywhere in a Deed of Trust state. There are currently thirty-two Deed of Trust states, and all other states are currently going through the process of going from standard mortgage agreements to Deeds of Trust. This will make it available for any bank to foreclose on any property owner at anytime, anywhere.

My follow up question to this is: Over 85% of all home real estate transactions have been securitized nationwide and packaged into mortgage-backed securities. To do this, the initial lender must SELL the note, so that the new trust can go through the securitization process in accordance with the rules of the SEC. How then can the initial lender come back to the table later down the road and foreclose on the borrower claiming they have standing to foreclose? They can't have standing to foreclose if they sold the note to another party. Also, this means that the trustee filed fraudulent paperwork to allow the courts to even THINK that the bank might have the right to foreclose.

Numerous studies have shown that over 95% of the securitizations have been filed incorrectly. This makes the note that was securitized VOID. If the note is void, then there is no standing.

Also, during the process of securitization, the rules of the SEC deal with the bifurcation process. In this, the note must be delivered to the securitizing trust free from all encumbrances. To accomplish this, they must separate the note from the Deed of Trust, or the encumbrance, thereby making the Deed of Trust void. Without a valid Deed of Trust and a void note, there is no standing for anyone to foreclose.

On March 14, 2011 (See Exhibit 5a-b), we sent a letter out to all the names and corporate players we could think of and find, as we thoroughly reviewed the Notice of Default letter that we received in the first days of the year 2011. This letter was sent out in addition to the Qualified Written Request (QWR). The Qualified Written Request rule allows a borrower a specific timeline and process in which to request and receive information and documentation that might help them answer questions they might have regarding the foreclosure documents the borrower is receiving in the mail. The law states that the borrower has an opportunity to submit a request for information and the recipient of the request has a specified timeframe in which to respond to this request. If the response doesn't include the answers to the questions, and/or isn't returned to the borrower who is requesting the information, then, by law, the foreclosure process is to stop. The financial institution may begin the foreclosure process again. However, it must comply with all the rules and regulations of the state and federal codes and statutes to move the foreclosure process forward. The Notice of Default was dated as being filed with the County Recorder's Office on Dec. 30, 2010. Then, a firm named NDEx West, Inc. had filed the Notice of Default against us.

This letter went unanswered. The reason for this was that we sent the first letter to the wrong parties. I began to learn—and you must very quickly—that you will make mistakes. It was a given, since I had never been in this position before and was totally lost as to the rules of foreclosure, as well as any rules of law that apply to foreclosure. I began to read. I began to read a lot. It was clear that it was imperative that I learn just what it was that we were undertaking. There was a new language, the language of law, which I had to become familiar with if we were to have any chance of successfully participating in this process.

The Qualified Written Request falls under 12 U.S. Code § 2605 - Servicing of mortgage loans and administration of escrow accounts. We originally didn't send this letter out to the firm NDEx West, Inc., as we had never heard of this firm prior to them filing the Notice of Default. When I reviewed our mortgage documents, which originated back in 2005, there was no such company named NDEx West mentioned in any of the paperwork.

I spent countless hours sitting quietly behind a computer terminal at the County Recorder's Office combing through hundreds of documents in the county archives hoping to find a document that named a substitution of trustee for NDEx West, as they were the firm now claiming to be an "original trustee, a substituted trustee, agent for the beneficiary ...." and other assertions as to who they claimed they were. However, I failed to find any legitimate filing to say who this company was within the agreement between the original lender and us, the borrower, or any other documents that had been filed to date. Yet, they filed the Notice of Default through a title company called LSI Title. So, we sent our first installment of the QWR letter to the names pertaining to the document and firm, LSI Title Co., to come up with some more information. It went unanswered.

I believe that there is an 'aha' moment in almost every story. It's like that part in a movie where everything changes. There becomes a paradigm shift for the participants in the storyline. I'm sure you've heard the saying "Does art imitate life or does life imitate art?"

I remember my 'aha' moment. There was a small bay area breeze that blew through the paralegal's office. It came at a specific second when my mind began to connect some of the dots. I knew that something wasn't right despite not knowing what that something was. *Right?*

After completing the original complaint with the paralegal and filling out the appropriate court documents that corresponded with this, it was time to file and send the summons to all the defendants named in the complaint.

By this time, I had certainly had a crash course in law. A key procedural part of any legal case is the necessity to summon the defendants. That is, to inform them that they are now included and party to a legal proceeding and to file proof of that service to the court. It creates the legal clock and evidentiary background to show that the accused party has been served the legal paperwork and has a specific legal limited timeline in which they need to respond to the arguments in the documents filed with the court.

What I found interesting was an address. In this case, a specific address. Most corporations have many different addresses and phone numbers for all the divisions or departments. Some of these divisions and departments can be located in different states. And in some cases, different countries. I found that, when serving legal documents to a corporation, there is a specific address that is deemed necessary to comply with the legal process. Due to this, and the fact that there were multiple defendants being named in the lawsuit, it took a little bit of research to come up with all the appropriate locations for service to all the various parties.

What caught my attention was the address of the original trustee in the Deed of Trust agreement, Golden West Savings Association. First of all, it wasn't not the same name as the entity listed on the foreclosure documents. That "substituted" trustee, named as NDEx, West, LLC, had simply appeared out of nowhere. They were in no other documentation registered with the county recorder's office prior to the filing of any of the foreclosure documents.

As I was writing down the service contact information of the original trustee in my notes, I felt as if I had written it before. Since I wasn't doing any of the address research in any order, it took a moment to set in. It seemed that Wells Fargo Bank had the exact same service address for legal documents as the original trustee, Golden West Savings Association, named in the original Deed of Trust contract. For some reason, this stood out to me as something that didn't feel right. I just hadn't learned enough about the position of a trustee in a Deed of Trust contract, yet.

Lis Pendens

We found the statute of frauds, a law which dates from 1677, that states any transfer of any rights or privileges to a real estate contract must be done in writing and signed by all parties involved. This is so that all parties involved in the transaction become privy to the changes and are knowledgeable of any changes and of any new parties in the contract. In U.S. law, a lis pendens is a written notice that a lawsuit has been filed concerning real estate, involving either the title to the property or a claimed ownership interest in it. The notice is usually filed in the County Land Records Office. Recording a lis pendens against a piece of property alerts a potential purchaser or lender that the property's title is in question, which makes the property less attractive to a buyer or lender. After the notice is filed, anyone who nevertheless purchases the land or property described in the notice takes it subject to the ultimate decision of the lawsuit.

Lis pendens is Latin for "suit pending." This may refer to any pending lawsuit or to a specific situation with a public notice of litigation that has been recorded in the same location where the title of real property has been recorded. This notice secures a plaintiff's claim on the property so that the sale, mortgage, or encumbrance of the property will not diminish the plaintiff's rights to the property, should the plaintiff prevail in its case. In some jurisdictions, when the notice is properly recorded, *lis pendens* is considered constructive notice to the other litigants or other unrecorded or subordinate lien holders. The term is sometimes abbreviated as "*lis pend*".

The County Recorder's Office will record a lis pendens upon request of anyone who claims to be entitled to do so (e.g., because they have filed a lawsuit). If someone else with an interest in the property (e.g., the owner) believes the lis pendens is not proper, they can then file suit to have it expunged. Some states' lis pendens statutes require the filer of the notice, in the event of a challenge to the notice, to establish that it has probable cause or a good likelihood of success on the merits of its case in the underlying lawsuit; other states do not have such a requirement.

Every time we met, this specific document had been on the forefront of the paralegal's mind, as we were preparing documents to initially file the case. Since there was a scheduled date set for the sale of the property, we had been under the gun to try to get all the necessary paperwork put together in order to file the lawsuit. The paralegal made sure to impress upon us the necessity to investigate also filing a lis pendens after we filed our case paperwork. This is because a lis pendens can be a legal document that helps to stop the foreclosure process in its tracks, and that is because a buyer at a foreclosure sale is much less likely to purchase a property in foreclosure if it has outstanding liens or litigation against the property. They would therefore move on to another property to purchase or wait until the liens or litigation on the property were settled. Furthermore, the parties orchestrating the foreclosure procedure might be inclined to take the property off the foreclosure timeline as they would hold liability for their actions if they were to wrongly or illegally sell a property that then ends up being litigated in favor of the plaintiffs.

One thing I found throughout my legal history is that the judicial system does not make, or wish to make, things easy for someone who is in the system acting as their own attorney. The system is filled with judges who used to be lawyers. Those judges understand that when someone is litigating their case as a pro per, or pro se, they are taking business away from a lawyer. The judges are simply looking out for their fellow golfing buddies. So, it is simply that judges can, and do make the process difficult for those acting on their own behalf. Perhaps, so that the pro per party might finally end up getting fed up with the system and subsequently would eventually hire an attorney. It is also because judges don't wish to deal with people who don't understand the legal procedures or perhaps don't have the acumen to argue their case in the same manner that a trained lawyer might. This would mean that the judge would have to do some real thinking in order to comprehend the thoughts and reasonings of a "normal" person, rather than the systemic legal authorities who are quoted on a daily basis, making the judge's decision easy. Plus, the judge will be unlikely to get any payola under the table to settle or end a case from a "normal" citizen who is acting as their own attorney. However, they might receive a payoff from a corporate law firm with whom the judge just might have stock in their own personal retirement portfolio of that financial institution. We will revisit this at the end of the book, but I digress ....

I say this because when I went to the County Recorder's Office to file our lis pendens I found that, in the state of CA, according to California Civil Code of Procedure 405.21, if you are acting as your own attorney you must have a judge review your case and sign off on your lis pendens before you can make it active and record it into the public record (See Exhibit 2 a-c). Therefore, we had to run back to the courthouse looking for an available sitting judge who would review the case documents to then sign off on the lis pendens. There was no guarantee that the judge would sign, and we were at the last days prior to the scheduled sale of the property, which was to take place in only a few short days after the weekend. The pressure was on.

We finally were able to see the judge. He took our case file to his chambers and reviewed the documents for about forty-five minutes before he came out of his chambers, handed the docs to the court secretary, who then asked us to approach. She gave us our documents. We turned the front page over to the next to see the judge had signed his approval. We ran over to the County Recorder's Office and filed the lis pendens and made it part of the public record.

One point I want to stress is that if someone else with an interest in the property believes the lis pendens isn't proper, they can file suit to have it expunged. I want to state that Wells Fargo Bank, after we filed our lawsuit and moved forward through the life of the lawsuit, they never attempted to have the lis pendens expunged. Interesting, to say the least.

Bona Fide Purchaser

The main reason it behooves someone to file a lis pendens is to make sure that the active court case pertaining to a real estate property becomes public knowledge. It legally becomes public knowledge when it is filed with the county recorder. This way, people can research property online, or at the County Recorder's Office computers and find out what liens or encumbrances are filed against the property. The process of a lis pendens is to file it with the court and then take the court-stamped copy to the County Recorder's Office and file it there. It becomes part of the paperwork, so that any party interested in the chain of title history on that property can find out about any encumbrances that are filed on the property and thoroughly research it. Professional real estate investors, banks, realtors, brokers, city inspectors, general contractors or appraisers frequently use the county records. It is part of their business practice as a professional in their field. This is where they find the crucial and up-to-date information prior to either submitting a bid to a realtor to purchase a property that is for sale or doing the necessary research before submitting a bid to an auctioneer during a trustee foreclosure sale.

I filed the lawsuit against Wells Fargo, and NDEx West, the acting substituted trustee, in April of 2011. Wells Fargo and NDEx immediately filed to have the case remanded to federal court. We had filed moving papers numerous times during the months that followed. What this means is that both Wells Fargo and NDEx knew of the lawsuit pending against the property. The open case meant that there were unlitigated questions pertaining to the property and being actively pursued in court. Since I immediately filed the lis pendens the same day as the lawsuit, it meant that the defendants had known for nearly a year that the case was opened against the property. During the case, I also filed the lis pendens with the court to become part and parcel of the case, just as an added measure to make sure everyone involved knew there was a lis pendens filed. I believe this one act helped stop Wells Fargo from moving forward with the foreclosure process for well over a year. Although, every month, and twice in December of 2011, I had to go down to the courthouse because the foreclosing trustee had the property scheduled for sale. Every month, on the day that the foreclosure was scheduled, I went down to the courthouse steps and announced to all prospective purchasers of the property, if it were to go on sale, it would become part of a current and ongoing court case against the property for fraud.

Black's Law Dictionary defines bona fide as: "In or with good faith; honestly, openly, and sincerely; without deceit or fraud. Merrill v Dept. of Motor Vehicles, 71 Cal.2d 907, 80 Cal.Rptr. 89, 458 P.2d 33. Truly; Actually; without simulation or pretense. Innocently; in the attitude of trust and confidence; without notice of fraud, etc. Real, Actual, genuine, and not feigned. Bridgeport Mortgage & Realty Corporation v. Whitlock, 128 Conn. 57, 20 A.2d 414, 416."

For me, the part that stands out in this definition is where it states, "without deceit or fraud", and further on with, "without notice of fraud, etc." You see, in order to make a true sale in a foreclosure sale, according to CA Civ Code Section 2924, it states that the sale is "true and correct" and that the buyer of the property sold at the foreclosure is a bona fide purchaser.

Let's go a little deeper then and find out what a bona fide purchaser is according to the law. *Black's Law Dictionary* states a bona fide purchaser to be: "One who purchased property for value without any notice of any defects in the title of the seller. Walter v Calderon, 25 Cal.App.3d 863, 102 Cal. Rptr. 89, 97. One who pays valuable consideration, has no notice of outstanding rights of others, and acts in good faith. J.C. Equipment, Inc. v. Sky Aviation, Inc., Mo. App., 498 S.W.2d 73, 75."

Now, when I read this, it seemed clear to me that if a legal case is opened against a property, and a lis pendens is filed pertaining to that legal action against the property, then this would mean that the public has been properly informed regarding the legal action, the encumbrance, and the defect in the title. It would mean that there had been proper notice of outstanding rights of others, which in my case, were under consideration because of the legal action pending.

Black's goes on to state that a bona fide purchaser for value: "is one who, without notice of another's claim of right to, or equity in, property prior to his acquisition of title, has paid vendor a valuable consideration. Snuffin v. Mayo, 6 Wash. App. 525, 494 P.2d 497." So, clearly this would mean that to be a bona fide purchaser in a foreclosure sale you would need to have not been notified of or have any knowledge of a lis pendens filed against the property. The lis pendens is filed because there is a claim of right to equity in the property prior to the sale. The fact that it is filed with the county recorder means it is public knowledge. Any professional purchaser who regularly buys properties at foreclosure sales would check with the county recorder prior to a sale.

Now, let us take this a little further still. It clearly states in the Universal Commercial Code or U.C.C. § 7-501 - Form of Negotiation and Requirements of Due Negotiation: "One who buys property or to whom a negotiable document of title is transferred in good faith and without notice of any defense or claim to the property or document. One who takes trust property for value and without notice of breach of trust and who is not knowingly part of an illegal transaction."

So, the requirements of due negotiation are defined in U.S. Legal online legal definitions as: "Due negotiation refers to a negotiation made after careful thought and deliberative consideration given to the matter at hand. A negotiable document of title is duly negotiated when it is negotiated to a holder who purchases it in good faith without notice of any defense against or claim to it on the part of any person and for value, unless it is established that the negotiation is not in the regular course of business or financing or involves receiving the document in settlement or payment of a money obligation. A holder of a duly negotiated document acquires title to the document, title to the goods, all rights accruing under the law of agency or estoppel, and direct obligation of the issuer to hold or deliver the goods according to the terms of the document."

Now, perhaps you might help me out here because I'm a bit confused.

I filed my lawsuit in April 2011. I filed a lis pendens pertaining to that lawsuit regarding my property in foreclosure in April 2011. I filed the lis pendens to make it public knowledge so that anyone who was looking to purchase my property at a foreclosure auction knew there was a lawsuit pending on my property. That way, if anyone were to look into the parcel number at the County Recorder's Office, they would find a claim of right being contested, they would find that there was in fact a defect in the title and there was an encumbrance on the property in the form of a lawsuit. They could look further and find that the lawsuit dealt with fraud. So, tell me how could the court find that the buyer was a bona fide purchaser in accordance with the rule of law? Based on what I had done to inform the public regarding the lawsuit pending on the property, there was no way that one could find the purchaser of the property to be a bona fide purchaser.

However, if the buyer isn't a professional buyer, then this specific rule has a bit more leniency to it. The reason for this is that a professional buyer would know the professional steps to take in order to properly research a property to purchase. It is what they do for a living, so they know to do the appropriate research on a parcel they are thinking of buying. But if it were simply a common person who has never purchased a home, or purchases less than one property every two years, they are considered a non-professional buyer, and this rule does not apply to them. They are considered to be less cognizant of the procedures for real estate.

Let us revisit the day my home was illegally sold in front of my eyes. It began with four bidders. I quickly extinguished two after they bid. I thrust my sign in front of them and told them they would be sued if they won this bid. They quickly decided to stop bidding for some reason. The other two bidders I had seen at the courthouse steps every time I had been there over the past year. I knew they were professionals. They ignored my sign and threat of inclusion in my lawsuit. They continued to bid. I listened to the price of the home rise by the thousands. They continued to bid. I soon watched my home being illegally sold in front of my eyes. I knew the banks were fraudulent, I knew the trustee was fraudulent and complicit, I knew the buyers were what I call institutional and professional in nature.

It made no sense.

I left the steps in shock, feeling as if I couldn't breathe. I immediately marched down the steps and around the corner so that I was away from the energy of my home being stolen from me. I sat down at a bus stop to regroup, not knowing what to do. So, I sat for a while waving a few buses on as they slowed thinking I was indeed waiting to board a bus. After about ten minutes, I hustled back to my car to go home.

I hadn't been home for much more than an hour when there was a knock on the door. I peeked out to see who it was knocking, only to find a stranger standing and waiting. I opened the door and stepped out onto the front porch, closing the front door behind me. The man smiled while trying to act as if he were my friend. He knew he was treading on dangerous territory. He was someone who I had never seen before and introduced himself by saying that he had just purchased my home at the foreclosure auction and wondered if anyone was living in the house. When he asked if he could come in and see the premises, I winced at hearing that. He seemed proud. I told him that I was aware that the house had just been sold, and that he wasn't the person who was bidding on it. I watched the auction take place and he wasn't part of the scenery.

Taking out his card, he slowly extended it to me. I took it and told him that it was best that he leave my porch immediately. He knew then that he wasn't welcome under any circumstance. As he began to slither down the front steps, he turned and stated that we had three days to leave the property. I moved toward him and descended a few steps. As I stood on the step above him, looking down at him, I told him that wouldn't be happening, and I would be seeing him in court for fraudulently stealing my home. I added, "Now, get off my property!"

I spent the rest of the day on the couch without saying a word.

Presumption of Correctness

We began to unravel evidence that the bank had never intended for us to have any protection in the bank's decision to use the non-judicial foreclosure process in event of our inability to pay the note. They knew at the time they wrote the Deed of Trust contract with us that the laws allowed them the "presumption of correctness" in California's non-judicial foreclosure procedure. It is called a non-judicial foreclosure because the state mandated an independent third party was to hold the equity title as collateral for both parties, it was also that party who was to oversee the process of the non-judicial foreclosure and make sure all the rules and procedures were done in compliance with the process in order to protect the title from both parties during the non-judicial foreclosure.

The bank also knew that the legislature of the state had given the banks the power to take the Deed of Trust from the named trustee whether the trustee agreed or not with the desires of the bank. The bank could simply reassign a new trustee if the old trustee wasn't acting in the best interests of the bank. In other words, the bank knew that the trustee held no power to protect the borrower's title and the trustee held no power to oversee and police any of the procedures pertaining to the non-judicial foreclosure process.

The Deed of Trust contract specifically outlined the position of the trustee. There were two simple actions that the trustee held and those were to reconvey the property upon full payment of the note balance and their position to oversee and protect the Deed of Trust from either party during the non-judicial foreclosure process. What the bank misrepresented and failed to inform us was that the trustee was simply a straw man who held no powers whatsoever as soon as we signed the Deed of Trust document.

We noticed that the very first notices and documents filed contained false information as to the bank stipulating their actions during the non-judicial foreclosure process and we couldn't figure out how these actions went unnoticed.

Part of the rules of procedure in the non-judicial foreclosure process is called the power of sale clause. This is a set of rules that the banks are to follow to legally begin and follow through the process of a non-judicial foreclosure. The bank must prove that they made every attempt to assist the borrower to rectify the unpaid balance and get the loan payments current again. There are specific rules that outline what the bank is to do, and in what order they are to do these actions if they are in contact with the borrower. There is also a set of rules to follow and an order in which to do so if they are unable to contact the borrower during this time, in order for the bank to complete the numerous procedural rules outlined regarding assisting the borrower. If the bank claims they attempted to contact the borrowers as outlined in the set of rules for this action, but were unable to contact the borrower, there are a set of rules for the bank to follow in order to substantiate this and prove that they took all the numerous steps outlined by the state. The bank is then able to submit the documents necessary to file a Notice of Default, because they can claim they have made every attempt to contact the borrowers and were unable to do so.

All these rules are to be overseen by the trustee to make sure that all of the detailed rules that are dictated in the California Civil Rules and Procedures are being followed by either party in order to make the non-judicial foreclosure procedure fair to both parties. The bank knew that the trustee held no power to police the actions of the bank or any papers they filed with the state and the County Recorder's Office and they could file robo-signed or forged documents if they wanted to because the trustee wasn't reviewing any documents in order to make sure that the bank was following the rules. The trustee was simply signing any documents the bank chose to file during the non-judicial foreclosure procedure.

The state had given the banks the "presumption of correctness" that they would abide by the rules of the power of sale clause. The "presumption of correctness" is based on the idea that there is a third party, the trustee, in between the bank and the borrower to oversee the non-judicial foreclosure procedures and to make sure that the rules and procedures were being followed accordingly. The power that the bank led us to believe existed when we were first given the Deed of Trust contract to sign, back in August of 2005, was misrepresented to us by the banks to misinform us so that we believed we had protection to our title that we were signing over to the trustee at that time. The bank failed to inform us that upon the signature of that document, the bank could take the title from the trustee and give it to another trustee who would work for the bank and make sure that the bank was able to do whatever it wanted to do with our title from that point forward.

In the state of California, there are legal steps to take that are outlined in part of what is called the California Civil Code. This is what is referred to as the power of sale clause, as part of a Deed of Trust. This was outlined in our contract which World Savings Bank had originally constructed for us to sign. Shortly after we had agreed to sign the contract with World Savings Bank, they were taken over by Wachovia Mortgage. Then, not long after that, there was a merger with Wachovia Mortgage and Wells Fargo Bank, who was the financial institution sending us the Notices dealing with the foreclosure.

The Law

I believe in the law. I think we have a great system of justice. But I do think that system of justice has been corrupted by racism and classism. I think it's difficult for 'poor people' - poor white people, brown people - to be treated fairly before the law in the same way that upper-class people are.

~ Henry Louis Gates ~

One of the biggest problems we face in this country is that the corporations are writing the laws. "But that isn't how things work," many people naïvely respond. To this day, people still think that the laws are written by legislators, who review the bills that they have submitted to Capitol Hill in the hope of someday becoming a law. After discussions and committees that pick apart the bills, sometimes adding phrases here and there—which can be referred to as Pork—or removing a word or two to make enough Congresspersons become comfortable to vote, YEA. After the point where a bill passes with enough YES votes in Congress, the bill is then sent to the Senate, where that body politic goes through the same process of review and subsequent voting. If it passes the Senate with enough yeses, the bill will then head to the president's desk in the Oval Office of the White House. The president has the option to either sign the bill, thereby creating a new law, or the president could veto the bill, which would send that bill back to Congress to start the process all over again.

The process for a bill to become a law is indeed that, as it was created within the context of the Constitution of the United States, except most bills are not written by politicians anymore. The politician used to be in place to serve the best interests of the people of the territory that the politician represented, in order to know what the needs of the people of that specific region of the country were, and to then go to Washington D.C. and act on their behalf. The position of the politician today has primarily become a talking head who is there to vote yea or nay on bills that were written and submitted to Congress by lobbyists acting on behalf of large corporations to do their bidding as that bill comes to the House floor for a vote. Now, most people know that these politicians are taking money from corporations to add to their campaign war chest to help them continue to campaign and raise money in their districts back in their home states. They take money from their constituents, as well as corporations. However, through the Citizens United ruling, the Supreme Court of the United States has made it easier for corporations to pay much larger donations to politicians than any regular person is able to as a means to have more leverage politically. This allows the corporations to receive a new tax deduction, or perhaps permits any corporation such as the international Nestlé Corp. to receive the good municipal water, all the while, the city of Flint, Michigan and its voters are given poisoned water to consume. The state politicians of Michigan literally voted YES to allow the Nestlé Corporation — one of the world's leaders in corporate ownership — rights of water throughout the world. They received the clean lake water that had been designated and delivered to the town of Flint, Michigan, while the people of Flint who voted for these politicians, began receiving water filled with toxins and lead. These poisons found in the Flint water supply are in a direct correlation to the illnesses, birth defects and deaths of the voters of Flint. Thanks to the elected officials who the residents of Flint, Michigan voted for, some of these same politicians turned their backs on their constituents, did deals with the corporations, and not only poisoned, but killed some of those same people who voted them into office. It sounds so surreal once we start to look at things and really define them by the basic facts. The saying that truth is stranger than fiction is true. Isn't that wild? How did we get to this place?

Most people think that the politicians in Washington D.C.—those men and women who the people voted for to act on behalf of their local constituents — sit and figure things out in order to do what is best for the American people. Although this was the basic idea of the founding fathers, back in the 1770s, when this country was beginning to stretch its wings and let loose the bonds the crown of England had on them, today, nothing seems to be further from the truth.

In January 1776, well before the internet, television and radio, it was the newspapers and pamphlets of the day that told the stories and plight of the dream that was to become the experiment called America. Thomas Paine, a political activist, author, political theorist and revolutionary penned what quickly became the bestselling document of the time, titled *Common Sense*. This pamphlet is described as the spark that was dropped on the powder keg that played to the emotions of the American people who were standing at the precipice of history during the Revolutionary War against the British.

In Common Sense, he wrote, "... O ye that love mankind! Ye that dare oppose not only the tyranny but the tyrant, stand forth! ... and let none other be heard among us, than those of a good citizen, an open and resolute friend, and a virtuous supporter of the rights of mankind, and of the free and independent states of America."

Barely six months after those words were disseminated throughout the young colonies, in 1825, a year before his death, Thomas Jefferson wrote to the Revolutionary War hero Henry Lee to explain his purpose in drafting the Declaration of independence in 1776. "It was intended to be an expression of the American mind, and to give to that expression the proper tone and spirit called for by the occasion." Jefferson scribed the Declaration of Independence, wherein he wrote, "... all men are created equal ... (and) are endowed by their Creator with certain unalienable rights ... life, liberty, and the pursuit of happiness ...."

It was in 1863 when President Abraham Lincoln referred to Jefferson's document and began his Gettysburg Address, "Four score and seven years ago our fathers brought forth on this continent a new nation, conceived in liberty, and dedicated to the proposition that all men are created equal... that this nation, under God, shall have a new birth of freedom; and that government of the people, by the people, for the people, shall not perish from the earth."

Going back only forty-four years before Abraham Lincoln said these words, the United States Supreme Court, in the case of Trustees of Dartmouth College v. Woodward, 17 U.S. 518 (1819), recognized corporations as having the same rights as natural persons. These rights include the right to contract and to enforce contracts. It formed the basis for the legal recognition of corporate personhood. It was noted in the Supreme Court case of Pembina Consolidated Silver Mining Co. v Pennsylvania, 125 U.S. 181 (1888), "Under the designation of 'person' there is no doubt that a private corporation is included [in the Fourteenth Amendment]. Such corporations are merely associations of individuals united for a special purpose and permitted to do business under a particular name and have a succession of members without dissolution."

When Lincoln stated that we are a "...government of the people, by the people, and for the people...", the people he was referring to then were not corporations. What he was referring to was the check and balance type of democracy that was created for the American Republic in the document entitled The Constitution of The United States and the Amendments." What the original fifty-five founding fathers, those delegates who met at Philadelphia during the hot summer days of 1787, set out to accomplish was a federal plan of government. They wanted to create a system with a separation of powers and a procedure for orderly change. This was accomplished in Article 1, Section 2, paragraph 1, "The House of Representatives shall be composed of members chosen every second year by the people of the several states, and the electors in each state shall have the qualifications requisite for electors of the most numerous branch of the state legislature."

In the following paragraph of Section 2, in paragraph 3, The Constitution goes on to outline how those Representatives are chosen. "Representatives shall be apportioned among the several states which may be included in this Union...the number of Representatives shall not exceed 1 for every 30,000, but each state shall have at least 1 Representative."

Lincoln was not referring to the corporations, but the individual people of America. Those people who stand and fall for their country. Primarily, he was referring to those thousands of men and women who lost their lives during the Civil War.

It was in 1913 that then President Woodrow Wilson signed into law what was called, The Federal Reserve Act. This bill, which became the law of the land, was enacted by Congress so that a small private group of investors would make up a corporation named the Federal Reserve System. This small group of wealthy individual stockholders of this newly formed corporation called, The Federal Reserve Bank, comprising a handful of extreme wealthy businessmen, was established in direct opposition to the fact that the United States Constitution itself, in Section 8(5), gives power to the Congress "To coin money, regulate the value thereof..."

What this action did was to take the power of printing money away from the American government, taking power away from the American people, and place it into the hands of a few wealthy individuals, through their small, private corporation called The Federal Reserve Bank.

Now, America was to stop printing its own money, and must now borrow money from The Federal Reserve Bank. The government of America would buy what was then termed as Federal Reserve Notes, now commonly called the U.S. Dollar. The American government would issue bonds, which the Federal Reserve Bank would buy using these Federal Reserve Notes as legal tender. The Federal Reserve Bank, now more commonly referred to as The Fed, would purchase these bonds from the American government and charge interest to the American government on the money that they printed in exchange for the bonds that the American government had printed. The money that the American government had purchased from The Fed would distribute these legal tender notes, or dollars, to the American people through the local banking system. The American government would then charge taxes against the people of the country to raise the money needed to pay the principal, as well as, all of the interest accrued to The Fed, for printing the money.

Despite that, prior to 1913, before Woodrow Wilson signed The Federal Reserve Act, the American government already had the power to print its own money, as outlined in the Constitution.

So, when the media stated in 2008 that the government was to be bailing out the banks, it was being deceptive. In simpler terms, it meant that the government of the people, by the people, for the people, or simply the American people, actually bailed out the banks. The government, in this case, is the people. The people bailed out the banks through taxes that would be levied against them to pay back the loans taken from The Fed to pay the failed institutional banks.

In 1887, it was Lord Acton who said, "...I cannot accept your canon that we are to judge Pope and King unlike other men, with a favorable presumption that they did no wrong. If there is any presumption it is the other way, against the holders of power, increasing as the power increases. Historic responsibility must make up for the want of legal responsibility. Power tends to corrupt, and absolute power corrupts absolutely. Great men are almost always bad men, even when they exercise influence and not authority, still more when you superadd the tendency or the certainty of corruption by authority."

When Lincoln was referring to 'a government of the people, by the people and for the people', these are the same people who voted for the Congressional and Senatorial politicians who were subsequently elected into office to 'oversee' the programs that had no oversight or regulations, then voted to give trillions of dollars of legal tender notes issued by The Fed to the American government on behalf of the American people so that the government could give that borrowed money to the failed financial corporations. Absolute power corrupts absolutely.

We elect the people to become representatives on behalf of the voting populace and entrust them to act in our best interests and that of our community. They get our votes by telling us what we want to hear. They prey on the public's emotions. Do they have to tell us the truth? Actually, no, they don't, and this is where it gets interesting. The Supreme Court has recently (2014) ruled in a unanimous decision allowing politicians to be able to lie while they campaign. They hide this in the context of the First Amendment of free speech. This came from a lawsuit that began in 2010 in Ohio, where Steve Driehaus, a former Congressman from that state filed a lawsuit against the organization The Susan B Anthony List. He filed a complaint with the Ohio Elections Commission alleging that petitioner Susan B. Anthony List (SBA) violated an Ohio law that criminalizes certain false statements made during a political campaign. Specifically, Driehaus alleged that SBA violated the law when it stated that his vote for the Patient Protection and Affordable Care Act (ACA) was a vote in favor of "taxpayer funded abortion." The ruling handed down by the Supreme Court opened up the possibility that a politician can tell untruths during the campaign process. The sad part is that I have read through this ruling and can see how they rationalized reaching this decision in the opinion that was authored by Justice Thomas.

Law is not logical. It should be, but it doesn't always work out that way. Judges are simply people doing a job. There is an old saying that "everyone has a price." In other words, anyone can be bought if the price is right. Judges can be bought to make decisions that might benefit one party over another. Judges have mortgages, children with college costs, retirement concerns, health concerns just like anyone else. Judges used to be lawyers. I have come to find and experience directly that some lawyers lie and cheat in order to win. They are only trying to look out for their interests and the interests of their families. Just like anyone else in this world.

I mean, let's face it, we all sell ourselves out to someone, or something at some point. We all have taken a job or done something we may not want, just to keep the bills paid and food on the table. We all have a point that we reach where we do something against our better judgement to receive something in return. There are numerous studies that show that we are all capable of selling ourselves out to the detriment of another. Yet, we all seem to want the world to be a place of truth, justice, and trust.

I have found that truth cannot be a part of law and our judicial process at all. Through my own personal experience, I have seen truth laid out clearly in the court of law. However, the presiding judge simply disregarded the truth and the law only to throw out the case without trial. They throw out the case without allowing the discovery process of law to delve further into the truth and evidence. But rather, they allow documents proven to be fraudulent in their content, disregard all rules of law and precedent, allow perjurious testimony, and allow the failure of procedures to circumvent truth and justice. The corruption of the judges disregards the rights of an innocent party trying to deliver truth in exchange for justice in favor of the fraudulent, perjurious party to fall in and comply with the corporate line.

Merriam-Webster defines Truth as:

    1. a: archaic: fidelity, constancy b: sincerity in action, character, and utterance

    2. a: (1) the state of being the case: fact (2) the body of real things, events, and facts: actuality (3) often capitalized: a transcendent fundamental or spiritual reality b: a judgment, proposition, or idea that is true or accepted as true <truths of thermodynamics> c: the body of true statements and propositions

    3. a: the property (as of a statement) of being in accord with fact or reality b: chiefly British: true c: fidelity to an original or to a standard

So, is it truth when there is no consistency in law? Is it truth when a judge defies the rule of law and decides the case on their own preferences? Is this sincerity in their action? Is this something we, as a society, would consider to be of character? Is it truth when a judge refuses to allow the facts to dominate a legal decision?

Truth is fundamentally transcendent. It does eventually prevail. I honestly believe this. We have to believe this if we are to continue to live in a society that is based on law. However, for this society to be based on law, truth must be respected and adhered to, regardless of the cost.

Is it truth when a judgment is based on misrepresentation, lies and perjury? Is it truth that the courts allow falsified documents to become truth by simply filing a declaration? Is this what makes something true? Is it truth that an idea that is not true but is accepted as true, makes it true? Is this where we have come to?

If truth is a property of being that is in accord with fact, then we must not allow the courts to find truth through falsified declarations. This is not truth if it is not reality. It is the reality to which the courts have become accustomed, however, I don't feel that the people would agree that truth can be or should be manipulated as such. It defies all logic. It defies all fairness.

Is it truth when a document can be submitted to the court as truth but is constructed of only falsities and misrepresentation of facts? If truth is fidelity to an original, then how can a bank foreclose on a borrower without having the original note to show that they have the right to foreclose? If truth is fidelity to an original, then why would the court not want to know if the foreclosing party is in fact in possession of the original.

I learned a lot about our judicial system. I kept thinking of the story of David and Goliath.

Merriam-Webster defines Philistine as:

Philistine

    1. a native or inhabitant of ancient Philistia (1000 B.C.)

> 2. a: often not capitalized: a person who is guided by materialism and is usually disdainful of intellectual or artistic values b: one uninformed in a special area of knowledge

Both the Hebrew Bible and the Old Testament Bible, in the book of 1 Samuel, tell a story of David and Goliath. Goliath was portrayed as a giant being. He was the greatest warrior who had defied all the armies of God throughout the land. Goliath was a Philistia, from the province of Gath, one of the five areas that make up Philistine. Goliath represents the behemoth Philistines who are only guided by materialism and have a lack of respect for art and science. It was in their minds that art, culture, and society serve no value if they cannot be capitalized. Domination through war and economic means was their modus operandi. So, when Saul led the Israelite army to defeat the approaching Philistine army, Goliath decided to give Israel the opportunity to spare the people of Israel their deaths and allow them to live out their lives in perpetual slavery. Unless, he offered, if the Israelites were to send in their best warrior for a one on one against Goliath himself to do battle, then both armies might eliminate the need for further bloodshed.

No one came forward for Israel. No one felt capable of defeating the great Goliath. Goliath was a master warrior. He was the best they had ever come against. He took careful preparation to take on another warrior in kind, so he protected himself with a full coat of battle dressings. He had his javelin, a bronze sword and shield. He was eager and ready for another soldier to defeat. He was not ready for what approached him.

A small boy, carrying a shepherd staff, emerged from the crowd. From out of the valley came a child of the poorest profession: that of a shepherd. His wooden staff was no match for the bronze-plated protections that Goliath had. Goliath was filled with arrogance and rage, expecting a soldier of contention only to be insulted with a boy with a stick.

Over time, it became the Christian point of view that the battle between David and Goliath was to show the victory of God's king of the enemies over the enemies of the disadvantaged. Much like the story of Jesus conquering sin by his death on the cross. The Catholic institution throughout the world eventually took it a step further as a metaphor to grant power to the church for its victory over Lucifer. Over time, the story of David and Goliath has found itself placed deep inside the daily conscience of the average person throughout the world, signifying the power of the underdog. It is the permeation of personal power to the commoner to exemplify the undeniable courage and ability to defy the odds of an opponent, and the power to stand up and face a much larger and stronger adversary.

I didn't have much time to stop and reflect on the fact that I was suing one of the largest corporations in the world. I just kept my mind on the fact that the truth will prevail. I would present the facts, so the truth could be heard, and justice would be served. It was the hardest thing I have ever done. It was as if I went through years of law school in a few weeks because I had to learn the rule of law and the rules of our judicial process at the same time as my lawsuit moved itself through our legal system. It was this process that ignited my passion for truth and justice that I thought could be found in the judicial framework I thought existed. To my own amazement, I found out just how naïve I was. Why should I have thought otherwise, knowing the injustices that occur throughout our country that I have and continue to advocate for? Why should I have thought otherwise, after living in Oakland, CA for nearly fifteen years. How could I have been so blinded with what I had seen, with what I had heard, and with what I had experienced? How could I have thought otherwise? How could I have been so naïve? I wanted to believe that we live in a world of truth and justice.

Corruption

You have heard me talk about the corruption of justice. You have heard me talk about corrupt judges. Well, let's delve a little into corruption. Let me share this story about my case.

We had a motion hearing scheduled on what was a misty, San Francisco bay area day. On that day, we were to discuss the third amended complaint that we had filed previously. I had never felt comfortable with the third amended complaint as I had rushed through it to submit it to the court in a timely fashion. I had been working on revising it to better state my cause of action to the court. I had also found some new case law that had allowed me to better focus my causes of action against Wells Fargo Bank.

As we hadn't yet received a response or demurrer from the defendants for the third amended complaint prior to thirty days after they were served, I wanted to submit my rewrite of the fourth amended complaint before the hearing. I prepared to file this under the rule of the Cal. Code of Civil Procedure 471.5 - 472. I thought I would use this strategy to put us in a more offensive position in the proceedings. We needed all the strategy help we could get. I felt as though I was always rushing to respond and react to the opposing counsel, rather than setting the pace from our side of the table.

I had been working days and nights for a few weeks to complete the new amended complaint. I decided to go down to the courthouse early to file the fourth amended complaint before we would head into the scheduled hearing. I gave myself a few hours just in case there would be lines at the courthouse windows where the tellers accepted the submissions of court documents. Usually, there would be about fifty people waiting in line to submit moving papers of some kind. Some of these people and I began to know each other as we would find ourselves on a seemingly similar filing schedule of documents. We would stand and make small talk, but never would anyone get too involved with discussing any of their legal issues. One must be careful as you never know who is listening. On this day, the line wasn't moving very fast, but at one point a clerk came through the line assisting special filings. I told her that I simply needed to file a fourth amended complaint.

She and I had been smiling at each other for a few years now. We would speak occasionally if I were to get her window when I was submitting documents. She seemed to appreciate my cause and my tenacity. She took me out of line and led me to the back where there were about twenty other people waiting. I handed her my documents, and she told me she should be right back with the stamped copies. I felt as though I was really getting the hang of all the procedures. I felt confident, which was good because in only a few more hours I had to be in court, alongside Wells Fargo's counsel, and in front of the judge.

After about five minutes, another woman came out of the back office. She called my name, and I went over to talk with her. She stated that she would not be able to file the moving papers because I didn't have permission from the judge. I informed her that I did not need permission as per rule 471.5 - 472 that mentions nothing about needing a judge's permission.

She disagreed with me in the interpretation of the rule and stated that she wouldn't accept it without the judge's permission.

So, I grabbed my documents in frustration and left the courthouse. I headed across the street to the other state law building where our upcoming hearing was to be held in about a half an hour. I met up with Michelle there and told her the news of the clerk's refusal to accept the amended complaint. She asked why I didn't know that I needed permission from the judge, as I should have looked that up in order to have the necessary documents with me as well. I told her that we didn't, and this woman didn't know what she was doing.

The courtroom where the hearing was being held was nearly full when we walked in. There were other cases being heard that afternoon, so plaintiffs, defendants and their counsel were milling about in the halls and sitting quietly waiting for the session to begin. We found our seats and settled in. I went over to the clerk of the court to check us in, and within a few more minutes, the hearings were ready to begin.

After a couple of other cases were heard by the judge, our case was called. We approached and sat down nervously. Even though we had been doing this now for a few years, I always became nervous when I had to argue in the court in front of the judge.

"Mr. Boggs, would you like to begin? We are going to discuss the amended complaint." He asked openly to the courtroom.

"I am, your honor." I responded politely.

Counsel for Wells Fargo interrupted saying, "Your honor, would this be the third amended complaint or the fourth amended complaint?"

At this point, I saw the judge wince in reaction to the statement, and then said, "Now, I know of a third amended complaint, but I am unaware of a fourth."

How did Wells Fargo know that only thirty minutes earlier I had tried and was unable to file a fourth amended complaint? How could they have known? Did the clerk of the court call them to inform them of my attempt to file? There was no other way that the defense's counsel could have known that I attempted to file because it was never entered into the system. They would have never received a notice via email or any other means of communication.

"Your honor, if I may?" I said raising my hand to interrupt the flow between the judge and the defense. "Your honor, not even a half hour ago I tried to file a fourth amended complaint. I am perplexed as to how the defendants would be privy to this information as we were not allowed to file the document. However, since we had never received an answer or demurrer from the opposing counsel, I thought via procedure code 471.5 through 472, I could file an amended complaint without the need for your permission. However, the clerk seemed to think otherwise, and informed me that I needed your permission to file that complaint. So, she didn't accept my filing. This brings the question as to how the defendants would know that this attempt was even made. So, I ask you now, your honor, if I could have your permission to file the fourth amended complaint. I have a copy for you right here if you'd like."

At that moment, there were a few quiet gasps and whispers from people in the courtroom. The hearings for our case had been garnering a number of spectators as we kept the case going. Each time we had a hearing, there would be a few new people in the crowd. Some were other lawyers, some law students, and I would guess a few public people as well. I used to do that when our case first began. I would go to visit different court proceedings that our judge was actively adjudicating in order to get a feel for what and how things go on in the courtroom.

The judge knew that there were people in the crowd who had picked up on what had just transpired. He knew that he had to backtrack to save the issue, so he took control.

"Well," he said with a slight chuckle, "I would enjoy reading that."

So, I went around our table and approached the bench, handing the documents to the clerk of court. The judge leaned over the bench smiling while saying, "You will need to file a copy with the clerk, as well. You have my permission. Don't leave without getting something from my office." He then sat back in his chair and said to the room, "In light of this new filing, the hearing for the third amended complaint is moot. This hearing is therefore adjourned."

So, did the judge have someone in the front clerk's office on the take informing Wells Fargo of any ongoing actions pertaining to certain cases? Did Wells Fargo have someone simply hanging out to listen to anyone randomly in the clerk's office waiting for some news to happen? Was the judge privy to the same information that Wells Fargo was receiving, or was the person in the judge's court who had informed Wells Fargo of our attempt to file an amended complaint, the only corrupt person in the judge's court? One thing was certain, as soon as this issue hit the courtroom floor, the judge wasted no time in trying to end the conversation, silencing the two parties, and dismissing our hearing for the day.

> *If experience demands a presumption that a judge will seize every opportunity presented to him in the course of his official conduct to line his pockets, no canon of ethics or statute regarding disqualification can save our judicial system.*
>
> ~ *Justice William Rehnquist* ~

Merriam-Webster defines Corruption as:

    1.   a: impairment of integrity, virtue, or moral principle; depravity b: decay, decomposition c: inducement to wrong

by improper or unlawful means (as bribery) d: a departure from the original or from what is pure and corrections

2. an agency or influence that corrupts

Our justice system is corrupt. We expect our judges to honor and adhere to the rule of law. Only in this way can we maintain any semblance of an attempt at fair law and justice. We expect our judges to accept their position and honor our rules of law and judicial process by setting an example and using their own moral compass. However, we are continually reminded that power corrupts, and absolute power corrupts absolutely.

No matter how many rules of law are created, or how many rules of ethics are written, without an adherence to truth and honesty in the quest for justice through transparency, there is little chance that a judiciary can execute any constitutional or moral guide to act for the public. Law should be bound in nothing but truth: the truths that lay within the solid, tangible evidence and the rule of law. Though, in many legal cases, there are facts and law that require interpretation. This interpretation is done by judges and juries. It is up to the judge or jury to decide what is justice, equity, and remedy, as they are reviewed and require judgment.

With each decision along the way in any court of law, judges are afforded a wide reach of discretionary latitude. Through each decision there is room for them to review and interpret the myriad case laws. This latitude reaches from granting a hearing to a motion or moving paper, to the interpretation of facts, precedents, and statutes. Every decision that is granted by the judge, including sentencing and damages, is an open invitation for interpretation and therefore corruption. We expect judges to be honest in their decisions. It is on this basis that we feel the justice system works to help the people meander their way through the maze of modern, western society. If we were to reduce any possibility of a judge becoming corrupt, we would need to begin by eliminating our current judicial system as we know it. The idea of a fair, independent, and malleable judicial system that grows with the lives of its society cannot exist within the structure of our current judicial system.

There have been many studies and books that have been written in the past on the corruption of judges. We have seen numerous recent cases that have exposed judges on the take. These stories seem to be larger than life and impossible but are found to be true. There are corrupt judges in PA that were paid more than $2.5M over a period of years to find juveniles guilty and send them to prisons for profit. Or there are corrupt judges, lawyers, and police on the take in Orange County, CA for traffic violations. Or there is the FL judge who was found to have taken bribes and texted prosecutors during trial to help facilitate their case.

In the beginning, our Constitution was written on the basis that only elected officials would be the lawmakers. However, over time, we have come to find that judges create their own law. They interpret the law and create new precedents through their own opinions and rulings. This is what is classified as case law, which is created and recreated by judges' rulings. When a ruling is given by a judge and that ruling survives an appeal, it becomes case law and legal precedent. This is constantly taking place throughout the nation daily. So much so, that we, as a society, have become subjected to the rule of law based on case rulings by judges, instead of the laws written by our state and federal lawmakers, which are outlined and defined within our Constitution. Allowing judicial power to become the lawmakers breaks down our initial ideals of what an independent judicial branch of government means. It means that we are no longer being guided by our constitutional intent but rather by case law. This system is dangerous as its actions constantly make small and subtle modifications to the Constitution itself.

The legal system was originally designed for anyone to be able to go to court and litigate their own case if they didn't have the money for an attorney. In the early days of the United States, most people were poor farmers and shopkeepers with little to no money to pay for a lawyer. So, the system allowed people to represent themselves in the courtroom. The legal system has changed. Through its case law system, it is difficult for a layman to keep up with the continuous, minute changes that occur in the judicial system. The judges used to be lawyers, and the lawyers want to become judges, so they look out for each other. They try to eliminate the person litigating the law by creating the façade that the law is technical and extremely complicated. At this point, due to the case law type of judicial structure we have all come to allow, it is too complicated for most people. The courts require myriad rules, timelines, and clerical structures to create and file documents, and through this, they attempt to eliminate the layman from clogging their courtrooms by confusing them so much that they will make enough errors to allow a judge the levity to throw out their case. This style of justice has created great business advancement for law firms, because the continually changing case law makes litigation of the law difficult, time consuming, complicated, and expensive. This process helps to reduce the commoner's access to the judicial process, thereby reducing the availability for the common person to have much effect on the rule of law. The common person doesn't have access to legal tools such as Lexus-Nexus or volumes of legal tomes that can assist one in their legal research. The judicial system began with a straightforward guideline through the Constitution, but due to the rise of the case law judicial structure, we see that a judge's interpretation of the law can ultimately end up changing the original meaning of the Constitutional intent.

Although there are many books and empirical studies on the evidence of judicial corruption, most are historical and not analytical. We find numerous works of anecdotal evidence of corruption, and we might find policy proposals, but there is little evidence that there is any attempt to analyze the effects of these actions in relation to the corruption of the judicial system and the policy proposals used to deal with the problem.

These subtle changes in the procedures of lawmaking have evolved over a period of decades. Over time, these changes have devolved the judicial process to such an extreme that few question these changes, and subsequently they have become part and parcel of our new and "evolved" legal system. We have reached a point where the law is out of reach of the average individual, making their involvement in the legal process nearly impossible unless one can afford an attorney. Due to the nature of these changes, the law has become so complex and expensive that the pro per or pro se litigant is no longer welcome in the courtroom. With the complications of the law, the corruption of the legal officials, and the difficulties found when attempting to litigate the law on one's own, the days where the courts served justice fairly and quickly are gone.

To understand judicial corruption, we need to define it so that we can put it into perspective. It is simply the sale and purchase of a legal decision. We must understand that when bribing a judge, one must know what the incentives might be for lawyers to buy a decision from a judge, or why a judge would decide to sell their decision.

Quite simply, a party might attempt to make a bribe if the gains for the decision from the judge are greater than the bribe itself, the expected costs of getting caught, and the expected gains from the corrupt decision. A judge might be willing to accept a bribe if it is safe to assume they will not be caught. Studies show that most judges do so by granting preliminary motions in favor of the bribing party as a way to signal the judge's loyalty. The judge might acquiesce to a few statements or motions being granted to the opposing party to show their fairness, only to cut the opposing party down some time later in the legal action.

Judges do not have the legal right to change law. We have allowed them this right by acquiescing to their decisions that make case law. The truth is getting mired through the interpretation of case law. (See Exhibit 6 a-o)

Fraud (18 U.S.C. 47 § 1001)

So, what is fraud? What does it mean?

Fraud would be if the president of the United States asked a leading official who was acting in an assumed capacity of an expert during a press conference if injecting people with disinfectant would help cure them of a virus. During a press briefing on April 23, 2020, regarding the coronavirus, Trump was seen asking Bill Bryan, the head of the Department of Homeland Security's science and technology division, "Then, I see the disinfectant that knocks it out in a minute, one minute. And is there a way we can do something like that by injection inside or almost a cleaning? As you see, it gets in the lungs, it does a tremendous number on the lungs, so it would be interesting to check that, so that you're gonna have to use medical doctors. But it sounds interesting to me." Prior to that, in March 2020, an Arizona man died after ingesting chloroquine phosphate, believing it would protect him from becoming infected with the coronavirus. The man's wife is known to have told NBC News that she had watched the prior press briefings by Trump talking about the potential benefits of chloroquine. He used his position of authority to deceive another. As a person who is perceived to know such information, being the president, and having access to the best and most knowledgeable scientists and research teams to initiate an idea by misleading allegations, or by concealment of facts he induced someone into doing something that caused himself injury.

Fraud is: "An intentional perversion of truth for the purpose of inducing another in reliance upon it to part with some valuable thing belonging to him or to surrender a legal right. A false representation of a matter of fact, whether by words or by conduct, by false or misleading allegations, or by concealment of that which should have been disclosed, which deceives and is intended to deceive another so that he shall act upon it to his legal injury. Any kind of artifice employed by one person to deceive another. Goldstein v. Equitable Life Assur. Soc. Of U.S., 160 Misc. 364, 289 N.Y.S. 1064, 1067. *Black's Law Dictionary 5th Edition 1979* West Publishing Co.

Fraud would be when a financial institution uses a Deed of Trust contract as a debt instrument while knowing that the trustee in the Deed of Trust agreement is not an independent party to the Deed of Trust. When a financial institution uses a Deed of Trust while they know a trustee holds no power in a Deed of Trust agreement, and the financial institution does not inform the borrower of their knowledge of this fact, the borrower is deceived by the "superior" knowledge of the financial institution. The borrower is misrepresented and relies on false representation of facts in order to make their decision to borrow. The borrower's decision comes with damaging results: "...false representation of a present or past fact made by defendant, action in reliance thereupon by plaintiff, and damage resulting to plaintiff from such misrepresentation." Citizens Standard Life Ins. Co. v. Gilley, Tex. Civ. App., 521 S.W.2d 354, 356.

The calculating and deceptive actions of a financial institution misrepresenting the legal use of a Deed of Trust when they know that the trustee is not an independent party in a Deed of Trust is an omission of fact, and a concealment of truth, creating an immediate breach resulting in serious damage to the borrower's title.

It comprises all acts, omissions, and concealments involving a breach of a legal or equitable duty and resulting in damage to another. It includes anything calculated to deceive, whether it be a single act or combination of circumstances, whether the suppression of truth or the suggestion of what is false, whether it be by direct falsehood or by innuendo, by speech or by silence, by word of mouth or by look or gesture.

Fraud, as it applies to contracts, is the cause of an error bearing on a material part of the contract, created or continued by artifice, with design to obtain some unjust advantage to the one party, or to cause an inconvenience, or loss to the other.

Fraud is either actual or constructive. Actual fraud consists in deceit, artifice, trick, design, some direct and active operation of the mind; it includes cases of the intentional and successful employment of any cunning, deception or artifice used to circumvent or cheat another. It is something said, done or omitted by a person with the design of perpetuating what he knows to be a cheat or deception. Constructive fraud consists in any act of duty, trust, or confidence justly reposed, which is contrary to good conscience and operates to the injury of another. Or as otherwise defined, it is an act, statement or omission that operates as a virtual fraud on an individual, or which, if generally permitted, would be prejudicial to the public welfare, and yet may have been unconnected with any selfish or evil design. Or constructive frauds are such acts or contracts, although not originating in any actual evil design or contrivance to perpetrate a positive fraud or injury upon other persons, are yet, by their tendency to deceive or mislead other persons, or to violate the public interests, deemed equally reprehensible with actual fraud. Constructive fraud consists in any breach of duty, which without an actually fraudulent intent, gains an advantage to the person in fault, or anyone claiming under him, by misleading another to his prejudice, or to the prejudice of anyone claiming under him; or in any such act or omissions as the law specially declares to be fraudulent, without respect to actual fraud.

The systemic use of inducing a borrower to transact their mortgage agreement using a Deed of Trust document in the transaction is not in the nature of the true legal ramifications of the document being signed. Fraud in the inducement is fraud connected with the underlying transaction and not with the nature of the contract or document signed.

This differs with intrinsic fraud, which is "...that which pertains to issues involved in original action or where acts of constitutional fraud were, or could have been, litigated therein." Fahrenbruch v. People ex Rel. Taber, 169 Colo. 70, 453 P.2d 601. Perjury is an example of intrinsic fraud.

The Statute of Frauds is the base mark of any contract fraud claim. This is the common designation of a very celebrated English statute (29 Car. II, c. 3) passed in 1677, which has been adopted, in a modified form, in nearly all the United States. Its chief characteristic is the provision that no suit or action shall be maintained on certain classes of contracts or engagements unless there shall be a note or memorandum thereof in writing signed by the party to be charged or by his authorized agent. Its object was to close the door to the numerous frauds and perjuries.

The Uniform Commercial Code U.C.C. § 2-201 provides that a contract for the sale of goods for the price of $500 or more is not enforceable by way of action or defense unless there is some writing sufficient to indicate that a contract for sale has been made between the parties and signed by the party against whom enforcement is sought or by his authorized agent or broker. A statement, or claim, or document, is "fraudulent" if it was falsely made, or caused to be made, with the intent to deceive. To act with "intent to defraud" means to act willfully, and with the specific intent to deceive or cheat; ordinarily this is for the purpose of either causing some financial loss to another or bringing about some financial gain to oneself.

Fraudulent concealment is the term for "...the hiding or

suppression of a material fact or circumstance which the party is legally or morally bound to disclose. The employment of artifice planned to prevent inquiry or escape investigation and to mislead or hinder the acquisition of information disclosing a right of action; acts relied on must be of an affirmative character and fraudulent." Fundunburcks v. Michigan Mut. Liability Co., 63 Mich. App. 405, 234 N.W.2d 545, 547. The test of whether failure to disclose material facts constitutes fraud is the existence of a duty, legal or equitable, arising from the relation of the parties; failure to disclose a material fact with intent to mislead or defraud under such circumstances is equivalent to an act of "fraudulent concealment." Fraudulent concealment justifying a rescission of a contract is the intentional concealment of some fact know to the party charged, which is material for the party injured to know to prevent being defrauded; the concealment of a fact, which one is bound to disclose, is the equivalent of an indirect representation that such fact does not exist.

Fraudulent intent can be a bit more difficult to prove in court. It can be difficult to show intent. "Such intent exists where one, either with a view of benefiting himself or misleading another into a course of action, makes a representation, which he knows to be false, or which he does not believe to be true." In re Orenduff, D.C.Okl., 226 F.Supp. 312, 413.

Fraudulent or dishonest act in fraud is defined as "...which involves bad faith, a breach of honesty, a want of integrity, or moral turpitude." Hartford Acc. & Indem. Co. v. Singer, 185 Va. 620, 39 S.E.2d 505, 507, 508.

Fraudulent representation refers to the opening paragraph to this section regarding the statement made by the president. "A false statement as to material fact, made with intent that another rely thereon, which is believed by another party and on which he relies and by which he is induced to act and does act to his injury, and the statement is fraudulent if the speaker knows the statement to be false or if it is made with utter disregard of its truth or falsity." Osborne v. Simmons, Mo. App., 23 S.W.2d 1102, 1104. As the basis for civil action establishment of representation, falsity, scienter, deception, and injury are generally required.

There are thirty-one words that affirm the values and freedom, which are represented by the American flag, and are recited while Americans face the flag and pledge their loyalty to their country. The Pledge of Allegiance was written in 1892 for the 400th anniversary of the "discovery" of America. It began in October 1892 on the "Columbus Day" holiday. School children across the country first recited the Pledge of Allegiance this way:

I pledge allegiance to my Flag and to the Republic for which it stands: one nation indivisible, with liberty and justice for all.

Over the years, the wording has changed. The words "my flag" were replaced by "the flag of the United States" in 1923. A year later, "of America" was added after "United States." The pledge finally received its first official recognition by Congress on June 22, 1942, when it was formally included in the U.S. Flag Code. The last change in language came on Flag Day 1954, when Congress passed a law that added the words "under God" after "one nation." The official name of "The Pledge of Allegiance" was adopted in 1945.

The Pledge of Allegiance now reads:

I pledge allegiance to the Flag of the United States of America, and to the Republic for which it stands, one Nation under God, indivisible, with liberty and justice for all.

...With liberty and justice for all. What does that really mean?

The modern concept of political liberty comes from the Greek concepts of freedom and slavery. To the Greeks, to be free meant to not have a master: to be independent from a master and to be able to live as one likes. This idea is closely linked to the concept of democracy. Aristotle explained: "This, then, is one note of liberty that all democrats affirm to be the principle of their state. Another is that a man should live as he likes. This, they say, is a privilege of a freeman, since, on the other hand, not to live as a man likes is the mark of a slave. This is the second characteristic of democracy, whence has arisen the claim of men to be ruled by none, if possible, or if this is impossible, to rule and be ruled in turns; and so, it contributes to the freedom based upon equality."

Some of the earliest recorded philosophers have pondered the question of liberty. It was Marcus Aurelius (121-180AD) who wrote: "A polity in which there is the same law for all, a polity administered with regard to equal right and equal freedom of speech, and the idea of a kingly government which respects most of all the freedom of the governed."

Merriam-Webster defines Liberty as:

Liberty

1. The quality of state of being free

    a. the power to do as one pleases

    b. freedom from physical restraint

    c. freedom from arbitrary or despotic control

    d. the positive enjoyment of various social, political, or economic rights and privileges

e. the power of choice

It was in 1776 when the United States began to outline its own definition of the meaning of liberty. Thomas Jefferson penned in *The Declaration of Independence* that all men have a natural right to "life, liberty, and the pursuit of happiness". However, this declaration of liberty was an issue from the outset because of the institutionalization of legalized slavery of the black people. Slave owners argued that their liberty was paramount since it involved property, their slaves, and that black people had no rights that any white man was obliged to honor. It was the Dred Scott decision of 1857 by the Supreme Court that upheld this principle. It was in 1866, just following the Civil War, that the United States Constitution was amended to extend these rights to persons of color, and it wasn't until 1920, only 100 years ago that these rights were extended to women.

Merriam-Webster defines Justice as:

Justice

    1. a: the maintenance or administration of what is just especially by the impartial adjustment of conflicting claims or the assignment of merited rewards or punishments

    b: judge: the administration of law; especially: the establishment or determination of rights according to the rules of law or equity

    2. a: the quality of being just, impartial, or fair

    b: (1): the principle or ideal of just dealing or right action

(2): conformity to this principle or ideal (3): righteousness

   c: the quality of conforming to law

   3. conformity to truth, fact, or reason: correctness

The United States is a country birthed out of the idea that it would be based on law. There would be equal legal representation for all citizens of the new world. However, since the beginning, we find that this simply means those monied people. Even today, we continue to see this played out. Washington continues to espouse the failed trickle-down theory of economics, which only favors the wealthy. In the bailouts of 2008, 2009, 2010, and more recently in 2019 and 2020, we see trillions of dollars going quickly to the largest corporations and their stockholders, while the average American or small business gets peanuts, delayed, pushed aside or forgotten.

Merriam-Webster defines Just as:

Just

   1. a: having a basis in or conforming to fact or reason: reasonable <a just but not a generous decision>

   b: archaic: faithful to an original

   c: conforming to a standard of correctness: proper <just proportions>

   2. a (1): acting or being in conformity with what is morally upright or good: righteous <a just war> (2): being

what is merited: deserved <a just punishment>

b: legally correct: lawful <just title to an estate>

For justice to prevail, we must first begin with liberty and follow it with justice. To have justice we must allow the facts and reasons to be presented. When courts, government officials, or administrations deny those facts and reasons to be admitted in an argument, justice is lost. When a judge dismisses the need for a bank or servicer to show proof that they are indeed holders of the note during a foreclosure proceeding, they simply flat out deny the justice of the party being foreclosed on. The refusal of the court to mandate the "standing" requirements for a party to foreclose is a flat denial of the foreclosed party's right to fair justice. When the foreclosed party requests the information showing cause for question, and the courts deny this need to show proof of ownership for jurisdiction or standing, justice cannot be served.

Now, hear me out and bear with me. For example, let's say that you were mugged. During this assault to you as a person, you were also stripped of your clothing. After stealing your car, the mugger left you sitting naked on the curb, next to where you had parked and were mugged. Thankfully, at least, your wallet and phone had fallen out onto the concrete during the scuffle before they grabbed your keys and drove off. Later, the police called your phone to inform you that your car was found in the middle of the street and was towed to the impound. You show up at the impound naked and ask for your car. They are not going to give you your car. You then show them your driver's license to prove that you are the person in the picture and listed as the owner of the vehicle. They are still not going to give you your car. It is customary in these situations that you must supply the proof of ownership of the vehicle or the pink slip for your car to be released. You explain that you were just mugged, they stole your keys and your car.

However, next, the person who stole your car comes up to the window and tells them that they have their car in the impound. They give the person behind the window the year, make and model of your vehicle. Then the thief gives them the keys they took from the car they just stole for a joyride and left in the road. The attendant gives the keys to their assistant to go get the car. When the car is driven around, the attendant says that it must have been their car because they had the keys to it. So, they give the thief your car.

You complain to the person behind the glass of the police impound booth stating that you have the pink slip for the car at home, but you were mugged by the person they just gave your car to.

This is the same as the court "assuming" that a party has standing to foreclose when they actually have none whatsoever. When a foreclosing party isn't required to show their position for standing in a foreclosure litigation, or when that standing is presumed by the court due to their filing of fraudulent documents in order to substantiate that premise, this is a denial of one's justice.

As of April 2020, we are seeing this again. During the coronavirus lockdown, we found the Trump administration giving mortgage relief to those borrowers who have a mortgage held by Fannie Mae or Freddie Mac through CARE. The homeowner holds the title, however, as we have come to realize, the holder of the note is the question. The only way to prove the true owner of a note is to do a forensic loan securitization audit. This will expose the fact that the true owner of the note cannot be found, so the government has placed the legal responsibility on the owner due to a discrepancy. It is assumed that Fannie and Freddie have everything correct and legally sound when all evidence shows that the possibility of Fannie and Freddie's information to be false is well over 80%.

In February 2012, a study completed by the City of San Francisco Assessor-Recorder, Phil Tang, was released as to the extent of mortgage fraud. When this study became public, it literally shocked the nation. The story became headline news throughout the country. A cursory review exposed widespread irregularities in foreclosure documents. This study came after a point when the banks had publicly announced that they had "fixed" their foreclosure documents' issues. But how could this happen? How could such a volume of fraudulent foreclosure documents be filed? It was the trustee, the independent party to the contract, who was tasked by the California Supreme Court and the state judicial system to make sure that this didn't take place. It was the trustee in the Deed of Trust contract who was acting independently on behalf of the judicial system in a non-judicial foreclosure proceeding. It was their position in the proceeding to act as the liaison for the court.

The presumption of correctness to the documents being filed by the trustee for the duration of a Deed of Trust contract was expected due to the independence of the position of the trustee. So, how could so much fraud be prevalent?

Assessor-Recorder Phil Tang, along with mortgage investigation firm Aequitas, announced the findings of an audit of 382 different San Francisco properties that had gone through the foreclosure process during 2009, 2010, or 2011. Their audit shows that 84% of the foreclosures audited contain at least one clear violation of California's foreclosure laws.

This is just one study in one town in all of California. The San Francisco City Assessor's audit served only as a benchmark in the evaluation of servicing settlements. This study managed to accomplish in only a few months what the Federal government and/or state attorneys general weren't able to do in over two years previous, with far fewer resources at their disposal. This study exposed the serious negative implications around the securitization process in general. This study also exposed the fraudulent nature of MERS and the hundreds of millions of dollars that system has deceptively taken from the state's tax base. This study showed how simple it was for an inquiry to expose the nation's largest consumer fraud in history being ignored by Attorney General Eric Holder, HUD Secretary Shaun Donovan, California's State Attorney General Kamala Harris, or Iowa's state Attorney General Tom Miller.

Tom Miller stated, "We will put people in jail," during a meeting in December of 2010 with homeowner advocates. Miller discussed the criminal investigation with the fifty attorneys general claiming to want criminal prosecutions. This nationwide probe was launched in the fall of 2010 in the wake of findings that most large banks were being exposed due to their fraudulent lending practices. They failed to track original mortgage documents after packaging the loans and selling them to investors to be placed in mortgage-backed securities. Also exposed were the ways in which banks would grant loans indiscriminately to feed the derivatives and market speculation. Due to this study, there were numerous banks that halted foreclosures for a period after their fraudulent practices were revealed. However, as the news of this began to fall from the headlines of news sources, they quickly began illegally seizing homes again.

Some components of the proposed settlement from this inquiry would require banks to modify home loans to reduce debt obligations on homes where the borrowers were found to be upside down. This might have helped borrowers if there were more stringent regulations attached to these programs. However, these programs eventually were exposed to show just how the financial institutions were being paid to "attempt" to modify a loan, rather than modifying a loan. Therefore, people by the millions found themselves locked into the quagmire of deceptive practices of constantly being "in the loan modification process" rather than receiving a modification. Then, when these borrowers finally reached the end of the modification options, the process left 95% of those who were modified with even more debt than they began the process with, due to additional penalties and interest accrued during the process. We were all asking why the largest consumer fraud settlement in the history of the country was proceeding with virtually no investigations.

On Sept. 16, 2015, an audit of land records was uploaded by Christopher King, to the website Scribd. His law degree with trial experience, coupled with his journalism experience, gives him his inquisitive mind that focuses on real estate issues. The file that was uploaded was a report that he worked on with the law offices of Scott Stafne. As the basis of the report, they included 195 mortgage assignments that were put through forensic loan analysis by the forensic loan auditing firm McDonnell Property Analytics. The Seattle City Council commissioned the firm to survey assignments from the first half of 2013. Their investigation was about those involving Mortgage Electronic Registration System (MERS), then owned by the GSEs Fannie Mae and Freddie Mac. In every single mortgage assignment reviewed, MERS attempted to transfer legal interest in the mortgage. The Washington State Supreme Court held in their 2012 Bain v. Metropolitan Mortgage Group decision that MERS violated state law by foreclosing on homeowners on behalf of a lender. In that decision, the court ruled that MERS is not a "lawful beneficiary" because it never held the promissory notes.

This is not an isolated litigation against MERS. In December 2009, Judge Dawson of the United States District Court, District of Nevada, found that "MERS provided no evidence that it was the agent or nominee for the current owner of the beneficial interest in the note, it has failed to meet its burden of establishing that it is a real party in interest with standing." This decision was issued in 5 (*Chong, Pilatich, Cortes, Medina, and O'Dell*) of the 18 cases on appeal, but declined to hold that "MERS would not be able to establish itself as a real party in interest had it identified the holder of the note or provided sufficient evidence of the source of its authority."

Although, earlier in September of that same year, the U.S. District Court for the District of Arizona, dismissed all federal and state law claims in Cervantes v. Countrywide Home Loans, Inc., et al., made by three borrowers in a complaint filed against a group of defendants that included MERS. The court discussed whether MERS was a proper beneficiary but only in the context of whether its involvement constituted the tort of fraud on the borrowers. The court found that the mere use of MERS was not common law fraud on the borrowers, finding that "Plaintiffs have failed to allege what effect, if any, listing the MERS system as a 'sham' beneficiary on the Deed of Trust had upon their obligations as borrowers". A few years later, in 2011, the U.S. Court of Appeals for the Ninth Circuit affirmed the trial court's judgement in favor of MERS in a published opinion. The court ruled that a borrower had no basis to challenge the standing of an entity such as MERS. It also, however, drew attention to a legal reference book's footnote that such a borrower still had a remedy to suing and have the trustee's sale set aside. The courts were setting the groundwork for the liability of fraud to only be able to be litigated by a homeowner once that homeowner had lost their home to the trustee sale.

This all seemed confusing because the prior year to this ruling, in April 2010, a Kansas appellate court in MERS v. Graham, 44 Kan App. 2D 547, 2010 WL 1873567, at **4-**5, interpreted Kesler to mean that MERS in fact does not have standing to foreclose on a mortgage in Kansas where there is no mention of MERS in the promissory note. MERS acts solely as a "nominee" for the lender, and there is no evidence that the promissory note has been assigned to MERS or that MERS otherwise possesses an interest in the promissory note.

Only a few months after this decision, in February 2011, the California Court of Appeal for the Fourth Appellate District affirmed the sustaining of a demurrer without leave to amend in Gomes v. Countrywide Home Loans. The California courts were solidifying the official takeover of Wall Street of homeownership and the whittling away of the perceived legal protections offered Californian homeowners. Keeping in line with a large portion of justices' retirement benefits that were held in banking stocks, the justice system was seemingly aligning itself with the banking industry to fend away any possible litigation snafus that might be pending on the horizon during the continued fallout of the 2008 economic collapse. Fraud be damned. In the opinion penned by Justice Joan Irion, the court ruled in favor of MERS in two ways. (1) California's non-judicial foreclosure statutes did not expressly or impliedly allow a lawsuit to determine whether the party initiating a foreclosure was authorized to do so; and (2) even if they did, the plaintiff consented to the use of MERS to initiate the foreclosure when they signed the Deed of Trust. Gomes cited and relied upon the supreme court's 2010 decision in Lu v. Hawaiian Gardens Casino, Inc., which clarified that a certain conservative method of statutory analysis applies to all California statutes, not just the California Insurance Code. Since the California legislators had not expressly written a cause of action into a statute, it simply did not exist. The Supreme Court of California denied Gomes' petition for review.

Then, later in September that same year, the California Court of Appeal for the Second District stated in Calvo v. HSBC that the complaint (an alleged violation of Section 2923.5 of the California

Code, which requires assignee of a mortgage to record an assignment before exercising a power to sell real property) was irrelevant as it applied only to mortgages, not to Deeds of Trust. The justice system was now whittling away at that same code, which was an integral part of my case that was going on at the time of this ruling.

The Robinson v. Countrywide case continued to further drive the nails into the coffin against homeowners in California. It was on that same day as the Gomes decision, September 12, 2011, the Fourth District Court cited its own May decision in Gomes v. Countrywide, stating that "the statutory scheme... does not provide for a preemptive suit challenging standing. Consequently, plaintiffs' claims for damages for wrongful initiation of foreclosure and for declaratory relief based on plaintiffs' interpretation of section 2924, subdivision (a), do not state a cause of action as a matter of law."

MERS is a system that is based on the electronic storage and transmission of legal documents. So, what happens to the original documents? What happens to the Deed of Trust and other documents in a real estate contract? At least, what happens in California. In Kansas, MERS was not allowed in the transaction. The question of notarization of electronic signatures and the honoring of notarized signatures across state lines was taken up with the U.S. House of Representatives. Congress had passed bills to legalize these steps, and in 2010, the U.S. Senate passed the legislation without debate. However, President Obama publicly opposed the legislation on Oct. 7, 2010. As a result, the bill died, and it was left to the states to decide whether electronic signatures can be notarized or whether a signature in one state must be accepted in another.

During the prolonged Covid-19 crisis, the United States Congress has attempted to push through what is known as the Electronic Notarization Act of 2020. Only twenty-three states allow the use of remote and electronic notarization. This is where a notary and signer are in different locations and use two-way audio-visual communication to securely execute electronic documents. The Republican from North Dakota who introduced the bill stated, "Americans shouldn't have to risk their health or safety to execute important financial legal documents, especially when they could do so from the safety of their own home." He went on to say, "The SECURE Notarization Act brings the notary process into the 21st century, allowing people to securely complete documents while still following recommended health and social practices amid the coronavirus pandemic." Some senators noted that as much as 55% of the country is unable to access the appropriate technology necessitated in the bill that would allow for it nationwide. This bill also requires tamper-evident technology to be used in electronic notarizations and encourages fraud prevention through use of multi-factor authentication.

As recently as May 5, 2020, Michigan is now under an Executive Order No. 2020-74. This order allows electronic signatures and remote witnessing, notarization, and visitation during the Covid-19 pandemic. This legislation paves the way for precedent to follow in its path where electronic signatures, electronic documents, electronic witnessing will be allowed, thereby eliminating the need for any "original" documents to become part of a real estate transaction. We will see what transpires with this in the coming months.

The lack of federal investigation was what led the nation to be shocked when in May 2011, CA Attorney General, Kamala Harris, announced the creation of a Mortgage Fraud Strike Force to protect homeowners. This strike force was tasked with monitoring and prosecuting violations at every step of the mortgage process, from the origination of loans through the marketing of mortgage-backed securities to investors on Wall Street.

When Harris announced her new mortgage fraud unit, she was joined by Los Angeles Mayor, Antonio Villaraigosa, representatives of HUD and others including homeowners who were harmed by fraudulent foreclosure practices. She stated, "Families are losing their homes, while those who perpetrated crimes and frauds against them walk free." She went on to say, "We will work to safeguard the homeowner at every step of the process from origination of a loan to its securitization, and we will prosecute to the fullest extent of the law those who take advantage of trusting California families. We are setting a high bar for other states and we insist that homeowners be protected, respected, and informed."

Nothing could be further from her truth.

In 2009 alone, there were foreclosure filings against 546,669 California homes. The Attorneys General of New York, California, and Delaware were among those AGs who chose to stay out of the national class action settlement investigations and vowed to till their own way. It was in 2012 that Kamala Harris introduced SB900 to the California State Legislature. This became better known as the California Homeowner's Bill of Rights. It was a set of laws that took effect on January 1, 2013, banning the practices of "dual-tracking". This became the catch phrase to the servicer and/or trustee processing the modification and foreclosure at the same time. This bill also covered robo-signing and giving homeowners a single point of contact at their lending institution. This bill also gave the California Attorney General more power to investigate and prosecute financial fraud. This was a multi-billion-dollar program designed to aid the homeowner. However, it became known as the smoke and mirrors bill that helped very few people. Despite these stories, Harris was elected as the state's Attorney General in 2014. Over time, volumes of evidence of fraud and corruption began to develop with regard to various corporations, one of which was One West, owned by Steve Mnuchin, the current Trump Administration

Treasury Secretary, yet Harris failed to prosecute. It was in 2016 that she was voted in as a United States senator and four years later as the Democratic nominee for the Vice President of the United States.

During her tenure as a state senator and the California Attorney General, I had written dozens of emails to her regarding the information that I was uncovering during my lawsuit against Wells Fargo. She failed to return one single phone call, or even reply to my emails. During this same timeframe, I can say the same about Nancy Pelosi, Kamala Harris, Diane Feinstein. The only politicians who ever responded to any of my information were Congresswoman Barbara Lee and Barbara Boxer. Their responses were a standard reply to any inquiry, and nothing further came from either of them. Despite over a five-year period of writing scores of emails and letters, they were largely ignored by every politician.

Eventually, news came out about massive document fraud and forgery throughout the United States when *60 Minutes* aired a story regarding the act of robo-signing. Their story involved a woman named Lorraine Brown who pled guilty to falsifying over 1 million documents, which then led to the 50-State Settlement against the banks on behalf of homeowners across the country. That settlement netted the homeowner a $300 check and maintained the use of falsified documents. Due to the fraudulent nature of all the documents being filed by this one person, it only delayed foreclosure of homes where it should never have happened at all. There were hundreds of other people across the country doing the same thing as Lorraine who were never litigated against. Again, how could this much fraud and misrepresentation be happening? Could we ever trust the financial institutions? Could we ever trust the judicial system?

Merriam-Webster defines Trust as:

Trust

    1.   a: assured reliance on the character, ability, strength, or truth of someone or something

        b: one in which confidence is placed

    2.   a: dependence on something future or contingent; hope

        b: reliance on future payment for property (as merchandise) delivered: credit<bought furniture on trust>

    3.   a: a property interest held by one person for the benefit of another

        b: a combination of firms or corporations formed by a legal agreement; especially: one that reduces or threatens to reduce competition

    4.   archaic: trustworthiness

    5.   a (1): a charge or duty imposed in faith or confidence or as a condition of some relationship (2) : something committed or entrusted to one to be used or cared for in the interest of another

        b: responsible charge or office: care, custody <the child committed to her trust.

We were supposed to be able to trust the trustee. It was built into the name of the position itself. It was ruled on by the California Supreme Court that the trustee was to be independent. Because of this independence of the trustee, one was to then trust that the laws were going to be adhered to. Because the judicial system created the position of the trustee in a Deed of Trust to act on behalf of the court system in a non-judicial foreclosure proceeding, we were supposed to trust that their position of independence was true and therefore recognized as such by the courts. It was this independence that gave way to the presumption of correctness of the documents filed by the trustee during a non-judicial foreclosure proceeding. Why did we trust that this was the case? Because it was designed to be that way by law.

Merriam-Webster defines law as:

Law

    1. a (1): a binding custom or practice of a community: a rule of conduct or action prescribed or formally recognized as binding or enforced by a controlling authority (2): the whole body of such customs, practices, or rules (3): common law

        b (1): the control brought about by the existence or enforcement of such law (2): the action of laws considered as a means of redressing wrongs; also: litigation (3): the agency of or an agent of established law

        c: a rule or order that it is advisable or obligatory to observed: something compatible with or enforceable by established law: control, authority

    2.   often capitalized: the revelation of the will of God set forth in the Old Testament capitalized: the first part of the Jewish

scriptures: Pentateuch, tor Cal. Civ. Code

3.   a rule of construction or procedure <the laws of poetry>

4.   the whole body of laws relating to one subject

5.   a: the legal profession: law as a department of knowledge: jurisprudence: legal knowledge

6.   a: a statement of an order or relation of phenomena that so far as is known is invariable under the given conditions

   b: a general relation proved or assumed to hold between mathematical or logical expressions.

Our society in America is governed by a set of laws. It was designed this way from the onset. It is these laws that allow the relative "freedoms" and privileges that we have become accustomed to today. However, what if we find that those same laws are not recognized as binding or being enforced by our authorities? Or that binding and enforcing is not held to the same standards for all? What if our laws, which were considered as a means of redressing wrongs through litigation, were not enforced? What if the rules of law and the rules of procedure were not adhered to or enforced by the authorities? What if our legal professionals in this country used their higher legal knowledge to circumvent the laws of jurisprudence? What if our laws and means of litigation and jurisprudence in relation to proof and logic are not abided by the judicial system as a whole? Where do we turn for justice? What if it is our judicial system itself that is not abiding by the rules of law or procedure? Would justice still even exist? That is, unless you are part of that judicial system, better known as "the good ole boys' club"? What I found was that to be a part of that club you needed to be a lawyer, a judge, or a financial institution. And I wasn't any of those things.

Did I experience the results of "good ole boys' club"? It was during the Unlawful Detainer litigation that began shortly after I watched my home being sold from under me, even though we were still in a lengthy litigation against Wells Fargo in Federal Court. You see, in a non-judicial foreclosure procedure, after a trustee's sale auction, the new owner is tasked with giving the foreclosed party a "3-Day Notice". If the foreclosed party refuses to leave the premises after the "3-Day Notice", the new owner is tasked to file an Unlawful Detainer action against them to evict them from the premises.

We knew that the foreclosure was done illegally. We had been arguing about fraudulent documents for the past year. We had proof that there were fraudulent documents that were filed, which instigated the foreclosure procedure allowing Wells Fargo to initiate the foreclosure process before we were given a chance to rectify the situation. After all, it was they who told us to stop paying the mortgage. We were current.

As per their instructions, we stopped payment of the mortgage in November 2010 in order to qualify for modification. Then, in December 2010 they began to foreclose on us. Although, as I had stated previously, they were claiming they had abided by the rule of the power of sale clause in order to foreclose on us, when they didn't follow the rules at all. It was this that began the litigation. The fact that this litigation was ongoing created another legal issue.

I had begun the case for fraud and breach of contract in the superior court. It didn't take long for the court to remand the case to federal court. Some of the causes of action included RICO and REMIC violations, as well as jurisdictional issues with some of the parties. The defendants Wells Fargo, NDEx, Inc., et al, were trying to use this tactic of remanding the case to federal court. It was their strategy to create as much confusion for us as possible since we were acting as our own attorneys. Now, we were tasked with learning how to deal with the rules and procedures of federal court, just as we were getting the hang of the process of superior court. During this process, I also had to learn the nuances of unlawful detainer court. The rules, procedures and timelines for this court were different than for the superior court. And now we found ourselves in both courts simultaneously. Our caseload had just doubled overnight.

Only a few months prior to the auction of the home, we had filed a motion for condition ruling to the court. We were wanting clarity on a point of law.

UNITED STATES DISTRICT COURT

NORTHERN DISTRICT OF CALIFORNIA – SAN FRANCISCO/OAKLAND DIVISION

Douglas J Boggs and   Case No. 4:11-cv-02346-SBA

Michelle A Moquin   [Assigned to the Hon. Saundra B. Armstrong]

Plaintiffs,

vs.   REQUEST FOR COURT ORDERED

Wells Fargo Bank, N.A.;   RULING OF CLARITY ON POINT OF LAW

Wachovia Mortgage, World Savings,

Golden W Sav. Assoc. Service Co.,

NDEx West, L.L.C., and

DOES 1 to 50

Defendants

PLEASE TAKE NOTICE that on October 24, 2011, the Honorable Judge /Saundra B. Armstrong filed the Order Granting Defendant's Motion to Dismiss and it was stipulated that the Deed of Trust, signed on August 8, 2005, by Plaintiff Moquin, secured by the property located at 1038 57th St, Oakland, CA 94608, identifies World Savings as the beneficiary and Golden West as the trustee. The ruling goes on to state that on July 5, 2007, Plaintiffs, Boggs and Moquin, obtained a line of credit secured against the property by a second Deed of Trust. This line of credit trust deed also identifies Golden West as the trustee and World Savings as the beneficiary. The ruling goes on to state that "NDEx, as agent for the beneficiary for the trust deed, recorded a Notice of Default against the Property on December 28, 2010. Then, on March 24, 2011, NDEx recorded a Notice of trustee's Sale, which set April 19, 2011 as the date of the foreclosure sale." The footnotes explain that "World Savings was later acquired by Wachovia, which in turn was acquired by Wells Fargo." and "Wells Fargo recorded a Substitution of trustee appointing NDEx as the substitute trustee in place of

Golden West on February 8, 2001." (Dkt.48 P2)

The Plaintiffs do hereby request from the Court a clarification and a ruling for a Point of Law as to the duly vested and legally appointed descriptions of all defendant parties involved.

The Plaintiffs point out that it is the right of the beneficiary to pick its desired trustee as a substitute trustee, however, it is clearly defined in the legislative intent of California State Senate Bill SB 1137 and ruled upon in 81 Cal. App.4 868 to state the definitive nature of the trustee to which it states "...A Deed of Trust differs from a mortgage in that (1) title passes to the trustee in case of a Deed of Trust, while, in the case of a mortgage, the mortgagor retains title; (2) the statute of limitations never runs against the power of sale in a Deed of Trust, while it does run against a mortgage; and (3) a mortgagor has a statutory right of redemption after foreclosure, while no such right exists under a Deed of Trust." (81 Cal. App.4 868) This outlines the legislative intent of SB 1137 as it states therein "...a trustee under an ordinary Deed of Trust is the common agent of both parties and is required to act impartially." This defines the arm's length separation of the trustee, the Beneficiary, and the Trustor in the Transaction. It is further defined by the California Supreme Court, who described the rationale behind the statutory scheme in Cal. Civ. Code § 2924 as follows: "The non-judicial foreclosure statutes—as an alternative to judicial foreclosure—reflect a carefully crafted balancing of the interests of beneficiaries, trustors and trustees. Beneficiaries, of course, want a quick and inexpensive recovery of amounts due on promissory notes in default. Trustors, on the other hand, need protection against the forfeiture of valuable property rights.

The trustees, the [persons in the middle], need to have clearly defined responsibilities to enable them to discharge their duties efficiently and to avoid embroiling the parties in time-consuming and costly litigation. In taking all these concerns into account, the statutes strike an overall balance favoring the protection of the trustors." (I.E. Associates v. Safeco Title Ins. Co. (1985) 39 Cal.3d 281, 216 Cal. Rptr. 438; 702 P.2d 596). It is this independence that is the crux of the legislative intent of the Deed of Trust contract process in the state of California versus that of a Mortgage contract lending agreement. The Plaintiffs point to the common law idea as to the importance of the independence of the three distinct parties namely the trustee, the Trustor, and the Beneficiary, as it pertains to the non-judicial foreclosure process versus the Mortgagee and the Borrower as they pertain in a Mortgage contract and Judicial Foreclosure process.

In the Mortgage contract it states the judicial foreclosure process is used solely because the Title to the said property in question is held by the borrower, or owner of the Title. The only means of remedy to a breach done by the borrower is for the beneficiary, or lender, to file a judicial foreclosure process and sue the owner for the right to said Title. In the non-judicial foreclosure process, as in the state of California, the courts instituted an independent party into the contract, named as trustee, to act as an intermediary in the transaction and to hold, at arm's length, the Title from both the trustor and the beneficiary. The Deed of Trust is the instrument used to separate the Trustor and the Beneficiary from the Title. The Title owner, or Trustor, subsequently hands the Title, as a security for the loan, to the trustee, an independent separate party, to hold until there is a Power of Sale or Reconveyance cause of action with which to act upon as per the state law. The California Civil Code has explicit instructions as to the actions and the order, which all parties, namely the trustee, the Trustor, or the Beneficiary must follow in fulfilling any and all actions regarding their position in the non-judicial foreclosure process. The trustee is only able to sell or reconvey that which it holds rights to (interests) in a real property. The Substitute of trustee is the party that is given certain rights to act upon as defined and outlined to the Original trustee within the original contract agreement from the Trustor, the Beneficiary, and the Power of Sale Clause of the state the contract originated from. The rights transferred or given to the Substitute trustee can only be those rights and interests in the real property that the Original trustee had. A Trust Deed Contract gives the Beneficiary the right to pick any trustee of his choosing, but it does not give the Beneficiary the right to vest in his pick of the powers of a duly appointed trustee. Statute of Frauds is the law in every state, which requires that certain documents be in writing, such as real property titles and transfers (conveyances), leases for more than a year, wills, and some types of contracts. The original statute was enacted in England in 1677 to prevent fraudulent title claims. Here, the Statute of Frauds requires that the original trustee transfer his interest in the real property via a recorded document. The right and possession of Title can only be transferred to a Substitute trustee from the original trustee, and that Substitute trustee can only redistribute any rights he legally possesses as were given to him.

The Plaintiffs stipulate that as the Court stated that as "Wells Fargo has recorded a Substitution of trustee appointing NDEx as the substitute trustee in place of Golden West on February 8, 2011", the Plaintiffs argue that recordation (See Exhibit B) did not legally record a Substitution of trustee because there is no instrument on record legally transferring the title from Golden West to NDEx as the Substitution of trustee as per the requirement for real property transfers or conveyances. Hence, the Plaintiffs assert that this appointment done by the Beneficiary does not give any rights to its appointed Substitute trustee, but only states the beneficiary's desire to name NDEx as its Substitution of trustee.

The Plaintiffs allege a most recent discovery of evidence found on October 31, 2011, through a full chain of title search done at the Clerk of the County Recorder's Office, in the county of Alameda, CA. A Deed of Trust between Michelle Moquin and Douglas Boggs, and Shirley M. Moquin ("Trustors"); Pacific Guarantee Mortgage Corp., and Mortgage Electronic Registration Systems, Inc. ("MERS") ("Beneficiaries"); and New Century Title Company ("trustee") was recorded on December 20, 2000 (Exhibit A). As the Plaintiffs found no continuance of vested title in the record, the Plaintiffs ask the Court to order the defendants to submit documentary evidence as required by Statute of

Frauds and Cal. Civ. Code § 2924 to show that New Century Title Co. had vested, transferred, or conveyed the title and interest it held in the Plaintiff's property through a subsequent or Substitute trustee.

The Plaintiffs allege that the defendant Golden West never had legal title to the Plaintiff's property because there is no legally recorded instrument as required by the California Civil Code 2924 and the Statute of Frauds that show legal transfer of title from a duly appointed previous holder of the Plaintiffs' title or previous trustee to Golden West. The Plaintiffs allege that All subsequent attempts by Wells Fargo to substitute a new trustee is merely an exercise in verbose wording to mislead the reader of the document into believing that a legal transfer of the Plaintiffs' title from one entity to another was taking place. (See Exhibits B &C). It is established law in all 50 states and U.S. territories that title to real property is evidenced by a written instrument that is backed by a continuous unbroken chain showing the transfer of the title to that property from one person(s) or entity(s) to another. If defendants cannot show that they have a contract with the Plaintiffs with the elements of a contract needed to form a legal Deed of Trust Contract, then the defendants and Plaintiffs don't have a Deed of Trust Contract. They have an oral agreement that amounts to a personal contract between the two parties. The Plaintiffs allege that when the Plaintiffs' Deed of Trust Contract was being sold from entity to entity until it was purchased from Wachovia by the Defendants, Wells Fargo Bank, the entity in this chain of purchasers that purchased from Pacific Guarantee Mortgage, the Original Beneficiary, failed to effect good, and legal transfer of title from the Original trustee, New Century Title Company, to the Substitute trustee picked by the succeeding Beneficiary. This failure to ensure that the elements of a Deed of Trust Contract, which are a Trustor, a Beneficiary and an impartial trustee were present were burdens of the purchasers. If the purchasers didn't meet that burden then they have issues with the party(s) that sold them what they assumed was a Deed of Trust Contract, they do not have claim of action with the Plaintiffs, i.e. breach of contract or anything else, arising out of a Deed of Trust Contract because they have no valid trustee and this indisputable fact means that the Defendant Wells Fargo Bank is missing an essential element of a Deed of Trust Contract, namely a duly recorded and vested impartial trustee. Therefore, according to Black, Wells Fargo didn't purchase a Deed of Trust Contract with the Plaintiffs from Wachovia. At most, what Wells Fargo purchased from Wachovia was an oral agreement that Wachovia had with the Plaintiff to pay back a loan. Based on the indisputable fact that Wells Fargo cannot show a legally recorded transfer of title to cure the failed Deed of Trust Contract that Wells Fargo purchased form Wachovia, the Plaintiffs ask for a summary judgement declaring that Wells Fargo has only an oral agreement with the Plaintiffs and therefore no right to a non-judicial foreclosure sale of the Plaintiffs' property.

A few days after filing this document, I received a phone call from the opposing counsel. Perhaps they were beginning to see where we were heading in our case? Perhaps we were beginning to make them a little nervous? I'd like to think so.

"Mr. Boggs, this is Gene Wu of Anglin, Flewelling, Rasmussen, Campbell & Trytten, LLP. Have you got a minute?" His voice had the sound of authority.

I wasn't buying whatever it was he wanted to sell. I didn't want to have a minute for him. I wanted it to be more on my terms. I know it was a strategy for them to have this unannounced contact with us in order to help throw us off balance. This is a business tactic used to attempt to dominate or take advantage of the opposition.

"No, I don't have a minute," I said to Wu on the other end of the line while pouring coconut milk over my cereal.

"Why don't I give you a call back in fifteen minutes? Would that work?" His voice sounded slightly defeated, clearly hoping I would have been caught off guard.

"Fine." I set the phone down and began to eat my cereal. Never get between a man and his food.

It was about thirty minutes later when the phone rang. I recognized the number from before. Prior to the second phone call, we had some time to sit and discuss what we thought they were calling for. We were mulling over the myriad of possibilities when he called again.

I answered.

"Mr. Boggs, it's Gene Wu again. Is this a good time?" he said with a strategic and measured politeness.

"What do you want?" I wanted my conversation style to be short. I wanted to minimize any of my vocal intonations by using as few words as possible. I didn't want them to hear the nervousness in my voice.

"Mr. Boggs, we see that you have filed for clarity on a point of law. We wanted to discuss something with you if you have a minute."

"Go." I was thinking by that response that they were beginning to understand where we were headed in our litigation.

"Uh, um, well, we wanted to discuss ways to keep this litigation from dragging on, as I am sure you are tired of all this."

There was a pregnant pause as if he were waiting for me to respond. Finally, after the extended silence, I said, "Wow, how sweet."

"Well, um, uh, would you consider discussing a means to ending this?"

"Perhaps."

"What would it take for us to come to some sort of an arrangement?" He was an associate to the law firm and not on the letterhead, so no matter what we agreed, he wouldn't be able to make any final decisions. They were fishing. They were wondering about our tenacity and perseverance to our cause.

"What do you have in mind?" I have learned that in the art of negotiation it is more advantageous that you let the other party begin.

"Well, sir, uh, I'm sure this is quite taxing on you both since you aren't attorneys and are going through such a difficult time." I didn't respond. He continued, "The legal arena is difficult enough to traverse even when someone is an attorney. I mean, we are considered one of the top law firms in the west and there are times when we can certainly feel that difficulty. Some cases can really take one through it."

It was obvious that he was trying to be friendly and create a common bond between us so that we might let our guard down. It was that phrase that triggered me to give a longer response. "And I'm sure having someone acting as their own attorney against one of the top law firms in the west, arguing in stride throughout the litigation process, doesn't make you look too good at the ol' watering hole at the good ol' boys' club, huh?"

He left the comment alone. There was a moment that we could feel that he was taking an extra moment to regroup and said, "Do you have an amount in mind?"

"An amount?" I was playing evasive even though I knew exactly what he meant.

"Yes, sir, is there an amount you have in mind that might bring a conclusion to this litigation?" It sounded as though he was getting a little frustrated with the conversation not running the way he thought it might go.

"Are you ready to write a check?"

"Well, that isn't my call, but I wanted to reach out and talk."

"Talk."

"Again, Mr. Boggs, we wanted to reach out to see if there was an amount you might have had in mind that we could take to our clients to discuss ending this whole process."

"You let me know when you're ready to cut the check. Then we might have that conversation." The entire discussion seemed like being in a tennis match. We were both lobbing the ball over the net, but neither of us were in the position to rush the net and put the ball out. I could tell that they were simply feeling out our resolve and were trying to bully us a bit. The call seemed to be done after he said for us to have a good day. I hung up.

The filing for clarity on a point of law was ignored and went unanswered by the judge.

For the next handful of months, we continued to file motions and responses in federal court. The judge eventually dismissed our initial breach of contract cause of action, which I disagreed with. She kept the fraud cause of action alive on the docket, which I agreed with. This signaled to the opposing counsel that I was constructing the arguments for fraud accordingly. At least enough for the court to be satisfied, thus far. However, the court asked us that we amend the four points of fraud to be outlined with more clarity. So, we constructed and filed a Second Amended Complaint, on the direction of the court.

I continued to spend hundreds of hours at the University of California Berkeley Law Library researching laws and codes. I would pour over volumes of legal reference books for hours on end. Between the frequent visits to the Berkeley Law Library and the San Francisco Law Library, I started to develop relationships with some of the other people there who were doing various research projects of their own. Because of the magnitude of the economic collapse, there were always a few other people also dealing with real estate issues.

There was one person in particular and we became study partners. They were doing their initial research to construct their own lawsuit against Wells Fargo Bank for fraud. It seemed that they were also in a foreclosure situation with them, and they were being foreclosed on while they were current on their mortgage. We tried to understand how Wells Fargo could file foreclosure documents against someone who was current on their mortgage. The process of foreclosure requires certain steps to be taken with specific results and being current on your mortgage defies them all.

One of the things I began discussing with my study partner was how I would go about filing a motion to counter the judge's removal of the breach of contract cause of action. My friend said that if I was going to be arguing about the contract, we would need to define exactly what a contract is in accordance with the rule of law. We would need to be able to show the court whether our Deed of Trust contract was true and correct in accordance with the codes and rules defined by law. If our contract wasn't found to be true and correct in accordance with those codes and rules, in order to prove this, I would need to bring in a contract that was. I would need to find a contract that abided by all the rules, codes and statutes relating to the legal structure of a contract and use that as an exhibit to show to the court.

World Savings

It was in 2005 when we walked into a downtown Oakland, California World Savings branch office to discuss the lending rates that we had seen advertised. We specifically inquired about the financial institution's "Pick-a-Pay Loan" program.

I had completed some home renovation plans and took them to the building department. With a few redline corrections from the city engineer, it eventually passed the review so that I could get a permit to begin construction. This loan was so that I could turn the 1200sf space downstairs into two more bedrooms, two more bathrooms, a family room with a fireplace, and a music room.

The benefits to this new loan program that World Savings had on the market was perfect for a project such as this. The idea of their loan was that you had four different payment options for your loan. Depending on your financial situation for that payment period, you could choose to pay the full payment of the loan principal plus the accrued interest for the month including taxes and insurance, or only the principle, or only the interest, or you could choose to pay the minimum amount due, referred as a negative amortization payment. That means your loan balance is not being paid down. In fact, the interest is accumulating, and the taxes and insurance also remain unpaid. We were not paying off our mortgage in any way. The choice to have this payment option defied all logic regarding the rules of contract law. How could there ever be an agreed pay off date?

These types of payment options were a perfect solution to saving money while in the construction process of the home renovation. Then, upon completion of the construction project, we would refinance the "Pick-a-Pay Loan" into a more conventional thirty-year fixed mortgage. After completing the construction, the value of the home would have increased dramatically, allowing us to refinance into the conventional loan program and letting us take out a profit from the increase in value if we wanted to.

At that time, I was in a position to self-finance the construction of the renovation, so we wouldn't need a construction loan. But it would be helpful to be able to choose which payment we would make to help us save a few thousand dollars every month during the construction process.

We sat down with the person in the loan department who explained the loan specifics and how being able to choose our payment every month would give us more choices for our monthly expenses while I was doing the construction. This loan would allow me to save money on the payment options so I could spend that money on materials for the project. They made it seem as if it were a golden opportunity.

Golden West Financial was the second largest savings and loan association in the United States, operating branches under the name of World Savings Bank. World Savings Bank was the only financial institution that had this kind of loan program on the market. They were a large financial organization that had been around since 1929. In 1990, *The New York Times* called them "the nation's best run savings and loan company. It was in the mid-90s, during the savings and loan crisis, that they expanded nationwide with assets totaling $32 billion, making it the third largest mortgage lender in the country. They convinced us to go ahead with this loan and we signed the paperwork.

The following year, in 2006, the company agreed to an acquisition of Golden West Financial, and its thrift, World Savings, by Wachovia Bank. The merger was completed in October of 2006 and expanded their branch network nationwide with an additional 285 locations in ten states. This merger also allowed Wachovia to pick up an additional $122 billion in option adjustable-rate mortgages.

This was the term the industry used for this type of loan package. It was what was better known as a subprime mortgage. The timing of the subprime mortgage crisis created financial hardship for Wachovia. Shortly after the acquisition, World Savings lending volume slowed, prompting World Savings to attract more new borrowers by writing new loans at an annual interest rate of 1% with low monthly payments. Their previous rates were never allowed to go so low. The steep losses generated by Golden West/World Savings did significant damage to Wachovia, which resulted in its eventual purchase by Wells Fargo Bank in 2008.

In contract law, there is supposed to be a date that is clearly defined whereby all parties would be aware of the commencement and completion of the contract. However, if I were to choose to ONLY pay the "negative amortization" option each month, I would never reach a date when the loan would be paid off. In fact, the loan balance would only rise with the accumulation of interest and outstanding principal that would remain unpaid overtime.

With this type of loan instrument, it seemed that World Savings Bank had been able to create an investment vehicle that could never be paid off. This created sort of an indentured servitude. If the borrowers chose to never pay additional principal, interest, taxes, and insurance, eventually their taxes would become a balloon payment that would be due. However, the principal and interest would only grow. This process would continue, thereby negating any means to calculate an end date to the contractual obligation.

The mere fact that this could take place makes this loan

fraudulent and void, since there is no true end date that exists to this loan. How could there be a true meeting of the minds? How could the bank say that the contractual loan duration has expired, and the loan should be paid in full? Perhaps, if there were a balloon payment clause that was worked into the language of the contract or would be legal, but there was not. In basic contract law there must be a definitive date that can be adhered to for the payoff of the loan.

Unlawful Detainer

Taking one step forward and two steps back, the rain had been making itself known all week. I'd prepared the night before by setting aside my umbrella next to the front door. It was one that I'd been given for being in a golf tournament the previous year at the course in Texas where I was building homes. Golf umbrellas are the best rain protection because they cover such a wide area. I needed this to not only cover myself, but the paperwork I was carrying along with the large sign that I would hold up. The sign I used was to inform any prospective buyer(s) that there is a Lis Pendens filed on the property due to the lawsuit that had been going on over the past year. I was simply making sure to cover all my tracks and all the legal rules. You see, by announcing to all possible buyers that there was an encumbrance—namely the lawsuit—associated with the property they would be bidding on, let anyone interested in bidding on the property know everything they were getting involved with when they made their bid. Because now they had legally been informed that there was a legal issue with the title filed against the property, the purchaser would therefore be purchasing a participating interest in the legal issue.

If you were a professional buyer of foreclosed properties, you would know this. It would be your job to know that information. Because, as a professional, your profit in a specific piece of property might depend on knowing if there were any legal injunctions with your property. That is a natural part of doing research as a professional foreclosure buyer. However, if you were simply trying to buy a home for your family and had never purchased a foreclosure before, you might not be fully aware that you would find that information from the County Records, whether online or by going into their office. So, if you were unfamiliar with that process, and someone at the courthouse steps showed you documents associated with that property stating that there was a legal issue currently in the courts, chances are you would pass and move on to a home with less headache involved from the onset. Either way, you would now be legally informed about the encumbrance that you would be inheriting if you were to purchase the property at the trustee sale.

In the eyes of the law there is a distinction of the quality of a real estate buyer named a bona fide purchaser. Someone who knows all the relevant facts regarding the purchase and the purchase process because it is their profession is not considered a bona fide purchaser. In real estate law and personal property, this term is used for an innocent party who purchases a property without notice of any other party's claim to the title of that property. It was for this reason that I filed the Lis Pendens. It is for this reason that I held a sign and delivered the court record cover sheet of the lawsuit to all the parties attending the foreclosure auction. If everyone who bid on the property at the auction was privy to the litigation encumbrance on the property, they could not then call themselves a bona fide purchaser. There is a distinction of an institutional buyer or a regular citizen buyer in the eyes of the law. Either way, it's a way of making sure the transaction is dealing with what the law defines as a bona fide purchaser.

I also kept my digital recorder turned on throughout the whole auction process. Only this time, I thought that it needed to remain in my shirt pocket. My hands were full between the sign in one hand with the papers under my arm and the umbrella in the other.

At least every month for the past year, and at times more frequently, I would go to Alameda County courthouse steps and listen to the auctioneer announce a list of properties that had been removed from the auction block for that day. This happened just at the last minute prior to the day's auction commencement. There would always be a fervor in the air from the investors there to purchase foreclosures. Most were bottom feeders eager to dive in for their kill. For over a year, I left the steps thankful that I heard my property being announced as one of those that would be canceled, postponed, or rescheduled. The lawsuit was working its way through state court for a few months, only then being remanded up to federal court for an additional handful of months of filings and responses, to then being remanded back to state court on jurisdictional issues. I filed papers to the court trying to have them put a stay on the foreclosure procedure until the lawsuit was completed, but to no avail. The judge left this motion sitting alone and unanswered, making me then wait at the courthouse steps every time there would be a noticed attempt to auction off my house. Every time.

I held the sign high for people to see while I handed out the documents detailing the Lis Pendens and the cover sheet of the lawsuit with its file number, judge information, etc.

This can be taxing on your nerves. The need to do this every month or more, and to hope that your home won't be stolen from under you, is difficult to manage. The fragility of your living circumstance being left in the balance for months, and for some people, years on end, creates an underlying feeling of failure and uneasiness that begins to sit within your core. The long-term effects of this kind of circumstance have led doctors to label the trauma as post-traumatic stress syndrome.

I do feel that it is an imperative legal strategy to file a temporary restraining order (TRO) and Lis Pendens during a foreclosure. Anything to help buy time and any legal advantage for you in a system that has shown itself to be filled with fraud and irregularities. Although someone would have to dig to find the fraud and irregularities, the chances are, your mortgage and title were filled with them. The fact that I had held off the auctions on my house for over a year was a small success given all the circumstances.

The mist had been heavy all morning, making the marble steps a little slick. The courthouse steps drew more and more people. As the economic collapse continued, it seemed there were more bidders every day. I rarely saw someone who was just trying to buy their next home for a discount. Perhaps there were some people who saw a late-night infomercial on foreclosure buying and purchased the DVD before coming down to buy their new piece of the American dream at a discount.

It was a crowd that was mainly filled with people representing companies that invest in foreclosed properties. The institutional investment groups would even come into these auctions buying bulk properties, sometimes dozens at a time. These companies knew exactly what they were doing and most of them had deep pockets. They were feeding off the economic cycle of those people who were financially incapable of fighting a system against any wrongdoing against them.

Most owners whose homes were being auctioned had no idea that they were being defrauded. Most thought that they had done something wrong. Most believed they failed, and it was their fault. This was what the press had been telling them. This was what the information they were receiving explained to them. Even though they knew something wasn't right with what they were going through, they either didn't or couldn't see their way through to the other side, if there was one.

When the auctioneer read off the list of postponed properties, this time, my property didn't make the list. My heart skipped a beat, and I felt the blood rush from my head. I'm sure I turned white with panic. Today would be the day. I was going to watch the home I had built with my own hands being auctioned off. After hearing the addresses come to a close and my property was not on the list, I immediately held my sign high for all bidders to see. I began announcing that the property had a lawsuit pending and if anyone were to bid for the property that they would indeed become part and parcel to a federal lawsuit for fraud. At this point, the case had been moved from superior court to the federal jurisdiction. We had been arguing motions for over eight months in federal court by this time. I was astounded that the property was going to be sold while it was in litigation. The sale would move forward despite that, creating a whole new set of legal issues that we were going to have to attend to straight away.

I immediately fled the scene and called my library study friend.

"They sold my house," I said, panting into the phone while I ran back to my car in utter disbelief. I was in a state of shock. We had been arguing in state superior court and federal court for over a year about mortgage fraud. The outstanding litigation on the Deed of Trust agreement did not stop the fraud, and in fact escalated it as it continued.

"Actually, this is a good thing, and it changes everything."

"What do you mean a good thing? I just lost my house."

"Yes, but that is the key phrase. You just "lost" something." I was dumbfounded, confused, and angry at my friend for being so callous. "You see, when you are proving fraud, the person who was defrauded has to have been harmed. You weren't harmed before this. You weren't out anything. Yes, you have had to deal with a few years of stress, but you chose to file the lawsuit against a fraudulent foreclosure. However, there was not a fraudulent foreclosure prior to this point. You were only arguing fraud against a process. In order to really get your teeth into the argument of fraud you need to be harmed by the fraudulent process."

"Oh, great. Now, I can argue about the harm while I go homeless. This is shit."

"You can't argue fraud without being harmed. It's that simple. Now, you've been harmed. That's a good thing, at least as far as the lawsuit goes. Now, we should meet up to construct so you can file a preliminary injunction to the federal court regarding the sale. This following the clarity to the point of law is all good to have in the file. Remember, you want your arguments and filings to hold up in court in preparation for the court that is higher. You are always writing for the higher court. You want to strategize for the appeal. And you will need to begin to strategize for your unlawful detainer case."

We had already discussed that we wouldn't leave the house if it were sold. That we would fight the buyers against a fraudulent sale if that were to take place. Even though we had prevented that from happening for the past year, the reality of an unlawful detainer was now front and center.

"I am overwhelmed. Now, we will have federal court, and UD court at the same time. Ever since we were remanded from the state superior court to the federal court, I've been on my own. I'm gonna lose it, and I don't necessarily mean the case, I mean my fucking mind!"

Once the paralegal heard that we were remanded to federal court, she called and politely told me that she had never dealt with the federal court and felt it best to bow out. She didn't want to give incorrect advice or assistance in an arena that she was inexperienced in. I told her I was more inexperienced than she was but understood where she was coming from professionally. But since that moment, I have felt alone against the Goliaths.

"I understand you are feeling overwhelmed. Keep breathing. Let's meet up at your place in an hour and we can begin a whole new line of attack. Turn this into a good thing."

I don't remember the handful of miles drive home from the courthouse steps of downtown Oakland. I was in a complete daze. When I got home, I simply walked in and collapsed on the couch. Michelle came in expecting to hear the same thing that she always heard after I came back from the scheduled auction. Only, this time, they sold our home rather than announce that the auction was postponed to another date.

"They sold our house." These were the only words I could muster. She stood there for a moment letting the reality set in and slowly sat down on the couch in silence.

"What do we do now?" She whispered.

"Well, my study partner says it's a good thing. We needed to be harmed. So, this is harmed. I guess we file for a preliminary injunction at the federal level. Although, we will need to prepare to also begin an unlawful detainer action against us if we defy their upcoming "3-Day Notice". Shit's about to get busy."

The knock on the door broke my daze. When I answered the door that was when I met the person who said they had purchased the house at the auction, and we now had three days to leave the house. That person who I quickly told to "get the hell off my property!"

Within the hour, I was researching and drafting the motion for a preliminary injunction to be submitted to the federal court. This would be following the most recent clarity of point of law that she had yet left unanswered.

UNITED STATES DISTRICT COURT

NORTHERN DISTRICT OF CALIFORNIA – SAN FRANCISCO/OAKLAND DIVISION

Douglas J Boggs and	Case No. 4:11-cv-02346-SBA
Michelle A Moquin	[Hon. Saundra B. Armstrong]
Plaintiffs,	MOTION FOR
vs.	PRELIMINARY INJUNCTION
Wells Fargo Bank, NA;	
Wachovia Mortgage, World Savings, Assoc. Service Co.,	(F.R.C.P. Rule 65)Golden W. Sav. Hearing Date: Feb. 10, 2012
NDEx West, L.L.C., and LSI Title Co.,	(or next convenient day)
DOES 1 to 50	Time: 1:00 p.m.
Defendants	Ctrm:1 (4th Fl)

TO THE HONORABLE COURT:

Please take notice that the Plaintiffs Douglas Boggs and Michelle Moquin (collectively, "Plaintiffs"), hereby seek an immediate Preliminary Injunction against, SGT Investments, LLC, Catalina Bay, LLC, and FAS Realty, Inc., all located at 14429 Catalina Street, San Leandro, CA 94577, from taking possession of the Plaintiff's property located at 1038 57th St., Oakland, CA.

1 The Plaintiffs currently have an active Federal Civil lawsuit ongoing as case no. 4:11-cv-02346-SBA in the Northern District Court of California, Oakland Division. (See Exhibit)

1   The Plaintiffs hereby request from the court for an immediate Preliminary Injunction against, SGT Investments, LLC, a 50% partner and Catalina Bay, LLC, a 50% partner, 14429 Catalina Street, San Leandro, CA 94577, for taking possession of the Plaintiff's property which is located at 1038 57th St., Oakland, CA. (See Exhibit)

1   Defendants filed an Unlawful Detainer case against the Plaintiffs and have secured a Master Jury Trial scheduled on 03/16/2012 at 8:45 AM in Dept. 1, 2nd fl of the Rene C. Davidson Alameda County Courthouse located at 1225 Fallon St. Oakland, CA.

LIKELIHOOD OF SUCCESS ON MERITS

1   Plaintiffs are bringing an instant action against Wells Fargo Bank("WFB") for fraudulent inducement to contract based on the fact that at the time of negotiations to contract WFB misled the Plaintiffs into believing that their Deed of Trust ("DOT") contract contained a binding agreement that WFB would not be the holder of the Plaintiffs Legal title and that a trustee would be the holder of the Plaintiffs' Legal title with the power to protect the Plaintiffs of misconduct by WFB in the event of a breach by the Plaintiffs and WFB used the Non-Judicial Foreclosure(NJF) process part of the contract as a remedy.

1   Fraudulent Misrepresentation is the instance of false statement where (1) the party making the statement is aware that it is false or disregards the possibility of it being false, (2) the party making the statement does so to induce another party to enter into a contract, and (3) the other party enters the contract as a result of the statement and consequently suffers a loss.

1   On _____ WFB presented a Deed of Trust (DOT) contract which contained a statement that the Plaintiffs' Legal title would be deeded to the trustee appointed by WFB as security for a loan. The contract further stated that the trustee would have the power to protect the Plaintiffs via the Power of Sale Clause (POSC) in the event WFB used its option to use the Non-Judicial Foreclosure (NJF) process as a remedy for the Plaintiffs' breach. Plaintiffs accepted this statement and thus signed the DOT. Plaintiffs were unaware that WFB knew that portion of the contract was untrue and in fact WFB would be the de facto owner of Plaintiffs' legal title upon any substitution of the original trustee by WFB. Plaintiffs' trust in the misrepresentation by WFB resulted in the loss of their property when WFB's misconduct in the pursuit of a quick foreclosure via NJF process was not detected by the trustee and could not have been enforced by the trustee if detected because of the actions and knowledge of WFB.

1   Plaintiffs feel they have a great likelihood of prevailing because they can present evidence to show that misconduct did occur by WFB when they employed

the NJF process; the Plaintiffs can present evidence to show that the trustee in Plaintiffs' contract was a "straw man" with no power to protect against that misconduct; and Plaintiffs can present facts that show that WFB knowingly misrepresented to the Plaintiffs that they would have that trustee with the power to protect them from that WFB's misconduct. Further the fact that WFB has sold the Plaintiffs' home without regard to the due process afforded them through the POSC as per CCC 2924 shows that Plaintiffs have suffered substantial damages.

LIKELIHOOD OF IRREPARABLE HARM TO THE MOVING PARTY IN THE ABSENCE OF PRELIMINARY RELIEF

1   In an effort by WFB to avoid Declaratory Relief for the Plaintiffs, WFB sold the Plaintiff's property in a trustee's sale thereby denying the Plaintiffs an early resolution of their rights. In the absence of preliminary relief preventing the defendant WFB from profiting by their attempt to prevent the plaintiffs from getting Declaratory Relief Plaintiffs may never be able to recover their property. The Plaintiff's home is very important to them as Plaintiff Douglas Boggs had to put a lot of personal work into the property because it was a fixer-upper purchase. The Plaintiffs enjoy the home and the neighborhood and wish to recover their home. Had the Defendants WFB not violated the POS clause to quickly foreclose upon the Plaintiffs, the Plaintiffs believe they would have come to some understanding with the Defendants to enable them to keep their home.

THE BALANCE OF EQUITIES TIPS IN THE MOVING PARTIES FAVOR

1   Plaintiffs purchased the property as their first home because it was in a neighborhood that was in their financial range, and for Douglas Boggs as a beginning contractor, Plaintiffs felt they could invest personal time and monies saved from their daily luxuries to make their home a place to live in and share with their friends and relatives. Plaintiffs have done extensive work on the property to include: replacement of the existing brick foundation with a new structural concrete foundation; upgraded the entire electrical, gas, sewer, and plumbing throughout; remodeled and updated the kitchen; added two new full custom bathrooms and remodeled the existing bath; installed a new gas fireplace and a new 30 year roof; a parking pad for one car; carefully attended the now fully grown landscaping that took ten years to complete which includes a rear patio area for entertaining and a full vegetable garden with fruit trees that are all protected by the installed fully fenced property.

1   Defendants, SGT Investments, LLC, and Catalina Bay, LLC, are institutional buyers who buy and sell homes not for personal use, but for resale or rental income. (See Exhibit) The Defendants have purchased numerous properties

through trustee sales represented by NDEx, either as the entities herein, (See Exhibit), as well as, Plaintiffs can show a lengthy list of properties purchased in foreclosure in association through other entities that they have partnered with dating back well over a decade.

1. A loss of the property by the Plaintiffs would not only result in a loss of a personal and financial investment of 12 years in the home, but it would present a substantial hardship if Plaintiffs now had to pack up and find a new place to live under the present economic circumstances. Defendants can indemnify themselves through WFB, the Defendant who is trying to profit from this by its precipitous sale of the Plaintiff's property. On balance, the harm to the Defendant SGT Investments, LLC, and Catalina Bay, LLC, would be the loss of a return on his investment. This can be made up by the court ordering WFB to compensate SGT Investments, LLC, and Catalina Bay, LLC for their loss should the Plaintiffs prevail in their lawsuit against WFB. If Plaintiffs lose their home because the court allows the Defendants to take possession and sell the home to another party, the Plaintiffs harm will be a loss of a place to live and the impossibility of recovering their home back.

AN INJUNCTION IS IN THE PUBLIC'S BEST INTEREST

1. An Injunction is in the public's best interest to return the property to the Plaintiffs to show that despite today's prolific economic climate of foreclosures throughout the state, and country that the financial institutions are not in the sole and seemingly enviable position to be able to thwart the law and abuse the systems that are in place that are supposed to be used to also protect borrowers in Real Estate loan contracts. It is in the public's best interest to return the property to the Plaintiffs to show that the homeowner/borrower is still allowed the opportunity to a fair means of justice in the foreclosure process and see that all parties must adhere to the rule of law and be able to see justice served in a balanced and fair way in order to find remedy to the financial institutions flagrant misconduct against the public. It is in the public's best interest to return the property to the Plaintiffs to show that institutional buyers of foreclosed properties are not allowed to be used as a conduit for the furthering of misconduct and corrupt business practices made by the financial institutions to deny a homeowner their Declaratory Relief.

CONCLUSION

1. Plaintiffs pray that the Honorable Judge Saundra B Armstrong find that the sale of the property be void and be reversed and quiet title given back to the Plaintiffs. If the judge doesn't see that the sale be reversed at this time, then it is

the Plaintiff's request that the judge hold and place a stay onto the possession of the property for the Plaintiffs until after the case is decided. The Plaintiff's request that the possession of the buyer be held in abeyance until the case is decided. The Plaintiffs believe that this is necessary because the Defendants violated the principle of the adversarial atmosphere in order to put undue pressure and hardships upon the Plaintiffs by forcing the Plaintiffs to address other issues for example; preparing and filing preliminary injunctions to prevent the buyer from taking possession, the time energy and expense required to pack up, vacate, and find another home all of which prevents the Plaintiff from concentrating on an active lawsuit pending on the property and filing an adequate claim of fraud against the Defendant and is an attempt by the Defendant to make the case moot now that the property has now been sold.

Dated: February 3, 2011

Respectfully submitted,

Douglas J Boggs Pro Se Plaintiff

Michelle A Moquin Pro Se Plaintiff

It was raining heavily the day we received the "3-Day Notice". As I pulled up to the driveway, I could see a pile of paperwork floating around in the street puddles next to the curb. The rainwater was flooding over them as they nestled themselves into a pile of sticks, leaves, and a discarded McDonald's fries' container. I parked my truck and went to the curb to see what the papers were. They were scattered as some had come unclasped from the staples that previously held them together. Picking them all up, on one sheet I saw the words "3-Day Notice to Quit". I guess that this meant that we were served.

As I laid out the papers to dry, I immediately noticed that the parties listed as the new owners were not the same as the guy who had come to the door a few hours after the auction. These were the names of two different companies. The first thing I knew to do was to research who these buyers were, since I had already been lied to. Something wasn't right.

I got online and began digging into who these companies were. Who were the owners? Were the companies legitimate? Had they ever worked together previously in other investments? Had they ever previously purchased foreclosures together? I tried to find anything I could on these two companies, because now I was also going to have to include them in the federal case that we had ongoing. They were now going to become another set of defendants to the case. Would I be able to find some connection between them and Wells Fargo? Or perhaps, I might find a link between them and the trustee who orchestrated the foreclosure sale. Or I might even find a connection between them and some judges. I was on a path to dig and was trying to upend every possible loose end.

After the three days had passed, we eventually received a lawsuit in Superior Court from the new buyers of our home. I was now going to be writing legal documents for two courts at the same time. Two related cases, however, two different schedules to adhere to. One schedule and procedure to deal with in federal court. I had become familiar with this process as we had been dealing with them for a year now. But now I also needed to learn the procedures, processes, and timelines for filing in an unlawful detainer court. Their rules and calendaring are substantially different. Plus, in the federal case I was listed as a plaintiff and now in the unlawful detainer case I was listed as a defendant. I would have to make sure I had the right hat on when I was writing any specific motion or response.

The further I researched, the more I noticed a trend of some seemingly shady kinds of evidence in the unlawful detainer case. I needed to assemble a response to the filing of their unlawful detainer cause of action. As I connected the dots, I became increasingly convinced about the larger picture of massive corruption between the banks, the trustees, the professional foreclosure buyers, and the courts.

In an unlawful detainer action, the time to respond to a cause of action and other filings is drastically reduced compared to the normal timeline of a superior court or federal court civil action. The timelines are shortened substantially to move the process forward. They do this so as not to delay the new owner from taking possession of their newly purchased foreclosed property. Notwithstanding that the whole foreclosure process against the previous owner was done in such an illegal manner, therein stealing their home from them. The wheels of justice turn quickly, leaving the foreclosed party behind as they can only try to keep up in an attempt to save their home. Within a few weeks after filing the preliminary injunction in the federal court, I was able to research, construct, and file our objection to unlawful detainer.

SUPERIOR COURT OF CALIFORNIA – COUNTY OF ALAMEDA

CIVIL – LIMITED JURISDICTION

SGT INVESTMENTS, LLC, and CATALINA BAY, LLC Plaintiffs, vs. MICHELLE MOQUIN DOUGLAS J BOGGS and DOES 1 to 10, inclusive, Defendants (in Pro Per)	Case No. RG 12616221 OBJECTION TO UNLAWFUL DETAINER ACTION BASED ON CODE OF CIVIL PROCEDURE SECTION 1161A

Defendants Douglas Boggs and Michelle Moquin (collectively, "Defendants"), hereby Object to the Cause of Action for Unlawful Detainer submitted to this court by Plaintiffs SGT Investments, LLC and Catalina Bay, LLC (collectively "Plaintiffs) as follows:

INTRODUCTION

The Defendants assert that the Plaintiffs have acquired the Defendant's property through fraudulent means and are not in fact good faith buyers. The Plaintiffs are speculators with large holdings of real property under various business entities who buy, sell and hold foreclosed properties on a regular basis. The Defendants assert that the Plaintiffs were well aware of the outstanding Lis Pendens associated with this property that had been filed in the Superior Court of CA, case no. RG 11570208 (See Exhibit A), which venue was subsequently transferred to the United States District Court as a Federal lawsuit that is currently associated with this property as case no. cv 11-02346 SBA. The Plaintiffs fraudulently purchased this property and are acting in collusion with NDEx West, LLC, the listed trustee of the sale of the property, in order to assist Wells Fargo Bank, a Defendant in the Federal case, to quickly foreclose on the Defendant's property despite the current litigation against the property. The Honorable Judge Saundra B Armstrong handling the Defendant's Federal case pertaining to this property has scheduled a hearing, as per Federal Rules of Civil Procedure 65, for a Preliminary Injunction filed against the Plaintiffs and for their participation in the Fraud being perpetrated against the Defendants to be held on April 10, 2012 at 1pm in courtroom 1 on the 4th floor in the United States District Court Northern District of California in Oakland, CA in Alameda County. Due to the scheduled Preliminary Injunction hearing associated with this property the Defendants hereby request from this court to allow the legal process to play out prior to moving forward with a decision that will seriously impact the Defendant and the rightful ownership of the property to which the speculating party, the Plaintiffs, have fraudulently purchased.

OBJECTION TO COMPLAINT FOR UNLAWFUL DETAINER

FIRST CAUSE OF ACTION

1   The Defendants asserts that the Plaintiffs acquired the property by fraudulent means and hereby request from this court for an immediate Preliminary Injunction against, SGT Investments, LLC, a 50% partner and Catalina Bay, LLC, a 50% partner, 14429 Catalina Street, San Leandro, CA 94577, for taking possession of the Plaintiff's property located at 1038 57th St., Oakland, CA.

1   The Defendants assert that the Plaintiffs were not good faith buyers. They are part of a group of speculators that buy foreclosed properties on a regular basis. (See Exhibit G)

1   The Defendants assert that on Friday, January 20, 2012, at 12:30pm, located at 1225 Fallon St., Oakland CA. a trustee sale auction was conducted by LPS. The Defendants assert that the trustee sale was wrongfully and fraudulently misrepresented and conducted by LPS, the parent company to LSI Title Co. LPS is currently being investigated for fraud by the states Attorney General of FL, MI, NV, NJ, CA and others. LPS is the parent company of LSI Title Co. LSI Title Co. is a defendant in the current fraud case the Defendants have in Federal court and is the Title Company listed on record in the Substitution of trustee documents that were submitted to the Defendants prior to the foreclosure sale of the Defendant's property.

1   The Defendants assert that the Substitute trustee of record, as it was submitted and recorded in the Substitution of trustee documents, is NDEx West, LLC. NDEx West, LLC is also a party to the Defendant's current Federal case.

1. The Defendants assert that NDEx West, the listed Substitute trustee did not conduct the sale of the property.

1. The Defendants assert that on the day of and at the auction the Defendants told all prospective bidders of the Defendant's property that there was an ongoing Federal lawsuit against the property for Fraud. The Defendants assert that every bidder at the auction heard this statement. The Federal case information is public record and was announced at the auction.

1. The Defendants assert that they held up a sign stating this same information and the sign included the Federal Court case number and showed the Lis Pendens that is filed against the property by the Defendants in the State Superior Court and is found in the public record.

1. The Defendants assert that on the afternoon of the auction, after the auction took place, one Vi Chau came to the Defendant's property. Vi Chau gave the Defendants his business card and claimed that he was the party that purchased the property for an FAS Realty, Inc. (See Exhibit)

1. The Defendants assert that Vi Chau fraudulently misrepresented himself as the purchaser of the property to give the Defendants wrong information. Vi Chau was aware that the Defendants would be filing an injunction against the wrongful sale and subsequent wrongful purchase of the Defendant's property, because the Defendants told Vi Chau directly.

1. The Defendants filed a Preliminary Injunction in the Federal court based on the misleading information the Plaintiff gave the Defendant. (See Exhibit)

1. The Defendants assert that Vi Chau misled the Defendants in order that the Defendants would be led astray and not file appropriate injunctions to the appropriate parties and would therefore not properly serve the appropriate parties in the action. The Defendants found out the true buyer's information upon receipt of a 3 Day Notice to Quit (See Exhibit). Defendants then went to the county recorder's office to print recorded information of new owners. (See Exhibit)

1. The Defendants were forced to file a Second Preliminary Injunction due to the misrepresentation of the Plaintiff. (See Exhibit)

1. The Defendants assert that upon learning of the true buyers of the property they went down to the county recorder's office and found it appears that this group of speculators work with NDEx to assist the complicitis action of NDEx filing fraudulent and Robo Signed documents to the County Recorder's Office that helps to perpetuate the Plaintiff's part of the complicit nature of the Fraud being perpetrated by Wells Fargo Bank to quickly foreclose on the Defendant's property. (See Exhibit)

1. The Defendants assert that the Defendant's Original trustee, Golden West Savings Assoc. Service Co., never legally transferred, in writing, their rights given to them by the Defendants(grantor), as per their Deed of Trust contract, to any other party to date and subsequently, Golden West, continues to retain the rights to the title as given them by the Defendants.

1. The Defendants assert that as according to the Statute of Frauds (1677), Contract Law as per Cal. Civ. Code § 1624(6) and Property Law that anything dealing with real property, all transactions and all legal actions pertaining to a property must be done in writing and signed by the party to be charged.

1. The Defendants assert that the Beneficiary was given none and therefore holds no right to the Defendant's title and is not in any way in a position to and therefore cannot convey perceived rights to a Substitute trustee. As per the Statute of Frauds (1677) and Cal. Civ. Code § 1624(6) all transactions dealing with real property must be done in writing and signed by the party to be charged.

1. The Beneficiary, Wells Fargo Bank, NA, executed a Substitute trustee, as per Cal. Civ. Code § 2934a.

1. The Defendants assert that they never agreed to a transfer of any of their rights of Legal title to any substitute trustee orally or in writing.

1. The Defendants assert that they did in fact transfer their right to title to the Original trustee, Golden West Savings Assoc. Service Co., in the Deed of Trust Contract signed July 2005.

1. The Defendants assert that there is no documentation, in writing and signed by the party to be charged, of the Original trustee, Golden West Savings Assoc. Service Co., transferring any rights of title, to the Defendant's property to any other party.

1. The Defendants assert that they have never given or agreed, either orally or in writing, to transfer to the Beneficiary any right to the Defendant's title. Therefore, the Beneficiary cannot hold any right to hold or to convey any rights or privileges of the Defendants title to any other party.

1. The Defendants do hereby request a Preliminary Injunction order by the court against the Plaintiffs, SGT Investments, LLC, and Catalina Bay, LLC, Vi Chau and Hoi Lam Chan, located at 14429 Catalina Street, San Leandro, CA 94577, for taking possession of the Defendant's property located at 1038 57th St., Oakland, CA until the Federal Court has reached its final decision as to Federal Court case No. 4:11-cv-02346-SBA and as to the Defendant's rights being violated.

1. As per California Code of Civil Procedure Section 170.6 and F.R.C.P.

Rule 65 the purpose is to maintain the status quo to ensure a Plaintiff that the Defendant will not either make him or herself judgement proof, or insolvent in some way, or to stop him or her from acting the harmful, complained of way until further judicial proceedings are available. In the Federal case pertaining to the current property the Defendants are the Plaintiffs and the Plaintiffs in this case herein are now named DOE Defendants.

1. The Defendants assert, as per F.R.C.P. Rule 65, as to the immediacy of the harm that will come to the Defendants from this foreclosure while the court has yet to rule on the pending case against the Plaintiffs for fraud through the undue burden, harassment, and stress that is associated with eviction and moving, along with the burden of a Federal Civil Court while acting in Pro Se, and now in Pro Per as per this Superior Court filing.

1. The Defendants assert that the Plaintiffs incorrectly and fraudulently claim to have issued the Three (3) Day Notice to Quit (See Exhibit D) pursuant to California Code of Civil Procedure Section 1161a(b)(3) which states: "Where the property has been sold in accordance with Section 2924 of the Civil Code, under a power of sale contained in a Deed of Trust executed by such person, or a person under whom such person claims, and the title under the sale has been duly perfected."

1. The Defendants assert that due to the current litigation that is pending on this property against the very fact that the Section 2924 was fraudulently used by the Beneficiary and an illegal trustee of record means that the Plaintiffs are in no position to assert that the property was sold in accordance with this Civil Code.

1. The Defendants assert that the Plaintiffs assertion of their pursuant use of California Code of Civil Procedure Section 1161a(b)(3) is wrong as the "title under the sale" was never duly perfected by the trustee of record.

1. The Defendants assert that in the Plaintiffs' First Cause of Action in Section 1 line 25 the Plaintiffs fraudulently claim they are "the real owners of the real property" to which the Federal Court has shown reason to believe that this is not the case and has not yet heard the full arguments pertaining to the Defendant's assertions to the Plaintiffs wrongful claim.

1. The Defendants assert that the Plaintiffs cannot rightfully make the claim that they are the real owners of a property that they have acquired fraudulently.

1. The Defendants assert that in the Plaintiffs' First Cause of Action on page 2 in Section 3 line 5 the Plaintiffs fraudulently claim that they are the real owners of the property. The Defendants assert that the Plaintiffs cannot rightfully make the claim that they are the real owners of a property that they have acquired fraudulently.

1. The Defendants assert that the Plaintiff's fraudulently claim that they hold a viable trustee's Deed that was executed on January 25, 2012 and are entitled to possession thereof. By the fact that the trustee of record did not rightfully hold the auction to which the Plaintiffs claim to have rightfully purchased the property, and that the trustee of record was never legally vested by the Defendant in writing of the right to hold equitable title of the property in which to affect a power of sale, there is no legal standing that the Plaintiffs can claim they are able to hold legal title and rightfully possess the property.

1. The Defendants assert that the Plaintiffs fraudulently claim that the premises were sold in accordance with Section 2924 of the Civil Code. The Defendants assert that because the Original trustee on the Defendant's Deed of Trust never conveyed in writing the rights to which the Defendants conveyed to the Original trustee in the Defendant's Deed of Trust the trustee that was assigned to sell the property to which the Plaintiffs claim rights to never held the legal power to transfer the title.

1. The Defendants assert that because the trustee that sold the Plaintiffs the property never held the right to legally sell the property it was not and could never be sold in accordance with Section 2924 of the Civil Code and was therefore never duly perfected.

1. The Defendant's request from the court that the court reverse the sale of the Plaintiff's property, as it was sold under fraudulent means, and return the ownership and Quiet Title back to the Defendants.

1. If the judge doesn't see that the sale be reversed at this time then it is the Defendant's request that the judge hold the possession of the property for the Defendants until after the Federal court's scheduled Preliminary Injunction is heard. The Defendants believe that should the judge find that the Defendants argument is not sufficient enough to reverse the sale the Defendant's request that the possession of the buyer be held in abeyance until the Federal court case is decided. The Defendants believe that this is necessary because the Plaintiffs violated the principle of the adversarial atmosphere in order to put undue pressure and hardships upon the Defendants by forcing the Defendants to address other issues for example; preparing and filing preliminary injunctions to prevent the buyer from taking possession, the time energy and expense required to pack up, vacate, and find another home all of which prevents the Defendants from concentrating on filing an adequate claim of fraud against

1. The Defendants assert that it would be extremely unfair to reward the Plaintiffs the property and this type of collusionary behavior of large landholding foreclosure speculating firms while litigation is still pending on issues that directly pertain to the Plaintiff's wrongful allegations of their rights to the Defendant's property all the while the Defendants will be substantially harmed and become insolvent due to the fraud being perpetrated against them and the current Federal

case has yet to be heard in order to maintain the status quo and to insure that the Plaintiffs will not either make themselves judgement proof, and to stop them from acting in a harmful, complained of way until further judicial proceedings are available.

1   The current Federal judicial proceedings on this issue are currently scheduled to be heard in the Federal Court on April 10, 2012, in Courtroom 1, 4th floor United States District Court, Oakland. (See Exhibit)

CONCLUSION

For the foregoing reasons, Defendants Douglas Boggs and Michelle Moquin request an order dismissing the entire complaint with prejudice. If the court does not see fit to dismiss the complaint with prejudice the Defendants hereby for the foregoing reasons request this complaint be held until the Federal Court can hold and rule on the outstanding Preliminary Injunction on this issue. If the court does not see fit to hold until the Federal Court can hold and rule on the outstanding Preliminary Injunction the Defendants hereby for the foregoing reasons request this court for a Preliminary Injunction as per California Code of Civil Procedure Section 170.6.

Dated: February 13, 2011

Respectfully submitted,

Douglas J Boggs

Michelle A Moquin

Pro Se Defendant Pro Se Defendant

Exhibit G

1.   County Recorder's file no. 2009214897 – trustee NDEx

FAS Realty, Inc., 1805 F Clement Ave., Alameda, CA 94501

2.   County Recorder's file no. 2009276301 – trustee NDEx

FAS Realty, Inc., 1805 F Clement Ave., Alameda, CA 94501

3. County Recorder's file no. 2010147422 – trustee NDEx

FAS Realty, Inc., 14429 Catalina St., San Leandro, CA 94577

4. County Recorder's file no. 2010189110 – trustee NDEx

FAS Realty, Inc., 14429 Catalina St., San Leandro, CA 94577

5. County Recorder's file no. 2009326002 – trustee NDEx

FAS Realty, Inc., 1805 F Clement Ave., Alameda, CA 94501

6. County Recorder's file no. 2009348087 – trustee NDEx

FAS Realty, Inc., 1805 F Clement Ave., Alameda, CA 94501

7. County Recorder's file no. 2011332602 – trustee NDEx

Catalina Bay, LLC, 14429 Catalina St., San Leandro, CA 94577

8. County Recorder's file no. 2010139254 – trustee NDEx,

SGT Investments, LLC, 14429 Catalina St., San Leandro, CA 94577

9. County Recorder's file no. 2011161481 – trustee NDEx

SGT Investments, LLC, 14429 Catalina St., San Leandro, CA 94577

10. County Recorder's file no. 2010225634 – trustee NDEx

FAS Realty, Inc., SGT Investments, LLC, 1805 F Clement Ave., Alameda, CA 94501

11. County Recorder's file no. 2011289009 – trustee NDEx

SGT Investments, LLC, FAS Realty, Inc., 14429 Catalina St., San Leandro, CA 94577

12. County Recorder's file no. 2009055973 – trustee NDEx

FAS Realty, Inc., SGT Investments, LLC, 1805 F Clement Ave., Alameda, CA 94501

13. County Recorder's file no. 2012031185 – trustee NDEx

SGT Investments, LLC, Catalina Bay, LLC, 14429 Catalina St., San Leandro, CA 94577

We received a package of interrogatories that didn't contain reference to our proper case number, there was another party that was listed as the defendants to the interrogatories, and the questions in the interrogatories referred to a different property address. It was entirely incorrect. So, I answered these interrogatories with "N/A" for every question. When the opposing counsel pressed in court for leave to amend and resubmit, the judge allowed the attorney leave to do so, although he never did. When they answered the interrogatories that we submitted to them, the plaintiffs perjured themselves. We asked them about the various companies they owned and had either of them ever done business together and they said, "No." This was asked in different ways due to the different corporations they owned. Each time they answered, "No." With each answer they perjured themselves. We brought up their numerous improper services, their failure to be present for the hearings, and their perjurious answers. The judge seemed blind and deaf.

SUPERIOR COURT OF CALIFORNIA – COUNTY OF ALAMEDA

CIVIL – LIMITED JURISDICTION

SGT INVESTMENTS, LLC and
    CATALINA BAY, LLC

    Plaintiffs,

vs.

MICHELLE MOQUIN,
DOUGLAS J BOGGS

and DOES 1 to 10, inclusive,

    Defendants (in Pro Per)

Case No. RG 12616221

ANSWER TO

REQUEST FOR PRODUCTION OF

Douglas J Boggs - DOCUMENTS -
SET ONE

RESPONDING PARTY: Defendant Douglas J BOGGS

DEMANDING PARTY: Plaintiff SGT INVESTMENTS, LLC and CATALINA BAY, LLC

SET NUMBER:ONE

Pursuant to the provision of Code of Civil Procedure section 2031, Defendant Douglas J Boggs hereby submits to the Plaintiff the answers for the Plaintiff's request for Production of Documents, Set One, as requested and further discussed in a meet and confer phone call between both parties done on Mar. 05, 2012. Defendant does hereby answer for the Production of Documents, under oath, separately and fully:

DOCUMENT REQUEST NO. 1:

We cannot answer this as requested because we are named Defendants and not Plaintiffs and line 15 as per your instructions defines "YOU" and "YOUR" as Plaintiff and his agents, employees, attorneys and to all other persons acting or purporting to act on his behalf.

DOCUMENT REQUEST NO. 2:

We cannot answer this as requested because we are named Defendants and not Plaintiffs and line 15 as per your instructions defines "YOU" and "YOUR" as Plaintiff and his agents, employees, attorneys and to all other persons acting or purporting to act on his behalf.

DOCUMENT REQUEST NO. 3:

We cannot answer this as requested because we are named Defendants and not Plaintiffs and line 15 as per your instructions defines "YOU" and "YOUR" as Plaintiff and his agents, employees, attorneys and to all other persons acting or purporting to act on his behalf.

Defendants were unable to respond to or produce the Documents in question due to the confusion in the directions and definitions as they were expressed and defined by the Plaintiff.

Dated Mar. 6, 2012

Defendant in Pro Per – Douglas J Boggs

The Unlawful Detainer (UD) case went on through several filings in a very short time. We had a handful of hearings that took place in a small court located on the second floor in the corner of the building. The old wood dominated the room. The columns in the room blocked the view depending on where you were sitting. The five rows of benches for the public to sit in were at their usual three-quarter capacity. We exchanged motions and responses, and we exchanged a set of interrogatories and answers.

At each of the hearings we had, I requested a court reporter to document the hearing. I wanted to prepare and have all the information available if this went south and we needed to take it to the appellate court. We would arrive early so we could try to calm our nerves. The stress had been escalating now that I had doubled my caseload overnight without having any staff. All this legal world was taxing and taking its toll. There was always something to do, always something to research, another code to look up, and more precedents to verify. I didn't have the blessings of the constant availability of Lexis-Nexis that law firms have to assist them in expediting the Shepardizing process.

Shepardizing refers to checking a citator or other legal references to see how and when another case has cited the case that you are researching. Shepardizing is important because it helps you check the status of a case or statute to ensure that it is still good law. It also helps to locate other cases, statutes, and legal resources that cite your case on a similar legal issue.

The term "Shepard's" comes from the original print version of citators, but now it is used to generically refer to the act of checking all citing cases. (Think of Shepard's as a brand name, like "Kleenex," that we use to refer to all things in that category even if it is not that brand). You can Shepardize both in print and electronically.

For me, it was a lot of reading and taking notes, writing and constructing for filing documents, scheduling and managing the caseloads, rehearsing and preparing for oral arguments.

Each hearing had a scheduled time for the hearing to begin. I liked to be there about fifteen minutes before the call time. However, in our hearings, the opposing counsel for SGT Investments and FAS Realty was never on time. In fact, we would be called to appear at least three times and the opposing counsel was not present. This happened at each of the hearings. I was livid. Overall, there were several times I requested a dismissal without leave to amend from the court, due to the opposing counsel's actions, I quoted the rule of law regarding this issue, and asked for sanctions. The judge never dealt with this. The opposing counsel was given numerous "bites of the apple" in order to stay in the case.

We had already begun to uncover large amounts of new evidence against the buyers showing that they were not good faith purchasers. We needed time to follow up on this evidence. And due to the voluminous paperwork filed by the opposing counsel in the superior court case that was just remanded, I filed an ex-parte continuance hearing for the unlawful detainer. The hearing was scheduled for March 15, 2012 at 9am.

We filed for this hearing appropriately and it was scheduled in the court. We quickly prepared for and went to the ex-parte hearing on March 15, 2012. The opposing counsel did not show for this hearing. The judge made a quick statement saying that he could not rule on this and would pass it to the judge to hear the following day just prior to the scheduled master jury trial on March 16, 2012.

At the hearing on March 16, 2012, that following morning, I opened the discussions by stating the following:

"Your honor, we filed an ex-parte motion for a trial continuance, which was scheduled for yesterday, Mar. 15, 2012, at 9 am. We filed all the appropriate documents, and it was accepted by the court. We had the plaintiff's counsel served with all the moving documents as prescribed by the Cal. Rules of Court. We notified the other party regarding the ex-parte appearance as per Cal. Rules of Court, Rule 3.1203. Time of notice to other parties. We attended the scheduled ex-parte hearing and no one for the plaintiff showed up. I know that when someone shows up for a scheduled court hearing for small claims or a traffic violation and the other party or police officer doesn't show, the case is dismissed. None of this seems fair. Yet here we stand in court again to ask for a continuance when this should have been handled yesterday. Now, we must show and plead for a second hearing. This doesn't seem to be fair justice. It seems that the plaintiff knew something we didn't, by not needing to show up for the court scheduled ex-parte hearing yesterday. This simply gives the plaintiff a second, or in this case, a tenth bite of the apple.

I would like the record to show that we filed the necessary moving documents to the court for an ex-parte hearing for a trial continuance and we showed up for the original scheduled hearing. Let the record also show that the plaintiff did not show for that hearing. Let the record also show that we were denied our hearing as scheduled by the court and are now here answering to a second hearing.

I would like to take a moment and quote some case law for the record regarding the granting of a continuance:

Courts will lend a defendant all practicable help in securing evidence necessary for a defense if it is sought in a timely manner. It is usual to grant a continuance if there is a problem in gathering evidence or the serving of subpoenas upon witnesses if the defendant is not at fault for the delay. Powell v. State, 39 Ala 246 100, So. 2nd 38, cert den 267 Ala 100, 100 So 2nd 46

One accused of a crime has a right to a reasonable opportunity to secure the personal attendance of a witness. A continuance is proper, if it appears due diligence has failed to procure the presence of a witness. It must be shown that it is reasonably certain that their presence will be subsequently secured, and that the expected testimony will be material to the accused's defense. State v. Wilcox, 21 SD 532, 114 NW 687

Whether the failure to grant a continuance in the proceeding would be a miscarriage of justice. 18 USCS section 3161 (h) (8) (B) (i)

The failure to grant such a continuance in a case is enough to deny the defendant reasonable time to obtain counsel, or effective preparation. 18 USCS section 3161 (h) (8) (B) (iv)

Continuances are traditionally granted to allow the defendant additional time for procuring an absent witness, or other evidence necessary for the defense or the prosecution of the applicant's case. State v. Humphreys, Utah, 707 P 2nd 109; Federal Rules of Procedure 50, Section 50:8; People v. Leary, 28 Cal 2nd 727, 172 P 2nd 34.

The expected evidence or witness is material and competent to the trial. 83 ALR 1349, 44 ALR 2nd 711, 42 ALR 2nd 1129, section 3 (American Law Reports).

There is a probability that the evidence will be forthcoming if the case is continued. 17 Am Jur 2nd "Continuance", section 70; 13 ALR 147 (American Law Reports)

The moving party (the party requesting the continuance) has exercised due diligence (issued a subpoena) to secure the evidence or witness. 18 ALR 2nd 789 (American Law Reports); 17 Am Jur 2nd "Continuance", section 73.

A continuance may be granted if the counsel is legitimately engaged in another professional proceeding. 31 ALR 198 (American Law Reports); 17 Am Jur 2nd. Section 98

A continuance may be granted because there has been unexpected evidence or testimony. This includes additional witnesses not named in the original indictment, or unanticipated testimony of witnesses, such as major differences of fact from deposition and trial. Minor differences in testimony do not constitute surprise. 66 ALR 360 (American Law Reports); 58 ALR 2nd 1141 (American Law Reports); 17 Am Jur 2nd "Continuance", sections 103-106

A party may have good grounds for a continuance of a civil case when through no fault of their own, it is taken by surprise by the conduct of its adversary and would be unjustly prejudiced if forced to proceed without being given an opportunity to prepare to meet the new situation. Hays v. Viscome 122 Cal App 2nd 135, 264 P 2nd 173; 39 ALR 2nd 1435 (American Law Reports)

A continuance may be granted because more time is needed to prepare for trial. People v. Murray 46 Cal App. 2nd 535, 116 P 2nd 141

I now request from the court to issue a summary judgement against the plaintiffs for their failure to appear at yesterday's scheduled hearing. This is a pattern of the plaintiff to ignore the rules of the court. This pattern also reflects a blatant disregard to the rights of the defendant in this court of law. We ask the court to rule on this summary judgement in favor of the defendants and that the court rule with prejudice. Thank you."

The judge thanked us for the opening remarks and began the rest of the proceeding. He simply ignored my request for a summary judgement. He walked through the case file thus far, and we discussed some of the new evidence we were uncovering that we purported to be damning to the plaintiffs in the case.

Now, I know that I am not privy to all the rules of the court. I know now that there was a more legitimate means of making this verbal request for the ruling. I also know that we were acting in pro per. We didn't know all the rules and procedures of the court, however, as pro per we were to be given latitude in those procedures. The judge, once again, simply disregarded my opening statement and moved on. It seemed that he was going through the motions to put the case to rest.

(The following motion document is the filing that I rushed home to write and file by the end of the previous day for the hearing.)

SUPERIOR COURT OF CALIFORNIA – COUNTY OF ALAMEDA

CIVIL – LIMITED JURISDICTION

SGT INVESTMENTS, LLC and
CATALINA BAY, LLC

Plaintiffs,

vs.

MICHELLE MOQUIN,

DOUGLAS J BOGGS

and DOES 1 to 10, inclusive,

Defendants (in Pro Per)

Courthouse Dept. 1, Second Floor

Case No. RG 12616221

DEFENDANT'S EX-PARTE APPLICATION FOR MOTION FOR ORDER CONTINUING TRIAL (Cal.Civ. Proc. Rule 3.1332)

Complaint filed: Feb. 7, 2012

Trial Date: Mar. 16, 2012, 8:45AM
Rene C.Davidson Alameda County

To SGT Investments, LLC(Plaintiff) and Catalina Bay, LLC(Plaintiff), and to Richard L. Beckman, attorney of record for named Plaintiffs, located at 703 Market St., ste. 1610, San Francisco, CA, 94103, telephone (415)495-8500 and Fax (415) 495-8590:

PLEASE TAKE NOTICE that on Mar. 15, 2012, at 9:00AM, the matter will be heard in Dept. 31 of the above-entitled court, located at 201 13th St., Oakland, CA, the Defendant submits this Ex-Parte Application for Motion for Order Continuing Trial to the Court pursuant to California Rule of Court 3.1332[Sec. 5,7] to continue the trial, presently scheduled for Mar. 16, 2012, at 8:45AM in Dept. 1, Second Floor, to April 27, 2012, at 8:45AM in Dept. 1, Second Floor, because upon Defendant's research of the Plaintiffs, the Defendants have found vital material evidence that supports the Defendant's assertion that the Plaintiffs are not Good Faith Purchasers. Considering this new evidence, the Defendants make their request as per Rule 3.1332(c)(5)(b) which states "The other parties have not had a reasonable opportunity to conduct discovery and prepare for trial in regard to the new party's involvement in the case". The Defendants assert as per Rule 3.1332(c)(7) which states "A significant, unanticipated change in the status of the case because of which the case is not ready for trial", the Defendant's request a trial continuance in order to fully explore this new evidence. The Defendants feel there will be several subpoenas necessary in light of this new evidence. On March 7, 2012, the Defendants submitted their Interrogatories to begin to get to the base of the new evidence discovered and needs to be reviewed by the court. Also, the Defendants set of Interrogatories to the Plaintiffs have yet to be answered by the Plaintiffs. The Defendants feel the continuance is necessary in order to be fair to opposing counsel to be able to also review the new evidence being found, and to be in the best interests of the public.

Notice of this Motion and this hearing was served on Beckman, Blair, LLP, Plaintiff's Counsel, via Fax, on March 14, 2012. See Certificate of Service attached.

As per California Rule of the Court Rule 3.1332(d) (1-11) the Defendants makes this request in the interest of justice and to make sure that this case is decided in the full disclosure of all of the evidence with which to allow justice to prevail. Regarding Rule 3.1332(d)(1), the Defendants feel that with the proximity of the trial date there is a need to allow more time to explore this new evidence and serve the necessary subpoenas. Regarding Rule 3.1332(d)(2), the Defendants assert that there has been no previous continuance, delays, or extensions. Regarding Rule 3.1332(d)(4), the Defendants point that in meet and confer discussions with Plaintiff's counsel there has not been any progress between counsel to stipulate or find any alternative means of addressing the evidence. Regarding Rule 3.1332(d)(5), the Defendants point out that in the fairness of justice, if the evidence presented finds for the Defendants it will show that the Plaintiffs are not Good Faith Purchasers and should not be granted title to the Defendant's property and the Defendants will therefore not be left homeless until all of the evidence can be allowed and shown in court in the fairness of justice. If the evidence presented finds for the Plaintiffs, since the Plaintiffs are institutional real estate investors and have no intention of living in the property, the Plaintiffs will only suffer the equivalent of the loss of one or two months' rent. Regarding Rule 3.1332(d)(6), the Defendants point out that in light of this new evidence found, under the current timeframe scheduled with the court the Defendants have no ability to obtain documents, subpoena and/or obtain testimony or fully explore the material evidence despite their due diligence thus far. Regarding Rule 3.1332(d)(7), the Defendants understand the effect this might have on the court's calendar and the impact of granting a continuance and what that might have on other pending trials and hope that the court will weigh this with the severity of the fact that without the Defendants being able to fully explore and present this evidence, they may lose their home without the full extent of the evidence in order for justice to be reviewed. Regarding Rule 3.1332(d)(8), the Defendants are involved in a Federal Court litigation on this property, which also directly pertains to this new evidence, and the new parties to be subpoenaed and the Defendants have requested the time of April 27, 2012, since the Defendant's Federal Case Management Conference hearing will be completed at that time. Regarding Rule 3.1332(d)(9), the Defendants have discussed this evidence with Plaintiff's counsel and are unable to achieve a stipulated continuance. Regarding Rule 3.1332(d)(10), the Defendants feel that the interests of justice will be best served by granting this continuance to explore this new evidence and allow time for more investigation and subpoenas.

This application is based on this notice, the records and files in this action, the attached Memorandum of Points and Authorities, and the attached Declaration.

Memorandum of Points and Authorities

1. The Defendants are certain that they can prevail in the Federal arena against WFB and have their property returned. The Defendants are certain they can win on the merits by showing fraud on the part of WFB to induce the Defendants to enter into a Deed of Trust Contract. The Defendants are asking the Superior Court to allow them to remain in possession of the property until the litigation has run its course. Plaintiffs knowingly accepted this encumbrance or should have known the property came with that encumbrance when they purchased it. The Defendants assert that the Plaintiffs are not good faith purchasers and should not be allowed possession of the Defendant's property until all claims and evidence can be fully investigated and presented to the court in the fairness of justice. Defendants have a suit against Wells Fargo Bank (herein referred as WFB) that sold defendants' property to plaintiff' asserting fraud in the formulation of the contract between defendants and WFB. Defendants can show that plaintiffs knew of this lawsuit or should have known of the lawsuit because of a Lis Pendens on record and the fact that defendants were present at every attempt of an auction to include the actual auction with an 8 1/2" x 11" sign claiming such. Defendants assert that since plaintiffs purchased the property anyway, they are not on good grounds presenting themselves to the court as put-upon good faith purchasers needing possession of their property to occupy as residents. Defendants can show that Plaintiffs are speculators in foreclosures and hence should be required to accept the legal encumbrances on the foreclosure properties they purchased. Not doing so allows banks like WFB to escape the pleas of declaratory relief by those owners like Defendants because speculators like Plaintiffs purchase those properties knowing the owners are involved in lawsuits against the banks. Plaintiffs purchased Defendant's property knowing it was party to a lawsuit with Defendants and WFB. The harm to Plaintiffs of not getting the property would be for them to wait until the litigation concerning the property which was part of the risk they took when they purchased a property in litigation. This harm is mitigated by the fact should Plaintiffs lose the property they can indemnify their loss by the courts order to WFB to return Plaintiffs purchase costs with any interest the court deems fair. The harm to the Defendants would be to force them to lose any chance of recovery of their property via Declaratory Relief since the Plaintiffs will

undoubtedly sell the property to avoid the same action that WFB is attempting to avoid by selling to Plaintiff. The Defendants harm is much greater because Defendants will be forced to spend time looking, moving, and having to use precious little finances needed to fight their case in federal court against WFB. The public interest in stopping the financial fraud and punishing the banks and all those who collaborate in the scheme to defraud unknowing mortgagees in the state of California is far more important than the public interest in allowing those who purchase properties that are part of such litigation to claim those properties under the standard Unlawful Detainer action.

2. A Good Faith Purchaser is defined as "Those who buy without notice of circumstances which would put a person of ordinary prudence on inquiry as the title of the seller.(*Black's Law Dictionary, Special Deluxe, 5th Edition, 1979*) a Bona Fide Purchaser of the Defendant's property, as a bona fide purchaser is one who has purchased property for value without any notice of any defects in the title of the seller.(Walters v. Calderon, 25 Cal.App.3d 863, 102 Cal.Rptr. 89, 97.) One who pays valuable consideration, has no notice of outstanding rights of others, and acts in good faith. (J. C. Equipment, Inc. v. Sky Aviation, Inc., Mo.App., 498 S.W.2d 73, 75.) The Plaintiffs are not "good faith purchasers" because they knew at the time of their purchase that there was another claim on the property, by the fact that Defendant, Douglas Boggs, marched with a sign with information to a Lis Pendens that has been properly filed and recorded in the Alameda County Recorder's Office at 1106 Madison St., Oakland, CA, for the last eleven (11) months. The Plaintiffs were put on notice by an oral declaration from the Defendants and by a sign the Defendants were displaying that the property's ownership was under litigation. Hence, for the Plaintiffs to pretend to be unduly burdened by the Defendants' resistance to their brazen purchase of a property bearing a Lis Pendens is disingenuous at best and an attempt to mislead the court at worst. The Plaintiffs are in the business of buying properties so they cannot claim to be ignorant of the need to check the county records on properties they intend to bid on. Negligence on the part of the Plaintiffs to check the records does not give them the right to claim to be "good faith purchasers."

3. The Defendants assert that the Plaintiffs cannot claim that they are a bona fide purchaser of the Defendant's property, as a bona fide purchaser is one who has purchased property for value without any notice of any defects in the title of the seller. (Walters v. Calderon, 25 Cal.App.3d 863, 102 Cal.Rptr. 89, 97.) The Defendants made oral announcements and carried a 8 1/2" X 11" sign with the notice "Lis Pendens!! Lawsuit pending on this property: 1038 57th St. Oakland, CA, APN# 015-1303-013, DO NOT BID!!" clearly displayed prior to every attempted auction of the property and the sale auction regarding the current litigation against the property. The Defendants filed a Lis Pendens in the Alameda County Recorder's office on the property. Plaintiffs are in the business of buying and selling foreclosures. Hence, they cannot claim they were not informed of any possible defects in the title of the seller. If Plaintiffs are claiming that they were not informed, then it was their negligence that caused them not to be informed

because the Lis Pendens is a matter of record.

4. The Defendants assert that the Plaintiffs acquired the property, 1038 57th St., Oakland, CA, 94608, by a trustee auction held on January 20, 2012, at 12:30pm located at 1225 Fallon St., Oakland, CA. The Plaintiffs are recorded as owners in the County Recorder's Office records as SGT Investments, LLC, a 50% partner and Batalina Bay, LLC, a 50% partner, 14429 Catalina Street, San Leandro, CA 94577.

5. The Defendants assert that on the afternoon of the auction, after the auction took place, one Vi Chau came to the Defendant's property. Vi Chau gave the Defendants his business card and claimed that he was the party that purchased the property. His card named him as Property Manager for a company named as FAS Realty, Inc. (See Exhibit)

6. The Defendants assert that Vi Chau misrepresented himself as the purchaser of the property to give the Defendants wrong information.

7. The Defendants assert that Vi Chau misled the Defendants in order that the Defendants would be led astray and not file appropriate injunctions to the appropriate parties and would therefore not properly serve the appropriate parties in the action. The Defendants found out the true buyer's information upon receipt of a 3 Day Notice to Quit (See Exhibit).

8. The Defendants assert that upon learning of the true names of the purported buyers of the property the Defendants went to the county recorder's office to verify. (See Exhibit)

9. The Defendants also found what appears to be that these two parties are part of a group of companies that make a front for two specific real estate investment speculators, named as Francis Ho and Wilson Young, who are listed as President, and members of multiple companies.

10. In our investigations we have discovered a possible collusion between SGT Investments, LLC, and Catalina Bay, LLC, in their relationship between various corporations namely FAS Realty, Inc., Clement Holdings, LLC, and Wyoming Investments, LLC to purchase properties without drawing attention to the number, and kind of foreclosure purchases they are making. We are investing whether these corporations have participated in fixing the bids on foreclosure properties by pretending to bid against themselves. The evidence shows that all the corporations are headed by two individuals Francis Ho and Wilson Young even though they make great efforts to disguise their connections to each other as in claiming to be different entities as SGT Investments, LLC, and Catalina Bay, LLC, when in fact they hold joint interests in both properties through the ownership of Clement Holdings, LLC, which owns all the previous named companies. Defendants need more time to investigate whether Defendant's

property was one of those incorporating fixed bidding.

11. Plaintiffs claim to be two separate corporations purchasing Defendant's property under the corporate titles of SGT Investments, LLC, and Catalina Bay, LLC. The implication being two separate entities coming together to make a good faith purchase. But Defendant's investigations show that Plaintiff SGT Investments, LLC, is jointly owned by both Wilson Young and Frances Ho (See Exhibit D). Defendant's investigations also show that Plaintiff Catalina Bay, LLC, is owned by Wilson Young (See Exhibit E). Defendant's investigations show that both Plaintiffs are owned with Clement Holdings, LLC, (See Exhibit F). Defendant's investigations show that Clement Holdings, LLC, is owned by both Frances Ho and Wilson Young (See Exhibit G). Hence, Defendant's property has been acquired by both Frances Ho and Wilson Young hiding behind corporate names to deceive the public into believing they are separate entities bidding against each other for properties or two unrelated corporations to become "good faith purchasers." Plaintiff's records of purchases show a pattern of purchasing properties in default sales conducted by FAS Realty, Inc., and their other companies they own or are partners in. (See Exhibit H).

12. Our research shows that FAS Realty, Inc., SGT Investments, LLC, and Catalina Bay, LLC, are purchasing properties in which WFB uses NDEx West, LLC (a party Defendants are suiting in their Federal case for collusion with WFB to defraud them) to unload properties that are subject to Declaratory Relief by owners suiting WFB as defendants are doing. (See Exhibit I).

13. The Defendant's request that this evidence be given time to be researched and reviewed by opposing counsel prior to trial as per Rule 3.1332(c)(5)(b) which states "The other parties have not had a reasonable opportunity to conduct discovery and prepare for trial in regard to the new party's involvement in the case".

14. The Defendant's request, as per F.R.C.P. Rule 65(b)(1), a Temporary Restraining Order to protect the Defendants from the immediacy of the extreme financial harm resulting from the possibility of Defendant's permanent loss of Declaratory Relief from WFB and the increased financial burden moving will put on the Plaintiffs ability to defend their legal position.

15. The Defendant's request from this court a continuance of this trial in order to have time to review the Interrogatories the Defendants hand delivered to Plaintiff's secretary on Mar 7, 2012, to newly discovered evidence described above, and time to file the required subpoenas to the parties that the Defendants believe are necessary to defend its position in this Unlawful detainer suit.

March 13, 2012

By Defendants: Douglas J. Boggs Michelle Moquin

Objection to Summary Judgement

After the final hearing of the unlawful detainer case, the judge filed a summary judgement in favor of SGT Investments, LCC and FAS Realty, LLC and that was that we lost our home. Our next move was to quickly file an objection to the summary judgement, which we did. It was a busy time indeed.

SUPERIOR COURT OF CALIFORNIA – COUNTY OF ALAMEDA

CIVIL – LIMITED JURISDICTION

SGT INVESTMENTS, LLC and CATALINA BAY, LLC Plaintiffs, vs. MICHELLE MOQUIN, DOUGLAS J BOGGS and DOES 1 to 10, inclusive,	Case No. RG 12616221 DEFENDANT'S OBJECTION TO PLAINTIFF'S AMENDED MOTION FOR SUMMARY JUDGEMENT OR SUMMARY ADJUDICATION (UCC Article 1 Defendants (in Pro Per) §1-201(9)) Date: April 3, 2012 Time: 10:30 AM Dept.: 31 Res. No 1276033

Defendants, Douglas Boggs and Michelle Moquin, Object to the Plaintiff's Amended Motion for Summary Judgement, or, in the Alternative, Summary Adjudication, pursuant to UCC Article 1 §1-201(9), against the Plaintiffs SGT Investments, LLC and Catalina Bay, LLC.

1. The Defendants object to the Plaintiff's claim that their motion is based on the grounds that there is no defense to the Complaint and there is no triable issue as to any material fact with respect to the allegations in either the Complaint or the Answer. The Defendants object to the Plaintiffs claim they have established its prima facie claim for Unlawful Detainer.

2. Plaintiff's attorney has forced Defendants into court on their motion for

Summary Judgement four separate times. Each of the three previous times Plaintiffs have been denied their request for Summary Judgement. Plaintiffs repeated bites at the apple have amounted to legal harassment of the Defendants. Defendants will be filing a motion asking for sanctions against Plaintiffs and their attorney.

3. Defendants ask this court to deny Plaintiffs request for Summary Judgement with prejudice because of the previous Procedural errors they made in filing the motion and or because they have failed to establish a prima facie case that shows there is not triable issue of fact that they are not Bona Fide Purchasers.

4. The triable issue is whether the Plaintiffs qualify as Bona Fide Purchasers of Defendants property which would enable them to avail themselves of the right to use the Unlawful Detainer statutes to remove Defendant. Defendants argue it has enough evidence to show that according to the United States Uniform Commercial Code Article 1 §1-201(9) the Plaintiffs do not qualify as Good Faith Purchasers since they knew at the time of purchase there was a lawsuit pending on Defendant's property in Federal court. There was a Lis Pendens filed and duly recorded on the property at the time Plaintiffs purchased the property. The burden of proof is on the Plaintiffs to show that they have established a prima facie claim for an Unlawful Detainer. They have not met that burden because they have not shown the court that they are Bona Fide Purchasers.

5. The burden of proof is on the Plaintiffs to prove that they are Bona Fide Purchasers. Plaintiffs have not met that burden of proof to show that they were unaware of any defect in the title of Defendant's property that would prevent Wells Fargo Bank from selling it. Since Plaintiffs have not met that burden of proof Defendants ask that the Plaintiff's Summary Judgement be denied with prejudice.

6. The Defendants assert that the Plaintiffs cannot make the claim of a prima facie claim for Unlawful Detainer and take possession of the Defendant's property due to the fact that the Plaintiffs are not in fact Good Faith Purchasers as it is defined in the United States Uniform Commercial Code Article 1 §1-201(9) which states "Where a non-merchant purchases property that the seller lacks legal title to convey, the issue of good faith is known both as the innocent purchaser doctrine and as the bona fide purchaser doctrine. If the purchaser acquires the property by an honest contract or agreement and without knowledge of any defect in the title of the seller or means of knowledge sufficient to charge the buyer with such knowledge, the purchaser is deemed innocent."

7. The Defendants assert that the Plaintiffs cannot claim that the property was acquired by an honest contract or agreement since that contract and agreement they are claiming to be honest is in litigation in the Federal Court. The Defendants also assert that the Plaintiffs cannot claim that they were without knowledge of any defect in the title of the seller when the Plaintiffs knew or should have known

of the Lis Pendens and Federal Litigation against the Defendant's property. The Plaintiffs cannot claim that the trustee's deed title was duly perfected when the Plaintiffs are not in fact Good Faith Purchasers.

8. The Defendants filed a Lis Pendens with the Alameda County Recorder's Office in April 2011. (See Exhibit)

9. The Defendants assert that the Plaintiffs are institutional investors and are in the business of buying foreclosed properties. The Defendants have shown that the Plaintiffs have been in the business of buying properties for well over two decades. (See Exhibit)

10. The Defendants assert that the Plaintiffs were well aware or should have been aware of the encumbrance upon the Defendant's property and the litigation that is still ongoing with the property. The Defendants were at the auction of their property and announced to every bidder at the auction that there was a lawsuit on the property. The Plaintiffs bid anyway. The Defendants held a sign for all bidders at the auction to see that there was a Lis Pendens filed with the Alameda County Recorder's office which included the case number and the Lis Pendens (See Exhibit), but the Plaintiffs bid anyway.

11. The Defendants assert that it is the business of the Plaintiffs to purchase foreclosed properties. Since the Plaintiffs are in the business of purchasing foreclosed properties, and they have been in this business for well over two decades, it is their business to do their due diligence on the properties that they are attempting to purchase. This due diligence would include a quick look at the County Records of the property, and they would have seen the Lis Pendens filed against the property.

12. Any person of sound mind would do even the minimal amount of due diligence before spending $250,000. Anyone in their right mind would agree that this due diligence would include a view of the County Records on the specific piece of property that the person was looking to purchase. This quick research would have shown any non-institutional buyer that there is a lawsuit on the Defendant's property and, anyone in their right mind would know that this is an encumbrance and would be sold with the property and therefore not bid on the property.

13. The Defendants assert that since the Plaintiffs have been purchasing foreclosed properties for such a long time it is their business to do this simple act of research. If they did not do this act, since they are in the business of purchasing foreclosed properties, they should have done this research.

14. The Defendants, in order to make sure that any prospective bidders on the property were well informed of the litigation and subsequent encumbrance on the property, they announced to all bidders at the auction of this encumbrance and

showed the appropriate documents substantiating this encumbrance on the property by holding up a sign which showed the Lis Pendens filed, as well as the filed case number associated with the Lis Pendens.

15. Just like any other encumbrance, such as an easement or a right to trespass, the purchaser buys the property with the encumbrance with it. The lawsuit that the Defendants have against the property that is in Federal Court has not been fully litigated and is an encumbrance to which the Plaintiffs must possess with the property. Until the lawsuit is fully litigated the Plaintiffs should not be legally entitled to take possession of the property until this encumbrance to which the Plaintiffs purchased is litigated. The Defendants ask the court for a Summary Judgement with Prejudice against the Plaintiffs for taking possession of the Defendant's property because the Plaintiff has committed perjury.

16. The Defendants also assert that the Plaintiffs, Francis Ho and Wilson Young, have committed perjury in their answers to the Defendant's Special Interrogatory 19, "Please identify the relationship of The Wolf Firm, to your and any of your current, previous owners, partners, employees, agents, or affiliates." The Plaintiffs stated that Catalina has no known "relationship" to "The Wolf Firm." Just naming the company Catalina and not the owners or others as the question states, is their attempt to hide the fact that the Plaintiffs Francis Ho and Wilson Young, in fact have a long relationship with The Wolf Firm. (See Exhibit) The Defendants ask the court for a Summary Judgement with Prejudice against the Plaintiffs for taking possession of the Defendant's property due to the fact that the Plaintiff has committed perjury.

17. The Defendants also assert that the Plaintiffs, Francis Ho and Wilson Young, have committed perjury in their answers to the Defendant's Special Interrogatory 20, "Please identify the relationship of Richard O Burke, to your and any of your current or previous owners, partners, employees, agents, or affiliates." The Plaintiffs stated that Catalina has no known "relationship" to "Richard O Burke." Just naming the company Catalina and not the owners or others as the question states, is their attempt to hide the fact that the Plaintiffs Francis Ho and Wilson Young, in fact have a long relationship with Richard O Burke. (See Exhibit) The Defendants ask the court for a Summary Judgement with Prejudice against the Plaintiffs for taking possession of the Defendant's property due to the fact that the Plaintiff has committed perjury.

18. The Defendants ask the court for a Summary Judgement with Prejudice against the Plaintiffs for taking possession of the Defendant's property because the Plaintiff has committed perjury numerous times.

19. The Plaintiffs continued to respond to the Defendant's Interrogatories 25-35 by stating "...objects to this interrogatory on the grounds that it is overboard, burdensome, oppressive, vague and ambiguous, and on the grounds that it seek information that is neither relevant to the subject matter of this litigation nor

reasonably calculated to lead to the discovery of admissible evidence." The Defendants assert that all of these questions are in fact relevant to show the historic pattern of the Plaintiffs use of manipulating various companies to hide the fact that they are manipulating bids of foreclosure properties and trustee sales. The pattern of using numerous properties to hide the fact that it is in fact two people that are the owners of all of the companies. The Plaintiffs use these numerous companies to bid against each other in the trustee sales in order to manipulate the market and be able to buy the properties for low purchase pricing from the trustee. This allows the Beneficiary to take a loss on the sale of the property and therefore does not have to give any profits to the previous foreclosed owner. This action also eliminates the possibility of the foreclosed owner having any means of Declaratory Relief if these properties are in fact in litigation with the Beneficiary.

20. The Defendants assert that the Plaintiffs have been buying properties from NDEx West, LLC for years. (See Exhibit) The company NDEx West, LLC, was the trustee of record on the Defendant's property. The property was sold while the property is in litigation, thereby eliminating the Defendant's opportunity for Declaratory Relief from the Beneficiary should the Defendant prevail in their Federal lawsuit against the Beneficiary. The Beneficiary, Well Fargo Bank, and NDEx West, LLC, is an opposing party in the Defendant's Federal lawsuit.

21. The Defendants have supplied a list of exhibits to show the court a sample of some of the firms that the Plaintiffs own either singularly or together, so that the court can see through the pattern of their use of these firms to hide the fact that only two owners own all the properties. (See Exhibit)

22. The Defendants also point out to the court the use of the Plaintiff's names to further hide their personal identity to make it seem that it is not only two people. The Plaintiff's use of their middle initial is used to help hide the fact that it is in fact only two people.

23. The Defendants found it interesting that the company name FAS Realty, Inc. seems to be owned by two people. The company, according to Dun and Bradstreet, is registered as having two owners. One name Francis Ho, and the other named Francis M Ho. Why would a company register themselves as being owned by two owners when both names as named owners are the same person? Francis Ho signed a document, as recently as March 05, 2010, as Francis Ho AKA Francis M Ho (See Exhibit). The Secretary of State in California shows that FAS Realty, Inc. is owned by a Francis M Ho. (See Exhibit) In the Plaintiff's Declaration in Support of Plaintiff's Amended Motion for Summary Judgement or Summary Adjudication to this court, the Plaintiff Francis Ho, again attempts to hide his true identity to the court by stating in Sec. 8 on page 2, line 21 that he was simply acting as an employee of FAS Realty, Inc. the property manager for the Plaintiffs. The evidence is clear that Francis Ho is not only an employee of FAS Realty, Inc., but is also the noted owner according to Dun and Bradstreet and the Secretary of State records. The fact that Francis Ho and Francis M Ho are the

same person, as it was declared by both Francis Ho and Francis M Ho by his own signature which included an AKA.

24. The Defendants clearly show a manipulation of company names to hide the true identities of only two owners. This action shows the court it is clear that the Plaintiffs do not come to the table with clean hands. The Defendant's prima facie evidence is clear that the Plaintiffs are not in fact Good Faith Purchasers and should not be given possession of the Defendant's property.

25. The Defendants assert that if the courts allow the Plaintiffs, who are clearly not Good Faith Purchasers, to take possession of the property it will leave the Defendants homeless. The Defendants will also lose their right to Declaratory Relief in the possibility of getting their property returned to them upon the decision for Boggs and Moquin in the Federal case against Wells Fargo Bank, et al. If this court rules for the Plaintiffs, the Defendants will have to locate and move to another home even while they are still in litigation to the property that they now would be no longer able to get back.

26. The Defendants assert that it is clear by the evidence submitted by the Defendants of the volumes of real estate property owned by the Plaintiffs that the Plaintiffs will not be financially harmed by the court's decision to not allow the Plaintiffs possession of the Defendant's property until the encumbrance, which the Plaintiffs purchased with the property, is fully litigated. During the time of the Federal litigation, or the encumbrance to which the Plaintiffs purchased, the Plaintiffs are already, and will continue to receive the rent of the tenant that resides in the unit at the Defendant's residence. It is further argued that should the Defendant's win their Federal case and the ruling of the court is that the Defendants are to get their property returned to them, the Plaintiffs are able to sue Wells Fargo Bank to return them their purchase costs and interests accrued. The Plaintiffs will be out nothing.

27. The facts show that Plaintiffs are not Bona fide Purchasers because they purchased the property knowing it had an encumbrance with a Lis Pendens amounting to a federal lawsuit. It is settled law that purchasers of property should inspect the title and be aware of all significant encumbrances. It is also settled law that a purchaser takes a property with the encumbrances that run with the title. Plaintiffs should not be permitted to benefit from their claim not to know about an encumbrance due to their own negligence.

28. The Defendants ask the court for a Summary Judgement with Prejudice against the Plaintiffs against taking possession of the Defendant's property until the matter is settled in court against Wells Fargo Bank.

April 2, 2012

Defendants Douglas Boggs   Michelle Moquin

The objection to the summary judgement was ignored and the summary judgement that was posted in our docket was final and we lost our home. We received notice from the sheriff shortly after that we would have to be out of the property on April 26, 2012. The sheriff would be at the property on that date to make sure we had abandoned the property. If we had not yet done so, it was the order of the court for the sheriff to physically remove us and any belongings that were left from the premises. This date was of significant importance to me.

It was my birthday.

Our next option was to now appeal that decision and take it to a higher court. So, I began to put together the documents and necessary pleading to submit to the appellate court. Part of the evidentiary material that I wanted to submit for the appeal included each of the court reporter transcriptions that I had done for all the hearings during the unlawful detainer litigation. I petitioned the court to supply me with the transcriptions while I completed the writing of the notice of appeal and the argument for the filing of the appeal. As the deadline to file the appeal approached, I had yet to receive the transcripts from the court. I couldn't get a straight answer from anyone in the courthouse until three days before the deadline to submit the appeal documents. The court informed me that they were unable to locate the transcripts or recordings completed by the court reporter for any of the hearings that we had with them. Oh, and they added that they were sorry. The negligence of the court left me without the court reported prima facie evidence that I could use in my appeal.

While this was going on, the case in federal court kept moving forward. Judge Armstrong never addressed the motion for the point of clarity of law or the motion for a preliminary injunction to stop the sale of our home. However, it seemed she wanted it off her desk, so she dismissed the breach of contract cause of action in the pleading and now was remanding the case back to the California Superior court. There were some points for remanding that I disagreed with, so we drafted a response to the remand. I knew the response was mostly done as a formality, but I wanted to get the document and information into the file. I rushed to do this because I had just experienced how the court mishandles important evidence and information.

UNITED STATES DISTRICT COURT

NORTHERN DISTRICT OF CALIFORNIA – SAN FRANCISCO/OAKLAND DIVISION

MICHELLE MOQUIN,	Case No. 4:11-cv-02346-SBA
DOUGLAS J BOGGS	[Hon. Saundra B. Armstrong]
Plaintiffs, (Pro Se)	PLAINTIFF'S RESPONSE TO
vs.	JUDGE'S ORDER TO SHOW
Wells Fargo Bank, NA, et al.	CAUSE RE REMAND
and DOES 1 to 50, inclusive,	
Defendants	

Plaintiffs Douglas Boggs and Michelle Moquin do hereby show cause why the instant action should not be remanded for lack of subject jurisdiction.

Plaintiffs Douglas Boggs and Michelle Moquin are natural born citizens of the United States of America. Plaintiffs are legal residents of the state of California.

The Defendants Wells Fargo Bank NA ("Wells Fargo"), Wachovia Mortgage ("Wachovia"), World Savings Bank FSB ("World Savings"), Golden West Savings Association Services Company ("Golden West"), NDEx West LLC ("NDEx"), and LSI Title Company ("LSI") are all citizens of the United States of America.

According to the California Secretary of State website data that is updated weekly and is current as of Friday, June 1, 2012, Defendant Wells Fargo is in the jurisdiction of the United States and resides at 101 N Phillips Ave., Sioux Falls, South Dakota, 57104. Defendants Wachovia and World Savings have been taken over by acquisition or merger and are now under the control of Wells Fargo. The Agent for Service of process is named as Corporation Services Company and is located at 2710 Gateway Oaks Drive, Ste. 150N, Sacramento, CA, 95833.

According to the California Secretary of State website data that is updated weekly and is current as of Friday, June 1, 2012, Defendant Golden West is in the jurisdiction of the state of California and resides at 2730 Gateway Oaks Drive, Ste. 100, Sacramento, CA, 95833. The Agent for Service of process is named as Corporation Services Company and is located at 2710 Gateway Oaks Drive, Ste. 150N, Sacramento, CA, 95833.

According to the California Secretary of State website data that is updated weekly and is current as of Friday, June 1, 2012, Defendant NDEx is in the jurisdiction of the state of Delaware and resides at 222 S 9th Street, Ste. 2300, Minneapolis, MN, 55402. All information on the Non-Judicial foreclosure documents submitted to the Court and to the Alameda County Recorder's Office show the location and contact information of NDEx to be in the state of Texas.

According to the California Secretary of State website data that is updated weekly and is current as of Friday, June 1, 2012, Defendant LSI is in the jurisdiction of the state of California and resides at 601 Jacksonville, Florida, 32204. The Agent for Service of process is named as CT Corporation System, located at 818 W Seventh St., Los Angeles, CA, 90017.

According to 28 U.S.C. § 1332, (a) The district courts shall have original jurisdiction of all civil actions where the matter in controversy exceeds the sum or value of $75,000, exclusive of interest and costs, and is between —

(1) citizens of different States;

(2) citizens of a State and citizens or subjects of a foreign state, except that the district courts shall not have original jurisdiction under this subsection of an action between citizens of a State and citizens or subjects of a foreign state who are lawfully admitted for permanent residence in the United States and are domiciled in the same State;

(3) citizens of different States and in which citizens or subjects of a foreign state are additional parties; and

Due to the fact of the varied diverse locations of residence of all the Defendants, and as according to the California Secretary of State listing the jurisdiction of Delaware for the Defendant NDEx, the Plaintiffs show that the subject matter jurisdiction lies with the District Court as based on the diversity of the parties.

The matter in controversy before this court is $293,200.00, the purchase value of the Plaintiff's home as it was sold in the Non-Judicial foreclosure sale held at 1225 Fallon St, Oakland CA, on January 21, 2012. The Plaintiffs also assert the additional punitive damages from each Defendant individually that is above and beyond the amount of the Plaintiff's property. Plaintiffs are asserting liability for that amount against each Defendant, Wells Fargo, Wachovia, World Savings, Golden West, NDEx, and LSI collectively and individually.

Plaintiffs have petitioned the court to file a Third Amended Complaint alleging fraud on the part of Wells Fargo, Wachovia, World Savings, Golden West, NDEx and LSI. The definition of fraud allows for each defendant to be jointly and separately liable for damages suffered by the Plaintiff(s). The damages asserted in Plaintiffs complaint will exceed $75,000 as the value of the property disposed of by Wells Fargo in a foreclosure sale largely exceeded that amount by over two hundred thousand dollars.

Therefore, Plaintiffs assert that under Zahn v. International Paper Co., 414 U.S. 291 (1973) this meets the requirement that original federal jurisdiction over a state law requires each member in the named to meet the amount in controversy threshold.

If the court disagrees that each party named does reach that threshold, Plaintiffs assert that 28 U.S.C. § 1367 eliminated the complete diversity rule of Zahn v. International Paper Co requiring that each party reach that threshold. Plaintiffs make that assertion based on a decision by this 9th Circuit court in the case of Gibson v. Chrysler Corp., 261 F.3d 927, 933-943 (9th Cir. 2001) (W. Fletcher, J, w/ Schroeder & Hall, JJ). In that case the court ruled in this fashion, ("[f]or the reasons that follow, we agree with the Fifth and Seventh Circuits in Abbott Laboratories and Stromberg Metal Works, and hold that Zahn is overruled by 28 U.S.C. § 1367."

Plaintiffs assert that this is still good law and therefore Plaintiffs meet the diversity requirements to continue the case in Federal Court. Plaintiffs ask the court to rule in favor of the Plaintiffs.

Plaintiffs do hereby request leave to amend the Second Amended Complaint (SAC).

Date:June 8, 2012

Douglas Boggs   Michelle Moquin

Plaintiffs (Pro Se)

Judge Saundra Armstrong never responded to this document or the numerous others that I previously mentioned. While not addressing these outstanding filed documents, she remanded our case back to the superior court and granted leave to amend the second amended complaint.

Things were very hectic and chaotic. With the various responsive filings and hearings, subsequently more ex-parte filings, in court arguments, and case management hearings and delays, we were constantly busy being "courted" by this highly prestigious law firm acting on behalf of Wells Fargo Bank. Also, during the following months the research became more honed. The evidence was shaping itself well and the argument idea was becoming clearer every time another document was filed.

I finally had some time over the 2012 holiday season to focus on creating a third amended complaint. The defense had been arguing and asking for a demurrer stating that we were not arguing the points of fraud correctly. They were claiming that, to argue fraud, we needed to be able to name a specific person who was guilty of perpetrating the fraud. It was our contention that the fraud was perpetrated by Wells Fargo Bank as a corporate policy to act in such a manner. The "person" in this situation was the corporation itself. There was no need for us to name a specific person to qualify that all points of fraud were being argued.

We were able to file the third amended complaint in March 2013.

SUPERIOR COURT OF THE STATE OF CALIFORNIA

COUNTY OF ALAMEDA - RCD COUNTY COURTHOUSE

DOUGLAS BOGGS AND	Case No. RG 11570208
MICHELLE MOQUIN	[Assigned for all purposes to:
Pro Per Plaintiffs	Judge Robert McGuiness – Dept.22]
v	
WELLS FARGO BANK, N.A., et al, and DOES 1-50, inclusive,	THIRD AMENDED COMPLAINT FOR ACTUAL FRAUD
Defendants	

1. Intentional or Negligent Misrepresentation of a fact or

2. Concealment of a material fact

No Jury Trial Requested

Plaintiffs Douglas Boggs and Michelle Moquin (collectively, "Plaintiffs"), hereby complain against defendants Wells Fargo Bank, Wachovia Mortgage, World Savings Bank, Golden West Savings Assoc. Services Co., NDEx West LLC, and LSI Title Co. (collectively, "Defendants"), as follows:

GENERAL ALLEGATIONS APPLICABLE TO

ALL CAUSES OF ACTION

On or about December 28, 2010 Defendants Wells Fargo Bank began a Non-Judicial foreclosure action against the Plaintiffs for a breach of contract alleging failure to pay their mortgage. Plaintiffs filed an action for rescission challenging the validity of the contract based on actual fraud by intentional or negligent misrepresentation and concealment of a material fact.

Issues May Be Raised by Affirmative Defenses In Answer or In Action for Rescission. If the opposing party has filed an action seeking to enforce a contract or recover damages for its breach, the party challenging the validity of the contract may assert fraud in an answer to the complaint. Cal.Civ.Proc. § 431.30(b)(2)

If the opposing party has not filed an action on the contract, the party challenging the validity of the contract may file an action for rescission. Cal. Civ. Code § 1689(b)(1)

PARTIES

1. Plaintiffs are:

A. Douglas Boggs and Michelle Moquin, husband and wife, and owners of the property in question, located at 1038 57th street, Oakland, CA 94608, described as LOT 26, BLOCK "G" OF THE GOLDEN GATE TRACT, FILED APRIL 28, 1890, MAP BOOK 10, PAGE 66, ALAMEDA COUNTY RECORDS, A.P.N. NO.: 015-1303-013.

Defendants are:

B. World Savings Bank f/s/b is a federal savings bank that has changed their name from World Savings Bank FSB to Wachovia Mortgage.

C. Wachovia Mortgage, FSB converted to Wells Fargo Bank Southwest, N.A., which then merged with and into Wells Fargo Bank, N.A.

D. Wells Fargo Bank, N.A. is successor by merger with Wells Fargo Bank, Southwest, N.A., f/k/a Wachovia Mortgage, FSB, f/k/a World Savings Bank, FSB.

E. Golden West Savings Assoc. Services Co. is the original trustee on the Deed of Trust between the Plaintiffs and World Savings Bank.

F. NDEx West LLC is based in Addison, TX and is a private company categorized under Trust Service.

DOES are:

G. DOES 1- LSI Title Co. is a division of Lender Processing Services, the nation's leading provider of integrated data, servicing, and technology solutions to mortgage lenders.

JURISDICTION

2. This Complaint alleges Fraud arising under ACTUAL FRAUD - Intentional or Negligent Misrepresentation Cal. Civ. Code § 1572. The Complaint also alleges violations of California law. This Court has supplemental jurisdiction over these claims pursuant to 28 U.S.C. § 1367(a).

VENUE

3. This Venue has been chosen by all Defendants and agreed to by the Plaintiffs and is proper in this district pursuant to the provisions of 28 U.S.C. §§ 1391 (b) and (c) because a substantial part of the events giving rise to this lawsuit occurred in this district and because Defendants conduct continuous and systematic business in this district, advertise in this district and have caused many of the injuries complained of to occur in this district.

FACTUAL BACKGROUND

4. The Plaintiffs are challenging the existence of the Deed of Trust contract between the Plaintiffs and World Savings Bank, commissioned on August 8, 2005, with which Wells Fargo Bank used to foreclose on the Plaintiffs on January 20, 2011. The Plaintiffs do not dispute that there is a contract between the Plaintiffs and World Savings Bank, but that the contract is not in fact a Deed of Trust contract. Plaintiffs allege that World Savings deceived the Plaintiffs into believing that material elements of the Deed of Trust contract which they represented to plaintiffs as elements designed to protect Plaintiffs rights as to the control of Plaintiffs legal title, would operate to do so. Plaintiffs also allege that World Savings misrepresented the ability of specific elements in the Deed of Trust contract that the Defendant claimed would protect the Plaintiffs rights and interests in the event World Savings filed an action for breach and instituted a non-judicial foreclosure action against the Plaintiffs.

World Savings used a Deed of Trust instrument to contract with Plaintiffs. World Savings regular business use of Deed of Trust contracts to conduct refinance transactions gave them a superior knowledge about material facts concerning how the law applied certain elements in the Deed of Trust which they knew were not known to or reasonably discoverable by Plaintiffs. Those transactions included but were not limited to: the general day to day profiting from the ownership of a borrower's Deed of Trust contract; filing actions of breaches and foreclosures; and using Agents and elements of a Deed of Trust contract; such as; the rules applying to the trustee, Recordation of Documents, alienating the title of the borrower, transferring legal title from one party to another, Power of Sale clause. World Savings' representations that certain elements of the Deed of Trust contract provided legal protections for the Plaintiffs legal title, and rights and interests in the event the lender filed action for breach or non-judicial foreclosure deceived Plaintiffs into using a Deed of Trust instrument to refinance their loan because Plaintiffs were not aware that those elements did not provide those protections of their legal title or protect their legal interest when a lender filed an action for breach or attempted to use a Non-Judicial Foreclosure action. Had Plaintiffs known of these material flaws in the Deed of Trust instrument they would have insisted that World Savings use a different instrument such as a general mortgage contract to conduct their refinance loan. Plaintiffs were never provided this option because World Savings concealed material facts concerning their ability to manipulate key elements in a Deed of Trust contract to give them superior advantage over the Plaintiffs in almost every area of the contract.

FIRST CAUSE OF ACTION – ACTUAL FRAUD

Cal.Civ. 1572

FIRST AFFIRMATIVE DEFENSE

Actual Fraud - Intentional or Negligent Misrepresentation

5. When determining the parties' consent to contract any of the following acts may constitute actual fraud, intentional misrepresentation of facts, concealment of facts, promissory fraud, are all recognized by statute as actual fraud. (Cal. Civ. Code §1572)

6. The apparent consent of the Plaintiffs Michelle Moquin and Douglas Boggs to the Deed of Trust between Defendant World Savings and the Plaintiffs was not real, mutual, or free in that it was obtained through fraud, as herein alleged.

7. On or about Aug. 5, 2005, Pacific Guarantee Mortgage (herein agent) for Defendant World Savings, represented to Plaintiffs Michelle Moquin and Douglas Boggs that a Deed of Trust contract was the instrument they should use to contract

with Defendant to refinance their loan with Defendant because it contained (A-F).

    A. an independent trustee that would protect the Plaintiffs' legal title from any and all alienations to that title except for specific instructions that would be provided in the contract in the event of a breach by Plaintiffs;

    B. three sections [1. ("Borrower's Transfer of Rights in the Property "Exhibit 1 Contract page 2, section 2)- 2. ("Description of the Property "Exhibit 2 Contract page 2, section 3)- 3. ("Borrower's Right to Grant a Security Interest in the Property and Borrower's Obligation to Defend Ownership of the Property" Exhibit 3 Contract page 3, section 4,)] which guaranteed that the trustee in a Deed of Trust contract would be the only one having access to the Plaintiffs' Legal title and that the trustee could only follow the instructions which were put into the Deed of Trust contract by the Plaintiffs as "the Borrower," and the Defendant as "the Lender.";

    C. the section of the Deed of Trust contract called the "Borrower's Right to Grant a Security Interest in the Property and Borrower's Obligation to Defend Ownership of the Property" (Exhibit 4 Contract page 3, section 4), would guarantee that Defendant as lender would only have a guarantee as to Warranty of the Borrower's title but would not have the ability to alienate the Plaintiffs' title to their property.

    D. Defendant falsely and fraudulently represented to Plaintiffs that in a Deed of Trust contract any new trustee named by the Defendant would be an Independent agent and bound by the instructions that were given to the Original trustee and the rules governing the transfer of real property titles in the state of California and therefore at no time would the Defendant have control of the Plaintiffs' Legal title. (Exhibit 5 Contract page 13, section 29)

    E. Defendant falsely and fraudulent represented to the Plaintiffs that in a Deed of Trust contract the trustee acts independently to ensure that the rules governing the Power of Sale Clause would protect the rights of the Plaintiffs before it was used.

    F. Defendant falsely and fraudulently represented to the Plaintiffs that the Power of Sale Clause in a Deed of Trust contract that would protect the Borrower's rights in the event the Lender chose to exercise its right to a Non-Judicial Foreclosure remedy to a breach.

8. The representations (A-F) made by the Defendant were false, the true facts were as follows:

    A. The trustee in a Deed of Trust contract does not protect the Borrower's Legal title because the trustee in a Deed of Trust contract cannot refuse to transfer the Borrower's legal title to any newly named trustee if the Lender or an agent of the Lender disagreed with his opinion. The Borrower's legal title can be transferred by the Lender or an agent of the Lender by either of their signatures alone without the consent of the trustee. The trustee in a Deed of Trust cannot object to who the Borrower's title is transferred to ergo the Lender or the agent of the Lender can break up the Borrower's title and transfer it to whomever they please as often as they please in a derivative or any manner they choose. The trustee cannot object to making the transfer of title if the Statute of Frauds isn't followed, or the transfer isn't recorded properly, or any or all of the CC rules for transfer of real property aren't followed. It really doesn't matter how you examine the trustee in a Deed of Trust contract, the fact is a trustee in a Deed of Trust is a straw man with no purpose but to deceive the Borrower into believing that there is someone between him and the Lender protecting his Legal title. Any objection by a trustee to any action of the Lender or an agent of the Lender is ineffective because the Lender or an agent of the Lender can simply replace the trustee at will and with an employee of the Lender or the agent if they chose to ignore the trustee's objection or performance. (Exhibit 6 Substitution of trustee), shows an example of the transfer of the Plaintiffs' Legal title by the signature of the Lender's agent, Joyce Copeland, without the signature of the previous trustee.

B. Those three sections in the Deed of Trust contract do not guarantee that the trustee in a Deed of Trust contract would be the only one having access to the Borrower's Legal title, the Lender or an agent of the Lender have total control over the Borrower's title immediately after the Borrower transfers his title to a trustee in a Deed of Trust. As a matter of fact the only time the transfer of the Borrower's title is made according to the Cal. Civ. Code is when the Borrower makes the initial transfer of his title to the trustee after that in a Deed of Trust contract in the state of California the Lender for, all practical purposes, has total control over the Borrower's Legal title. The fact that the Lenders using Deed of Trust contracts regularly spilt up their Borrower's titles into various forms of derivatives and sold them at will shows that a Deed of Trust contract offered no protection from the alienation of a Borrower's Legal title by the Lender or an agent of the Lender. Need a case that says the lender can record on his signature alone.

C. The "Borrower's Right to Grant a Security Ownership of the Property" does not guarantee that the Lender or an agent of the Lender would not have the ability to alienate the Borrower's Legal title. As a matter of fact, in a Deed of Trust contract the Lender or an agent of the Lender could alienate the Borrower's Legal title by converting it into a form of security derivative and selling the parts. It has been accepted by the U.S. Federal government and the state government of California, and the lending institutions that the ability was available to Lenders before and during the time Plaintiffs were induced to use a Deed of Trust contract to refinance their loan. THE OCTOBER 2008 BAILOUT PAID OFF THE HOLDERS OF MORTGAGE-BACKED

SECURITIES AND DERIVATIVE INSUREDS World Savings, Wachovia Mortgage, and Wells Fargo Bank were among the institutions who benefited from the bailout. COURT: S.D. New York, DOCKET NUMBER: 09-CV-00833. JUDGE NAME: Hon. Leonard B. Sand. DATE FILED: 01/29/2009.

D. The representation made by the Defendant was false, the true fact is as follows in a Deed of Trust contract the Lender or an agent has the right to not only name anyone the Lender or agent wishes to appoint as the trustee, they can name a person who is employed by them in another capacity to act as the trustee and maintain the trustee as an employee. (See Exhibit)

E. The representation made by the Defendant was false, the true fact is as follows; that if the trustee objected to the Lender or his agent not following the prescribed rules to follow before the Lender or his agent could enact the Power of Sale Clause, the Lender has the power in a Deed of Trust contract to name a trustee would allow the Lender or an agent of the Lender to skirt the rules.

F. The representation made by the Defendant was false, the true fact is as follows; the Power of Sale Clause in a Deed of Trust contract poses no actual prohibition to its misuse. The state of California gives the "power of presumption of correctness" (Exhibit 8 Contract page 13, section 28) to the filing of any documents by the Lender or an agent of the Lender as required to satisfy the Power of Sale Clause when filing a Non-Judicial Foreclosure action. Hence the Lender or an agent of the Lender can forge, robo-sign, and or back date documents without fear of legal penalty. (See Exhibit)

9. When the agent for Defendant World Savings made these representations, he knew them to be false or had no reasonable grounds for believing them to be true.

10. The agent for Defendant World Savings made these representations with the intent to deceive and induce Plaintiffs Michelle Moquin and Douglas Boggs to enter into the contract. Plaintiffs Michelle Moquin and Douglas Boggs relied on the truth of the representations in entering into the contract. Plaintiffs Michelle Moquin and Douglas Boggs would not have given their consent to the contract had it not been for the fraud. The reliance of Plaintiffs Michelle Moquin and Douglas Boggs was justified because neither Plaintiffs were familiar with the difference between a Deed of Trust or a mortgage contract and the agent held himself out to be a person that dealt regularly with the Deed of Trust contracts, World Savings had a reputation of being a respected refinance company, Plaintiffs had heard nothing about institutions splitting up a mortgage in to derivatives and trading in them, or " robo signing accusations and there was no reason for Plaintiffs to suspect that the state of California would give Lenders the power to alienate their title on the signature of the Lender absence the trustee who Plaintiffs had deeded their Legal title to having to deed it to another trustee. Indeed it would be difficult to convince the ordinary person who had been involved in deeding an

interest in real property in the state of California that a person who did not have a deed to real property could on his signature convey that property to any one he wished and record the transaction without the slightest oversight as his recordation of the required documents to complete such a transaction would be taken on his word and the documents would be accepted by the Court as legally correct under the doctrine of the "Presumption of Correctness."

11. As a result of the fraud, Plaintiffs were injured in that they did not get the opportunity to select a standard mortgage contract over the Deed of Trust. Had they contracted with a standard mortgage contract the Defendant Wells Fargo Bank would have had to go to court to get a judicial foreclosure. The Plaintiffs could have found the funds to remedy the contract defect or the Plaintiffs could have worked out a way to save their house since it was more than $200,000 overvalued by the bank. Hence the injury to the Plaintiffs was the loss of their home and the years of material and emotional investment they put into it when Wells Fargo Bank used a feature, the Non-Judicial Foreclosure action with all the other advantages the Deed of Trust gave them to take and sell the Plaintiffs home.

REQUEST LEAVE TO AMEND

12. The Plaintiffs request leave to amend Third Amended Complaint as defined by Cal.Civ. Proc. 472, and Fed. R. Civ. P. 9(b).

NO DEMAND FOR JURY TRIAL

13. Plaintiffs, Douglas Boggs and Michelle Moquin do not demand a trial by jury.

PRAYER FOR RELIEF

WHEREFORE, Plaintiffs pray judgement against Defendants, and each of them, as follows:

ON FIRST CAUSE OF ACTION

A. Plaintiffs realize because of part performance that some loan contract does exist between the two parties, and Plaintiffs request that the Deed of Trust loan be rescinded, but that loan contract should be converted to a personal one and allow the two parties to negotiate.

B. Plaintiffs request their property to be returned to them.

C. Plaintiffs request additional damages as the court deems necessarily sufficient to deter Defendants from profitably practicing similar conduct.

D. For costs of suit incurred herein.

Dated: March 23, 2013

Respectfully submitted,

Douglas Boggs

Michelle Moquin

Pro Se Plaintiff

Pro Se Plaintiff

I knew as soon as I had filed the third amended complaint that it wasn't written very well. I had to submit it because I was running under some time constraints and it needed to be filed. There was still so much research being done to properly argue the fraud claim, but I wanted to get the third amended complaint filed by the deadline that we were given by the court.

My intention was that we would file this as it was, and deal with the fallout of the demurrer from the defendants. We could add more details into the response to the demurrer, but we could also file a motion to amend and draft up a fourth amended complaint. Regardless, as soon as I filed the third amended complaint, I was back in front of the computer beginning to construct the fourth.

The late-night study sessions were taking their toll. We had been into the case now for over two years, every day, all day long and into the night. It became the total consumption of who I was. It was all I could think about. It was all I had time for. The lengthy discussions would bring about questions. Those questions became avenues of research. We would look up current law to find precedent court cases to validate our theory and answer those questions.

My friend came up with a question that eventually took us down a very deep rabbit hole of information. His query gestated from when he began receiving his foreclosure documentation. At that point, our litigation was well under way. By this time, we had been remanded from the superior court to the district court, and then back again. The benefit of this was that we were getting better at our research, more proficient at writing motions and responses. One of the primary benefits to our experience was that he had the same parties in his case committing fraud against him. Beginning as far back as World Savings, to Wachovia, to Wells Fargo Bank, the trail of trustee and substitute trustees was the same, as well.

He was current on his monthly payments and he began receiving foreclosure notices seemingly out of the blue. He contacted the bank to discuss the foreclosure paperwork he was receiving from them. He wanted to discuss their mistakes as he could show them that he was current on his mortgage and wanted to put it all behind him. One might think it would have been easy. However, the representatives who he spoke with said that they couldn't assist him due to the fact that the foreclosure procedure had already begun. He asked for a manager who he could be transferred to. He went on to explain to them that they were making a grave mistake.

First, he explained to the managing representative that he was in fact current on his mortgage, so he couldn't understand why the bank would be filing foreclosure documents. How could a trustee filing those documents make such a careless error like that? He went on to explain that the foreclosure documents were being filed by a trustee who was not even authorized as the trustee to the Deed of Trust. There were no documents filed with the county records that showed any substituted trustee ever taking place. Therefore, how could this company act as a legal trustee named in the foreclosure documents?

He went on and indicated that Wells Fargo was foreclosing on a loan that they claimed was refinanced in May of 2005. He had never done such an action. The loan Wells Fargo referred to was a "non-existent" loan. It never happened. However, Wells Fargo claimed it was signed by his partner, June, who they stated was the original note holder on the property beginning back in 2000 with World Savings.

He had become a silent partner in this property in the year 2003 when a friend of his, named June, approached him for financial assistance to help her save her home. He took over the payments for June to help her get back on her feet again. Then, in the latter part of

2004, June began to have health problems. During this time of healing, she had inquired with Wells Fargo about refinancing the property. She felt she might need some money that she could pull out of the property to use for her medical assistance. He and June discussed the situation and he agreed he would sign off on refinance documents if she could put something together. The bank tried to put a loan refinancing package together for her that she could afford but were unable to come to a decision and she never signed any loan documents. Frustrated and in need of healing, she finally let go of the idea of refinancing the property and focused on her healing. In March of 2005, June's health progressively worsened, and she passed away. June had no other family, so prior to her death she had quitclaimed her part of the property over to my friend.

His concern, as discussed with the managing representative from Wells Fargo, was that the foreclosure documents they were submitting to the court were based on a refinanced loan on the property, which they claim took place in May of 2005 that had been signed by June. The problem with this was that June had died in March of 2005. Prior to her death, she hadn't refinanced the property. However, after her death, it seems that Wells Fargo was able to get her to sign new mortgage documents for a refinance, which they claimed took place.

The representative thanked him for the information and said that she would get back with him on the issue. What took place was that they simply stopped any further foreclosure proceedings against his property. The paperwork just stopped.

Throughout all of this, we had been dealing with writing and filing our third amended complaint. However, his process took us down a new rabbit hole. We would sit and discuss his foreclosure issues as we studied, and the question that stood out the most was how could a trustee, who is not a legal trustee, file documents that were totally false in order to initiate a foreclosure proceeding? Everything about it was fraudulent.

We also discussed that in our case, for us to clearly state to the court that the Deed of Trust was fraudulent, we needed to review contract law and find a Deed of Trust contract that we would argue was in fact a valid contract in the eyes of the law.

I began to spend days on end at the Alameda County courthouse searching through thousands of filed documents. I was looking for a contract that included signatures by all parties to the agreement. It needed to have a start date to the contract and an end date, so a specified timeline could be agreed to. The terms of the contract would be included and clearly outlined. As I reviewed the rules of contract law again and reviewed our Deed of Trust agreement that was being foreclosed on, things weren't matching up. I stared at the computer screens at the county offices for days on end.

I went through random filings of mortgage documents that were filed and reviewed them thoroughly. I kept going back further into the historical archives of the county records and couldn't find any Deed of Trust mortgage agreements that included all the necessary legal parameters that would constitute a valid contract.

Eventually, the computer records ran out and the person behind the counter told me I needed to switch to their microfiche in order to review documents further back than the year 2000. This was probably due to the Y2K computer scare that swept across the world in 1999. It was the fear that computer systems would crash. At any rate, any documents that I wanted to research prior to January 1, 2000, must be reviewed by microfiche.

So, I began combing through those records. This task was much more cumbersome as unlike the computer, there were no search parameters or indexes I might be able to type in to reference. This was simply time spent viewing the film and rolling it forward: Image after image, reel after reel.

I spent an additional week weeding through the rolls of microfiche until I eventually found a Deed of Trust contract from Oakland, California that seemed to contain every nuance of contract law that we had agreed was to be included in the document for it to be a valid contractual agreement according to California law and contract law. That contract document was dated December 28, 1997. Then I found another similar contract that was filed on December 29, 1997. There was another on December 24, 1997, and another on December 30, 1997. As I looked ahead again into 1998, I couldn't find any documents written in the correct way by rule of law. It seemed that there was a change that took place in Deed of Trust contracts that were being filed. Something happened that was changing the structure of the Deed of Trust agreements that were being filed after January 1, 1998.

At least now, I had found what a true legal Deed of Trust agreement looked like that I could use as an example to the court to help my arguments about our contract. But this brought up the question of, "what took place for such a change to happen on January 1, 1998?" It was another rabbit hole to venture down.

As the defendants had not yet responded to the third amended complaint within the thirty-day timeline to file, I attempted to then file the fourth amended complaint on those grounds. The teller at the courthouse did not accept the filing of this, citing that that rule only applied to the original complaint. This was not how the rule of law read. I raised my questions and concerns as to the code regarding this issue. And I protested this to no avail.

I explained to her that according to California Code of Civil Procedure 585 (CCP § 585) based on the fact that the defendants had failed to file their response to the third amended complaint in the appropriate time, I should be able to file a fourth amended complaint. In fact, we were supposed to be issued a default judgement. End of game. She would not take my filing.

We had a hearing only about an hour later regarding a summary judgement that had been filed against the third amended complaint. However, this filing had been done after the time in which the court was allowed to accept such a filing. But we were having a hearing nonetheless.

SUPERIOR COURT OF THE STATE OF CALIFORNIA

COUNTY OF ALAMEDA - RCD COUNTY COURTHOUSE

DOUGLAS BOGGS AND	Case No. RG 11570208
MICHELLE MOQUIN	Assigned for all purposes to:
Pro Per Plaintiffs	Judge Robert McGuiness – Dept.22]
V	
WELLS FARGO BANK, N.A., et al.,	FOURTH AMENDED
and DOES 1-50 Inclusive,	COMPLAINT FOR ACTUAL
Defendants	FRAUD

1. Intentional or Negligent Misrepresentation of a fact or

2. Concealment of a material fact

No Jury Trial Requested

Plaintiffs Douglas Boggs and Michelle Moquin (collectively, "Plaintiffs"), hereby complain against defendants Wells Fargo Bank, Wachovia Mortgage, World Savings Bank, Golden West Savings Assoc. Services Co., NDEx West LLC, and LSI Title Co. (collectively, "Defendants"), as follows:

GENERAL ALLEGATIONS APPLICABLE TO ALL CAUSES OF ACTION

1. On or about December 28, 2010 Defendants Wells Fargo Bank began a Non-Judicial foreclosure action against the Plaintiffs for a breach of contract alleging failure to pay their mortgage. Plaintiffs filed an action for rescission challenging the validity of the Deed of Trust (herein "DOT") contract based on actual fraud by intentional or negligent misrepresentation and concealment of a material fact to induce Plaintiffs to use a Deed of Trust contract to secure their loan.

2. Statute of Limitations-----Discovery Rule Tolls Statute of Limitations.

In William I. Lyon & Associates, Inc. v. Superior Court (2012)204 CA 4th 1294 1309- 1310, the court held that the discovery rule tolled the statute of limitations for a breach of contract claim for the purchase of a home when the buyers alleged they were unaware of the breach of contract because the broker failed to disclose their knowledge of construction defects and the sellers concealed the defects with dark paint.

Plaintiffs were unaware of Wells Fargo Bank's (herein "WFB") fraud because the bank failed to disclose their knowledge that they could manipulate the rules governing the normal expectations of the transfer of a legal title to real estate under a DOT Contract.

Plaintiffs did not discover that lenders could avoid the rules governing the pre-execution of the Power of Sale Clause until WFB violated rule 2923.5(g) which states that proper notice must be given prior to executing the Power of Sale Cause because plaintiffs were unaware of the fact that the lender can manipulate the third Party in a Deed of Trust Contract, the trustee, so that the borrower has no independent party to protect the borrower's rights under the Power of Sale Clause.

Plaintiffs were not aware that the state of California did not have in place a legal procedure that was set up to prevent the lender from converting the "independent trustee" in a Deed of Trust Contract to a straw man without any of the powers and duties it explicitly stated and or implied that a trustee had in a Deed of Trust Contract. Plaintiffs were not at fault for not discovering this because WFB failed to disclose this knowledge when they disguised their failure to comply by having their agent perform as the straw man, trustee, Index West who approved WFB's actions as in compliance to the Plaintiffs as if it was independent and serving as such to protect both entities interest.

Plaintiffs lacked knowledge of the fact that WFB was well aware there was no independent policing if they failed to comply either by a "trustee" in the Deed or Trust contract or the state of California in the recordation of any documents involved in enacting a Non-judicial Foreclosure Procedure.

Plaintiffs' excuse for lack of discovery of these facts is that the only way a plaintiff would discover those facts is after they were victims of the fraud and in the litigation of pursuing it.

Plaintiffs exercised reasonable diligence in discovering their cause or action, but it also seems that each new discovery of what WFB knew it could get away with is rife with other acts of misconduct that only WFB as players in the business of Non-judicial Foreclosures would be aware of; such as while they knew that they could alienate Plaintiffs legal title without the normal steps required and properly executed and filed documents under California law to transfer a legal real property title using a Deed of Trust by classifying it as a "security instrument," plaintiffs could discover this until they were deep into researching what happened to them under their original cause of action.

Under the delayed discovery rule, a cause of action accrues and the statute of limitations begins to run when the plaintiff has reason to suspect an injury and some wrongful cause, unless the plaintiff pleads and proves it's a reasonable investigation at that time would not have revealed a factual basis for that particular cause of action; in that case, the statute of limitations for that cause of action will be tolled until such time as a reasonable investigation would have revealed its factual basis[Fox v. Ethicon Endo-Surgery, Inc. (2005) Fox v. Ethicon Endo-Surgery, Inc.(2005) 35 C4th 797, 803]. Ignorance of the identity of the defendant does not delay accrual of a cause of action, but ignorance of a generic element of the cause of action does [Norgart v. Upjohn Co. (1999)21 C4th 383, 399, 87 CR 2d 453, 981 P2d 79; Burdette v.Carrier Corp. (2008) 158 CA4th 1668,1693, 71 CR 3d 185] Plaintiffs did not have reason to suspect that WFB knew they could manipulate the parts of the Deed of Trust Contract involving the independence of the trustee to honor the parts of the DOT that declares that the purpose of the trustee in the DOT was to protect the interests of both parties and to insure that the Lender would at all times obey the terms of the contract in the event the Lender chose to exercise his option to use the Non-Judicial Foreclosure Sale option of the contract.

Plaintiffs suffered appreciable harm in at least two ways, one is the harm that occurred by World Savings Bank (herein "WS") deceiving Plaintiffs into entering into a contract that deceived Plaintiffs into giving WS total control over Plaintiffs title without just compensation for that right. WFB may argue that Plaintiffs received a sizable sum for the lien on their property. But the loss to the Plaintiffs is in the interest rate and the amount of the loan that the Plaintiffs could have bargained for had the Plaintiffs known they would be giving more than they intended for the rate and the amount they received. Since the interest rate directly involves the amount of the monthly note how can the defendant plead that Plaintiffs are in default as their defense when Plaintiffs may not have been in default if Plaintiffs had been free to bargain for a lesser monthly mortgage rate.

If defendants argue that this is mere speculative harm, Plaintiffs argue that the case of [San Francisco United Sch. Dist. V. W.R. Grace & Co. (1995) 37 CA4th 1318 1326, 44 CR2d 305] defined the difference between Speculative Harm and appreciable harm.

In that case the harm was ruled Speculative because the harm had not yet occurred. In Plaintiffs case here the harm occurred when the lower mortgage rate that could have been negotiated had the Plaintiffs known of the additional opportunity, they were giving WS to make money on the breaking up of their title in? transactions without their permission. If WFB argues that this did not occur with Plaintiffs property title that hardly matters because it would have been a business decision by WFB and not one of the Plaintiffs. The fact remains that WS was aware of the option because of their ability to make the trustee a "straw man" and Plaintiffs were not and hence were fraudulently deprived of the right to bargain with WS for that right.

If WFB argues that Plaintiff's argument fails because the amount they could have bargained for has or cannot be declared, Plaintiffs argue that the amount of the appreciable harm suffered need not be certain. In [Davies v. Krasna (1975) 14 C3d 502, 121 CR 705, 535 P2d 1161: Barton v. New United Motor Mfg. (1996) 43 CA4th 1200, 1209, 51 CR2d 328] the court declared that the harm suffered need not be certain in amount.

The fact is that WS knew they were getting the benefit to make money off breaking up Plaintiffs title into derivatives, and WS knew they were getting the right to foreclose on the plaintiff anytime they wished whether the Plaintiff paid on time or didn't because the contract they deceived Plaintiffs into signing was a one sided one that gave WS all the power with total control over Plaintiffs' legal title and left the Plaintiffs with nothing but the sole right or obligation to pay for the contractual terms they would not have agreed to had they known about the deceptive terms in the agreement.

Plaintiffs did not have a reason to investigate the nature of the contract until WFB used its "straw man" position of the trustee in their DOT contract to illegally foreclose on Plaintiffs. It was during the Plaintiffs reasonable and diligent investigations of how WFB was able to legally get away with passing Plaintiffs' legal title to anyone they wished without the normal procedures and documentation required to transfer a legal title of real property that plaintiffs discovered another kind of wrongdoing by WS and WFB.

Issues May Be Raised by Affirmative Defenses In Answer or In Action for Rescission.

3. If the opposing party has filed an action seeking to enforce a contract or recover damages for its breach, the party challenging the validity of the contract may assert fraud in an answer to the complaint. Cal.Civ.Proc. § 431.30(b)(2). If the opposing party has not filed an action on the contract, the party challenging the validity of the contract may file an action for rescission. Cal. Civ. Code § 1689(b)(1)

The Court's Decision in Riverisland Cold Storage Inc. v. Fresno-Madera Production Credit Association has several ramifications for parties contracting in CA -Code of Civil Procedure section 1856(f).

4. The Court's decision in Riverisland broadly expands the evidence a party may introduce to support invalidating a contract based upon fraud. On or about Aug 6, 2005 Plaintiffs, Michelle Moquin and Douglas Boggs, met with an in-house loan officer of World Savings Bank, at the bank located at 1970 Broadway Ave., Oakland, CA 94612, to ask more detained questions of the bank representative in order to gain more clarity to some key points the Plaintiff's still had in question after their meeting, on or about Aug 5th, 2005, with the Pacific Guarantee loan broker. Plaintiffs discussed the degree of independence the trustee would have to enforce their written instructions which WS said they could give to the trustee to protect their interest and protect their legal title. Plaintiffs and the WS loan officer discussed the trustee's abilities and the authority the Deed of Trust and the Power of Sale clause, which was within the contract, gave to the trustee. Plaintiffs discussed the instructions given to the trustee by the Power of Sale Clause to protect the Plaintiffs rights and to insure that WS would obey those instructions prior to enacting the Power of Sale clause as a prelude to a non-judicial foreclosure procedure in the event of a breach by Plaintiffs.

During contract negotiations WS failed to disclose that the trustee in a Deed of Trust contract does not have the powers or independence that the contract purports to give to the trustee to force WS to obey the terms of the contract that require WS to obey a set of rules set forth by CA statute to ensure proper performance by WS prior to exercising a Non-Judicial procedure or employing the Power of Sale Clause in the contract. The trustee is merely a Straw man employed by WS as an agent to do its bidding.

During the contract negotiations WS failed to disclose that they knew that the state of California in a DOT gave them the right to file documents which could transfer Plaintiffs legal title virtually at will without the normal recording requirements when an exchange of the legal title of real property takes place. WS savings withheld the fact that the state gave them the legal presumption of correctness of all documents filed with the county recorder's office for purposes of transfer of Plaintiffs legal title.

WS failed to disclose that the DOT would give them the ability to alienate Plaintiffs title without regard to the power of the trustee named in the contract to be the sole holder of Plaintiffs legal title. WS failed to disclose that ability would enable WS to profit from the splitting and/or pooling of Plaintiffs legal title without his permission or the ability of the contract appointed trustee. WS failed to inform Plaintiffs of their right to bargain for the unfair enrichment they stood to make. Thereby depriving Plaintiffs of the right to bargain for a lesser mortgage or interest rate.

The true amount owed WS by the Plaintiffs cannot be arrived at based on the current figures and calculations by WFB because the Plaintiffs right to make a fair bargain was denied them by WS' concealment of the above facts.

Plaintiffs would not have consented to contract with WS using a DOT if they had known what WS knew about how the terms and conditions of the DOT contract operated as opposed to the way it was misrepresented to Plaintiffs.

PARTIES

5. Plaintiffs are:

A. Douglas Boggs and Michelle Moquin, husband and wife, and owners of the property in question, located at 1038 57th street, Oakland, CA 94608, described as LOT 26, BLOCK "G" OF THE GOLDEN GATE TRACT, FILED APRIL 28, 1890, MAP BOOK 10, PAGE 66, ALAMEDA COUNTY RECORDS, A.P.N. NO.: 015-1303-013.

Defendants are:

B. World Savings Bank f/s/b is a federal savings bank that has changed their name from World Savings Bank FSB to Wachovia Mortgage.

C. Wachovia Mortgage, FSB converted to Wells Fargo Bank Southwest, N.A., which then merged with and into Wells Fargo Bank, N.A.

D. Wells Fargo Bank, N.A. is successor by merger with Wells Fargo Bank, Southwest, N.A., f/k/a Wachovia Mortgage, FSB, f/k/a World Savings Bank, FSB.

E. Golden West Savings Assoc. Services Co. is the original trustee on the Deed of Trust between the Plaintiffs and World Savings Bank.

F. NDEx West LLC is based in Addison, TX and is a private company categorized under Trust Service.

DOES are:

G. DOES 1- LSI Title Co. is a division of Lender Processing Services, the nation's leading provider of integrated data, servicing and technology solutions to mortgage lenders.

JURISDICTION

6. This Complaint alleges Fraud arising under ACTUAL FRAUD - Intentional or Negligent Misrepresentation Cal. Civ. Code § 1572. The Complaint also alleges violations of California law. This Court has supplemental jurisdiction over these claims pursuant to 28 U.S.C. § 1367(a).

VENUE

7. This Venue has been chosen by all Defendants and agreed to by the Plaintiffs and is proper in this district pursuant to the provisions of 28 U.S.C. §§ 1391 (b) and (c) because a substantial part of the events giving rise to this lawsuit occurred in this district and because Defendants conduct continuous and systematic business in this district, advertise in this district and have caused many of the injuries complained of to occur in this district.

FACTUAL BACKGROUND

8. This action by Plaintiffs arises out of the action by Wells Fargo Bank to foreclose on Plaintiffs for breach of a Deed of Trust contract which gave Defendants the right to choose an optional remedy to a breach by Plaintiffs called a Non-Judicial Foreclosure which was unique to the Deed of Trust contract that would not have been available to the Defendants if Plaintiffs had elected to choose a different loan instrument as a means of securing their loan with World Savings. The Plaintiffs are challenging the validity of the Deed of Trust contract between the Plaintiffs and World Savings Bank, commissioned on August 8, 2005, with which Wells Fargo Bank used to foreclose on the Plaintiffs on January 20, 2012. The Plaintiffs are challenging the amount WFB says is owed by Plaintiffs because Plaintiffs were deprived of the right to bargain for a lesser mortgage and interest rate on the mortgage when WS concealed they stood to make additional profit from the contract because they could circumvent the part of the contract that would act to prevent a lender from alienating the legal title of the borrower at will. Plaintiffs allege that World Savings deceived the Plaintiffs into believing that material elements of the Deed of Trust contract which they represented to plaintiffs as elements designed to protect Plaintiffs rights as to the control of Plaintiffs legal title, including who would have control, but are not limited to who would have the authority to decide if the contractual protections provided by the Deed of Trust were met, would operate to do so. Plaintiffs also allege that World Savings misrepresented the ability of specific elements in the Deed of Trust contract that the Defendant claimed would protect the Plaintiffs

rights and interests in the event World Savings filed an action for breach and instituted a non-judicial foreclosure action against the Plaintiffs.

9. Plaintiffs also allege that WS misrepresented the ability of specific essential elements in the DOT(the abilities of the trustee and the ability of the Power of Sale Clause) which the DOT claimed would protect the Plaintiffs' legal rights as detailed by the POSC contained in the DOT and the powers and authority the DOT contract gave the trustee to act on the Plaintiffs' behalf should the lender violate the borrower's legal rights as defined by the POSC and the instructions given to the trustee by the state of CA.

10. Plaintiffs' also allege that the WS fraudulently misrepresented the control over and the interest in Plaintiffs' legal title WS would hold once the DOT contract was signed in an attempt to deprive Plaintiffs of the right to bargain for that benefit. As a result, WS profited from a higher mortgage and interest rate than the Plaintiffs would have agreed to if they had known about the ability of WS to profit from a derivatives scheme and or polling of the legal titles of borrowers which allowed WS to transfer in whole or part Plaintiffs' legal title for profit without Plaintiff's knowledge, agreement or right to strike a better bargain for giving WS the right to conduct such transfers. WS was fully aware that Plaintiffs would have no reason to know that hidden elements inherent to a DOT contract as opposed to a standard mortgage contract permitted a Lender to parcel up a Borrower's title without regards to the usual safeguards a Borrower would expect when engaging in a mortgage with a Lender using his title as collateral.

11. Plaintiffs allege that WS having fraudulently induced Plaintiffs to enter into a contract Plaintiffs would not have made with WS, under the interest terms that WS proposed and received because they withheld the fact that they could profit from an unknown derivative scheme, is now attempting to collect fully for the higher interest rate and mortgage amount they fraudulently gained through their deceit.

12. Plaintiffs allege that agents of WS orally fraudulently assured Plaintiffs that a DOT contract was a safe instrument to do business with WS and that it was safe to transfer Plaintiffs legal title to the "trustee" WS named in the contract because the contract provided safeguards to give the "trustee" independent powers to protect a Borrower's legal title from the use and control of Plaintiffs title by the lender and that protection extended to any situation in which the lender accused the Borrower of breach.

13. World Savings used a Deed of Trust instrument to contract with Plaintiffs. World Savings regular business use of Deed of Trust contracts to conduct refinance transactions gave them a superior knowledge about material facts concerning how the law applied certain elements in the Deed of Trust which they knew were not known to or reasonably discoverable by Plaintiffs. Those transactions included but were not limited to: the general day to day profiting

from the ownership of a borrower's Deed of Trust contract; filing actions of breaches and foreclosures; and using Agents and elements of a Deed of Trust contract; such as; the rules applying to the trustee, Recordation of Documents, alienating the title of the borrower, transferring legal title from one party to another, Power of Sale clause. World Savings' representations that certain elements of the Deed of Trust contract provided legal protections for the Plaintiffs legal title, and rights and interests in the event the lender filed action for breach or non-judicial foreclosure deceived Plaintiffs into using a Deed of Trust instrument to refinance their loan and to accept a higher mortgage and interest rate on that mortgage because Plaintiffs were not aware that those elements did not provide those protections of their legal title or protect their legal interest when a lender filed an action for breach or attempted to use a Non-Judicial Foreclosure action. Had Plaintiffs known of these material flaws in the Deed of Trust instrument they would have insisted that World Savings use a different instrument such as a general mortgage contract to conduct their refinance loan or give them a lesser mortgage and interest rate on that mortgage. Plaintiffs were never provided this option because World Savings concealed material facts concerning their ability to manipulate key elements in a Deed of Trust contract to give them superior advantage over the Plaintiffs in almost every area of the contract deprived them of the bargaining power to make a better deal.

ESTABLISHING ACTUAL FRAUD

Intentional or Negligent Misrepresentation of a Fact

INTRODUCTION

14. On or about Dec. 28, 2010, Defendants Wells Fargo Bank, N.A. (herein "WFB") began a Non-Judicial foreclosure action against the Plaintiffs for a breach of contract between World Savings Bank (herein "WS") and Plaintiffs alleging the failure of Plaintiffs to pay their mortgage. The Deed of Trust (herein "DOT") contract that WFB used as a basis for its foreclosure action was purchased from Wachovia Mortgage (herein "WM") who had purchased it from WS. Plaintiffs filed an action for rescission challenging the validity of the contract based on actual fraud by intentional or negligent misrepresentation and concealment of a material fact by WS.

15. The Parties' Consent Is an Essential Element of a Valid Contract. The consent of the parties is required for a valid contract. [CC § 1550] The consent must be mutual and freely given. [CC § 1565]

16. Fraud, Duress, Menace, or Undue Influence May Negate Consent. An

apparent consent is not real or free when obtained through fraud, mistake, duress, menace, or undue influence. [CC § 1568]. Consent is deemed to have been given had that cause not existed [CC § 1566].

17. A Party May Unilaterally Rescind If The Rescinding Party's Consent to the Contract Was Given by Mistake, or Obtained Through Duress, Menace, Fraud, or Undue Influence [CC § 1689] In the case of duress, menace, fraud, or undue influence, a party is entitled to rescind only if another party to the contract was responsible for the duress, menace, fraud or undue influence, or knows that it has taken place and takes advantage of it by enforcing the contract.

DEFINITIONS

18. Deed of Trust - An instrument in use in many states, taking the place and serving the uses of a common-law mortgage, by which the legal title to real property is placed in one or more trustees, to secure the repayment of a sum of money or the performance of other conditions. Bank v. Pierce, 144 Cal. 434, 77 Pac. 1012. (*Black's Law Dictionary 2nd Edition.*)

A Deed of Trust is a document that embodies the agreement between a lender and a borrower to transfer an interest in the borrower's land to a neutral third party, a trustee, to secure the payment of a debt by the borrower. (*West's Encyclopedia of American Law, edition 2. Copyright 2008*)

19. Trustee - A trust agreement is a complicated legal relationship involving the trustor, the trustee, and one or more beneficiaries. The trustee holds only "legal" title to the property and the beneficiaries hold what the law calls "equitable" title. As a result, the trustee only has authority to transfer trust property as provided in the trust agreement instructions. The trustee's title to the property is always limited to the provisions of the trust agreement.

20. Straw Man - A front; a third party who is put up in name only to take part in a transaction. Nominal party to a transaction; one who acts as an agent for another for the purpose of taking title to real property and executing whatever documents and instruments the principal may direct respecting the property. Person who purchases property for another to conceal identity of real purchaser, or to accomplish some purpose otherwise not allowed. [Emphasis added] (*Black's Law Dictionary, 6th Edition*)

21. Material Fact - Crucial to the interpretation of a phenomenon or a subject matter, or to the determination of an issue at hand this is a specific type of confirmed or validated event, item of information, or state of affairs. (*Black's Law Dictionary 2nd Ed.*) A Material Fact is an occurrence, event, or information that is sufficiently significant to influence an individual into acting in a certain way, such

as entering into a contract. In formal court procedures, a material fact is anything needed to prove one party's case or tending to establish a point that is crucial to a person's position. (*West's Encyclopedia of American Law, edition 2. Copyright 2008*)

22. Caveat Emptor - Let the buyer take care. This maxim summarizes the rule that the purchaser of an article must examine, judge, and test It for himself, being bound to discover any obvious defects or imperfections. Miller v. Tiffany, 1 Wall. 309, 17 L. Ed. 540; Barnard v. Kellogg, 10 Wall. 388, 19 L. Ed. 9S7; Slaughter v. Gerson, 13 Wall. 3S3, 20 L. Ed. 627; Hargous v. Stone. 5 N. Y. 82; Wissler v. Craig. SO Va. 32; Wright v. Hart, 18 Wend. (N. Y.) 453. Caveat emptor, qui ignorare non debuit quod jus alienum emit. Hob. 99. Let a purchaser beware, who ought not to be ignorant that he is purchasing the rights of another. (*Black's Law Dictionary Free 2nd Ed.*)

FIRST CAUSE OF ACTION – ACTUAL FRAUD

Cal.Civ. 1572 Code of Civil Procedure section 1856(f).

23. Intentional or Negligent Misrepresentation of Fact, Concealment, or Promissory Fraud may Constitute Actual Fraud. Fraud is either actual or constructive [CC§1571]. When determining the parties' consent to contract any of the following acts may constitute actual fraud [CC § 1572]:

A. The suggestion, as fact, of something that is not true, by one who does not believe it to be true.

B. The positive assertion, in a manner not warranted by the information of the person making it, of that which is not true, though that person believes it to be true.

C. The suppression of that which is true, by one having knowledge or belief of the fact.

D. A promise made without any intention of performing it.

E. Any other act intended to deceive.

Thus, intentional, or negligent misrepresentation of facts, concealment of facts and promissory fraud, are all specifically recognized by statute as "actual fraud" which may be raised to attack the existence of a contract.

FIRST AFFIRMATIVE DEFENSE

Actual Fraud - Intentional or Negligent Misrepresentation

24. When determining the parties' consent to contract any of the following acts may constitute actual fraud, intentional misrepresentation of facts, concealment of facts, promissory fraud, are all recognized by statute as actual fraud. (Cal. Civ. Code §1572), (See also- Code of Civil Procedure section 1856(f), Riverisland Cold Storage Inc. v. Fresno-Madera Production Credit Association.)

25. The apparent consent of the Plaintiffs Michelle Moquin and Douglas Boggs to the Deed of Trust between Defendant World Savings and the Plaintiffs was not real, mutual, or free in that it was obtained through fraud, as herein alleged.

26. On or about Aug. 6, 2005, in house loan officer of WS (herein "agent") for Defendant World Savings, falsely and fraudulently represented to Plaintiffs Michelle Moquin and Douglas Boggs that a Deed of Trust contract was the instrument they should use to contract with Defendant to refinance their loan with Defendant because it contained the following set of elements (A-F).

27. (A.) An independent trustee that would protect the Plaintiffs' legal title from any and all alienations to that title except for specific instructions that would be provided in the contract in the event of a breach by Plaintiffs, but at no time would the independent trustee allow the lender to exercise control over the Plaintiffs legal title.

28. (A1) The representations made by the agent of the Defendant and implications in the DOT contract were false, the true facts were as follows: The trustee in a Deed of Trust contract does not protect the Borrower's Legal title because the trustee in a Deed of Trust contract cannot refuse to transfer the Borrower's legal title to any newly named trustee if the Lender or an agent of the Lender disagreed with his opinion. The Borrower's legal title can be transferred by the Lender or an agent of the Lender by either of their signatures alone without the consent of the trustee. The trustee in a Deed of Trust cannot object to who the Borrower's title is transferred to ergo the Lender or the agent of the Lender can break up the Borrower's title and transfer it to whomever they please as often as they please in a derivative, Pooling Service Agreement, or any manner they choose. The trustee cannot object to making the transfer of title if the Statute of Frauds isn't followed, or the transfer isn't recorded properly, or any or all of the CC rules for transfer of real property aren't followed. It really doesn't matter how you examine the trustee in a Deed of Trust contract, the fact is a trustee in a Deed

of Trust is a Straw Man with no purpose but to deceive the Borrower into believing that there is someone between him and the Lender protecting his Legal title, and to act as an employed agent of the Lender. Any objection by a trustee to any action of the Lender or an agent of the Lender is ineffective because the Lender or an agent of the Lender can simply replace the trustee at will and with an employee of the Lender or the agent if they chose to ignore the trustee's objection or performance. (Exhibit 6 Substitution of trustee), shows an example of the transfer of the Plaintiffs' Legal title by the signature of the Lender's agent, Joyce Copeland, without the signature of the previous trustee.

29. (A2) When the agent for Defendant World Savings made these representations, they knew them to be false or had no reasonable grounds for believing them to be true.

30. (A3) The agent for Defendant World Savings made these representations with the intent to deceive and induce Plaintiffs Michelle Moquin and Douglas Boggs to enter into the contract.

31. (A4) Plaintiffs Michelle Moquin and Douglas Boggs relied on the truth of the representations in entering into the contract. Plaintiffs Michelle Moquin and Douglas Boggs would not have given their consent to the contract had it not been for the fraud. The reliance of Plaintiffs Michelle Moquin and Douglas Boggs was justified because neither Plaintiffs were familiar with the difference between a Deed of Trust or a mortgage contract and the agent held himself out to be a person that dealt regularly with the Deed of Trust contracts, World Savings had a reputation of being a respected refinance company, Plaintiffs had heard nothing about institutions splitting up a mortgage into derivatives and trading in them, or Pooling Service Agreements, or "robo signing" accusations and there was no reason for Plaintiffs to suspect that the state of California would give Lenders the power to alienate their title on the signature of the Lender absence the trustee who Plaintiffs had deeded their Legal title to having to deed it to another trustee. Indeed it would be difficult to convince the ordinary person who had been involved in deeding an interest in real property in the state of California that a person who did not own a deed to certain piece of real property could on his signature convey that property to any one he wished and record the transaction without the slightest state policing of the recordation or check of the required documents to complete such a transaction, nor would the Plaintiff suspect that the transaction would be taken on his word and the documents would be accepted by the Court as legally correct under the doctrine of the "Presumption of Correctness."

32. (A5) As a result of the fraud, Plaintiffs were injured in that they lost their home in a Non-Judicial Foreclosure sale. The Plaintiffs were deprived of the benefit of being able to bargain for a lower mortgage and lower interest rate. Therefore, the Plaintiffs suffered the real harm of paying more for the loan then they would have every month. The loss of the extra income deprived the Plaintiffs

of the benefit of the goods and services that extra income would have given them. The increased mortgage contributed to the Plaintiffs lack of ability to meet the high monthly mortgage and hence contributed to plaintiff's default on the fraudulent loan. The deception prevented the Plaintiffs from getting the opportunity to select a standard mortgage contract or any other instrument for securing their loan over the Deed of Trust which is by any stretch of the imagination is merely a deceptive device that gives the lender total control over and free reign to profit in any manner the lender can devise by alienating the borrower's title for profit. In the state of CA, a DOT contract is a license for lenders to contract in real estate without regard to the standard protections afforded to a borrower by a standard mortgage contract or to the right of the borrower to knowingly bargain for the benefits that the DOT bestows upon a lender who knows that the borrower is unaware of his unconscionable one-sided advantage. Without the benefit of the Non-Judicial Foreclosure action, the Defendants would have been more likely to work with Plaintiffs to save their house since it was $200,000 over valued by the Defendant thus making it underwater by $200,000. If Defendants were forced to use a judicial action rather than a non-judicial action the harm to the Plaintiffs would have been lessened because both parties would have incentives for settling thereby lowering the overall costs for litigation. But Defendants gain of the use of a Non-Judicial action by their deception increased the harm to the Plaintiffs because Plaintiffs were left with only one option, which was to pay in full or lose their property in a non-judicial foreclosure sale. Plaintiffs suffered additional loss due to the unequal bargaining power and lack of knowledge concerning the WFB's ability to profit from making the trustee a Straw Man. The loss in the lower interest rate that knowledge would have produced should the Plaintiffs have been willing to accept the DOT under the present conditions of CA law giving the lender the power to alienate the Plaintiff's legal title for profit should be calculated and deducted from any amounts defendant is claiming before a rescission is granted. Plaintiffs' harm was further exacerbated by the additional benefit that was gained through WFB's deception of having no one check their abuse of the requirements to activate the power of sale clause. Without the availability of the Power of Sale clause the Plaintiffs would still be in their home, since a drawn-out judicial process would require economic sacrifices by both parties thereby reducing the economic and psychological and emotional harm the Plaintiffs have suffered and giving Plaintiff's the new right under "Capacity Argument" that would force WFB to produce proof they were not in violation of their Pooling and Servicing Agreement before they could foreclose on the Plaintiffs. Under that theory the harm becomes the value of the property. Hence, the injury to the Plaintiffs is in the economic value of the loss of their home and the years of material and emotional investment that they put into it when Wells Fargo Bank used the non-judicial foreclosure benefit they gained by the deception of inducing the Plaintiffs to use the instrument called a Deed of Trust contract to secure their loan.

33. (B1) A guarantee in Three sections [1. ("Borrower's Transfer of Rights in the Property "Exhibit 1 Contract page 2, section 2)- 2. ("Description of the

Property "Exhibit 2 Contract page 2, section 3)- 3. ("Borrower's Right to Grant a Security Interest in the Property and the Borrower's Obligation to Defend Ownership of the Property" Exhibit 3 Contract page 3, section 4,)] which would guarantee that the trustee in a Deed of Trust contract would be the only one having access to the Plaintiffs' Legal title and that the trustee could only follow the instructions which were put into the Deed of Trust contract by the Plaintiffs as "the Borrower," and the Defendant as "the Lender." This section would guarantee that the Lender would have to bargain fairly for the right to alienate the borrower's property for profit in a derivative scheme, or Pooling Service Agreement or any other profit-making scheme the Lender thought of.

34. (B2) The representations made by the Defendant were false, the true facts were as follows: Those three sections in the Deed of Trust contract do not guarantee that the trustee in a Deed of Trust contract would be the only one having access to the Borrower's Legal title, the Lender or an agent of the Lender have total control over the Borrower's title immediately after the Borrower transfers his title to a trustee in a Deed of Trust. As a matter of fact the only time the transfer of the Borrower's title is made according to the Cal. Civ. Code is when the Borrower makes the initial transfer of his title to the trustee after that in a Deed of Trust contract in the state of California the Lender for, all practical purposes, has total control over the Borrower's Legal title. The fact that the Lenders using Deed of Trust contracts regularly spilt up their Borrower's titles into various forms of derivatives and sold them at will shows that a Deed of Trust contract offered no protection from the alienation of a Borrower's Legal title by the Lender or an agent of the Lender. (Exhibit 10)

35. (B3) The agent for Defendant World Savings made these representations with the intent to deceive and induce Plaintiffs Michelle Moquin and Douglas Boggs to enter into the contract.

36. (B4) Plaintiffs Michelle Moquin and Douglas Boggs relied on the truth of the representations in entering into the contract. Plaintiffs Michelle Moquin and Douglas Boggs would not have given their consent to the contract had it not been for the fraud. The reliance of Plaintiffs Michelle Moquin and Douglas Boggs was justified because neither Plaintiffs were familiar with the difference between a Deed of Trust or a mortgage contract and the agent held himself out to be a person that dealt regularly with the Deed of Trust contracts, World Savings had a reputation of being a respected refinance company, Plaintiffs had heard nothing about institutions splitting up a mortgage in to derivatives and trading in them, or "robo signing" accusations and there was no reason for Plaintiffs to suspect that the state of California would give Lenders the power to alienate their title on the signature of the Lender absence the trustee who Plaintiffs had deeded their Legal title to having to deed it to another trustee. Indeed it would be difficult to convince the ordinary person who had been involved in deeding an interest in real property in the state of California that a person who did not have a deed to real property could on his signature convey that property to any one he wished and record the

transaction without the slightest oversight as his recordation of the required documents to complete such a transaction would be taken on his word and the documents would be accepted by the Court as legally correct under the doctrine of the "Presumption of Correctness."

37. (B5) As a result of the fraud, Plaintiffs were injured in that they lost their home in a Non-Judicial Foreclosure sale. The deception prevented the Plaintiffs from getting the opportunity to select a standard mortgage contract or any other instrument for securing their loan over the Deed of Trust. Without the benefit of the Non-Judicial Foreclosure action, the Defendants would have been more likely to work with Plaintiffs to save their house since it was $200,000 over valued by the Defendant thus making it underwater by $200,000. If Defendants were forced to use a judicial action rather than a non-judicial action the harm to the Plaintiffs would have been lessened because both parties would have incentives for settling thereby lowering the overall costs for litigation. But Defendants gain of the use of a Non-Judicial action by their deception increased the harm to the Plaintiffs because Plaintiffs were left with only one option, which was to pay in full or lose your property in a non-judicial foreclosure sale. This harm was further exacerbated by the additional benefit that was gained through their deception of having no one check their abuse of the requirements to activate the power of sale clause. Without the availability of the Power of Sale clause the Plaintiffs would still be in their home, since a drawn-out judicial process would require economic sacrifices by both parties thereby reducing the economic and psychological and emotional harm the Plaintiffs have suffered. Hence, the injury to the Plaintiffs was in the economic value of the loss of their home and the years of material and emotional investment that they put into it when Wells Fargo Bank used the non-judicial foreclosure benefit they gained by the deception of inducing the Plaintiffs to use the instrument called a Deed of Trust contract to secure their loan.

38. (C1) A guarantee the section of the Deed of Trust contract called the "Borrower's Right to Grant a Security Interest in the Property and Borrower's Obligation to Defend Ownership of the Property" (Exhibit 4 Contract page 3, section 4), which would guarantee that Defendant as lender would only have a guarantee as to Warranty of the Borrower's title but would not have the ability to alienate the Plaintiffs' title to their property.

39. (C2) The representations made by the Defendant were false, the true facts were as follows: The "Borrower's Right to Grant a Security Ownership of the Property" does not guarantee that the Lender or an agent of the Lender would not have the ability to alienate the Borrower's Legal title. As a matter of fact, in a Deed of Trust contract the Lender or an agent of the Lender could alienate the Borrower's Legal title by converting it into a form of security derivative and selling the parts. It has been accepted by the U.S. Federal government and the state government of California, and the lending institutions that the ability was available to Lenders before and during the time Plaintiffs were induced to use a Deed of Trust contract to refinance their loan. It is widely known and accepted

that "...the October 2008 bailout paid off the holders of mortgage-backed securities and derivative insureds. World Savings, Wachovia Mortgage, and Wells Fargo Bank were among the institutions who benefited from the bailout." (COURT: S.D. New York, DOCKET NUMBER: 09-CV-00833. JUDGE NAME: Hon. Leonard B. Sand. DATE FILED: 01/29/2009.) WFB uses Pooling and Servicing Agreement notes to foreclose in No-Judicial Foreclosure sales in CA. WFB's motion for a summary judgment failed because the court ruled they did not own the note. Wells Fargo Bank, N.A. v. Erobobo, NYSC – REMIC FAI: 04/29/13

40. (C3) The agent for Defendant World Savings made these representations with the intent to deceive and induce Plaintiffs Michelle Moquin and Douglas Boggs to enter into the contract.

41. (C4) Plaintiffs Michelle Moquin and Douglas Boggs relied on the truth of the representations in entering into the contract. Plaintiffs Michelle Moquin and Douglas Boggs would not have given their consent to the contract had it not been for the fraud. The reliance of Plaintiffs Michelle Moquin and Douglas Boggs was justified because neither Plaintiffs were familiar with the difference between a Deed of Trust or a mortgage contract and the agent held himself out to be a person that dealt regularly with the Deed of Trust contracts, World Savings had a reputation of being a respected refinance company, Plaintiffs had heard nothing about institutions splitting up a mortgage in to derivatives and trading in them, or "robo signing" accusations and there was no reason for Plaintiffs to suspect that the state of California would give Lenders the power to alienate their title on the signature of the Lender absence the trustee who Plaintiffs had deeded their Legal title to having to deed it to another trustee. Indeed it would be difficult to convince the ordinary person who had been involved in deeding an interest in real property in the state of California that a person who did not have a deed to real property could on his signature convey that property to any one he wished and record the transaction without the slightest oversight as his recordation of the required documents to complete such a transaction would be taken on his word and the documents would be accepted by the Court as legally correct under the doctrine of the "Presumption of Correctness."

42. (C5) As a result of the fraud, Plaintiffs were injured in that they lost their home in a Non-Judicial Foreclosure sale. The deception prevented the Plaintiffs from getting the opportunity to select a standard mortgage contract or any other instrument for securing their loan over the Deed of Trust. Without the benefit of the Non-Judicial Foreclosure action, the Defendants would have been more likely to work with Plaintiffs to save their house since it was $200,000 over valued by the Defendant thus making it underwater by $200,000. If Defendants were forced to use a judicial action rather than a non-judicial action the harm to the Plaintiffs would have been lessened because both parties would have incentives for settling thereby lowering the overall costs for litigation. But Defendants gain of the use of a Non-Judicial action by their deception increased the harm to the Plaintiffs

because Plaintiffs were left with only one option, which was to pay in full or lose your property in a non-judicial foreclosure sale. This harm was further exacerbated by the additional benefit that was gained through their deception of having no one check their abuse of the requirements in order to activate the power of sale clause. Without the availability of the Power of Sale clause the Plaintiffs would still be in their home, since a drawn-out judicial process would require economic sacrifices by both parties thereby reducing the economic and psychological and emotional harm the Plaintiffs have suffered. Hence, the injury to the Plaintiffs was in the economic value of the loss of their home and the years of material and emotional investment that they put into it when Wells Fargo Bank used the non-judicial foreclosure benefit they gained by the deception of inducing the Plaintiffs to use the instrument called a Deed of Trust contract to secure their loan.

43. (D1) Defendant falsely and fraudulently represented to Plaintiffs that in a Deed of Trust contract any new trustee named by the Defendant would be an Independent agent and bound by the instructions that were given to the Original trustee and the rules governing the transfer of real property titles in the state of California and therefore at no time would the Defendant have control of the Plaintiffs' Legal title. (Exhibit 5 Contract page 13, section 29)

44. (D2) The representations made by the Defendant were false, the true facts were as follows: In a Deed of Trust contract the Lender or an agent has the right to not only name anyone the Lender or agent wishes to appoint as the trustee, they can name a person who is employed by them in another capacity to act as the trustee and maintain the trustee as an employee. (Exhibit 7 Contract page 12, section 27)

45. (D3) The agent for Defendant World Savings made these representations with the intent to deceive and induce Plaintiffs Michelle Moquin and Douglas Boggs to enter into the contract.

46. (D4) Plaintiffs Michelle Moquin and Douglas Boggs relied on the truth of the representations in entering into the contract. Plaintiffs Michelle Moquin and Douglas Boggs would not have given their consent to the contract had it not been for the fraud. The reliance of Plaintiffs Michelle Moquin and Douglas Boggs was justified because neither Plaintiffs were familiar with the difference between a Deed of Trust or a mortgage contract and the agent held himself out to be a person that dealt regularly with the Deed of Trust contracts, World Savings had a reputation of being a respected refinance company, Plaintiffs had heard nothing about institutions splitting up a mortgage in to derivatives and trading in them, or "robo signing" accusations and there was no reason for Plaintiffs to suspect that the state of California would give Lenders the power to alienate their title on the signature of the Lender absence the trustee who Plaintiffs had deeded their Legal title to having to deed it to another trustee. Indeed it would be difficult to convince the ordinary person who had been involved in deeding an interest in real property

in the state of California that a person who did not have a deed to real property could on his signature convey that property to any one he wished and record the transaction without the slightest oversight as his recordation of the required documents to complete such a transaction would be taken on his word and the documents would be accepted by the Court as legally correct under the doctrine of the "Presumption of Correctness."

47. (D5) As a result of the fraud, Plaintiffs were injured in that they lost their home in a Non-Judicial Foreclosure sale. The deception prevented the Plaintiffs from getting the opportunity to select a standard mortgage contract or any other instrument for securing their loan over the Deed of Trust. Without the benefit of the Non-Judicial Foreclosure Action the Defendants would have been more likely to work with Plaintiffs to save their house since it was $200,000 over valued by the Defendant thus making it underwater by $200,000. If Defendants were forced to use a judicial action rather than a non-judicial action the harm to the Plaintiffs would have been lessened because both parties would have incentives for settling thereby lowering the overall costs for litigation. But Defendants gain of the use of a Non-Judicial action by their deception increased the harm to the Plaintiffs because Plaintiffs were left with only one option, which was to pay in full or lose your property in a non-judicial foreclosure sale. This harm was further exacerbated by the additional benefit that was gained through their deception of having no one check their abuse of the requirements in order to activate the power of sale clause. Without the availability of the Power of Sale clause the Plaintiffs would still be in their home, since a drawn-out judicial process would require economic sacrifices by both parties thereby reducing the economic and psychological and emotional harm the Plaintiffs have suffered. Hence, the injury to the Plaintiffs was in the economic value of the loss of their home and the years of material and emotional investment that they put into it when Wells Fargo Bank used the non-judicial foreclosure benefit they gained by the deception of inducing the Plaintiffs to use the instrument called a Deed of Trust contract to secure their loan.

48. (E1) Defendant falsely and fraudulent represented to the Plaintiffs that in a Deed of Trust contract the trustee acts independently to ensure that the rules governing the Power of Sale Clause would protect the rights of the Plaintiffs before it was used.

49. (E2) The representation made by the Defendant was false, the true fact is as follows: if the trustee objected to the Lender or his agent not following the prescribed rules to follow before the Lender or his agent could enact the Power of Sale Clause, the Lender has the power in a Deed of Trust contract to name a new trustee who would allow the Lender or an agent of the Lender to skirt the rules.

50. (E3) The agent for Defendant World Savings made these representations with the intent to deceive and induce Plaintiffs Michelle Moquin and Douglas Boggs to enter into the contract.

51. (E4) Plaintiffs Michelle Moquin and Douglas Boggs relied on the truth of the representations in entering into the contract. Plaintiffs Michelle Moquin and Douglas Boggs would not have given their consent to the contract had it not been for the fraud. The reliance of Plaintiffs Michelle Moquin and Douglas Boggs was justified because neither Plaintiffs were familiar with the difference between a Deed of Trust or a mortgage contract and the agent held himself out to be a person that dealt regularly with the Deed of Trust contracts, World Savings had a reputation of being a respected refinance company, Plaintiffs had heard nothing about institutions splitting up a mortgage in to derivatives and trading in them, or "robo signing" accusations and there was no reason for Plaintiffs to suspect that the state of California would give Lenders the power to alienate their title on the signature of the Lender absence the trustee who Plaintiffs had deeded their Legal title to having to deed it to another trustee. Indeed it would be difficult to convince the ordinary person who had been involved in deeding an interest in real property in the state of California that a person who did not have a deed to real property could on his signature convey that property to any one he wished and record the transaction without the slightest oversight as his recordation of the required documents to complete such a transaction would be taken on his word and the documents would be accepted by the Court as legally correct under the doctrine of the "Presumption of Correctness."

52. (E5) As a result of the fraud, Plaintiffs were injured in that they lost their home in a Non-Judicial Foreclosure sale. The deception prevented the Plaintiffs from getting the opportunity to select a standard mortgage contract or any other instrument for securing their loan over the Deed of Trust. Without the benefit of the Non-Judicial Foreclosure Action the Defendants would have been more likely to work with Plaintiffs to save their house since it was $200,000 over valued by the Defendant thus making it underwater by $200,000. If Defendants were forced to use a judicial action rather than a non-judicial action the harm to the Plaintiffs would have been lessened because both parties would have incentives for settling thereby lowering the overall costs for litigation. But Defendants gain of the use of a Non-Judicial action by their deception increased the harm to the Plaintiffs because Plaintiffs were left with only one option, which was to pay in full or lose your property in a non-judicial foreclosure sale. This harm was further exacerbated by the additional benefit that was gained through their deception of having no one check their abuse of the requirements in order to activate the power of sale clause. Without the availability of the Power of Sale clause the Plaintiffs would still be in their home, since a drawn-out judicial process would require economic sacrifices by both parties thereby reducing the economic and psychological and emotional harm the Plaintiffs have suffered. Hence, the injury to the Plaintiffs was in the economic value of the loss of their home and the years of material and emotional investment that they put into it when Wells Fargo Bank used the non-judicial foreclosure benefit they gained by the deception of inducing the Plaintiffs to use the instrument called a Deed of Trust contract to secure their loan.

53. (F1) Defendant falsely and fraudulently represented to the Plaintiffs that the Power of Sale Clause in a Deed of Trust contract that would protect the Borrower's rights in the event the Lender chose to exercise its right to a Non-Judicial Foreclosure remedy to their breach.

54. (F2) The representations made by the Defendant were false, the true facts were as follows: The Power of Sale Clause in a Deed of Trust contract poses no actual prohibition to its misuse. The state of California gives the "power of presumption of correctness" (Exhibit 8 Contract page 13, section 28) to the filing of any documents by the Lender or an agent of the Lender as required to satisfy the Power of Sale Clause when filing a Non-Judicial Foreclosure action. Hence the Lender or an agent of the Lender can forge, robo-sign, and or back date documents without fear of legal penalty. The Defendants can hardly use the defense that they did not know of the ease by which they could readily commit such abuse because over the last five years the mainstream media has been full of accounts concerning the fine imposed upon lenders for those violations. (Exhibit 9 MERS)

55. (F3) The agent for Defendant World Savings made these representations with the intent to deceive and induce Plaintiffs Michelle Moquin and Douglas Boggs to enter into the contract.

56. (F4) Plaintiffs Michelle Moquin and Douglas Boggs relied on the truth of the representations in entering into the contract. Plaintiffs Michelle Moquin and Douglas Boggs would not have given their consent to the contract had it not been for the fraud. The reliance of Plaintiffs Michelle Moquin and Douglas Boggs was justified because neither Plaintiffs were familiar with the difference between a Deed of Trust or a mortgage contract and the agent held himself out to be a person that dealt regularly with the Deed of Trust contracts, World Savings had a reputation of being a respected refinance company, Plaintiffs had heard nothing about institutions splitting up a mortgage in to derivatives and trading in them, or "robo signing" accusations and there was no reason for Plaintiffs to suspect that the state of California would give Lenders the power to alienate their title on the signature of the Lender absence the trustee who Plaintiffs had deeded their Legal title to having to deed it to another trustee. Indeed it would be difficult to convince the ordinary person who had been involved in deeding an interest in real property in the state of California that a person who did not have a deed to real property could on his signature convey that property to any one he wished and record the transaction without the slightest oversight as his recordation of the required documents to complete such a transaction would be taken on his word and the documents would be accepted by the Court as legally correct under the doctrine of the "Presumption of Correctness."

57. (F5) As a result of the fraud, Plaintiffs were injured in that they lost their home in a Non-Judicial Foreclosure sale. The deception prevented the Plaintiffs from getting the opportunity to select a standard mortgage contract or any other

instrument for securing their loan over the Deed of Trust. Without the benefit of the Non-Judicial Foreclosure action, the Defendants would have been more likely to work with Plaintiffs to save their house since it was $200,000 over valued by the Defendant thus making it underwater by $200,000. If Defendants were forced to use a judicial action rather than a non-judicial action the harm to the Plaintiffs would have been lessened because both parties would have incentives for settling thereby lowering the overall costs for litigation. But Defendants gain of the use of a Non-Judicial action by their deception increased the harm to the Plaintiffs because Plaintiffs were left with only one option, which was to pay in full or lose your property in a non-judicial foreclosure sale. This harm was further exacerbated by the additional benefit that was gained through their deception of having no one check their abuse of the requirements in order to activate the power of sale clause. Without the availability of the Power of Sale clause the Plaintiffs would still be in their home, since a drawn-out judicial process would require economic sacrifices by both parties thereby reducing the economic and psychological and emotional harm the Plaintiffs have suffered. Hence, the injury to the Plaintiffs was in the economic value of the loss of their home and the years of material and emotional investment that they put into it when Wells Fargo Bank used the non-judicial foreclosure benefit they gained by the deception of inducing the Plaintiffs to use the instrument called a Deed of Trust contract to secure their loan.

58. When the agent for Defendant World Savings made these representations, they knew them to be false or had no reasonable grounds for believing them to be true.

59. The agent for Defendant World Savings made these representations with the intent to deceive and induce Plaintiffs Michelle Moquin and Douglas Boggs to enter into the contract. Plaintiffs Michelle Moquin and Douglas Boggs relied on the truth of the representations in entering into the contract. Plaintiffs Michelle Moquin and Douglas Boggs would not have given their consent to the contract had it not been for the fraud. The reliance of Plaintiffs Michelle Moquin and Douglas Boggs was justified because neither Plaintiffs were familiar with the difference between a Deed of Trust or a mortgage contract and the agent held himself out to be a person that dealt regularly with the Deed of Trust contracts, World Savings had a reputation of being a respected refinance company, Plaintiffs had heard nothing about institutions splitting up a mortgage in to derivatives and trading in them, or "robo signing" accusations and there was no reason for Plaintiffs to suspect that the state of California would give Lenders the power to alienate their title on the signature of the Lender absence the trustee who Plaintiffs had deeded their Legal title to having to deed it to another trustee. Indeed it would be difficult to convince the ordinary person who had been involved in deeding an interest in real property in the state of California that a person who did not have a deed to real property could on his signature convey that property to any one he wished and record the transaction without the slightest oversight as his recordation of the required documents to complete such a transaction would be

taken on his word and the documents would be accepted by the Court as legally correct under the doctrine of the "Presumption of Correctness."

60. As a result of the fraud, Plaintiffs were injured in that they did not get the opportunity to select a standard mortgage contract over the Deed of Trust. Had they contracted with a standard mortgage contract the Defendant Wells Fargo Bank would have had to go to court to get a judicial foreclosure. The Plaintiffs could have found the funds to remedy the contract defect or the Plaintiffs could have worked out a way to save their house since it was more than $200,000 overvalued by the bank. Hence the injury to the Plaintiffs was the loss of their home and the years of material and emotional investment they put into it when Wells Fargo Bank used a feature, the Non-Judicial Foreclosure action with all the other advantages the Deed of Trust gave them to take and sell the Plaintiffs home.

61. II. Negligent Misrepresentation - Most American courts now recognize liability for negligent misrepresentation. In California, negligent misrepresentation is given statutory recognition as a form of deceit: Under section 1710, subdivision 2, of the Civil Code, it is the assertion, as a fact, of that which is not true, by one who has no reasonable ground for believing it to be true; under section 1572, subdivision 2, of the Civil Code, it is the positive assertion by a contracting party, in a manner not warranted by the information of the person making it, of that which is not true, though he believes it to be true.CC § 1572(2) gives statutory recognition to negligent of fact as a form of deceit.

62. The mere assertion of liability begs the real question: whether plaintiff's interests are entitled to legal protection against the defendants' conduct. In other words, whether a duty exists depends on those considerations of policy which lead the law to say that the plaintiff is entitled to protection. (Dillon v. Legg, 734 [69 Cal.Rptr. 72, 441 P.2d 912, 29 A.L.R.3d 1316].) The policy factors to be considered in determining whether a duty exists have been judicially defined as follows: "the foreseeability of harm to the plaintiff, the degree of certainty that the plaintiff suffered injury, the closeness of the connection between the defendant's conduct and the injury suffered, the moral blame attached to the defendant's conduct, the [48 Cal. App. 3D 87] policy of preventing future harm, the extent of the burden to the defendant and consequences to the community of imposing a duty to exercise care with resulting liability for breach, and the availability, cost, and prevalence of insurance for the risk involved." (Rowland v. Christian, 69 Cal. 2d 108, 113 [70 Cal. Rptr. 97, 443 P.2d 561, 32 A.L.R.3d 496]; Biakanja v. Irving, 49 Cal. 2d 647, 650 [320 P.2d 16, 65 A.L.R.2d 1358]; Hanberry v. Hearst Corp., supra, 276 Cal. App. 2d 680, 685.)

63. In Hale v. George A. Hormel & Co (1975) 48 CA3d 73, 84, 121 CR 144 (CC § 1572(2), the Court then affirmed the summary judgements against the Plaintiff in favor of Defendants Hormel & Co because it did not believe Hale met those policy factors. The Plaintiff's case differs significantly in every area. Whereas no "foreseeability of harm factor" was found for Hale because neither

Welch nor Hormel could have reasonably foreseen that their activity in selling juices to Universal would have caused Hale to part with $25,000 in cash without receiving a single machine. WS being in the business of conducting Non-Judicial Foreclosures could reasonably foresee that Plaintiffs could lose a substantial sum because of the value of their property if a dispute arose between Plaintiffs and WS concerning a possible breach by Plaintiffs or misconduct by WS.

64. The degree of certainty factor that the Plaintiffs would suffer injury if the trustee turned out to be a straw man and there was misconduct by the Lender or merely haste on the Lender's part if there was a disagreement as to contract differences that involved the Lender's choice to foreclose by his Non-Judicial Foreclosure is almost 100%. WS is in a business involving regularly using the Non-Judicial Foreclosure process to sell properties of those they have DOTs with. They were fully aware that the "trustee" in their DOTs with their borrowers could be either "the Original trustee, duly appointed Substituted trustee, or acting as Agent for the trustee or Beneficiary under a Deed of Trust. (Exhibit 10 – Substitution of trustee)

65. On the "close connection" factor in Hale could not show a close connection between Hormel & Co and his $20,000 loss, but Plaintiffs loss of their home is a direct result of the misrepresentation by WS that the trustee would be there to stand between the premature selling of their home whether it was due to misconduct by the Lender merely his haste to sell. The connection between WS conduct of deceiving Plaintiffs into believing that the trustee was the person who held Plaintiffs' Legal title in trust and the Plaintiff's loss of their home because the trustee was a straw man and as a straw man the trustee had no power to stand between the Lender and whatever he chose to do with the trustee's legal title is as direct as cause and effect. But for Plaintiffs believing WS misrepresentation of the trustee's power and thereby consenting to contract with WS, Plaintiffs would not have been subject to a Non-Judicial Foreclosure sale of their property without being able to litigate their differences in court.

66. Whereas in Hale, the court found that no moral blame could be attributed to the defendants' conduct because nothing Hormel or Welch did can be said to be closely related to Universal's fraud or breach of contract, in Plaintiffs' case the moral blame of Plaintiffs' loss of their home without the ability to litigate the arguable issues in Court is directly related to the fact that as a Straw man the trustee in a DOT could do nothing to prevent the Lender prematurely selling the Plaintiffs' home, nor could the trustee force WFB to obey the terms of the Notice of Default before WFB could require the trustee to enact the Power of Sale clause. As a Straw Man, the trustee had no power to act independently to protect Plaintiffs' Legal title interests.

67. As to the [48 Cal. App. 3d 87] policy of preventing future harm, the extent of the burden to the defendant and consequences to the community of imposing a duty to exercise care with resulting liability for breach, and the availability, cost,

and prevalence of insurance for the risk involved," (Rowland v. Christian, 69 Cal. 2d 108, 113 [70 Cal. Rptr. 97, 443 P.2d 561, 32 A.L.R.3d 496]; Biakanja v. Irving, 49 Cal. 2d 647, 650 [320 P.2d 16, 65 A.L.R.2d 1358]; Hanberry v. Hearst Corp., supra, 276 Cal. App. 2d 680, 685.) In the Hale case the Court ruled this factor was not met because the burden of requiring Welch and Hormel to investigate every firm or person which might be interested in vending their products would be onerous: too many individuals and organizations are involved in a national marketing system to require a financial check on each one. [48 Cal. App. 3d 88]

68. However, in Plaintiffs' case the policy of preventing future harm to property owners like the plaintiffs when it comes to lenders defrauding borrowers is enormous. It is in almost every conversation in which the very balance of our State and Federal economies is discussed. A huge step in the right direction would be to correct a mistake which allows the banks to ignore the rules governing the transfer of the legal title of property when the owner of that title is a borrower in a DOT. It was certainly not the intent of legislators of the state of California when they drafted the definition of a DOT to allow the Lender to corrupt the definition of the third necessary party to a DOT, the trustee. The California Supreme called the trustee an independent party in the DOT who is to be at arm's length between the Borrower and the Lender. The indisputable fact that arises out of the Legal Definition of a trustee in a Deed of Trust in the state of California is that it is an entity that the Beneficiary chooses but that choice MUST be independent and by "independent" the Legislature as interpreted by the Supreme Court of the state of California (81 Cal. App.4 868) must be at arm's length between the Trustor and the Beneficiary(I.E. Associates v. Safeco Title Ins. Co. (1985) 39 Cal.3d 281, 216 Cal. Rptr. 438; 702 P.2d 596) to ensure that independence the State of California enacted Civil Code § 2934(a) and required all duly appointed trustees to a Deed of Trust to abide by them.

69. The burden of requiring the Lender to inform the borrower that the trustee is a Straw man for all practical purposes when it comes to protecting the Legal title the borrower transfers to the trustee is hardly onerous. A simple statement or clause added to the DOT explaining that once the Borrower transfers his Legal title to the Original trustee, he has effectively transferred his title to the Lender because the Lender can transfer that Legal title at will without any of the regular requirements an ordinary transfer of real property title requires such as the signature of the actual title holder. From that point on a borrower would be free to consent to the use of a DOT or a Mortgage Note or whatever instrument he was free to negotiate to use his real property as lien for a loan.

70. Defendant could argue that the question of whether a trustee in a DOT is a strawman was a material fact. The question of whether a misrepresentation is a material fact is directly addressed in Costello v. Roer, "... if it would be likely to affect the conduct of a reasonable man with reference to the transaction in question." (Costello v. Roer 77 Cal. App. 2D 174) The fact that Plaintiffs did not

know that they would be giving up their Legal title to the Lender via a Straw man posing as a trustee was material in their consent since with this knowledge the Plaintiffs would have not consented to borrowing using the DOT as the instrument for contracting.

71. In Wood vs Kalbaugh, a distinction is made between an innocent misrepresentation and a fraudulent misrepresentation. "a distinction must be drawn between a fraudulent representation and an innocent one. For example, if A, with knowledge of B's idiosyncrasy or personal belief, willfully conceals a fact related to the idiosyncrasy or belief, to induce B to enter into a contract, A should not reap the fruit of his deception merely because it is unlikely that the misrepresentation would have affected a reasonable man (Wood v. Kalbaugh 39 Cal. App. 3D 926). That distinction becomes glaringly clear when we examine the facts in Plaintiffs case. WS with knowledge, coming from their daily experience of using DOTs, of the general beliefs of borrowers using a DOT(WS was fully aware that most Plaintiffs negotiating a DOT had no knowledge that a trustee was essentially a straw man when it came to having the powers normally legally ascribed to a trustee to real property) took advantage of that belief when they told Plaintiffs that the trustee would hold only "legal" title to their property and that they, as the borrowers, would hold what the law calls "equitable" title and as a result, the trustee would only have authority to transfer their legal title as was provided in the instructions that both the Borrower and the Lender put in writing in the DOT. WS assured the Plaintiffs that the trustee's title to the property is always limited to the actions necessary to obey those instructions given in writing in the DOT. Thereby suggesting to the Plaintiffs that the Lender would have no control, legal or otherwise of their Legal title. WS should not reap the benefits of a DOT because of their deception in inducing the Plaintiffs to enter into a DOT. Wood v. Kalbaugh emphasizes that this should be true even if this misrepresentation would not have affected a reasonable man.

72. Defendants could argue that if the misrepresentation was made it was an innocent one. However, we see no reason this should allow Defendant to benefit from any of the provisions that a DOT bestows upon Defendant such as the right to a Non-Judicial Foreclosure action. If Defendants have no right to that Non-Judicial benefit because Defendant induced the Plaintiffs to give him that benefit because of Defendant's innocent mistake. Plaintiffs property gained through the Non-judicial Foreclosure remedy should be returned forth with. Wood v. Kalbaugh expressly speaks additionally to this issue when it states, "As the Restatement of Contracts puts it, the "... materiality of the mistake induced by innocent misrepresentation is essential while materiality is not essential if a mistake induced by fraud produces the intended consequences." (§ 476, com. b.) As to innocent misrepresentations, the right to rescind is based on equitable principles, and equity dictates that in determining whether the misrepresentation was of a material fact the objective test is applicable. In fact, it is basic that the effect of an innocent misrepresentation is destroyed "... if the facts subsequently accord with the representation." (Rest., Contracts, § 476, com. b.) (Wood v.

Kalbaugh 39 Cal. App. 3D 926)

73. CONCLUSION

Plaintiffs should be granted rescissions with general damages, which the Court feels are just and punitive damages as the court feels would act to discourage this type of behavior by WFB in the future. Plaintiffs should be allowed to rescind their contract with WFB because they were fraudulently induced to use a contract that WS knew at the time was a device designed to take total control over the Plaintiffs legal title so that the Defendants could gamble with it for profit in various schemes from derivative splitting of the Plaintiff's title into Defendant's lucrative Pooling and Servicing Agreements.

WS knew at the time they were negotiating with Plaintiffs that none of the provisions that they were assuring Plaintiffs that were in the contract to help protect them in the event of a disagreement with WS would work because they knew something that the Plaintiffs didn't know. And that something, was the flaws in the enforcement of a DOT contract gave them the right to commit fraud with virtual impunity.

WS knew at the time that the state of California had basically given them the legal right to police their own conduct, beginning with allowing the lender to pick the supposedly "independent" trustee to giving them the "presumption of correction" when they filed documents with the county recording office to assuming they would on their own good conduct obey the rules of notification before using the very generous provision Crown Jewel of a DOT, the Non-Judicial Foreclosure option, given to them by a foolish legislature. WFB owns the conduct of WS because they purchased it with the business that is the law. But WFB itself continued in the line of WS using the flaws in the DOT to foreclose on the Plaintiffs knowing they could essentially ignore the parts of the DOT that required them to follow the rules.

WFB fully utilized the Straw Man portion of the fraud to appoint an "independent" trustee of their own, NdeX West, Inc. Together they deprived Plaintiffs of every shred of protections that the DOT guaranteed them when they innocently signed on the dotted line believing that the "trustee" would indeed do what the terms of the contract and the agent of WS told them he would do. That was to insure that WFB obeyed the terms and instructions of the DOT.

The law is clear about rescission concerning fraud. A party may unilaterally rescind if the consent of the rescinding party was [CC § 1689(b)(1)]: obtained through fraud and the other party is responsible for the fraud.

Plaintiffs and the facts have clearly shown that the defendant is clearly responsible for the fraud.

Plaintiffs are aware that the court may not award "benefit of the bargain" damages in a rescission action. Hence the court is inclined to accept the defendant argument that Plaintiffs should repay the loan before they can ask for a rescinding of the contract. But Plaintiffs argue this would be unfair on three grounds:

1. It would require the Plaintiffs to pay a sum to the defendant they are not entitled to. The amount in question is in question because had the defendants not concealed their ability to profit from the alienation of Plaintiffs title without the Plaintiff's consent, the amount of the loan and the subsequent interest rate on that loan would be substantially different.

2. The excessive interest paid on the loan amounts, because the Plaintiffs were deceived as to the potential additional benefit the defendants stood to profit from, and therefore were deprived of the right to bargain for that benefit, amounts to an unjust reward for the defendants. Until a formula for or an agreement to resolve the issue is attained Plaintiffs should not be forced to reward defendants for their fraud with a sum they are not entitled to.

3. The interest of the public demands that defendants with practically unlimited resources not be allowed to use those resources to defraud the citizens of California and walk away free because the weaker party financially cannot afford to repay in full before receiving the justice they are entitled to.

4. Defendants have sold Plaintiffs property in a Non-Judicial Foreclosure Sale. Until and unless they are willing to return Plaintiffs' property, they have no legal right to ask for the benefit of a contract they have dissolved with the sale.

Plaintiffs should be granted rescission with general damages, which the Court feels are just and punitive damages as the court feels would act to discourage this type of behavior by WFB in the future.

After all damages to the Plaintiffs have been awarded, including the return of Plaintiffs property, the Court can order Plaintiffs to enter into an agreement with WFB to work out a formula or agreement to pay WFB what it is actually owed minus the unjust enrichment of the higher interest rate and the loss of interest Plaintiffs would have received on the extra amount of interest they paid for years towards the higher interest rate on their mortgage.

This is not an admission that Plaintiffs would have contracted with defendants using a DOT contact had they known that it was not the document they thought they were agreeing to. The only fair and equitable solution to the intentional fraud by WFB that does not reward their bad behavior and serves public policy by not defying the public interest to discourage this type of conduct is to grant Plaintiffs an immediate rescission of the contract with General and Punitive Damages.

REQUEST LEAVE TO AMEND

74. The Plaintiffs request leave to Amend Fourth Amended Complaint as defined by Cal. Civ. Proc. 472, and Fed. R. Civ. P. 9(b).

NO DEMAND FOR JURY TRIAL

75. Plaintiffs, Douglas Boggs and Michelle Moquin, do not demand a trial by jury at this time.

PRAYER FOR RELIEF

WHEREFORE, Plaintiffs pray judgement against Defendants, and each of them, as follows:

ON FIRST CAUSE OF ACTION

A. Plaintiffs realize because of part performance that some loan contract does exist between the two parties, and Plaintiffs request that the Deed of Trust loan be rescinded, but that loan contract should be converted to a personal one and allow the two parties to negotiate.

B. Plaintiffs request a new calculation be formulated to calculate the true amount owed WFB based on a logical formula to determine what the value of benefit WS and WFB gained as a result of their ability to alienate the Plaintiffs legal title not just on whether or not they took advantage of that benefit. Regardless of whether they had the business acumen to use the benefit they acquired it at the expense of the Plaintiffs not being able to negotiate a lower mortgage rate which in turn forced Plaintiffs to pay much more in interest and service fees on a monthly basis for years.

C. Plaintiffs request their property to be returned to them.

D. Plaintiffs request additional damages as the court deems necessarily sufficient to deter Defendants from profitably practicing similar conduct.

E. For costs of suit incurred herein.

Dated:

Respectfully submitted,

Douglas J Boggs   Michelle A Moquin

Pro Se Plaintiff   Pro Se Plaintiff

Here is my dialogue of the hearing that I recorded on my tablet:

"A demurrer that attacks an entire pleading should be overruled if one of the counts therein is not vulnerable to the objection raised (Lord v. Garland (1946) 27 Cal. 2d 840, 850, 168 P.2d 5; Knickerbocker v. City of Stockton (1988) 199 Cal. App. 3D 235, 245, 244 Cal. Rptr. 764). Defendants assert in the Statement of Demurrer p3 Sec. 1 ln 4-6 that "Plaintiffs fail to state a claim for fraud in their third amended complaint because: (i) the misrepresentations plaintiffs allege resulted in their property being foreclosed concerned a Deed of Trust that was not foreclosed upon." Under defendant's heading on p4 of their Memorandum of Points and Authorities, defendants claim on ln 8 of p4 that it was the second trust deed that was used to foreclose upon the Plaintiffs. Defendants cite that deed as being recorded on 07/11-2007 as Instrument # 2007255632. This is a misrepresentation of a material statement of fact. The truth is that the second trust deed the defendant is referring to as Instrument # 2007255632, which WFB claims used to foreclose on plaintiffs, was rescinded on May 25, 2011 and filed in the Alameda County Recorder's Office (See Exhibit.1), and hence could not be the instrument used to foreclose on the defendants. The trustee's deed upon sale recorded on Jan 31, 2012, 11 days after the sale of plaintiffs' property used the First DOT dated 08/08/2005 and executed, by MM, Trustor, and recorded on 08/16/2005 as instrument #2005348480 to convey the sale to the New Owners, SGT Investments, LLC, and Catalina Bay, LLC the property located 1038 57th street, Oakland, CA 94608, Lot #26, Block G ... (See exhibit 2). The true fact is the DOT used by WFB to foreclose on the plaintiffs was the First DOT, Instrument # 2005348480. Therefore, this demurrer attacks a material fact asserted by the plaintiffs, which is not vulnerable to their objection. (See Exhibit 3, Statement of Demurrer, page 3 sect. 4-6. and Exhibit 4 Memorandum of Points and Authorities Defendant's claim on ln 8 of p4)."

SUPERIOR COURT OF THE STATE OF CALIFORNIA

COUNTY OF ALAMEDA - RCD COUNTY COURTHOUSE

DOUGLAS BOGGS AND	Case No. RG 11570208
MICHELLE MOQUIN	[Assigned for all purposes to:
Pro Per Plaintiffs	Judge Robert McGuiness – Dept.22]
V	MEMORANDUM OF POINTS
WELLS FARGO BANK, N.A., et al.,	AND AUTHORITIES TO
And DOES 1-50, Inclusive OPPOSITION TO	PLAINTIFF'S
Defendants	DEFENDANT WELLS FARGO
	BANK'S DEMURRER TO
	PLAINTIFF'S FOURTH
	AMENDED COMPLAINT
	Date:11/21/13Time:3PM
	Dept: 22 Action filed: 04/11/11
	Trial Date: tbd Res. #: R1427493

No Jury Trial Requested

TO DEFENDANT'S WELLS FARGO BANK and GOLDEN WEST SAVINGS ASSOC.: Plaintiffs MICHELLE MOQUIN and DOUGLAS BOGGS (herein "Plaintiffs") oppose the Demurrer and Request for Judicial Notice of Defendants WELLS FARGO BANK, N.A., and GOLDEN WEST SAVINGS ASSOCIATION SERVICES CO. (herein "Defendants"); as follows:

THE GENERAL DEMURRER SHOULD BE OVERRULED BECAUSE THE COMPLAINT HAS STATED FACTS SUFFICIENT TO CONSTITUTE A CAUSE OF ACTION.

TABLE OF CONTENTS

I. INTRODUCTION

II. STATEMENT OF FACTS

III. MEMORANDUM OF POINTS AND AUTHORITIES ARGUMENT

A. PLAINTIFF HAS ADEQUATELY PLEAD EACH AND EVERY CAUSE OF ACTION

IV. CONCLUSION

TABLE OF AUTHORITIES

Case Law:

Bank v. Pierce, 144 Cal. 434, 77 Pac. 1012

Title 17 U.S. Code - RESTATEMENT (SECOND) OF AGENCY § 1(1)

Countrywide Financial Corporation, 601 F. Supp. 2d 1201, 1220 (S.D. Cal. 2009)

Hatch v. Collins (1990) 225 Cal. App. 3d 1104, 1111-1112 Stephens, Partain & Cunningham v. Hollis (1987) 196 Cal. App.3d 948, 955 [242 Cal. Rptr. 251] (Hollis)

4 Miller & Starr, op. cit. Supra, § 9.3

Fleisher v. Continental Auxiliary Co. (1963) 215 Cal. App.2d 136, 139 [30 Cal. Rptr. 137]

Baron v. Colonial Mortgage Service Co. (1980)111 Cal. App.3d 316, 323 [168 Cal. Rptr. 450]

Bank of Seoul & Trust Co. v. Marcione (1988)198 Cal. App.3d 113, 118[244 Cal. Rptr. 1]

Block v. Tobin (1975)45 Cal. App.3d 214, 221 [119 Cal. Rptr. 288]

Civil Codes, Civil Procedures, Business Codes, Professional Codes, United States Codes:

California Business and Professions Code § 17200

Cal. Civ. Code § 2923.5

Cal. Civ. Code § 2923.6

Cal. Civ. Code §§ 2923.4 – 2944.7

References:

(3 Witkin, Summary of Cal. Law(9th ed. 1987)Security Transactions in Real Property, §7, p.520

I.INTRODUCTION

In a classic use of a Deed Of Trust (herein "DOT") to mortgage your property scheme, Defendants, World Savings Bank, Wachovia Mortgage, Wells Fargo Bank, NA, Golden West Savings Assoc., NDEx West, LSI Title Co.(herein "Defendants"), individually and collectively, caused Plaintiffs to suffer damages as a result of being unable to prevent an illegal non-judicial foreclosure process which they knew or reasonably should have known the Plaintiffs would not have known that a DOT would not provide the protections against an illegal non-judicial foreclosure of their property in the event they were accused of defaulting on their loan or could not repay their loan.

Plaintiffs entered into a DOT agreement with World Savings Bank (herein "WS") believing they were mortgaging their home with a contract that would protect their interest in their property and deal fairly with them if they were to suffer a financial setback and were forced to default. They trusted the agents of the bank and their broker when they were told by them that the agreement which they signed, a DOT contract, would do just that.

Plaintiffs were not aware that WS knew that the legislature of the state of CA had put in place a certain set of rules and regulations that would allow an unscrupulous lender to take advantage of those provisions to defraud the borrower in several ways, but especially in the event of a default by the borrower.

Plaintiffs' cause of action for Actual Fraud arises out of the discovery of how this lender, WS, used those rules and regulations to defraud them and illegally foreclose on their home, causing them to lose their home, their credit rating which prevents them from purchasing a new one, and the emotional distress involved in going through the process.

A "Deed of Trust" (DOT) in California is a document in which a person who takes out a home loan pledges to repay that loan according to the terms spelled out in the document. The Deed of Trust serves the same purpose as a mortgage note, with a couple of key distinctions. They are: Even though home loans are almost universally referred to as "mortgages," a mortgage is not technically a loan, but rather a way of guaranteeing repayment of the loan--which is why the term "mortgage loan" is not redundant. People who borrow money to buy a house must sign a pledge to pay back the loan. This promissory note is either a mortgage note or a Deed of Trust. It's not a matter of choice; individual jurisdictions require one or the other, and in California it's usually a Deed of Trust. Home loans backed by a Deed of Trust are called "trusts." WS knew that the Plaintiffs were not in a position to question why they were taking out their mortgage using a DOT rather than a Mortgage contract to secure their loan. WS knew that they would accept the document put before them to enter into the mortgaging of their home.

Mortgage loans are agreements strictly between lenders and borrowers, with one of them holding the title to the house and the mortgage note acting as a lien—an obligation that must be fulfilled before the house can be sold. In loans backed by a Deed of Trust, however, a third party, known as the trustee, actually holds the title to the house. Once the borrower has paid off the loan, the lender notifies the trustee that the obligation has been fulfilled, and the trustee turns the title over to the borrower. Here the WS informs the Plaintiffs that they get to choose who the trustee will be.

The trustee in a deed-of-trust loan can be a law firm, a title company, a bank or an individual. The trustee must be a neutral third party, meaning a person or company with no pre-existing personal or financial relationship with either the borrower or the lender. The possibility to defraud the borrower begins here because unbeknownst to the Plaintiffs or for that matter to the average borrower this explanation of the requirement of a DOT that the trustee to their contract who will be holding their legal title has to be a "neutral third party." But WS knew that it did not have to be true. WS knew at the time of contracting that the original trustee, Golden West Savings Assoc. (herein "GW") could be an employee, agent, or anyone WS chose to appoint as the trustee. This fact makes the DOT a misleading document on its face, one that is known to the Lenders but not necessarily to the borrower. It is particularly damaging to the borrower because it gives the Lender the power to manipulate who has control over the borrower's title over the length of the loan and control over the process governing how the borrower's property will be handled in the event of a foreclosure.

Under California law, a Deed of Trust must identify the property in question and identify all parties to the agreement—lender, borrower, and trustee. The document must be signed by both the borrower and lender. Although a Deed of Trust does not have to be officially recorded with the county recorder in order to be in force, most usually are. Only deeds of trusts that have been notarized can be recorded.

The DOT gives the trustee the power to sell the home if the borrower's obligation is not met. This is a significant difference from a mortgage loan, in which the lender must go to court to get permission to take the house back from the borrower and sell it. The fact that the Lender has complete control over the trustee, in all practicality gives the power to sell the home if the borrower's obligation is not met to the Lender. WS knew at the time or should have known this fact and WS knew that the Plaintiffs did not know this. The average mortgagee would have no reason to suspect that a document accepted as the standard form for conducting mortgages in the state of CA was not just misleading as to its representation of what it meant, was composed of or how it affected the interests of the two parties, it was basically fraudulent on its face because it gave one party such a superior position without the knowledge of the other party as to be unconscionable. It gave the lender the ability to speculate with the borrower's title in derivatives and other pooling and servicing schemes without his knowledge and the ability to record documents anyway the lender wished to facilitate a quick disposal of the borrower's property in the event of a default.

WS knew or should have known that the DOT they used to contract a mortgage with the Plaintiffs represented to Plaintiffs that the Plaintiffs could count on GW, the trustee, in their DOT contract to enforce the terms in the Power of Sale clause to prevent the Defendants from illegally foreclosing on the Plaintiffs if they defaulted on their loan. Defendants used the fact that a trustee in a DOT is merely a "straw man" because he has no power to prevent any illegal actions by the defendants during a non-judicial foreclosure of their loan and immediately set out to illegally skirt the requirements of the Power of Sale Clause. The title company, LSI Title Co.(herein "LSI") filed documents on behalf of the Beneficiary and the trustee without regard to the expectation of the Plaintiffs when they entered the contract that this action could not be done without the expressed permission and signature of the trustee, GW, and the trustee, or Substitute trustee, namely NDEx West (herein "NDEx") having the power to nix any such action if he suspected the Defendant of wrongdoing.

Defendants were fully aware at the time of the contracting that they could do this procedure while the terms and the rules and regulations of the state of CA governing DOT contracts implied otherwise because they were doing it regularly as a course of doing business. They were also aware that the Plaintiffs could not discover the fact that the Defendants could file any document via the signature of the Defendant or an agent for the Defendant, or an agent of that agent to affect a non-judicial foreclosure and that the California courts would give them a free pass under its "Presumption of Correctness" doctrine which had the effect of making any illegal transaction occurring during the recordation of those documents effective for their foreclosure purposes.

Plaintiffs were left with the untenable task of trying to refute the times, dates, signatures, and contents on the documents the Defendants filed under the "Presumption of Correctness" doctrine. Plaintiffs could not contact the trustee with any expectation of the trustee having an "arm's length" relationship with the Defendant as the Defendant hid from the Plaintiffs the fact that the trustee in a DOT was essentially a "straw man" and the entity named in the DOT as the trustee, GW, was an employee of the Defendant, as well as, the Substitute trustee, NDEx. The result was that Plaintiffs were prevented from even being able to reasonably ascertain with whom they were supposed to be dealing with. Inevitably and predictably, Plaintiffs lost their home through an illegal non-judicial foreclosure.

As a consequence of the wrongful conduct in the contracting practices of the Defendants, individually and acting in concert, Plaintiffs were deprived of their ability to finance their home using a contract that provided the proper safeguards to prevent Defendants from illegally foreclosing on their home and in the process ruining their credit standing by way of an illegal non-judicial foreclosure which will take them years to repair, thereby effectively preventing Plaintiff from being able to purchase a home of their own for the foreseeable future.

The means and mechanism by which this result was accomplished by the various Defendants proceeded by way of a complicated scheme involving fraud, misrepresentation, civil conspiracy, and breaches of the general negligence duties of due care and due diligence, the fiduciary duty of trust and confidence existing between financial institutions and their customers, the duties of good faith and fair dealing that underlie all contractual relationships in the state of California, as well as, violations of a number of statutory and regulatory duties imposed by the California Civil and Business & Professions Codes.

The Defendants submitted a demurrer challenging whether the Plaintiffs have presented a cause of action for Actual Fraud, with a suggestion to the Court that Plaintiffs not be allowed to pursue any new discoveries of wrong doing on the part of WS. In light of the fact that the state of CA and the federal are continuing to discover new violations committed by lenders such as WS and Wells Fargo Bank (herein "WFB") to grant either would be a signal to those lenders that their illegal use of the DOT to profit at the expense and agony of the borrowers of the state of CA will go unpunished.

II. STATEMENT OF FACTS

In and before 2005, Defendant WS engaged in a business practice of marketing home loans using a DOT. The business plan of WSB was to quickly bundle the loans in pools and unload them to investors on international securities markets as high interest, "mortgage-backed securities." To put this scheme into effect, WSB cultivated a cadre of mortgage brokers with established ties in minority and lower income communities.

WS used a security instrument (DOT) to contract that gave them the ability to alienate the Plaintiffs' title without their knowledge, without the ability of the trustee charged with protecting the mortgagee's title to do so, and without the ability of the state of California to discover what they were doing.

The scheme worked because the definition of a DOT contract as regulated by the state of CA allowed the Defendants to deceive the mortgagees into believing that the trustee in the security instrument had the power to police the actions of the lender.

That was not true at the time the Plaintiffs used a DOT to contract with Defendants and still is not true today. At no time during the contract could the trustee to that contract deny the Lender any course of action he chose to affect a mortgagee's legal title. With that assurance WSB also developed relationships with banks and loan servicers who would bundle the loans into mortgage-backed securities and/or pooling and servicing agreements so that the loans would be impossible to trace and, thus, allegedly limit liability once the loans became toxic which was inevitable.

The banks got to profit again when the loans went into default because they could skirt any regulation set by the state of California because the person, the trustee, who by the terms of the security instrument, was charged with protecting the legal title of the mortgagee had no legal means to do so. If a trustee objected to anything the banks did, that trustee could be replaced with a signature of the Defendant or an agent of the Defendant without recourse.

On Aug 5, 2005, Pacific Guarantee Mortgage (herein "PGM") directed Plaintiffs to sign a mortgage application that it would submit to WS. What PGM proposed was no money down, 100% financing consisting of an 80% first Trust Deed/Mortgage. While the sale and loan application were pending, Plaintiffs went to WS, located at 1970 Broadway St., Oakland, CA, on Aug. 6th, 2005, to see if they could get a better deal and more questions answered. They made it clear that they were shopping around for a better deal. WS's in house loan agent made material misrepresentations and omitted material facts from its sales pitch. Among other things, Plaintiffs were not told that the trustee, GW, in the security instrument was a Straw Man.

To the contrary Plaintiffs were reminded that their signature on the DOT was in part their approval to the trustee concerning what he could do and what he could not do. They were assured that the trustee was part of the security instrument called a DOT to protect the interests of the mortgagee and the lender. WS' agents left out the part about WS being able to fire the trustee at will, thereby rendering any protection of the mortgagee's interest by a trustee ineffective contractually.

After their default, Plaintiffs attempted to discuss modification of their loan. They were told that their foreclosure would be suspended while it was in process. While they were exploring their options with WFB, WFB violated the terms in the Power of Sale Clause concerning notification before filing a non-judicial foreclosure. The Defendants knew they could get away with filing papers saying they couldn't reach the Plaintiffs while they were talking to the Plaintiffs in a Loan Modification because the state gave them "The Presumption of Correctness" on any documents they filed during a non-judicial procedure process. WS also knew that the trustee worked for them and could not object to any action they took that would impede their desire for a quick foreclosure whether or not it was legal. The inevitable result was that Plaintiffs lost their home at a non-judicial foreclosure when the Defendants refused to work with them in a good faith attempt to modify their loan.

In accordance with the overall scheme, the Defendants, WFB and NDEx West, became, respectively, the servicing agent and substitute trustee for the loan.

In Defendant's Demurrer, it attempts to establish that its foreclosure of the Plaintiffs' property was proper. However, at the very least, Defendants' own documents establish that there is a triable issue of fact as to whether it had the right to foreclose on the Plaintiffs' property. Specifically, Defendants' Request for Judicial Notice fails to attach a copy of the actual Note. Instead, Defendants request judicial notice of the Deed of Trust and an Interest Only Period Fixed/Adjustable-Rate Rider, both of which reference a separate Note, the original of which apparently has not been assigned to and is not in the possession of Defendants. Accordingly, the foreclosure of the Subject Property was improper and in violation of applicable law.

In Defendant's Demurrer it tries to prove that the Plaintiff's claim is a nonspecific fraud claim by attempting to focus the Court's attention only on its foreclosure of the Plaintiffs' loan because of the Plaintiff's' default. Plaintiffs' assert that the true issue before the court is whether WS deceived the Plaintiffs into using a security instrument that they knew or should have known would not protect Plaintiffs interest in their property in the event the Plaintiffs' defaulted or were accused of default.

The issue is not that complicated. The lenders are taking advantage of a flaw in a DOT which renders the neutrality of the trustee void. Defendants like WS and WFB come to court with an arrogance that asks the Courts to ignore that fact. They are asking the Court to ignore the fact that the king is naked, forget that what the Plaintiffs expected, indeed what any average mortgagee would expect a trustee to be in their DOT is just not true. If Plaintiffs can show that the DOT is not what it is held out to be and that the Defendants knew that or should have known that when they were using it to conduct business with it, and the result to the Plaintiffs was a loss of property, credit worthiness to purchase a new property, or other emotional or other tangible loss, then the Plaintiffs have a cause of action for fraud. Plaintiffs should be allowed to let a court decide whether the DOT is a misleading document on its face and whether the knowledge of that fact and the use of it by the Defendants without informing the user is fraudulent.

4A 18p12 - "Deed of Trust – An instrument in use in many states, taking the place and serving the uses of a common-law mortgage, by which the legal title to real property is placed in one or more trustees, to secure the repayment of a sum of money or the performance of other conditions. Bank v. Pierce, 144 Cal. 434, 77 Pac. 1012. (*Black's law Dictionary 2nd Edition*.) A Deed of Trust is a document that embodies the agreement between a lender and a borrower to transfer an interest in the borrower's land to a neutral third party, a trustee, to secure payment of a debt by the borrower. (*West's Encyclopedia of American Law, edition 2. Copyright 2008*)

In the Defendants Demurrer it attempts to sell the court on an idea that since the Plaintiffs had time to read the contract, and the contract was signed in 2005, Plaintiffs should be time-barred by the Statute of Limitations from asserting their cause of action. But the facts show that at least two incidents would have to occur before the Plaintiffs would ever have reason to suspect fraud on the part of the Defendants: (1.) The Plaintiffs would have to default on their loan or be accused of it, and then (2.) Defendants would have to choose to exercise their option to use the Non-judicial Foreclosure Process and arguably (3.) violate one or more of the regulations, rules, and/or laws governing or impacting the exercise of that option.

While there are variations on the principle, well established law clearly states that time begins to run when the cause of action is discovered or should have been discovered. The fact is the Plaintiffs could not have asserted fraud until they were confronted with the fact that they had been misled to believe that the person(trustee), who by definition of a DOT contract was a necessary element in order to make the security instrument Defendant used to be legally a DOT, was a Straw Man. The three essential elements of a DOT by definition as noted in the Plaintiff's Fourth Amended Complaint (herein "4AC") ...are the Borrower, Lender and the trustee.

III. MEMORANDUM OF POINTS AND AUTHORITIES

ARGUMENT

A. PLAINTIFF HAS ADEQUATELY PLEAD EACH AND EVERY CAUSE OF ACTION AGAINST DEFENDANTS

With regard to Plaintiffs' cause of action for Actual Fraud; Intentional, or Negligent Misrepresentation of a fact or Concealment of a material fact.

In Defendant's Demurrer for 4AC page 4 of their Memorandum of P&A line 12 Defendants assert that Plaintiffs did not identify the name of anyone who made any alleged misrepresentation. Plaintiffs assertion is that its cause of action arises out of the fact that a DOT contract is fraudulent on its face because it purports to guarantee a protection of the Plaintiffs interests that it does not do. The particular interests that it does not protect are those that the trustee in a DOT is charged with protecting by the legal definition of a DOT contract (4AC ¶ 18, p12). Plaintiffs cause of action is since the trustee in a DOT is a Straw Man and as such has no true function but to pose as an independent actor who will protect the interests of both the borrower and the lender when he is merely an employee of the lender acting to protect the interest of that lender.

Defendants have continued to dodge this fact by filing numerous demurrers claiming Plaintiffs failed to identify the speaker who claimed their DOT promised such protections. Plaintiffs' assertion is that the entity that made the assertion is WS or any agent that signed the DOT for them. It is well established law that a contract is construed against the drawer. WS can hardly deny they are the producers of the DOT since they are in the business of using DOTs to contract with mortgagees. The mortgagee doesn't come to WS or WFB with a DOT to contract requesting a loan, the mortgagee is presented with a DOT as the means of contracting for a loan by WS or WFB. Plaintiffs can hardly be more specific when it declared that WS's agent was the person who made the misrepresentation about the nature of a DOT as to the protections it provided the Plaintiffs via the contractual obligations the legal definition of a DOT imputes to its trustee. (Title 17 U.S. Code - RESTATEMENT (SECOND) OF AGENCY § 1(1))

In Defendant's Demurrer for 4AC page 4 of their Memorandum of P&A line 12 Defendants assert that Plaintiffs made an allegation in an earlier pleading that directly contradicted the 4AC pleading. This was a typing error. It was meant to say agent for Plaintiffs. The point that Plaintiffs were attempting to make was that even their own agent believed that a DOT provided the protections that it purports to in its legal definition, indeed many lawyers and judges believed it until it became apparent during recent lawsuits that the trustee in a DOT is merely a STRAW MAN with no power to force a lender to obey the requirements of the Power of Sale Clause or prevent the lender from alienating the borrower's legal title. The lenders know that they have the right to fire a trustee at will and substitute a willing trustee.

In Defendant's Demurrer for 4AC page 5 of their Memorandum of P&A line 6 Defendants assert that Plaintiffs do not adequately plead a false representation. Again, we are forced to use time to defend frivolous allegations by Defendant the Plaintiffs clearly pleaded "falsely and fraudulently." (4AC 26, P15, ln 8).

In Defendant's Demurrer for 4AC page 5 of their Memorandum of P&A lines 12-16. Defendants assert that the Plaintiffs failed to make an allegation that the characteristics of the DOT were part of the misrepresentation. Again, it seems that the Defendant has not versed himself in the issues. The Plaintiffs are asserting that their cause of action arises out of the fact that the DOT is fraudulent on its face and that the WS knew or should have known that the DOT did not provide the protections of the mortgagees' interests that it purports to do.

In Defendant's Demurrer for 4AC page 5 & 6 of their Memorandum of P&A lines 20-28, 1. Defendants assert that the descriptions of the law and trust terms governing the trustee are simply wrong. Defendants offer no facts that prove this. The fact that any lender has the power to fire a DOT trustee at will is ipso facto that the trustee has no power to deny the transfer of a borrower's legal title if the foreclosure rules are not followed. As a matter of fact, while the Defendant is frivolously making that statement, he knows that the DOT allows the lender to alienate the borrower's legal title with the lender's signature or any agent of the lender.

In Defendant's Demurrer for 4AC page 6 of their Memorandum of P&A lines 11-28. Defendants assert that the lender or an agent of the lender could not alienate the borrower title or skirt the rules of the Power of Sale Clause. The courts are full of cases and incidents where the lenders have done all the above. Defendants are just playing with words and making denials it knows has been disproven by thousands of court cases.

When Defendant asserts that Plaintiffs failed to plead knowledge and intent, Plaintiffs assert that they have adequately pleaded that WS was aware that they were using an instrument that on its face could not protect the interests of the Plaintiffs as it purports to do.

The causal connection has been established by the Plaintiffs that it was WS choice of the security instrument(DOT) that enabled WFB to use the Non-judicial Foreclosure procedure to illegally foreclose on the Plaintiffs thereby depriving them of their home, their credit rating to buy a new one and contributing to the emotional distress that would be expected when one is confronted by a monied entity that has the ability to use a contract to deprive them of their home and the means to purchase another.

Defendant asserts that Plaintiffs are attempting to add a negligent misrepresentation claim. Plaintiffs are merely pleading in the alternative for the cause of action of Actual Fraud. The negligent misrepresentation was that the security instrument (DOT) that was chosen by WS represented a false fact at the time that a trustee in a DOT had no power to protect the interests of the Plaintiffs. This was true whenever the occasion arose where the actions of the trustee were required to insure that protection.

Defendants assert that Plaintiffs Concealment claims fail but Plaintiffs assert that they have met the burden to show that WS concealed that the security instrument (DOT) they chose to contract with the Plaintiffs could not protect the interests of the Plaintiffs because they knew that the trustee was a Straw Man.

IV. CONCLUSION

Defendant's scheme to use a DOT to gain control over the Plaintiffs' legal title and enable it to quickly foreclose on the Plaintiffs without the protections they fraudulent led Plaintiffs to believe the trustee in a DOT would provide was, not only unlawful; it was "unreasonable" and "unfair." It is in violation of the law, the harm to Plaintiff outweighs any benefit to Defendants, and it was likely to deceive. Defendants argue that they are immune from liability because they did not make the actual misrepresentations to Plaintiff. However, Defendants cannot avoid liability under B&P § 17200 because Plaintiff has properly alleged a scheme which includes not just the individual broker who made the representations but all the entities that aided and abetted, profited, benefited, and participated in the joint venture and conspiracy. See In re Countrywide Financial Corporation, 601 F. Supp. 2d 1201, 1220 (S.D. Cal. 2009).

However, if the Court doesn't agree, then surely the fact that the Defendants were aware that the definition of a foreclosure trustee for the purposes of a Deed of Trust is found in California case law. In Hatch v. Collins (1990) 225 Cal. App. 3d 1104, 1111-1112, the California 1st District Court of Appeals provides a detailed discussion of the Deed of Trust trustee's legal obligations: (4) A trustee under a Deed of Trust has neither the powers nor the obligations of a strict trustee; rather, he serves as a kind of common agent for the trustor and the beneficiary. (3 Witkin, Summary of Cal. Law (9th ed. 1987) Security Transactions in Real Property, § 7, p. 520; Stephens, Partain & Cunningham v. Hollis (1987) 196 Cal. App.3d 948, 955 [242 Cal. Rptr. 251] (Hollis).) The Defendants knew at the time of contracting with the Plaintiffs that they could compromise the common agency status of the trustee by and/or his ability to be a common agent for the Plaintiffs by firing the trustee if he attempted to perform any duty they were not in agreement with. They also knew at the time of the contracting that they could compromise the trustee in this way without the knowledge of the Plaintiffs. His agency is a passive one, for the limited purpose of conducting a sale in the event of the trustor's default or reconveying the property upon satisfaction of the debt. (4 Miller & Starr, op. cit. Supra, § 9.3, p. 16; see Fleisher v. Continental Auxiliary Co. (1963) 215 Cal. App.2d 136, 139 [30 Cal. Rptr. 137].) Often the trustee is a title company, which is unaware of its selection as trustee and has no knowledge of either the transaction or the identity of the beneficiary. (4 Miller & Starr, op. cit. supra, § 9.3, p. 15.) Consequently, "The use of the term `trustee' in the Deed of Trust is unfortunate and misleading. The `trustee' of a Deed of Trust is not a trustee at all in 1112*1112 a technical or strict sense.... He does not assume the obligations which are imposed on a trustee by operation of law, and the statutes applicable to trustees of express trusts do not apply to deeds of trust. The trustee of a Deed of Trust does not possess the personal confidence for the benefit of another required for a true trust relationship." (4 Miller & Starr, op. cit. Supra, § 9.3, at pp. 13-14, italics added; see also Hollis, supra,196 Cal. App.3d at pp. 955-956, holding that trustee may acquire the property at a foreclosure sale for his own benefit.) A trustee, therefore, while an agent for both the beneficiary and the trustor, does not stand in a fiduciary relationship to either. (Baron v. Colonial Mortgage Service Co. (1980) 111 Cal. App.3d 316, 323 [168 Cal. Rptr. 450].) [4] (1d) This court dicta points out the claim of Plaintiffs that the DOT is misleading to the point of being both fraudulent, as to its intentions by the CA legislature to provide a Contract with a neutral trustee who would be able to protect the interest of the mortgagee, and unconscionable as to the effect of being a viable contract since it gives one party, the lender, an unconscionable advantage contractually. The lender can assume all the duties of the trustee as described in Cal. Civ. Code §§ 2923.4 – 2944.7 and foreclose on the mortgagee in any manner he wishes. The actor acting as the trustee on behalf of the lender can avoid legal responsibility and if he objects the lender is free to fire him and replace him with a willing trustee of his choice. It is true, as the Hatches repeatedly points out, that a trustee has a general duty to conduct the sale "fairly, openly, reasonably, and with due diligence," exercising sound discretion to protect the rights of the mortgagor and others. (Baron v. Colonial Mortgage Service Co., supra, 111 Cal. App.3d 316, 323; Bank of Seoul & Trust Co. v. Marcione (1988) 198 Cal. App.3d 113, 118 [244 Cal. Rptr. 1]; Block v. Tobin (1975) 45 Cal. App.3d 214, 221 [119 Cal. Rptr. 288].) It by no means follows, however that this duty is a fiduciary one. These dicta that only the Lenders would be aware of on average. Concealment of this fact from the mortgagee gives the lender an unfair advantage and allows him to contractually take advantage of the mortgagee.

Thus, Defendants conduct constitutes a violation of B&P § 17200 pursuant to the unlawful, unfair, and fraudulent prongs, and they can be held liable for said conduct. Moreover, as set forth above, the violations of Cal. Civ. Code § 2923.5 and 2923.6 also provide a basis for a claim for relief based on violation of B&P § 17200. Accordingly, Plaintiffs' claim should not be dismissed.

The Plaintiffs have shown herein that the demurrer to Fourth Amended Complaint should not be granted and that the Plaintiffs have all the facts that are sufficient to state the associated cause of action, and/or the allegations of the Plaintiffs show enough theory to allow the Plaintiffs to amend the complaint. At this stage of pleading the allegations must be taken as true, and the complaint is to be construed liberally.

For the reasons stated herein, Plaintiffs respectfully request that the demurrer to Fourth Amended Complaint be denied, and Plaintiffs be allowed to have their day in court to have the merits of whether a DOT is misleading on its face and argue that Defendant committed fraud when they used the non-judicial foreclosure process illegally to foreclose Plaintiffs.

Dated: August 29, 2013

Respectfully submitted,

Douglas J Boggs   Michelle A Moquin

Pro Se Plaintiff   Pro Se Plaintiff

After I submitted this information in the fourth amended complaint and the defense attempted to argue various points of law to demurrer the complaint, I chose not to argue or respond to any of their legal points or case law they were spewing out. Because, none of it was relevant. I responded by stating that they must first prove that they had a true and legitimate contract to begin with. They must first prove that they had and were in possession of a true and legitimate Deed of Trust contract as outlined by the rule of law. I was now holding them to task to prove that the Deed of Trust was legitimate as per the rules of law in the state of CA. They must show the court that the trustee held an independent position in the Deed of Trust agreement. They must show the court that the trustee would be able to hold the banks accountable for wrongdoing against a borrower's title without recourse against them by the banks if the banks chose to do so. They must show that all parties had signed off on all documents and changes to the Deed of Trust agreement throughout the duration of the contract.

The defense was unable to do so. The court was now in the unenviable position to side with a homeowner who had proven to the court how all the Deeds of Trust in the state of CA were based on VOID paperwork dating back from Jan 1, 1998.

After this information was presented in the courtroom and there was no response available from the defense, the judge looked at me and smiled and said, "Mr. Boggs, I know exactly what you are trying to state now. I understand your argument and see where you are going with this. Since we have nothing else from the defense," he stated, "I will have to take this under consideration in my chambers." Note that when he said this, the courtroom was filled with other people from other cases and other witnesses who were listening to and following our case quite intently. So, his "taking into consideration" meant that he would not rule in the courtroom so that all the people would hear his response or decision.

He then subsequently dismissed our case and took the documents from public view and access. This was how he silenced my court documents. His decision was to allow Wells Fargo Bank to issue a fraudulent contract. His reasons why should be clear at this point.

Again, it is fraudulent because of the fact that there was no legitimate trustee participating in the contract. Since the bank failed to represent this fact to me prior to the signing of the contract, it made the contract void. This meant that all other Deed of Trust agreements in the state of CA could now file an actionable defense against the lender in the other contracts, therefore negating every Deed of Trust in the state of CA. This also meant that, by law, all the money spent on all the contracts should be returned to the borrowers who were lent money under the banks' deceptive practices and misrepresentation of facts. This meant that the entire non-judicial foreclosure system was a fraud and broken. This meant that all foreclosures in CA must immediately be stopped and reviewed. He also knew that there were thirty-two Deed of Trust states in the United States, which all had similar rules allowing similar practices across the nation. This would have set a precedent with a domino effect that would have collapsed Wall Street much more than what took place in 2008. Not only would this have set a precedent that could negate all Deed of Trust contracts in thirty-two states, but it would have also negated every mortgage-backed security that used any of those mortgage agreements that the Deeds of Trust were held with. No judge is going to sign off on that. Perhaps you now understand why the judge silenced my court documents? Is this justice? Is this corruption? Is this complacency?

This is our judicial system. There won't be a ruling on truth, but only a ruling that works in the best interest of keeping the flow of capitalism as we have come to know it: despite the fraud, despite the corruption, despite any truth.

The court ruled the case closed without leave to amend. Not only was it without leave to amend, but if you were to look at the courthouse files, you could no longer find the case files of over 114 filings of various motions and responses. The judge removed any relevant documents to my points of fact from the public record. There were only a couple of documents that were able to be found in the courthouse files online for public view, and those were documents written by the defendants and that only benefited Wells Fargo Bank.

None of the information that I had uncovered was made public. None of my points of law that were laid out definitively were able to be viewed by the public any longer. The case was silenced.

I couldn't let go. I couldn't move on. I still couldn't understand why the contracts changed in their construction back in 1998. Why was it that the signatures of all parties were no longer "deemed necessary" by the courts from this point forward? Why was there seemingly no oversight to the Deed of Trust contracts that were being used and submitted to the county recorder. Or why were any of the substitutions of trustee changes to the contracts being submitted without all parties signing or even being notified of those changes to the contract? What were the new changes in contract law or to the statute of frauds that would allow contracts to be handled so differently than the law had dictated for nearly 400 years?

If I were going to take this any further and appeal this ruling as well, I needed to find that silver bullet of evidence. I needed a smoking gun.

The Making of Senate Bill 1638 to Amend CA Civil Code 2934a

The history of property recordation takes us back to the Greeks. Our more modern means and standardized processes come out of old English Common Law and the Statute of Frauds. This has been a rule since 1677 and is still valid law throughout the United States today. It requires that all real property contract agreements, such as leases to sales, and conveyances of transfer, were to be in writing, dated, and signed by all parties involved in the contract agreement. The purpose of the law was to help eliminate the fraudulent practices that many people had been attempting. It helped to prevent perjury and gave the courts of the day more information with which to adjudicate land title disputes. It also helped to stabilize true land prices of the day, creating a valuable and appreciable asset for the title holder. The monarchies had found a way to appreciate and control assets of their holdings through their ability to trade and sell a property with a legal value. The landholders with more grand estates held the keys to the kingdom, although the commoner began to feel the stability of being a landowner.

Society was coming out of the feudal period when rich landholding monarchs owned the property and had serfs working the land. Serfs is a term used for someone who works a piece of land for someone else but is given a stipend to survive and food to eat. Gradually, privately held real estate began to take hold. As there were little to no standing armies during this time outside of the monarchies such as the French, English, and a few others, for landholders to protect their land, they would have to travel away from their property and families to fight for their rights and freedoms. When they left to head off to battle, the landholders would leave their property in the care of a friend or neighbor, who at times would refuse to give the land back upon the return of the owner who had gone to battle.

The Statute of Frauds created a set of written documents that held a legal standing for someone to prove their ownership of a parcel of land. Eventually, a notary became commonplace as a means of true legal assurance through the act of notarization of documents. This action would simplify the legal verification that all parties who signed the documents were the true and correct persons who were party to the contract. Without a set of these documents, no one in their right mind would want to invest in property as anyone could come in and claim it to be their own. This means of a legal binding document was necessary to possess in such a developing world as it showed the accurate property recordation of the landowner and who was the true title holder.

California became part of the United States after being admitted to the Union on September 9, 1850. Coming straight out of the gold rush, California quickly became a leader in legislation for real estate issues. One of the very first acts that the legislature of the new state named California performed was to adopt a recording system in order to create public notice or evidence of title or interests in the title, which could be conveniently collected and maintained in a safe public place. The intent behind the idea of this recording system was to inform interested parties planning to purchase or otherwise deal with land about the ownership and condition of the title.

California has a long 170-year history of the way its courts have applied legal principles regarding the title to real property and the conveyance/transfer of the title. The development and evolution of these principles also apply to encumbering a title to real property through mortgages or Deeds of Trust and to provide notice of and to evidence monetary claims against the title in the form of liens. This history is documented by the creation of constitutional provisions and statutes, and subsequently by a long line of case law. In the absence of some specifically applicable constitutional or statutory provisions, the common law/case law prevails.

This design of the system was to protect lenders and purchasers against secret or private party sales, transfers, or conveyances, and from undisclosed encumbrances/liens. The purpose of this system is to allow the title to the real property to be freely transferable. The California Legislature adopted a recording system modeled after the system established by the original American Colonies. It was strictly an American device for safeguarding the ownership of and the encumbering of land/property. Recording of sales, transfers, or conveyances and encumbrances/liens as part of a public record was established to impart constructive notice. This system of recording is known as the "race recording", or as the "race-notice recording" statute/law.

California got its basic principles of law governing title to real property from England's Common Law, which has been generally implemented by case law known as stare decisis. Stare decisis is a Latin phrase that means "to stand by a decision". As it is applied, stare decisis is a doctrine to bind a trial court by higher court decisions, such as appellate and supreme court decisions that become precedents on a legal question raised in the lower trial court. Reliance on such precedents is required of lower courts until a higher court changes the rule.

So, not only does our judicial system have a set of rules or laws as they are created by the legislature, but those rules, those laws that the legislature has created are then interpreted by lawyers and judges in every case brought to court. Lawyers attempt to litigate their arguments in their case in a way that will best serve their clients' side of the story. They do this by interpreting the intent of the rule of law, or the intent with which the legislature was acting when they voted on a specific rule of law. Or, this was true of the intent of the society in which the law was originally written, and how that intent might reflect on how our society is today. The lawyers argue about the intent of the wording of the law to the court, and the judge then takes this argument into consideration in his or her ruling, based on the arguments and the existing rule of law and precedents set since the law was put on the books. This means that the law isn't simply the law as it is written, but it must also deal with the intent of the legislature and the judge's perceptions of the intent, along with the precedents that have become part and parcel of the framework of the original law as it was written.

The one thing that is true about the making of a bill into a law is that it takes a lot of time, taxpayers' dollars, and many different people to orchestrate the entire bill into becoming a law or an amendment to an existing law. There are numerous legal and legislative channels that must be dealt with, and in each of those channels there can be compromising opinions and views that create hurdles for the parties who are interested in finally getting the bill to the floor for its legislative vote. The parties involved want to make sure that after all the time and money spent on the preparation of the bill to reach its voting day, the proposal passes, and the bill's constructors find the sense of victory and success of their bill becoming law.

The story behind Senate Bill 1638 began in the year 1984. It was more than a decade prior to the conception of Bill 1638, but the wheels began turning to create the chaos of what was to come.

In February of 1996, attorneys Michael J. Arnold and Kristian E. Foy, on behalf of the Mortgage Association of California, wrote a statement of support for Senate Bill 1638. The Mortgage Association of California sponsored this bill, which Senator Ross Johnson, of La Habra, Orange County, CA, supported. Johnson and his staff worked on this issue for months before the senator took the bill's third draft and amended form to the floor for a vote.

The background of the bill held to the premise that the bill would be specific to what was known as "multi-lender loans or loans that had more than one, but as many as ten different lenders that would be involved in one specific real estate transaction.

In July of 1982, the CA Department of Corporations adopted a regulation called the "Multi-Lender Rule". This regulation was known as Regulation 260.105.30 and it permitted mortgage brokers to arrange loans involving up to ten private investors. This "Multi-Lender Rule" became increasingly important to the brokerage and lending industries as the price of real estate continued to rise to a point where most larger loans were being conducted using multiple lenders. This new rule allowed the investors to spread their risk by investing their capital in a series of loans, rather than having to commit such a large portion of their investment capital to only one loan. In subsequent years, this rule soon became a mainstay to the brokerage borrowing and lending industries.

The problem—claimed by the Mortgage Association of California who sponsored the bill—that seemed to be arising in the real estate industry was that the prices across the board for real estate were rising dramatically. So much so, that there were more and more transactions needing multiple investors to make the transaction work. In nearly all multiple lender transactions, the appointment of a trustee was involved.

The appointment of a trustee is an integral part of any note using a Deed of Trust, as well as being a vital part of any transaction using multiple lenders. The trustee is empowered to take action on behalf of the multiple beneficiaries in the event of a foreclosure. It is also the trustee's position to make sure that the rules and regulations of the lenders are followed in accordance with the rules of law to protect the borrower's title against any wrongdoing on behalf of the beneficiary. There are various circumstances that might arise in which a substitution of the trustee is either desired or necessary. As an example, the original trustee named in the Deed of Trust might no longer be in business, or the lender has elected to change the servicing agent, and the servicing agent might prefer to use a trustee with which they are more familiar and have done business with previously. Under the current law at that time, the substitution of a new trustee required the written approval from each of the investors.

The reason for this is that this is basic contract law. It is imperative that ALL parties to the transaction must be informed of any changes to the contract agreement, not simply the beneficiaries.

However, it seemed that the Mortgage Association of CA wanted the wording to specify beneficiary and have no mention of the borrower, or trustor, having any needs or protections allotted them by the trustee in the transaction. Their position was solely on behalf of the lenders. So much so, that they went on to state that obtaining the required approval is frequently difficult and time consuming. An example they used was that one of the investors may be away for an extended vacation, medically incapacitated, or be unreachable for other reasons. Additionally, they claimed there had been instances where a small investor in a multi-lender transaction would demand that he or she be paid in full before agreeing to allow substitution of the new trustee. It was also their claim that it was frequently essential that a new trustee be appointed expeditiously to accomplish foreclosure proceedings or to take other appropriate action in connection with the protection of the interests of the beneficiaries.

The Mortgage Association of California seemed to have the solution. In February of 1996, Senator Ross Johnson began backing a new bill, Senate Bill 1638 ("SB 1638"), which was sponsored by the Mortgage Association of California. The requirement at that time was that there needed to be a 100% approval from the beneficiaries. This, according to Michael J. Arnold and Kristian E. Foy, on behalf of the Mortgage Association of California, was that this was costly, time consuming, and created the opportunity for one investor to take advantage of the others by withholding consent until other demands were met. Moreover, it gave equal power to all beneficiaries in the transaction. It was therefore the intention of the new bill, SB 1638, to redistribute that power to the largest investor in the transaction and strip away any power and position to the lesser investors in the transaction. So, this new bill would permit the substitution of a new trustee under a multi-lender transaction with the approval of beneficiaries holding a majority interest (more than 50%) in the note and Deed of Trust. They claimed this was a fair proposal that would protect the interests of all multi-lender beneficiaries by allowing a new trustee to expeditiously execute the actions, which were in the best interests of the note holders. It seemed in their position to the CA Senate for SB 1638 that they appeared to have no regard for the welfare of the smaller investors in a multiple-lender transaction (MLT), or the borrower's position, or of the protection of the borrower's title.

However, a few months later, on April 17, 1996, Senator Ross Johnson received a letter from the Department of Corporations stating their opposition to this new proposed bill. The letter held the department's position to oppose the bill unless there were amendments, and until such time they would only remain neutral to the bill. It was the position of the Department of Corporations that SB 1638 sets forth procedures for substituting a trustee under a Deed of Trust upon real property in connection with multi-lender transactions that are exempt from qualification with the Commissioner of Corporations. Let's make note that all these proposals at this time were very clear in that the bill was being structured to deal with multi-lender transactions, and there was no mention of any need to change any rules or any reason that single lender transactions were to be of any issue.

The Department of Corporations went on to state their concern that this bill had the potential to result in self-dealing and conflicts of interests. It was their position to name specifically real estate brokers in this concern, but we have now come to see that the concern held much merit, however, the parties of concern were the financial corporations themselves. The example used in their letter to Senator Johnson was that a broker or its affiliate holding 50% or more of the interest or notes may appoint itself as the trustee of the note and Deed of Trust. Let this sink in for a moment. The concern was clear from the beginning that this possibility could take place: the idea of corruption of a party holding a major interest in the note to make itself beneficiary AND trustee to the transaction. Although, at this time, the concern was hidden in the rhetoric of a corrupt broker, we have come to experience this corruption head-on as corporations, more specifically financial corporations, are the main parties guilty of this action. Another example that the Department of Corporations cited was that the bill might create the potential for misappropriation of funds for the purpose of selling the property and receiving funds for distribution to investors.

The department voiced their concern that they were unaware of any demonstrable evidence to support the need for this bill. Nor was the department aware of any information to demonstrate whether the lack of an existing trustee is a pervasive problem. In addition, a multi-lender transaction typically involves only ten investors, so it begs the question whether it is difficult to obtain consent from such a small group. They went on to say that existing law already sets forth procedures for substituting a trustee without the need for a new code section. The new code section was unnecessary and confusing.

In closing, however, the Department of Corporations added that,

"Assuming there is justification to support this bill, the Department of Corporations recommends amendments to: (1) exclude the interest or notes held by a real estate broker or its affiliate from the provision that allows a majority interest to substitute a new trustee; (2) conform the procedures for substituting a trustee to the provisions of the multi-lender rule; and (3) insert the amendments into an existing code section relating to substitution of trustee."

The department attached the amendments that they referred to in their letter in Legislative Counsel format to make those changes easier for Senator Johnson to add into the wording of the bill.

Through the submission of the Department of Corporations amendments, there was a rewrite of the proposed bill. This rewrite was sent to the State Senate floor again for a vote on June 26, 1996. It was approved unanimously in a 33-0 vote. The summary of this bill addressed the substitution of trustees and collective decisions made by beneficiaries in the context of "multi-lender transactions" (MLT's). I want to express the importance of that line in the summary. This bill was designed specifically for MLT transactions to help multiple lenders in a transaction eliminate the necessity for a unanimous agreement. It was not designed or put to the floor to be a part of the substitution of trustee in a single-lender transaction. It was originally set up to clean up and streamline the multiple-lender transactions needed to substitute a trustee. It would help to not restrict the ability of beneficiaries in MLTs to agree by contract to allow substitutions. It would allow a substitution by a simple majority, or allow the larger stake holders, or those with 50% or more in the transaction, to have more voice should all the investors be unavailable to make the substitution move forward. It did not require the beneficiaries in a MLT to have a unanimous consent for trustee substitution for other decisions.

There was one thing that struck me when I was reviewing the

analysis to this bill, which was written by a lawyer named Carrie-Lee Early, was her manipulation of the current law. The senators were reading this information and were basing their decisions on this information from a licensed attorney of the CA state bar who was to have known, understood, and educated the senators on the subject well enough for them to make informed decisions prior to their vote. No senator is knowledgeable on all the issues, rules of law, and other necessary policies that dictate the background of each bill that comes across the floor to a vote. These elected officials can be doctors, dentists, businesspersons, activists, or simply concerned citizens who were eventually elected to their positions. They are normal people who are relying on the information that is supplied in the analysis to help educate them on some of the issues pertaining to each individual proposed bill. The senators use this analysis to learn about the existing law and summary legal advice that is given to them by lawyers who are employed by the State Legislature.

Carrie-Lee Early was an attorney for the Assembly Judiciary Committee. It was the Assembly Judiciary Committee's task to help clear up questions and to inform the senators of the nuances of the proposed bill or amended bill by constructing the analysis of the Mortgage Association of California who was sponsoring the bill being supported by Senator Johnson. In her analysis, there was a section titled EXISTING LAW. The first section of this analysis read: "1) Governs and defines right and duties of the parties to a DOT, which is a real property security device given to secure a payment of indebtedness. There are three types of party to a DOT: the trustor (mortgagor and usually, debtor), the trustee (title company, bank or other person who holds the legal title with power to sell on default of the trustor), and the beneficiary (creditor). As a practical matter, a DOT functions as a mortgage agreement containing a power of sale that allows the trustee to sell the property upon the default of the trustor. This procedure is known as a "non-judicial foreclosure". Procedures for exercising the power of sale are set forth in statute. Foreclosure may also be obtained by a beneficiary through judicial foreclosure. 2) Allows the trustee identified in a Deed of Trust to be substituted by the recording of a document acknowledging the substitution by all the beneficiaries under the DOT. The substitution document must contain specified information, such as the date on which the underlying DOT was recorded, and the name of the new trustee. Depending upon when the substitution is made, the beneficiaries may have to notify the trustee of record and those persons entitled to receive notice of default. 3) Does not restrict the ability of beneficiaries in MLTs to agree by contract to allow substitutions by a simple majority or to be governed by majority decisions with respect to other decisions (such as whether to foreclose)."

The background of the analysis states that the Multi-Lender Rule exempts MLTs from certain securities regulations. MLTs are lending agreements secured by real estate that involve no more than ten lenders/investors (beneficiaries). To qualify for the exemption, a MLT must comport with various rules pertaining to the mortgage broker's solicitation, the structuring of the loan, and the qualifications of the beneficiaries. The Multi-Lender Rule states that the transaction documents must require that beneficiaries who hold 50% or more interest in the unpaid dollar amount of the applicable interest or votes may "determine and direct the actions to be taken on behalf of all holders in the event of default or with respect to other matters requiring the direction or approval of the holders, and that they may designate the broker, servicing agent, or other person to so act on their behalf". The Multi-Lender Rule has become important in recent years due to high real estate values and the need for larger loans by borrowers.

The arguments in support attempt to make clear that according to the Mortgage Association of California—the bill's sponsor—that the bill is necessary to address situations in which the substitution of a trustee is necessary, but not all the beneficiaries (lenders/investors) in a multi-lender loan are readily available to authorize the substitution. For example, one of the investors may be away on an extended vacation, medically incapacitated, or simply unreachable for other reasons. The sponsor also states that there have been cases in which a small investor in a multi-lender transaction had demanded that he or she be paid before agreeing to allow substitution of a new trustee. In these examples, the current requirement for 100% approval from the beneficiaries is costly and time-consuming.

There were never any arguments in opposition to this bill as its analysis was written in this manner. But what if it were written in a way that held true to the rule of law to allow the senators who were to vote on this bill to be given a more well-rounded depiction of the rule of law as it pertains to real estate and contract law? What if it were written in a way that gave the senators more detailed information on the legal statutes set forth by the CA Supreme Court only eight years prior to the bill being pushed through the CA Senate.

In May of 1978, in Garfinkle v. Superior Court of Contra Costa County (Wells Fargo Bank - respondent), the supreme court ruled through a unanimous view. In the opinion, authored by Justice Manuel (Wiley W Manuel), they were careful to include "Similarly, we are not convinced that the state has encouraged or facilitated non-judicial foreclosure by enacting comprehensive and detailed regulations governing that process. As we stated earlier, these statutory regulations were enacted primarily for the benefit of the trustor and for the greatest part limit the creditors' otherwise unrestricted exercise of the contractual power of sale upon default by the trustor..." They knew and expressed their concern pertaining to the non-judicial foreclosure process and how it can act against the interest of the trustor, or more generally, the borrower and title owner. They could envision the unrestricted exercise of the contractual power against the borrower in a non-judicial foreclosure action. This case specifically was in relation to the argument that Wells Fargo was attempting to present that the state or the federal courts had no jurisdiction in a non-judicial foreclosure action since there was a trustee involved, thereby creating a private action, and contending that it did not satisfy the state action requirements of the due process clause of the State Constitution. The court went on to clarify how a non-judicial foreclosure action did in fact satisfy the due process clause of the State Constitution, however, they were careful to include wording stating that "...it cannot realistically be claimed that the state, by acting to protect the debtor, has thereby become the partner of the creditor so that the creditor's actions are converted into the actions of the state. (; Barrera v. Security Building & Investment Corporation, supra.) fn. 17[21 Cal. 3D 280].

In the 1978 Garfinkle v. Contra Costa County ruling it was clearly stipulated by the unanimous opinion and the intention of that ruling was made clear that "...the trustee has an independent duty, as the common agent of the parties," (See Ainsa v. Mercantile Trust Co. (1917) 174 Cal. 504, 510 [163 P. 898]; Pacific S. & L. Co. v. N. American etc. Co. (1940) 37 Cal. App. 2D 307, 310 [99 P.2d 355]).

Only seven years had passed when in August 1985, the Supreme Court of CA heard I. E. Associates v. Safeco Title Ins. Co. (1985) 39 Cal.3d 281, 216 Cal. Rptr. 438; 702 P.2d 596. This was also a unanimous decision with the opinion authored by Justice Kaus. It was in this decision that the details of a trustee were more narrowly defined, once again as they "cited in Garfinkle—merely contain the general statement that a trustee under an ordinary Deed of Trust is the common agent of both parties and is required to act impartially." The opinion of California's highest court went on to state "... In short, there is no authority for the proposition that a trustee under a Deed of Trust owes any duties with respect to exercise of the power of sale beyond those specified in the deed and the statutes. There are, moreover, persuasive policy reasons that militate against a judicial expansion of those duties. The non-judicial foreclosure statutes — an alternative to judicial foreclosure — reflect a carefully crafted balancing of the interests of beneficiaries, trustors, and trustees. Beneficiaries, of course, want quick and inexpensive recovery of amounts due under promissory notes in default. Trustors, on the other hand, need protection against the forfeiture of valuable property rights. Trustees, the middlemen, need to have clearly defined responsibilities to enable them to discharge their duties efficiently and to avoid embroiling the parties in time-consuming and costly litigation. In taking all these concerns into account, the statutes strike an overall balance favoring the protection of trustors. (Garfinkle v. Superior Court, supra, 21 Cal.3d at p. 278; Smith v. Allen (1968) 68 Cal.2d 93, 96 [65 Cal. Rptr. 153, 436 P.2d 65].)

The Legislature's decision not to require the trustee to search for the trustor's current address, but to compel him to use it if it is known, is consistent with this careful balancing of competing interests to maintain the overall working of the system under which a trustor should normally [39 Cal.3d 289] receive actual notice. The beneficiary ordinarily would know if the trustor had moved, and the statute requires him to notify the trustee of any new address he knows. The efficacy of the system supports striking the balance in favor of requiring the trustor to keep the beneficiary and trustee informed of his current address. It is a simple task for the trustor, whereas imposing on the trustee a duty of taking reasonable steps to discover the trustor's current address would bring far more cost and uncertainty into the system. Litigation would be likely any time a person failed to receive actual notice, since one could always argue that the steps taken were insufficient.

This wording clearly shows the intention of the Supreme Court of

California to specify the independence of a trustee in a Deed of Trust agreement. The opinion talks of "... a carefully crafted balancing of the interests of beneficiaries, trustors, and trustees."

Using the word "middlemen" and detailing the balance of interests by naming the three independent parties in a Deed of Trust agreement as the beneficiaries, trustors, and trustees, the detailed wording makes clear the independent position of the trustee in a Deed of Trust agreement.

With all that said, this brings us back to the wording used by attorney Carrie-Lee Early for the Assembly Judiciary Committee. Remember that she cited in the EXISTING LAW section of her Analysis that "... There are three types of party to a DOT: the trustor (mortgagor and also usually, debtor), the trustee (title company, bank or other person, who holds the legal title with power to sell on default of the trustor), and the beneficiary (creditor)."

So, here was an attorney giving the legal advice in her analysis of the bill to the senators, many of whom may or may not be learned in the rule of law. In this, she states that the trustee can be a bank. This statement on its own might be true, but what she does not stipulate and clarify to the senators who might read her analysis is that the trustee cannot be the bank who is also the beneficiary to the Deed of Trust. This was never cleared and stipulated. The California Supreme Court has ruled with clarity that the trustee must be independent in a Deed of Trust agreement. The wording in the analysis did not clarify enough, which might have misrepresented the truth to the senators. Also, the analysis stated that the trustee was the party who holds the legal title with power to sell on default. The misrepresentation here is the wording that the trustee holds legal title. The trustee holds title on behalf of the title owner who is the trustor. The trustee does not hold legal title whatsoever. The supreme court was clear in this when they wrote their concern on this specific issue "... In short, there is no authority for the proposition that a trustee under a Deed of Trust owes any duties with respect to exercise of the power of sale beyond those specified in the deed and the statutes." Their intention in the 1985 ruling was to build more defined clarity as to the position of the trustee. They were showing their concern about the necessity of the independence of the trustee, and to not have the beneficiary and the trustee able to intermingle their positions, as it would clearly inflict on the rights of the **Fourteenth** Amendment of the Constitution of the United States. "The Fourteenth Amendment prohibits the State from depriving any person of life, liberty, or property, without due process of law; but it adds nothing to the rights of one citizen as against another." (United States v. Cruikshank (1875) 92 U.S. 542, 554 [23 L. Ed. 588, 592].)

In the I.E. Associates v. Safeco Title Insurance Co. (1985) ruling, the supreme court wanted to give more detail and specificity to the position of the trustee than the held and quoted previous ruling from Garfinkle v. Contra Costa County (1978). They were expressing their concern for the delicacy of the situation to make sure that the expansion of the power of the trustee is held in check. This was noted specifically to protect the title and the trustor, who is the owner of the title.

If the beneficiary is also able to act as the trustee, then there is no separation of the parties, no independence of the trustee, and therefore the idea of a true Deed of Trust as defined by the California Supreme Court is in fact a falsity.

Once you see behind the proverbial curtain, you will find that "it's actually all quite simple, but so corrupt." Why do we call it a justice system when justice is gone? Why do we call it a trustee when it is in fact a strawman? Why do we call it a Deed of Trust when there is no trust involved? Why do we call it a non-judicial foreclosure procedure when the courts are partisan to the fraud?

Perhaps it is called non-judicial because you will never find true justice.

It all comes down to this: "The banks are incapable of proving that the trustee is in fact independent in the Deed of Trust contract that the bank used as the instrument to attach the home as collateral against the mortgage. The bank is incapable of proving that the trustee has the power to protect the homeowner from any wrongdoing by the bank during the life of the Deed of Trust contract as described by the need for the trustee to be recognized as an independent party to the Deed of Trust transaction. If the banks are unable to prove the independence of the trustee in a Deed of Trust agreement, then they are in fact committing fraud when using a Deed of Trust agreement when they do not inform the borrower of the fact that the trustee is not independent and is incapable of looking out for the best interests of the borrower in the Deed of Trust. If the bank uses a Deed of Trust agreement, knowing that the trustee is not independent as described by the CA Supreme Court in 1978; Garfinkle v. Superior Court of Contra Costa County, they are in fact committing fraud against the borrower at the inception of the contract, which makes the contract in fact VOID."

Because the bank knows that they are in control of the trustee in a non-judicial foreclosure action, they can foreclose on anyone, anytime, anywhere, whether they have a mortgage or even paid cash for their property. Because the banks know that they have the power to replace the trustee at any time for any reason they see fit, they know that if they wish to, they can file fraudulent paperwork to the County Recorder's Office in a non-judicial foreclosure. Because there is no party looking out for the interest of the property owner and the courts have handed over the justice system to the trustee in a non-judicial foreclosure action. Because the courts have entrusted the trustee, and the CA Supreme Court has ruled that the trustee is to be independent in a Deed of Trust agreement, they have given the judicial power of correctness to all the documents that are filed into the court in a non-judicial foreclosure procedure. The reason the bank or other party can file whatever paperwork they choose in order to foreclose on someone is due to a 1998 rule that changed the rules to the Power of Sale clause. This rule comes from the 1996 Senate bill 1638:

> SB 1638, Johnson. Deeds of Trust: trustee substitution. Existing law sets forth the procedures for the substitution of trustees under a Deed of Trust upon real property or an estate for years therein. This bill would, as an alternative procedure, set forth the procedures for the substitution of trustees under a Deed of Trust upon real property or an estate for years, given to secure an obligation to pay money, by the beneficiary or beneficiaries under the trust deed who hold more than 50% of the record beneficial interest of a series of notes secured by the same real property or of undivided interests in a note secured by real property equivalent to a series transaction. The bill would also establish a process through which all the beneficiaries under a trust deed can agree to be governed by beneficiaries holding more than 50% of the record beneficial interest of a series of notes in real property or interests in a note equivalent to a series transaction, as specified. In order to substitute trustees or agree to be governed by the majority interest holders, all parties to the transaction would be required to sign and record a document containing specified information.

This rule gave the bank power to substitute a new trustee at the will of the bank. This removed the independence of the trustee, thereby destroying any semblance of law to the Power of Sale clause known as CA Civ Code 2924. The use of a Deed of Trust contract without informing the borrower to the fact that the bank will have full control of their title as soon as they sign the contract is misrepresentation. This misrepresentation of the facts constitutes fraud, therein making any Deed of Trust agreement fraudulent on its face and therefore void. Which makes EVERY Deed of Trust agreement in the state of California since Jan 1, 1998, in fact VOID.

There have been some recent attempts to make "changes" to some California law regarding the exact issue that I was litigating in my case about the independence of a trustee. This new change is an attempt to create the façade that the trustee is independent. That the trustee can act in an independent fashion to guard any wrongdoing of the beneficiary to the trustor in a Deed of Trust contract. This does nothing to change the ruling of SB 1638 negating the independence of the trustee. What this does though is gloss over the insinuation that a trustee has independence. Although, there is a big difference between a trustee having the power to not accept appointment of the beneficiary as a new substituted trustee, and the substituted trustee having absolutely no power to protect the borrower's title in a Deed of Trust agreement because of their lack of independence in the Deed of Trust agreement.

Senate Bill No. 306 CHAPTER 474

An act to amend Section 2934a of the Civil Code, relating to mortgages.

[Approved by Governor October 02, 2019. Filed with the Secretary of State October 02, 2019.]

LEGISLATIVE COUNSEL'S DIGEST

SB 306, Morrell. Mortgages and deeds of trust: trustee substitutions. Existing law regulates the terms and conditions of mortgages and deeds of trust. Existing law authorizes a beneficiary of a Deed of Trust to substitute a new trustee for the existing trustee in accordance with certain statutory requirements, and that substitution is not effective in certain cases unless it is signed by the respective parties under penalty of perjury. Under existing law, a trustee named in a recorded substitution of trustee is deemed to be authorized to act in this capacity under the mortgage or Deed of Trust for all purposes from the date the substitution is executed by the mortgagee, beneficiaries, or by their authorized agents. Existing law provides specified methods by which a trustee may resign, including as provided in the trust instrument or, in the case of a revocable trust, with the consent of the person holding the power to revoke the trust. This bill would authorize a trustee to resign or refuse to accept appointment as trustee at that trustee's own election without the consent of the beneficiary or by their authorized agents, under a trust deed upon real property or an estate for years. The bill would require the trustee to give prompt written notice of resignation or refusal to accept appointment to the beneficiary or their authorized agents by mailing, as specified, an envelope containing a notice of resignation of trustee by recording the notice of resignation in each county in which the substitution of trustee under which the trustee was appointed is recorded, and by attaching to the recorded notice an affidavit stating that notice has been mailed to all beneficiaries and their authorized agents, as specified. The bill would make the resignation or refusal to accept appointment of that trustee effective upon the recording of the notice of resignation in each county in which the substitution of trustee under which the trustee was appointed is recorded. The bill would also require the trustee and any successor in interest to that trustee to retain and preserve every writing relating to the trust deed or estate for years under which the trustee was appointed for at least 5 years after a notice of resignation is mailed and recorded. The bill would specify that the resignation of the trustee does not affect the validity of the mortgage or Deed of Trust, except that no action required to be performed by the trustee under those provisions or under the mortgage or Deed of Trust may be taken until a substituted trustee is appointed. The bill would make related conforming and non substantive changes to those provisions. By expanding the crime of perjury, the bill would impose a state-mandated local program. The California Constitution requires the state to reimburse local agencies and school districts for certain costs mandated by the state. Statutory provisions establish procedures for making that reimbursement. This bill would provide that no reimbursement is required by this act for a specified reason.

DIGEST KEY

Vote: majority Appropriation: no Fiscal Committee: yes Local Program: yes

BILL TEXT

THE PEOPLE OF THE STATE OF CALIFORNIA DO ENACT AS FOLLOWS:

SECTION 1.

Section 2934a of the Civil Code is amended to read:

2934a.

(a) (1) The trustee under a trust deed upon real property or an estate for years given to secure an obligation to pay money and conferring no other duties upon the trustee than those which are incidental to the exercise of the power of sale therein conferred, may be substituted by the recording in the county in which the property is located of a substitution executed and acknowledged by either of the following:(A) All of the beneficiaries under the trust deed, or their successors in interest, and the substitution shall be effective notwithstanding any contrary provision in any trust deed executed on or after January 1, 1968.(B) The holders of more than 50 percent of the record beneficial interest of a series of notes secured by the same real property or of undivided interests in a note secured by real property equivalent to a series transaction, exclusive of any notes or interests of a licensed real estate broker that is the issuer or servicer of the notes or interests or of any affiliate of that licensed real estate broker.(2) A substitution executed pursuant to subparagraph (B) of paragraph (1) is not effective unless all the parties signing the substitution sign, under penalty of perjury, a separate written document stating the following:(A) The substitution has been signed pursuant to subparagraph (B) of paragraph (1).(B) None of the undersigned is a licensed real estate broker or an affiliate of the broker that is the issuer or servicer of the obligation secured by the Deed of Trust.(C) The undersigned together hold more than 50 percent of the record beneficial interest of a series of notes secured by the same real property or of undivided interests in a note secured by real property equivalent to a series transaction.(D) Notice of the substitution was sent by certified mail, postage prepaid, with return receipt requested to each holder of an interest in the obligation secured by the Deed of Trust who has not joined in the execution of the substitution or the separate document. The separate document shall be attached to the substitution and recorded in the office of the county recorder of each county in which the real property described in the Deed of Trust is located. Once the document is recorded, it shall constitute conclusive evidence of compliance with the requirements of this paragraph in favor of substituted trustees acting pursuant to this section, subsequent assignees of the obligation secured by the Deed of Trust and subsequent bona fide purchasers or encumbrancers for value of the real property described therein.(3) For purposes of this section, "affiliate of the licensed real estate broker" includes any person as defined in Section 25013 of the Corporations Code that is controlled by, or is under common control with, or who controls, a licensed real estate broker. "Control" means the possession, direct or indirect, of the power to direct or cause the direction of management and policies. (4) The substitution shall contain the date of recordation of the trust deed, the name of the trustor, the book and page or instrument number where the trust deed is recorded, and the name of the new trustee. From the time the substitution is filed for record, the new trustee shall succeed to all the powers, duties, authority, and title granted and delegated to the trustee named in the Deed of Trust. A substitution may be accomplished, with respect to multiple deeds of trust that are recorded in the same county in which the substitution is being recorded and that all have the same trustee and beneficiary or beneficiaries, by recording a single document, complying with the requirements of this section, substituting trustees for all those deeds of trust.(b) If the substitution is executed, but not recorded, prior to or concurrently with the recording of the notice of default, the beneficiary or beneficiaries or their authorized agents shall mail notice of the substitution before or concurrently with the recording thereof, in the manner provided in Section 2924b, to all persons to whom a copy of the notice of default would be required to be mailed by Section 2924b. An affidavit shall be attached to the substitution that notice has been given to those persons, as required by this subdivision.(c) If the substitution is effected after a notice of default has been recorded but prior to the recording of the notice of sale, the beneficiary or beneficiaries or their authorized agents shall mail a copy of the substitution, before, or concurrently with, the recording thereof, as provided in Section 2924b, to the trustee then of record and to all persons to whom a copy of the notice of default would be required to be mailed by Section 2924b. An affidavit shall be attached to the substitution that notice has been given to those persons, as required by this subdivision. (d) (1) A trustee named in a recorded substitution of trustee shall be deemed to be authorized to act as the trustee under the mortgage or Deed of Trust for all purposes from the date the substitution is executed by the mortgagee, beneficiaries, or by their authorized agents. A trustee under a recorded substitution is not required to accept the substitution and may either resign or refuse to accept appointment as trustee pursuant to this subdivision. (2) (A) A trustee named in a recorded substitution of trustee may resign or refuse to accept appointment as trustee at that trustee's own election without the consent of the beneficiary or beneficiaries or their authorized agents. The trustee shall give prompt written notice of that resignation or refusal to accept appointment as trustee to the beneficiary or beneficiaries or their authorized agents by doing both of the following:(i) Depositing or causing to be deposited in the United States mail an envelope containing a notice of resignation of trustee, sent by registered or certified mail with postage prepaid, to all beneficiaries or their authorized agents at the address shown on the last-recorded substitution of trustee for that real property or estate for years in that county.(ii) Recording the notice of resignation of trustee, mailed in the manner described in clause (i), in each county in which the substitution of trustee under which the trustee was appointed is recorded. An affidavit stating that notice has been mailed to all beneficiaries and their authorized agents in the manner provided in clause (i) shall be attached to the recorded notice of resignation of trustee.(B) The resignation of the trustee or refusal to accept appointment as trustee pursuant to this subdivision shall become effective upon the recording of the notice of resignation of trustee in each county in which the substitution of trustee under which the trustee was appointed is recorded.(C) The resignation of the trustee or refusal to accept appointment as trustee pursuant to this subdivision does not affect the validity of the mortgage or Deed of Trust, except that no action required to be performed by the trustee under this chapter or under the mortgage or Deed of Trust may be taken until a substituted trustee is appointed pursuant to this section. If a trustee is not designated in the Deed of Trust, or upon the resignation, incapacity, disability, absence or death of the trustee, or the election of the beneficiary or beneficiaries to replace the trustee, the beneficiary or beneficiaries or their authorized agents shall appoint a trustee or a successor trustee.(D) A notice of resignation of trustee mailed and recorded pursuant to this paragraph shall set forth the intention of the trustee to resign or refuse appointment as trustee and the recording date and instrument number of the recorded substitution of trustee under which the trustee was appointed.(E) A notice of resignation of trustee mailed and recorded pursuant to this paragraph shall contain an address at which the trustee and any successor in interest will be available for service of process for at least five years after the date that the notice of resignation is recorded.(F) For at least five years after a notice of resignation of trustee is mailed and recorded pursuant to this paragraph, the trustee and any successor in interest to that trustee shall retain and preserve every writing, as that term is defined in Section 250 of the Evidence Code, relating to the trust deed or estate for years under which the trustee was appointed.(3) For purposes of this section, paragraph (2) sets forth the exclusive procedure for a trustee to either resign or refuse to accept appointment as trustee.(4) Once recorded, the substitution shall constitute conclusive evidence of the authority of the substituted trustee or their authorized agents to act pursuant to this section, unless prompt written notice of resignation of trustee has been given in accordance with the procedures set forth in paragraph (2).(e) Notwithstanding any provision of this section or any provision in any Deed of Trust, unless a new notice of sale containing the name, street address, and telephone number of the substituted trustee is given pursuant to Section 2924f after execution of the substitution, any sale conducted by the substituted trustee shall be void.

Today's law as Amended – SEC. 2.

No reimbursement is required by this act pursuant to Section 6 of Article XIII B of the California Constitution because the only costs that may be incurred by a local agency or school district will be incurred because this act creates a new crime or infraction, eliminates a crime or infraction, or changes the penalty for a crime or infraction, within the meaning of Section 17556 of the Government Code, or changes the definition of a crime within the meaning of Section 6 of Article XIII B of the California Constitution.

Another recent change to the exact argument that I had in my unlawful detainer case was the primary argument of the bona fide purchaser. This has also been of some obvious concern to the state legislature that they created the Assembly Bill 354. This deals with the idea and the legal delineation of what it means to be an institutional investor. The very definition of this goes to the base arguments of being a bona fide purchaser in a foreclosure proceeding.

The key take away from this is the legislative change to the definition of an institutional investor. It used to be a measure of how many transactions an investor, an investment group, corporation, or the like would do in a calendar year. This could help to define the knowledge base of that foreclosure purchaser. This knowledge base is also what helps to delineate what a bona fide purchaser is. It would be the reason someone might file a Lis Pendens to help stop an illegal foreclosure is to help weed out those who are innocent buyers to a tainted foreclosure property or those whose business it is to know all about the encumbrances to a foreclosure property.

An institutional investor, no matter how many properties they purchase in a year, will no longer include a lien holder that acquires ownership of a single-family home through a judicial or non-judicial foreclosure. As many institutional investors purchase multiple-unit property, it is a given that they are professional real estate investors. The definition of bona fide purchaser in a multiple-unit property can be a little more easily defined based on the business model of the real estate itself. However, it is not a given.

But now, the legislature has even deemed that a buyer of a single-family home purchased through a judicial or non-judicial foreclosure will not be construed as an institutional investor, and will, therefore, have the levity of being a bona fide purchaser in fact. The idea of corporate and institutional investing in real estate has been leveled.

Amended August 17, 2018 – AB-354 Institutional investors: housing. (2017-2018) (SEE THE FINE PRINT IN BLUE BELOW) Date Published: 08/17/2018 12:10 PM

Amended in Senate August 17, 2018

Amended in Senate June 26, 2018

Amended in Senate July 03, 2017

Amended in Assembly May 1, 2017

Amended in Assembly April 18, 2017

Amended in Assembly March 28, 2017

California Legislature – 2017-2018 Regular Session

Assembly Bill No. 354

Introduced by Assembly Member Calderon

February 08, 2017

An act to add Division 21 (commencing with Section 60000) to the Financial Code, relating to housing investors.

LEGISLATIVE COUNSEL'S DIGEST

AB 354, as amended, Calderon. Institutional investors: housing.

Existing law establishes the Department of Business Oversight within the Business, Consumer Services, and Housing Agency.

Existing law, the Economic Revitalization Act, establishes the Governor's Office of Business and Economic Development, also known as GO-Biz, under the control of a director. Existing law requires GO-Biz to serve the Governor as the lead entity for economic strategy and authorizes it to undertake specified activities, including marketing business and investment opportunities in California by working in partnership with local, regional, federal, and other state public and private institutions.

This bill would require an institutional investor, as defined, to register by July 1, 2019, and annually thereafter, with the Department of Business Oversight by providing a statement containing certain information, including, among other things, the total number of single-family homes in the state that are owned by the institutional investor, including the number owned in each county, and the number occupied by renters throughout the state, and in each county. The bill would authorize the department to charge a reasonable fee to process the registration. The bill would require the department to submit a report to the Legislature by July 1, 2020, and annually thereafter, regarding the information collected from institutional investors during the prior calendar year pursuant to the provisions of this bill.

Vote: majority Appropriation: no Fiscal Committee: yes, Local Program: no

THE PEOPLE OF THE STATE OF CALIFORNIA DO ENACT AS FOLLOWS:

SECTION 1.

Division 21 (commencing with Section 60000) is added to the Financial Code, to read:

DIVISION 21. Institutional Investors 60000.

(a) An institutional investor shall register by July 1, 2019, and annually thereafter, with the department by providing the Department of Business Oversight with a written statement of all of the following for the prior calendar year:

(1) The total number of single-family homes in the state that are owned by the institutional investor, including the number that are owned in each county, and the number that are occupied by renters throughout the state, and in each county.

(2) The total number of single-family homes in the state annually purchased by the institutional investor.

(3) The total number of offers to purchase single-family homes in the state

made by the institutional investor.

(4) The total dollar value of single-family homes owned by the institutional investor in the state and the total dollar value of single-family homes owned by the institutional investor that are occupied by renters.

(5) The total number of single-family homes that are sold to existing tenants.

(b) The department may charge a reasonable fee to administer the registration required pursuant to subdivision (a).

(c) For purposes of this section, "institutional investor" means a publicly traded company or corporation that owns more than 100 single-family homes in the state during a calendar year that are occupied by renters and that have a total value of more than ten million dollars ($10,000,000). An institutional investor may use an automated valuation model to estimate the value of homes it owns for purposes of determining whether the ten-million-dollar ($10,000,000) threshold required by this subdivision is met. An institutional investor does not include a lienholder that acquires ownership of a single-family home through a judicial or non-judicial foreclosure.

(d) For purposes of this section, "single-family home" means a home that is alienable separate from the title to any other dwelling unit or is a subdivided interest in a subdivision.

(e)(1) Notwithstanding Section 10231.5 of the Government Code, the department shall submit a report to the Legislature by July 1, 2020, and annually thereafter, regarding the information collected pursuant to subdivision (a) during the prior calendar year.

(2) A report required to be submitted pursuant to this subdivision shall be submitted in compliance with Section 9795 of the Government Code.

Securitization

Securitization is a term used for the bundling of bank loans to create tradeable bonds. This type of investment strategy in the mortgage industry began in the 1970s. It was at this time that Government Sponsored Enterprises (GSEs) began to pool "relatively safe", conventional, "conforming" or "prime" mortgages, creating "mortgage-backed securities" (MBS) from the pool. These GSEs would then sell them to investors, guaranteeing these securities/bonds against default on the underlying mortgages.

This is the catch phrase of the millennium, "...guaranteeing these securities/bonds against default on the underlying mortgages". The federal government would guarantee these securities, along with the elimination of oversight within the financial industry. This, coupled with Moody's and other rating agencies selling their ratings for profit, created a cesspool of investments in the mortgage industry that was a house of cards built on a foundation of fraud. All this combined with greed and corruption created the Bush 2008 "too big to fail" bailouts and the subsequent Obama bailouts that continued. Despite all the exposing of the fraudulent process of securitization and the corruption of the mortgage industry since 2008, there have been no governmental restrictions or regulations to control any of this. And presently, we are well into thirty or more million people being forced into unemployment created by the "shelter-in-place" orders throughout the country, new government restrictions or regulations are needed now more than ever.

The Trump administration was known for their background in the foreclosure industry, beginning with the president on down the chain of command. The former Treasury Secretary, Mnuchin, owns hundreds of thousands of properties throughout the country that he was able to acquire by taking many of these funds and mortgages off the government's balance sheets. He was able to do this through investors for pennies on the dollar. In fact, their purchase balance was given back to them in incentives, in essence, allowing his company to purchase over $1.5B of loans for free. So, I didn't feel that there would be much change to that administration's regular business model. I was not proven wrong. It was Wall Street as normal.

The securitization of the "originate-to-distribute" model had advantages over the previous model known as "originate-to-hold". This model is where the bank that originated a loan to the borrower/homeowner would retain the credit (default) risk. The process of securitization removed the loans from a bank's books, thereby enabling the bank to remain in compliance with capital requirement laws. More loans could be made with proceeds from the MBS sale. The liquidity of a national and even international mortgage market allowed capital to flow where mortgages were in demand and funding was short. However, securitization created a moral hazard. This new model allowed the bank/institution making the loan to no longer worry if the mortgage was paid off. This gave them incentive to process mortgage transactions but not to ensure their credit quality. Bankers were no longer around to work out borrower problems and minimize defaults during the mortgage. The guaranteed returns given by the federal government gave the investors in the MBS no risk and no liability. This is not a very stable business model, unless there is a "too big to fail" understanding to the investors.

With the high down payments and credit scores of the conforming mortgages used by GSE, this danger was minimal. Investment banks, however, wanted to enter the market and avoid competing with the GSEs. They did so by developing mortgage-backed securities in the riskier non-conforming subprime and Alt-A market. Unlike the GSEs the issuers generally did not guarantee the securities against default of the underlying mortgages.

What these "private label" or "non-agency" originators did was to use "structured finance" to create securities. Structured financing involved "slicing" the pooled mortgages into "tranches", each having a different priority in the stream of monthly or quarterly principal and interest streams. Tranches were compared to "buckets" catching the "water" of principal and interest. More senior buckets didn't share water with those below until they were filled to the brim and overflowing. This gave the top buckets/tranches considerable creditworthiness (in theory) that would earn the highest "triple A" credit ratings, making them salable to money market and pension funds that would not otherwise deal with subprime mortgage securities. These "triple A" ratings were found to be bought and paid for at a price.

Next came the highly creative investment tools used to pool the lower rated tranches that a conservative fixed income market would not buy. The investment banks developed another security known as the collateralized debt obligation (CDO). Although a smaller market share, it was crucial unless buyers were found for the non-triple-A or "mezzanine" tranches. If buyers were not found, it would not be profitable to make a mortgage-backed security in the first place. These CDOs pooled the leftover BBB, A-, etc. rated tranches, and produced new tranches. Of these tranches, as much as 70% to 80% were rated triple A by rating agencies. The profits from selling these ratings helped fuel the profits for the rating agencies. The 20–30% remaining mezzanine tranches were sometimes bought up by other CDOs, to make so-called "CDO-Squared" securities, which also produced tranches rated mostly triple A.

This was a process that was later disparaged as "ratings laundering". It was a way of transforming "dross into gold" by some business journalists. At the time, this process was justified by the belief that home prices would always rise. However, in physics it is widely known that what goes up must come down. The model used by underwriters, rating agencies, and investors to estimate the probability of mortgage default was based on the history of credit default swaps, which unfortunately went back "less than a decade", a period when house prices soared. There was not a realistic historical statistic that would allow the outcomes for the probability of default.

In addition, the model that postulated the correlation of default risks among loans in securitization pools could be measured in a simple, stable, tractable number, suitable for risk management or valuation also purported to show that the mortgages in CDO pools were well diversified or "uncorrelated". The smoke and mirrors of this system allowed the risks to expound infinity. The defaults on mortgages in Orlando, for example, were thought to have no effect on, i.e. were uncorrelated with the real estate market across the country such as in Laguna Beach. When prices corrected, which took shape in an economic collapse, the resulting defaults were not only larger in number than predicted but far more correlated.

Still another innovative security criticized after the bubble burst was the synthetic CDO. Cheaper and easier to create than original "cash" CDOs, synthetics did not provide funding for housing, rather synthetic CDO-buying investors were in effect providing insurance (in the form of "credit default swaps") against mortgage default. The mortgages they insured were those in "cash" CDOs the synthetics "referenced". So, instead of providing investors with interest and principal payments from MBS tranches, payments were the equivalent of insurance premiums from the insurance "buyers". If the referenced CDOs defaulted, investors lost their investment, which was paid out to the insurance buyers. Another means of a guarantee to the investors risk. After the meetings in August 2008 and the trillion-dollar bailouts of Wall Street, AIG, and other insurance and reinsurance firms, it became clear that there was no downside for Wall Street or investors.

Unlike true insurance, credit default swaps were not regulated to ensure that providers had the reserves to pay settlements, or that buyers owned the property (MBSs) they were insuring, i.e. were not simply making a bet that a security would default. Because synthetics "referenced" another (cash) CDO, more than one, in fact, numerous synthetics could be made to reference the same original CDO. This multiplied the effect if a referenced security defaulted. As with MBS and other CDOs, triple A ratings for "large chunks" of synthetics were crucial to the securities' success, because of the buyer/investors' ignorance of the mortgage security market and trust in the credit rating agencies ratings. However, Wall Street knew that they were covered on their investments in the front end, as well as the back end. They also were aware of their fraudulent ratings, thereby guaranteeing a win no matter how things played out.

Securitization began to take off in the mid-1990s. Wall Street was always trying to find new ways to expand their portfolios without decreasing their lending ability. Accounting practices be damned. In 1997, the Credit Default Swap (CDS) came from the mind of Blythe Masters. At that time, she was a mathematics graduate employed by J.P. Morgan. The Wall Street juggernaut was trying to find ways to keep the five billion dollars they had loaned to Exxon for oil spill damages as liquid as the oil that they spewed into the Arctic waters. The Wall Street firm didn't want to tie up any cash that they could use to chase other new loans. Her idea was to sell off all the risk of that loan to the European Bank of Reconstruction and Development. The CDS played a pivotal role in the tearing down of Bear Stearns, Washington Mutual, AID, and other corporations, including Enron. The shell games of Wall Street were being played in the boudoir of Washington, and the American taxpayers were always the ones who had to leave the cash on the nightstand.

The total amount of mortgage-backed securities issued almost tripled between 1996 and 2007, to $7.3 trillion. The securitized share of subprime mortgages (i.e., those passed to third-party investors via MBS) increased from 54% in 2001, to 75% in 2006. In the mid-2000s, as the housing market was peaking, GSE securitization market share declined dramatically, while higher-risk subprime and Alt-A mortgage private label securitization grew sharply. As mortgage defaults began to rise, it was primarily mortgages securitized by the private banks. GSE mortgages, securitized or not, which continued to perform better than the rest of the market. Picking up the slack for the dwindling cash CDO market, synthetics were the dominant form of CDOs by 2006, valued "notionally" at an estimated $5 trillion.

By the autumn of 2008, when the securitization market came to a halt, and investors would "lend at any price", securitized lending made up about $10 trillion of the roughly $25 trillion American credit market. The credit market is measured by what the American homeowner, consumer, and corporations owed. In February 2009, Treasury Secretary, Timothy Geitner, stated that securitization markets remained effectively shut, except for conforming mortgages, which could be sold to Fannie Mae and Freddie Mac. The relations with these GSEs created a deep well of complicity to the fraud and corruption of Wall Street and Washington.

Criticizing the argument that complex structured investment securitization was instrumental in the mortgage crisis, Paul Krugman points out that the Wall Street firms issuing the securities "kept the riskiest assets on their own books", and that neither of the equally disastrous bubbles in European housing or U.S. commercial property used complex structured securities. Krugman does agree that what is "arguable is that financial innovation... spread the bust to financial institutions around the world" and its inherent fragmentation of loans has made post-bubble "cleanup" through debt renegotiation extremely difficult. Since then, it has been shown the assumption of Krugman was off substantially. Also, since then, nothing has changed on Wall Street and it is business as usual.

Michael Spence, the Nobel Prize winning economist and senior fellow at Stanford University's Hoover Institute states, "Systemic risk escalates in the financial system when formerly uncorrelated risks shift and become highly correlated. When that happens, then insurance and diversification models fail. There are two striking aspects of the current crisis and its origins. One is that systemic risk builds steadily in the system. The second is that this buildup went either unnoticed or was not acted upon. That means that it was not perceived by the majority of participants until it was too late. Financial innovation, intended to redistribute and reduce risk, appears mainly to have hidden it from view. An important challenge going forward is to better understand these dynamics as the analytical underpinning of an early warning system with respect to financial instability."

The leverage ratios of investment banks showed a significant increase between 2003 and 2007. The Financial Crisis Inquiry Commission reported in January 2011 that: "From 1978 to 2007, the amount of debt held by the financial sector soared from $3 trillion to $36 trillion, more than doubling as a share of gross domestic product." The very nature of many conservative private partnerships that made up most of the Wall Street firms changed to publicly traded corporations taking greater and more diverse kinds of risks. Ten of the largest U.S. commercial banks held 55% of the industry's assets, by 2005. "...This was more than double the level held in 1990. As the impending crisis began to show its face, in 2006, financial sector profits constituted 27% of all corporate profits in the

United States, up from 15% in 1980."

Many financial institutions — investment banks in particular — issued large amounts of debt during 2004-07 and invested the proceeds in mortgage-backed securities (MBS), essentially betting that house prices would continue to rise, and that households would continue to make their mortgage payments. This was true even though their insuring and re-insuring practices showed that they were aware of the downside risks that they were also preparing for. Borrowing at a lower interest rate and investing the proceeds at a higher interest rate is a form of financial leverage. This is analogous to an individual taking out a second mortgage on his residence to invest in the stock market. This strategy proved profitable during the housing boom but resulted in large losses when house prices began to decline, and mortgages began to default. Beginning in 2007, financial institutions and individual investors holding MBS also suffered significant losses from mortgage payment defaults and the resulting decline in the value of MBS. By August 2008, it came to a point of no return. The only way out for Wall Street was a bailout with no oversight and no regulations. So, the conservative "free market capitalists" of the financial industry held their hands out for the largest socialistic assistance program ever created in human history.

In 2004, the U.S. Securities and Exchange Commission (SEC) made a decision related to the net capital rule. This decision allowed U.S. investment banks to issue substantially more debt, which was then used to purchase MBS. The repercussions of this decision over the next three years, from 2004–07, was that the top five U.S. investment banks each significantly increased their financial leverage. This increase in their financial leverage subsequently increased their vulnerability to the declining value of MBS. These five institutions reported over $4.1 trillion in debt for fiscal year 2007. This debt load equated to approximately 30% of U.S. nominal

Gross Domestic Product (GDP) for 2007. Further, the percentage of subprime mortgages increased from below 10% in 2001–03 to 18–20% from 2004 to 2006. This increase was due in part to financing from investment banks.

In August of 2008, one of the three largest investment banks on Wall Street, Lehman Brothers, went bankrupt. Bear Stearns and Merrill Lynch, the two other largest U.S. investment banks, were sold at fire sale prices to other banks. These failures augmented the instability in the global financial system. In a move to protect themselves, the remaining two investment banks, Morgan Stanley, and Goldman Sachs, opted to become commercial banks, thereby subjecting themselves to more stringent regulation. However, with their smoke and mirrors approach to MBS and CDO investments, their payola schemes to Moody's and the other rating agencies, and their insurance and reinsurance practices, it was as if the sun never set for them.

In the years leading up to the crisis, the top four U.S. depository banks, including Bank of America and Wells Fargo Bank, moved an estimated $5.2 trillion in assets and liabilities off-balance sheet and into special purpose vehicles and other entities in the shadow banking system. This enabled them to essentially bypass existing regulations regarding minimum capital ratios, thereby increasing leverage and profits during the boom, but increasing losses during the crisis. New accounting guidance required them to put some of these assets back on to their books during 2009. This new accounting process significantly reduced their capital ratios. This reduced capital was estimated to be between $500 billion and $1 trillion. This accounting practice was considered part of the stress tests performed by the government during 2009. This "stress test" action was a public relations ploy to pacify a weary populace that was becoming quite irate that there were no Wall Street firms or personnel held accountable for their fraudulent actions that crippled the global economy. Iceland jailed the CEOs and board members of their large financial institutions that were responsible for actions in their country, but America seemed to hold the fraud and corruption of Wall Street to some higher standard.

Martin Wolf, the British economics journalist, wrote in June 2009: "… an enormous part of what banks did in the early part of this decade — the off-balance-sheet vehicles, the derivatives and the 'shadow banking system' itself — was to find a way round regulation."

According to the New York State Comptroller's Office, in 2006, Wall Street executives took home bonuses totaling $23.9 billion. "Wall Street traders were thinking of the bonus at the end of the year, not the long-term health of their firm. The whole system — from mortgage brokers to Wall Street risk managers — seemed tilted toward taking short-term risks while ignoring long-term obligations. The most damning evidence is that most of the people at the top of the banks didn't really understand how those investments worked."

The incentive traders received in compensation was focused on fees generated from assembling financial products. These incentives had nothing to do with the performance of those products and profits generated over time. Their bonuses were heavily skewed towards cash rather than stock, and not subject to the recovery of the bonus from the employee by the firm in the event the MBS or CDO created did not perform. In other words, the trading staff from the largest Wall Street firms showed no care for their shareholders. It is now widely known that they were selling these MBSs and CDOs to their investors as prime triple A investments, despite knowing that they were loser funds. In addition, the increased risk, in the form of financial leverage, taken by the major investment banks, was not adequately factored into the compensation of senior executives. The stockholders be damned.

The following information comes from a friend of mine going through their own foreclosure procedures with the same parties that we dealt with in our case. The legal documents that follow represent the filings that we constructed that were included in their legal action. The homeowner name has been changed to John Doe and the property address has been changed as per the request of the homeowner.

The homeowner performed a Forensic Loan Securitization Audit to accompany their legal filings against Wells Fargo Bank for their illegal foreclosure actions being taken against them.

John Doe 123 Main St

San Francisco, CA 94122

NDEx File Number: 2012001500xxxx

(415) 555-1212

Wells Fargo Bank, N.A.

45 Fremont Street, 27th Floor

San Francisco, CA 94104

NDEx WEST, L.L.C.

15000 Surveyor Boulevard

Suite 500

Addison, TX 75001-9013

APN #: 14-1905- 000-00

NDEx File Number: 2012001500xxx

Property Address: 123 Main St

San Francisco, CA 94122

October 26, 2014

You have sent me a notice of intending to perform a trustee Sale of my property on October 29, 2014. I have had an audit of the loan pursuant to the Deed of Trust **Recorded on 06/21/2005** as **Instrument No. 2005-H9755xx-00, Book No. 1915 and Page No. 0000**. The audit was done by:

Certified Forensic Loan Auditors, LLC.

2750 West Main Street, Suite C

League City, TX 77573

(310)432-6304

Their conclusion is that the loan was Securitized and sold by **World Savings Bank, FSB** to a Trust and that therefore your employer **Wells Fargo Bank, N.A** does not own the loan and hence does not have the right to use this Non-judicial Foreclosure process to foreclose on my property.

According to the documents in my loan audit, the **Master Servicer** of the Trust in which my loan is located is not **NDEx West**, it is the **Bank of New York**. Yet, **NDEx WEST, LLC**, sent me a notice that as the duly appointed trustee, they have the right to sell my property in a Non-judicial Foreclosure sale.

You are acting as the lawful trustee and claiming to be using the Mortgage Deed of Trust on the Loan on my property as the instrument giving you the right to act as trustee to sell my property in a Non-judicial Foreclosure Sale. Please send me any proof you have that **Wells Fargo Bank, NA** is the holder of the **Promissory Note** to the Mortgage Loan on my property. Only the holder of the **Promissory Note** is entitled to the payment of the obligation.

Unless you are the agent of the holder of the **Promissory Note** on my property, you, **NDEx West, LLC** or **World Savings Bank, FSB**, or **Wells Fargo Bank, NA** as merely the holder(s) of the Deed of Trust have no legal authority to foreclose on my property.

This is my notice to you, **NDEx WEST, LLC** that you have been put on notice that there is a claim that **Wells Fargo Bank, NA** does not own the **Promissory Note** to the Loan on my property and that their claim to a valid Deed of Trust which would entitle **Wells Fargo Bank, NA** to a legal remedy if they owned the corresponding Promissory Note and the Loan on my property was in default is not valid.

NdeX West, you have asserted that you are the trustee empowered to sell my property in a Non-judicial Foreclosure Sale. You are also simultaneously asserting that you are an agent of **Wells Fargo Bank, NA**, the Servicer of the Loan acting as an agent collecting a debt. Holding both titles simultaneously while claiming to hold only one depending on what you are asserting in the notice to me seems to present a conflict of legal standing under the California and UCC regulations governing those legal positions.

As such I have no way to know who to contact with concerns about the legality of this Non-judicial Foreclosure Sale of my property. My frustration is compounded by the fact that Wells Fargo Bank, NA has refused to tell me if the Loan is even Assumable. Therefore, I am asking you **NDEx West, LLC**, to send me proof that you are the duly assigned trustee of the Deed of Trust that **Wells Fargo Bank, NA** claims to have legally used to name you as such.

If you are the trustee entitled to perform this Non-judicial trustee sale on my property (which I am also contesting), then it is your legal responsibility to check on my claim that **Wells Fargo Bank, NA** doesn't have the power to institute foreclosure proceedings because my loan was sold to a Remic Trust by **World Savings Bank, FSB** before **Wachovia** purchased **World Savings Bank, FSB** on May 7, 2006. That was years after **Wells Fargo Bank, NA** purchased **Wachovia** in 2008.

Wells Fargo Bank, NA, purchased **World Savings Bank, FSB's** assets when it purchased **Wachovia**. Whether or not your appointment as the trustee in the Deed of Trust on my property entitles you to legally perform a Non-judicial sale of my property depends on whether the Loan on my property was owned by **World Savings Bank, FSB** or **Wachovia** when **Wells Fargo Bank, NA** purchased **Wachovia** in 2008.

If you proceed without providing me proof that you have made a good faith effort to ascertain your legal position in this matter, I will be forced to file a lawsuit against you for Fraud, Slander of Title, and the Intentional Infliction of Emotional Distress to include all damages that result from your actions.

I am also requesting you to tell me if you are claiming to be the trustee on the Deed of Trust on the Loan on my property or merely the Servicing Agent to whom I am to submit the balance to make the loan on my property current.

I will be happy to provide you with copies of the expert testimony by **Certified Forensic Loan Auditors** which shows from a Bloomberg Audit that the loan on my property was sold to a Trust and that **World Savings Bank, FSB** was paid in full for the loan plus interest. Therefore, it was a **True Sale** to the Sponsor of the Trust and all ownership interests were transferred to that Sponsor.

REMICs are investment instruments of pooled mortgage loans that have been broken down into the individual principal payments and interest payments associated with each mortgage. The issuer repackages the principal and interest payments according to their payout and risk characteristics into "tranches" or slices of the mortgage pool. A bank invests in REMIC by purchasing bonds that correspond to the different classes that the various tranches represent and that have stated payment terms.

Remic Trusts are not secured transitions because issuers do not pledge any property as security for the investments. Investors who purchase REMIC certificates are beneficiaries of a trust and they have contractual rights under the pooling and servicing agreement, but they are not secured investors.

Wells Fargo Bank, NA's, investments in the Remic Trust containing my property's mortgage were not primarily secured by first mortgages or deeds of trust because **Wells Fargo Bank, NA,** had no power to institute foreclosure proceedings.

If on the other hand as you also claim you are an agent servicing the loan as a debt collector, then you are amassing servicing fees on my property which you are not legally entitled to unless you are the **Master Servicer** for the Remic Trust my property is in.

Please send me a copy of the documents showing me that you have been legally appointed by that Trust to be such a trustee empowered to collect service fees and to perform a Non-judicial Foreclosure sale on my property **BEFORE** you put my property up for sale.

Your right to proceed against my property is based on the rights given to you by **Wells Fargo Bank, NA.** I am putting you on notice that **Wells Fargo Bank, NA,** has no right to proceed directly against my property if I fail to make payments under the Promissory Note, or Deed of Trust, and **Wells Fargo Bank, NA,** does not have a right to require the respective trustees of any investments it may have in the Trust my property Loan is in to proceed against my property to satisfy the trustees' financial obligations to **Wells Fargo Bank, NA.**

Wells Fargo Bank, NA (World Savings Bank, FSB) has rights against the trustees that issued bonds to **World Savings Bank, FSB** but these rights do not extend to actions on the underlying mortgages or trust deeds. In the event of a trustee's default (perhaps because of homeowners' defaults under their mortgages or trust deeds), **Wells Fargo Bank, NA** may be able to replace the trustee, but the successor trustee still takes legal title to the underlying mortgages and trust deeds. **Wells Fargo Bank, NA** may have the right to require a trustee to sell tranches or classes to satisfy its obligation to **Wells Fargo Bank, NA** but **Wells Fargo Bank, NA** does not have the right to require the sale of the underlying mortgages or trust deeds:

Therefore, **Wells Fargo Bank, NA** cannot assign to you, **NDEx West, LLC**, what it does not have, or legally own, the power to perform a Non-judicial Foreclosure sale on my property.

I realize that as the purported **Servicer of the Loan** on my property, your incentive is to make as much money in servicing fees as possible and then sell my property as soon as possible in a Non-judicial Foreclosure sale. But since, in the same notice to me in which you claim to be acting as the Servicer of the Loan on my property, you also claim to be the duly appointed **trustee** on the Mortgage Deed of Trust entitled to perform the Non-judicial Foreclosure sale on my property, I am assuming that it is you to whom I should be sending this notice. If I do not hear from you in 3 business days, I will file a lawsuit naming you in the fraud to obtain service fees that you are not legally entitled to and to Slander the title to my property and other damages and claims that arise from your willful misconduct.

John Doe (415) 555 1212

SUPERIOR COURT OF THE STATE OF CALIFORNIA –

IN AND FOR THE COUNTY OF SAN FRANCISCO

JOHN DOE; an individual Plaintiff, In Pro Per

vs.

WORLD SAVINGS BANK, FSB; THE BANK OF NEW YORK AS TRUSTEE FOR SECURITIZED TRUST

WORLD SAVINGS BANK MORTGAGE PASS-THROUGH CERTIFICATES

REMIC 19 TRUST; MORTGAGE ELECTRONIC REGISTRATION SYSTEM, AKA "MERS" AND DOES 1 THROUGH 100, INCLUSIVE

Defendants.

Case No. _____

COMPLAINT FOR:

LACK OF STANDING TO FORECLOSE;

FRAUD IN THE CONCEALMENT;

FRAUD IN THE INDUCEMENT;

INTENTIONAL INFLICTION OF EMOTIONAL DISTRESS;

QUIET TITLE;

SLANDER OF TITLE;

DECLARATORY RELIEF;

VIOLATIONS OF TILA;

VIOLATIONS OF RESPA;

RESCISSION.

PLAINTIFF'S ORIGINAL PETITION COMES NOW

The Plaintiff, JOHN DOE ("Plaintiff"), complaining of the Defendants as named above, and each of them, as follows:

I. THE PARTIES

3. Plaintiff is now, and at all times relevant to this action, a resident of the County of SAN FRANCISCO, State of CALIFORNIA.

4. Defendant, WORLD SAVINGS BANK, FSB (herein referred to as "WORLD SAVINGS") is a National Banking Association, doing business in the County of SAN FRANCISCO, State of CALIFORNIA. Plaintiff is further informed and believes, and thereon alleges that WORLD SAVINGS is the Originator of the loan.

5. Defendant, THE BANK OF NEW YORK (herein referred to as "BANK OF NEW YORK"), as trustee for securitized trust WORLD SAVINGS BANK MORTGAGE PASS-THROUGH CERTIFICATES REMIC 19 TRUST (herein referred to as "REMIC 19 TRUST"). Plaintiff is informed and believes, and thereon alleges that, Defendant BANK OF NEW YORK, is a national banking association, doing business in the County of SAN FRANCISCO, State of CALIFORNIA and is the purported Master Servicer for Securitized Trust and/or a purported participant in the imperfect securitization of the Note and/or the Mortgage/Deed of Trust as more particularly described in this Complaint.

6. Defendant, WORLD SAVINGS BANK, FSB. Plaintiff is informed and believes, and thereon alleges that, Defendant WORLD SAVINGS BANK, FSB, is a corporation, doing business in the County of SAN FRANCISCO, State of CALIFORNIA and is the purported Sponsor for Securitized Trust and/or a purported participant in the imperfect securitization of the Note and/or the Mortgage/Deed of Trust as more particularly described in this Complaint.

7. Plaintiff is informed and believes, and thereon alleges that, Defendant, is a corporation, doing business in the County of SAN FRANCISCO, State of CALIFORNIA and is the purported Depositor for Securitized Trust and/or a purported participant in the imperfect securitization of the Note and/or the Mortgage/Deed of Trust as more particularly described in this Complaint.

8. Defendant, WORLD SAVINGS BANK, FSB Plaintiff is informed and believes, and thereon alleges that, Defendant WORLD SAVINGS BANK, FSB, is

a corporation, doing business in the County of SAN FRANCISCO, State of CALIFORNIA and is the purported Master Servicer for Securitized Trust and/or a purported participant in the imperfect securitization of the Note and/or the Mortgage/Deed of Trust as more particularly described in this Complaint.

9. Defendant, MORTGAGE ELECTRONIC REGISTRATION SYSTEMS, INC., aka MERS ("MERS"), Plaintiff is informed and believes, and thereon alleges that MERS is a corporation duly organized and existing under the laws of CALIFORNIA, whose last known address is 1818 Library Street, Suite 300, Reston, Virginia 20190; website: http://www.mersinc.org. MERS is doing business in the County of SAN FRANCISCO, State of CALIFORNIA. Plaintiff is further informed and believes, and thereon alleges that Defendant MERS is the purported Beneficiary under the Mortgage/Deed of Trust and/or is a purported participant in the imperfect securitization of the Note and/or the Mortgage/Deed of Trust, as more particularly described in this Complaint.

10. Defendant, WACHOVIA MORTGAGE, Plaintiff is informed and believes, and thereon alleges that, Defendant WACHOVIA MORTGAGE is a corporation, doing business in the County of SAN FRANCISCO, State of CALIFORNIA and is the purported Corporation to have become sole owner of World Savings Bank through acquisition.

11. Defendant, WELLS FARGO BANK, NA, Plaintiff is informed and believes, and thereon alleges that, Defendant WELLS FARGO BANK, NA is a corporation, doing business in the County of SAN FRANCISCO, State of CALIFORNIA and is the purported Corporation to have become sole owner of Wachovia Mortgage through merger.

12. Defendant, GOLDEN WEST SAVINGS ASSOC. SERVICES CO., Plaintiff is informed and believes, and thereon alleges that, Defendant GOLDEN WEST SAVINGS ASSOC. SERVICES CO. is a corporation, doing business in the County of SAN FRANCISCO, State of CALIFORNIA and was the Original trustee on the loan.

13. Defendant, NDEx WEST, LLC, Plaintiff is informed and believes, and thereon alleges that, Defendant NDEx WEST, LLC is a limited liability company, doing business in the County of SAN FRANCISCO, State of CALIFORNIA and is the purported Company to have become the Substituted trustee on the loan acting on behalf of WELLS FARGO BANK.

14. Defendant, LSI TITLE CO., Plaintiff is informed and believes, and thereon alleges that, Defendant LSI TITLE CO. is a corporation, doing business in the County of SAN FRANCISCO, State of CALIFORNIA and is the purported Corporation to have become Title company acting for NDEx WEST LLC, and WELLS FARGO BANK.

15. At all times relevant to this action, Plaintiff has owned the Property located at 123 MAIN STREET. SAN FRANCISCO, CA 94122 (the "Property").

16. Plaintiff does not know the true names, capacities, or basis for liability of Defendants sued herein as Does 1 through 100, inclusive, as each fictitiously named Defendant is in some manner liable to Plaintiff, or claims some right, title, or interest in the Property. Plaintiff will amend this Complaint to allege their true names and capacities when ascertained. Plaintiff is informed and believes, and therefore alleges that at all relevant times mentioned in this Complaint, each of the fictitiously named Defendants are responsible in some manner for the injuries and damages to Plaintiff so alleged and that such injuries and damages were proximately caused by such Defendants, and each of them.

17. Plaintiff is informed and believes, and thereon alleges that at all times herein mentioned, each of the Defendants were the agents, employees, servants and/or the joint ventures of the remaining Defendants, and each of them, and in doing the things alleged herein below, were acting within the course and scope of such agency, employment and/or joint venture.

II. JURISDICTION

18. The transactions and events which are the subject matter of this Complaint all occurred within the County of SAN FRANCISCO, State of CALIFORNIA.

19. The Property is located within the County of SAN FRANCISCO, State of CALIFORNIA with an address of 123 MAIN STREET. SAN FRANCISCO, CA 94122

III. INTRODUCTORY ALLEGATIONS

20. This is an action brought by Plaintiff for declaratory judgment, injunctive and equitable relief, and for compensatory, special, general and punitive damages.

21. Plaintiff, homeowner, disputes the title and ownership of the real property in question (the "Home"), which is the subject of this action, in that the originating mortgage lender, and others alleged to have ownership of Plaintiff's mortgage note and/or Mortgage/Deed of Trust, have unlawfully sold, assigned and/or transferred their ownership and security interest in a Promissory Note and Mortgage/Deed of Trust related to the Property, and, thus, do not have lawful ownership or a security interest in Plaintiff's Home which is described in detail

herein. For these reasons, the Court should Quiet Title to the property in Plaintiff's name.

22. Additionally, Plaintiff homeowner brings causes of action against all defendants for fraud, intentional infliction of emotional distress, rescission, declaratory relief based, and violations of T.I.L.A., R.E.S.P.A., and H.O.E.P.A, upon the facts and circumstances surrounding Plaintiff's original loan transaction and subsequent securitization. Defendants' violations of these laws are additional reasons this Court should quiet title in Plaintiff's property in Plaintiff and award damages, rescission, declaratory judgment, and injunctive relief as requested below.

23. From 1998 until the financial crash of 2008-2009, over 60 million home loans were sold by originating lender banks to investment banks to be securitized in a complex series of billions of transactions. The Plaintiff's home loan was one of the 60 million notes that were securitized.

24. Securitization is the process whereby mortgage loans are turned into securities, or bonds, and sold to investors by Wall Street and other firms. The purpose is to provide a large supply of money to lenders for originating loans, and to provide investments to bond holders which were expected to be relatively safe. The procedure for selling of the loans was to create a situation whereby certain tax laws known as the Real Estate Mortgage Investment Conduit (hereinafter "REMIC") Act were observed, and whereby the Issuing Entities and the Lenders would be protected from either entity going into bankruptcy. In order to achieve the desired "bankruptcy remoteness," numerous "True Sales" of the loans had to occur, in which loans were sold and transferred to the different parties to the securitization.

25. A "True Sale" of the loan would be a circumstance whereby one party owned the Note and then sold it to another party. An offer would be made, accepted and compensation given to the "seller" in return for the Note. The Notes would be transferred, and the Deeds of Trust assigned to the buyers of the Note, with an Assignment or Transfer made every step of the way, and, furthermore, each Note would be endorsed to the next party by the previous assignee or transferee of record.

26. Each REMIC Trust created by the investment banks, usually under New York Law, would be funded with thousands to tens-of-thousands of mortgage notes. In order to maintain their bankruptcy-protected status, REMIC's had to have closing dates by which every mortgage note and/or security device like a Mortgage of Mortgage/Deed of Trust was to be sold to the REMIC and had to be "owned" by the REMIC. Once the REMIC closed, it could accept no more mortgage notes under the terms of REMIC law, and it would begin selling securities backed by payments from homeowners on the notes it "owned".

27. How a particular mortgage loan ended up being transferred to a REMIC in the securitization process is governed by a contract known as a Pooling and Servicing Agreement ("PSA"). The PSA is a Trust Agreement required to be filed under penalty of perjury with the United States Securities and Exchange Commission ("SEC") and which, along with another document, the Mortgage Loan Purchase Agreement ("MLPA"), is the operative securitization document created by the finance and securitization industry to memorialize securitization transactions.

28. When the Plaintiff in this case closed on his/her property, her original lender (or other entity claiming original or near original ownership of the note) signed a PSA that governed the plaintiff's particular mortgage note. The PSA agreement, as described in more detail below, detailed the closing date by which the homeowner's loan must be "sold" to the REMIC, and described exactly how the homeowner's note is to find its way from the original lender to the REMIC trust.

29. A typical PSA calls for a homeowner's note to be transferred at least four times to different key parties before it comes into possession of the REMIC trustee.

30. As part of the process, the banks almost universally separated the promissory note from the Mortgage/Deed of Trust. Under the common law, the owner of the note has the right to payments on the note, and the owner of the Mortgage/Deed of Trust has the right to foreclose on the homeowner if the homeowner defaults on the note. Traditionally, before investment banks began securitizing mortgage notes, the holder of the note would universally hold the Mortgage/Deed of Trust. This made sense because the party with the right to collect payments on the note would want to be able to foreclose using the Mortgage/Deed of Trust if the homeowner defaulted.

31. However, to streamline the securitization process, the investment banks created an entity called Mortgage Electronic Registrations System ("MERS"), who is one of the defendants in this case. The investment banks, in addition to using MERS' electronic database to track the buying, selling, and assignments of securitized mortgage notes (bypassing the county clerks' offices), would transfer deeds of trust to MERS, thereby separating the mortgage note from the Mortgage/Deed of Trust. MERS would hold the Mortgage/Deed of Trust for whoever later claimed to be the "owner" of the homeowners' mortgage note.

32. Plaintiff alleges that Defendants, and each of them, cannot show proper receipt, possession, transfer, negotiations, assignment and ownership of the borrower's original Promissory Note and Mortgage/Deed of Trust, resulting in imperfect security interests and claims.

33. Plaintiff further alleges that Defendants, and each of them, cannot

establish possession and proper transfer and/or indorsement of the Promissory Note and/or proper assignment of the Mortgage/Deed of Trust herein; therefore, none of the Defendants have perfected any claim of title or security interest in the Property. Defendants, and each of them, do not have the ability to establish that the mortgages that secure the indebtedness, or Note, were legally or properly acquired.

34. Plaintiff alleges that an actual controversy has arisen and now exists between the Plaintiff and Defendants, and each of them. Plaintiff desires a judicial determination and declaration of its rights with regard to the Property and the corresponding Promissory Note and Mortgage/Deed of Trust.

35. Plaintiff also seeks redress from Defendants identified herein for damages, for other injunctive relief, and for cancellation of written instruments based upon:

a. An invalid and unperfected security interest in Plaintiff's Home hereinafter described;

b. Void "True Sale(s)" violating CALIFORNIA law and express terms of the Pooling and Servicing Agreement ("PSA") governing the securitization of Plaintiff's mortgage;

c. An incomplete and ineffectual perfection of a security interest in Plaintiff's Home;

IV. SPECIFIC ALLEGATIONS

36. On or about JULY 22, 2005 (hereinafter referred to as "Closing Date") Plaintiff entered into a consumer credit transaction with WORLD SAVINGS by obtaining a $500,000.00 mortgage loan secured by Plaintiff's principal residence, (Subject Property). This note was secured by a First Mortgage/Trust Deed on the Property in favor of WORLD SAVINGS.

37. Plaintiff's loan was securitized, with the Note not being properly transferred to Defendant, BANK OF NEW YORK, acting as the trustee for the REMIC 19 TRUST Trust holding plaintiff's note. Documents filed with the SEC by the securitization participants allegedly claim that the note and Mortgage/Deed of Trust at issue in this case were sold, transferred, and securitized by Defendants, with other loans and mortgages into the REMIC 19 TRUST Trust, which is a Common Law Trust formed pursuant to New York law. A detailed description of the mortgage loans which form the REMIC 19 TRUST Trust is included in Form 424B5 ("the Prospectus"), which has been duly filed with the SEC and which can be accessed through the above-mentioned footnote.

38. An expert, certified, forensic audit of the Plaintiff's loan documents reveals that Plaintiff's mortgage note was required to at least go through this assignment chain of key parties before it reached the REMIC trustee it was destined for.

39. The Plaintiff's PSA requires that his/her note or Mortgage/Deed of Trust had to be endorsed and assigned, or transferred, respectively, to the trust and executed by multiple intervening parties in the above chain of assignment before it reached the REMIC trustee.

40. Plaintiff executed a series of documents, including but not limited to a Note and Mortgage/Deed of Trust, securing the Property in the amount of note. The original beneficiary and nominee under the Mortgage/Deed of Trust was MERS.

41. Plaintiff is informed and believes, and thereon alleges that the purchase mortgage on the Property, the debt or obligation evidenced by the Note and the Mortgage/Deed of Trust executed by Plaintiff in favor of the original lender and other Defendants, regarding the Property, was not properly assigned and/or transferred to Defendants operating the pooled mortgage funds or REMIC trusts in accordance with the PSA and/or CALIFORNIA law to the entities making and receiving the purported assignments to this trust.

42. Plaintiff alleges that the PSA requires that each Note or Mortgage/Deed of Trust had to be endorsed, assigned, or transferred, respectively, to the trust and executed by multiple intervening parties before it reached the Trust. Here, neither the Note and/or the Mortgage/Deed of Trust, or both, was assigned to the Securitized Trust by the closing date. Therefore, under the PSA, any assignments of the Mortgage/Deed of Trust beyond the specified closing date for the Trust are void.

43. Plaintiff further alleges that even if the Mortgage/Mortgage/Deed of Trust had been transferred into the Trust by the closing date, the transaction is still void as the Note would not have been transferred according to the requirements of the PSA, since the PSA requires a complete and unbroken chain of transfers/assignments to and from each intervening party.

44. Plaintiff is informed and believes, and thereon alleges that the REMIC 19 TRUST Trust had no officers or directors and no continuing duties other than to hold assets and to issue the series of certificates of investment in mortgage-backed securities as described in the Prospectus identified herein below. A detailed description of the mortgage loans which form the REMIC 19 TRUST Trust is included in Form 424B5 ("the Prospectus"), which has been duly filed with the SEC and which can be accessed through the below mentioned footnote. that

45. Plaintiff also alleges that the Note was secured by the Mortgage/Deed of Trust. Plaintiff alleges that as of the date of the filing of this Complaint, the Mortgage/Deed of Trust had not been legally assigned to any other party or entity.

46. Plaintiff is informed and believes that Defendant BANK OF NEW YORK, alleges that it is the "holder and owner" of the Note and the beneficiary of the Mortgage/Deed of Trust. However, the Note and Mortgage/Deed of Trust identify the mortgagee and note holder as the original lending institution or Mortgage Originator. Documents state that the original lender allegedly sold the mortgage loan to REMIC 19 TRUST Trust.

47. Plaintiff further alleges that no documents or records can be produced that demonstrate that prior to the closing date for REMIC 19 TRUST Trust, the Note was duly endorsed, transferred and delivered to REMIC 19 TRUST Trust, including all intervening transfers. Nor can any documents or records be produced that demonstrate that prior to the closing date, the Mortgage/Deed of Trust was duly assigned, transferred and delivered to REMIC 19 TRUST Trust, via the trustee BANK OF NEW YORK, including all intervening transfers/assignments.

48. Plaintiff further alleges that any documents that purport to transfer any interest in the Note to REMIC 19 TRUST Trust after the Trust closing date are void as a matter of law, pursuant to New York trust law and relevant portions of the PSA. Plaintiff's debt or obligation did not comply with New York law, and/or other laws and statutes, and, thus, do not constitute valid and enforceable "True Sales." Any security interest in the Property was thus, never perfected. The alleged holder of the Note is not the beneficiary of the Mortgage/Deed of Trust. The alleged beneficiary of Plaintiff's Mortgage/Deed of Trust does not have the requisite title, perfected security interest or standing to proceed in a foreclosure; and/or is not the real party in interest, or agent or nominee of the real aprt in interest, with regard to any action taken or to be taken against the Property.

49. Plaintiff is also informed and believes, and thereon alleges that at all times herein mentioned, and any assignment of a Mortgage/Deed of Trust without proper transfer of the obligation that it secures is a legal nullity.

50. In order for a defendant, including the trustee of the Securitized Trust, to have a valid and enforceable secured claim against Plaintiff's Home, the party claiming the right to foreclose must prove and certify to all parties that, among other things required under the PSA:

    a. There was a complete and unbroken chain of indorsements and transfers of the Note from and to each party to the securitization transaction (which should be from the (A) Mortgage Originator to the (B) Sponsor to the (C) Depositor to the (D) Trust/trustee, and that all these endorsements and transfers were completed prior to the Trust closing dates (See discussion below); and

    b. The trustee of the Securitized Trust had actual physical possession of the

Note at that point in time when all endorsements and assignments had been completed. Absent such proof, Plaintiff alleges that the Trust cannot demonstrate that it had perfected its security interest in Plaintiff's Home that is the subject of this action. Therefore, if the Defendants, and each of them, did not hold and possess the Note on or before the closing date of the Trust herein, they are estopped and precluded from asserting any secured or unsecured claim in this case, through their agents or otherwise.

51. Plaintiff is informed and believes, and thereon alleges that pursuant to the terms of the PSA, the Mortgage Originator (i.e., the original lender herein) agreed to transfer and indorse to the trustee for the Securitized Trust, without recourse, including all intervening transfers and assignments, all its right, title and interest in and to the mortgage loan (Note) of Plaintiff's herein and all other mortgage loans identified in the PSA.

52. Plaintiff is further informed and believes, and thereon alleges that the PSA provides that the transfers and assignments are absolute, were made for valuable consideration, to wit, in exchange for the certificates described in the PSA, and were intended by the parties to be a "bona fide" or a "True Sale." Since, as alleged herein below, True Sales did not actually occur, Plaintiff alleges that the Defendant trustees are estopped and precluded from asserting any secured or unsecured claim in this case.

53. Plaintiff is further informed and believes, and thereon alleges that as a result of the PSA and other documents signed under oath in relation thereto, the Mortgage Originator, sponsor and Depositor are stopped from claiming any interest in the Note that is allegedly secured by the Mortgage/Deed of Trust on Plaintiff's Home herein.

54. Plaintiff is informed and believes, and thereon alleges that the Note in this case and the other mortgage loans identified in the PSA, were never actually transferred, and delivered by the Mortgage Originator to the Sponsor or to the Depositor nor from the Depositor to the trustee for the Securitized Trust. Plaintiff further alleges, on information and belief that the PSA herein provides that the Mortgage Files of the Mortgages were to be delivered to REMIC 19 TRUST Trust, which Mortgage Files include the original Deeds of Trust, herein.

55. Based upon the foregoing, Plaintiff is further informed and believes, and thereon alleges that the following deficiencies exist, in the "True Sale" and securitization process as to this Mortgage/Deed of Trust, which renders invalid any security interest in the Plaintiff's mortgage, including, but not limited to:

a. The splitting or separation of title, ownership and interest in Plaintiff's Note and Mortgage/Deed of Trust of which the original lender is the holder, owner and beneficiary of Plaintiff's Mortgage/Deed of Trust;

b. When the loan was sold to each intervening entity, there were no Assignments of the Mortgage/Deed of Trust to or from any intervening entity at the time of the sale. Therefore, "True Sales" could not and did not occur;

c. The failure to assign and transfer the beneficial interest in Plaintiff's Mortgage/Deed of Trust to BANK OF NEW YORK, in accordance with the PSA of the Defendants, as Securitization Participants;

d. The failure to indorse, assign and transfer Plaintiff's Note and/or mortgage to Defendant BANK OF NEW YORK, as trustee for REMIC 19 TRUST Trust, in accordance with the PSA and applicable New York law and/or the Uniform Commercial Code;

e. No Assignments of Beneficiary or Endorsements of the Note to each of the intervening entities in the transaction ever occurred under CALIFORNIA law, which is conclusive proof that no true sales occurred as required under the PSA filed with the SEC; and

f. Defendants, and each of them, violated the pertinent terms of the PSA.

56. Plaintiff, therefore, alleges, upon information and belief that none of the parties to neither the securitization transaction, nor any of the Defendants in this case, hold a perfected and secured claim in the Property; and that all Defendants are estopped and precluded from asserting an unsecured claim against Plaintiff's estate

57. Furthermore, the terms of the finance transaction with WORLD SAVINGS are not clear or conspicuous, nor consistent, and are illegal, which violates several statutes and in essence creates a fraudulent and unenforceable loan. Further, this loan was underwritten without proper due diligence by WORLD SAVINGS as evidenced by their failure to verify borrower's income utilizing signed IRS Income Tax Disclosure Form 4506T, which would have provided past borrower tax returns. WORLD SAVINGS also used a "GDW Cost of Savings" as the Index for the basis of this loan. Because the Lender controls this Index and it is directly based upon the average rate of interest WORLD SAVINGS parent company, it was not a valid index for the basis of the loan.

58. In addition, and unbeknownst to Plaintiff, WORLD SAVINGS illegally, deceptively and/or otherwise unjustly, qualified Plaintiff for a loan, which WORLD SAVINGS knew or should have known that Plaintiff could not qualify for or afford by, for example, the underwriter has approved this loan based upon credit scores and the borrower's Stated Income only. Had WORLD SAVINGS used a more accurate and appropriate factor, such as Tax Forms and a more determinative level of scrutiny of determining comply with the requirement to provide Plaintiff with a Mortgage Loan Origination Agreement the debt-to-income ratio, Plaintiff would not have qualified for the loan in the first place.

Consequently, WORLD SAVINGS sold Plaintiff a loan product that it knew or should have known would never be able to be fully paid back by Plaintiff. WORLD SAVINGS ignored long-standing economic principles of underwriting and instead, knowingly, liberally, greedily and without any regard for Plaintiff's rights sold Plaintiff a deceptive loan product.

59. There was no determination of the ability of the borrower to repay the loan, with complete disregard for the Guidance Letters issued by Federal Agencies and even Federal and State Law.

60. Additionally, Defendants, and each of them, neither explained the workings of the entire mortgage loan transaction, how the rates, finance charges, costs and fees were computed, nor the inherent volatility of the loan product(s) provided by Defendants.

61. The purpose of entering into the above-described mortgage loan transactions was for Plaintiff to eventually own the Property. That purpose was knowingly and intentionally thwarted and indeed made impossible by Defendants' combined actions as alleged herein.

V. FIRST CAUSE OF ACTION:

LACK OF STANDING/WRONGFUL FORECLOSURE

A. No Defendant has Standing to Foreclose

62. Plaintiff re-alleges and incorporates by reference all preceding paragraphs as though fully set forth herein.

63. An actual controversy has arisen and now exists between Plaintiff and Defendants specified hereinabove, regarding their respective rights and duties, in that Plaintiff contends that Defendants, and each of them, do not have the right to foreclose on the Property because Defendants, and each of them, have failed to perfect any security interest in the Property, or cannot prove to the court they have a valid interest as a real party in interest to foreclose. Thus, the purported power of sale, or power to foreclose judicially, by the above specified Defendants, and each of them, no longer applies.

64. Plaintiff is informed and believes and there upon allege that the only individual who has standing to foreclose is the holder of the note because they have a beneficial interest. The only individuals who are the holders of the note are the certificate holders of the securitized trust because they are the end users and

pay taxes on their interest gains; furthermore, all the banks or other entities holding the note in the middle of the chain of transfers were paid in full.

65. Plaintiff further contends that the above specified Defendants, and each of them, do not have the right to foreclose on the Property because said Defendants, and each of them, did not properly comply with the terms of Defendants' own securitization requirements (contained in the PSA) and falsely or fraudulently prepared documents required for Defendants, and each of them, to foreclose as a calculated and fraudulent business practice.

66. Plaintiff requests that this Court find that the purported power of sale contained in the Note and Mortgage/Deed of Trust has no force and effect at this time, because Defendants' actions in the processing, handling and attempted foreclosure of this loan involved numerous fraudulent, false, deceptive and misleading practices, including, but not limited to, violations of State laws designed to protect borrowers, which has directly caused Plaintiff to be at an equitable disadvantage to Defendants, and each of them. Plaintiff further requests that title to the Property remain in its name, with said Mortgage/Deed of Trust remaining in beneficiaries' name, during the pendency of this litigation, and deem that any attempted sale of the Property is "unlawful and void".

B. Defendant MERS Cannot be a Real Party in Interest in a Securitized Mortgage

67. Since the creation of Plaintiff's Note herein and Mortgage/Deed of Trust, Defendant MERS was named the "beneficiary" of the Mortgage/Deed of Trust.

68. Plaintiff is informed and believes, and thereon alleges that Defendant MERS lacks the authority under its corporate charter to foreclose a mortgage, or to own or transfer an interest in a securitized mortgage because MERS charter limits MERS' powers and duties to functioning as an electronic registration system of certain types of securities.

69. Plaintiff is informed and believes, and thereon alleges that in order to conduct a foreclosure action, a person or entity must have standing.

70. Plaintiff is informed and believes, and thereon alleges that pursuant to New York law, to perfect the transfer of mortgage paper as collateral, the owner should physically deliver the note to the transferee. Without physical transfer, the sale of the note is invalid as a fraudulent conveyance or as unperfected.

71. The Note in this action identifies the entity to whom it was payable, the original lender. Therefore, the Note herein cannot be transferred unless it is endorsed; the attachments to the notice of default do not establish that endorsements were made, nor are there any other notices, which establish that the

original lender endorsed and sold the note to another party.

72. Furthermore, insofar as the parties to the securitization of Plaintiff's Note and Mortgage/Deed of Trust base their claim that the Note was transferred or assigned to Defendant BANK OF NEW YORK, the trustee of the Securitized Mortgage herein, by the original lender, it is well established state law that the assignment of a Mortgage/Deed of Trust does not automatically assign the underlying promissory note and right to be paid and the security interest is incident of the debt.

73. Pursuant to state law, to perfect the transfer of mortgage papers as collateral for a debt, the owner should physically deliver the note to the transferee. Without physical transfer, the sale of the note is invalid as a fraudulent conveyance, or as unperfected. The Note herein specifically identifies the party to whom it was payable to and the Note, therefore, cannot be transferred unless it is endorsed.

74. Defendants, and each of them, cannot produce any evidence that the Promissory Note has been transferred; therefore, Defendant MERS could only transfer whatever interest it had in the Mortgage/Deed of Trust herein. The Promissory Note and Mortgage/Deed of Trust are inseparable: an assignment of the Note carries the mortgage (i.e., Mortgage/Deed of Trust) with it, while an assignment of the Mortgage/Deed of Trust alone is a nullity. Therefore, if one party receives the Note and another party receives the Mortgage/Deed of Trust (as in this case), the holder of the Note prevails regardless of the order in which the interests were transferred.

75. Defendants MERS has failed to submit documents authorizing MERS, as nominee for the original lender, to assign the subject mortgage to the foreclosing trustee. Hence, MERS lacked authority as a mere nominee to assign Plaintiff's mortgage, making any assignment from MERS defective.

76. In the instant action, MERS, as the nominee not only lacks authority to assign the mortgage but cannot demonstrate the trustee's knowledge or assent to the assignment by MERS to the foreclosing trustee.

77. Any attempt to transfer the beneficial interest of a trust deed without actual ownership of the underlying note, is void under law. Therefore, Defendant, MERS, cannot establish that it is entitled to assert a claim in this case. For this reason, as well as the other reasons set forth herein below, MERS cannot transfer an interest in real property, and cannot recover anything from Plaintiff.

78. Defendants, and each of them, through the actions alleged above, have or claim the right to illegally commence foreclosure under the Note on the Property via a foreclosure action supported by false or fraudulent documents. Said unlawful foreclosure action has caused and continues to cause Plaintiff's great and

irreparable injury in that real property is unique.

79. The wrongful conduct of the above specified Defendants, and each of them, unless restrained and enjoined by an Order of the Court, will continue to cause great and irreparable harm to Plaintiff. Plaintiff will not have the beneficial use and enjoyment of its Home and will lose the Property.

80. Plaintiff has no other plain, speedy, or adequate remedy and the injunctive relief prayed for below is necessary and appropriate at this time to prevent irreparable loss to Plaintiff. Plaintiff has suffered and will continue to suffer in the future unless Defendants' wrongful conduct is restrained and enjoined because real property is inherently unique, and it will be impossible for Plaintiff to determine the precise amount of damage it will suffer.

VI. SECOND CAUSE OF ACTION:

FRAUD IN THE CONCEALMENT

81. Plaintiff re-alleges and incorporates by reference all preceding paragraphs as though fully set forth herein.

82. Defendants concealed the fact that the Loans were securitized as well as the terms of the Securitization Agreements, including, inter alia: (1) Financial Incentives paid; (2) existence of Credit Enhancement Agreements, and (3) existence of Acquisition Provisions. By concealing the securitization, Defendant concealed the fact that Borrower's loan changed in character since no single party would hold the Note but rather the Notes would be included in a pool with other notes, split into tranches, and multiple investors would effectively buy shares of the income stream from the loans. Changing the character of the loan in this way had a materially negative effect on Plaintiff that was known by Defendant but not disclosed.

83. Defendant knew or should have known that had the truth been disclosed, Plaintiff would not have entered into the Loans.

84. Defendant intended to induce Plaintiff based on these misrepresentations and improper disclosures.

85. Plaintiff's reasonable reliance upon the misrepresentations was detrimental. But for failure to disclose the true and material terms of the transaction, Plaintiff could have been alerted to issues of concern. Plaintiff would have known of Defendants true intentions and profits from the proposed risky loan. Plaintiff would have known that the actions of Defendant would have an adverse effect on the value of Plaintiff's home.

86. Defendants' failure to disclose the material terms of the transaction induced Plaintiff to enter into the loans and accept the Services as alleged herein.

87. Defendants were aware of the misrepresentations and profited from them.

88. As a direct and proximate result of the misrepresentations and concealment Plaintiff was damaged in an amount to be proven at trial, including but not limited to costs of Loan, damage to Plaintiff's financial security, emotional distress, and Plaintiff has incurred costs and attorney's fees.

89. Defendants are guilty of malice, fraud and/or oppression. Defendants' actions were malicious and done willfully in conscious disregard of the rights and safety of Plaintiff in that the actions were calculated to injure Plaintiff. As such Plaintiff is entitled to recover, in addition to actual damages, punitive damages to punish Defendants and to deter them from engaging in future misconduct.

VII. THIRD CAUSE OF ACTION:

FRAUD IN THE INDUCEMENT

90. Plaintiff re-alleges and incorporates by reference all preceding paragraphs as though fully set forth herein.

91. Defendants intentionally misrepresented to Plaintiff those Defendants were entitled to exercise the power of sale provision contained in the Mortgage/Deed of Trust. In fact, Defendants were not entitled to do so and have no legal, equitable, or actual beneficial interest whatsoever in the Property.

92. Defendants misrepresented that they are the "holder and owner" of the Note and the beneficiary of the Mortgage/Deed of Trust. However, this was not true and was a misrepresentation of material fact. Documents state that the original lender allegedly sold the mortgage loan to REMIC 19 TRUST Trust. Defendants were attempting to collect on a debt to which they have no legal, equitable, or pecuniary interest in. This type of conduct is outrageous. Defendants are fraudulently foreclosing on the Property, which they have no monetary or pecuniary interest. This type of conduct is outrageous.

93. Defendant's failure to disclose the material terms of the transaction induced Plaintiff to enter into the loans and accept the Services as alleged herein.

94. The material misrepresentations were made by Defendants with the intent to cause Plaintiff to reasonably rely on the misrepresentation in order to induce the Plaintiff to rely on the misrepresentations and foreclosure on the Property. This material misrepresentation was made with the purpose of initiating the securitization process as illustrated above, in order to profit from the sale of the Property by selling the note to sponsors who then pool the note and sell it to investors on Wall Street and other New York investment banks.

95. Defendants were aware of the misrepresentations and profited from them.

96. As a direct and proximate result of the misrepresentations and concealment, Plaintiff was damaged in an amount to be proven at trial, including but not limited to costs of Loan, damage to Plaintiff's financial security, emotional distress, and Plaintiff has incurred costs and attorney's fees.

97. Defendants are guilty of malice, fraud and/or oppression. Defendants' actions were malicious and done willfully in conscious disregard of the rights and safety of Plaintiff in that the actions were calculated to injure Plaintiff. As such Plaintiff is entitled to recover, in addition to actual damages, punitive damages to punish Defendants and to deter them from engaging in future misconduct.

VIII. FOURTH CAUSE OF ACTION:

INTENTIONAL INFLICTION OF EMOTIONAL DISTRESS

98. Plaintiff re-alleges and incorporates by reference all preceding paragraphs as though fully set forth herein.

99. The actions of Defendants, as set forth herein, have resulted in the Plaintiff being threatened with the loss of the Property.

100. This outcome has been created without any right or privilege on the part of the Defendants, and, as such, their actions constitute outrageous or reckless conduct on the part of Defendants.

101. Defendants intentionally, knowingly and recklessly misrepresented to the Plaintiff those Defendants were entitled to exercise the power of sale provision contained in the Mortgage/Deed of Trust. In fact, Defendants were not entitled to do so and have no legal, equitable, or actual beneficial interest whatsoever in the Property.

102. Defendants' conduct – fraudulently attempting to foreclose or claiming the right to foreclose on a property in which they have no right, title, or interest – is so outrageous and extreme that it exceeds all bounds, which is usually tolerated in a civilized community.

103. Such conduct was undertaken with the specific intent of inflicting emotional distress on the Plaintiff, such that Plaintiff would be so emotionally distressed and debilitated that he/she would be unable to exercise legal rights in the Property; the right to title of the Property, the right to cure the alleged default, right to verify the alleged debt that Defendants are attempting to collect, and right to clear title to the Property such that said title will regain its marketability and value.

104. At the time Defendants began their fraudulent foreclosure proceedings, Defendants were not acting in good faith while attempting to collect on the subject debt. Defendants, and each of them, committed the acts set forth above with complete; utter and reckless disregard of the probability of causing Homeowners to suffer severe emotional distress.

105. As an actual and proximate cause of Defendants' attempt to fraudulently foreclose on Plaintiff's home or claim of the right to foreclose on Plaintiff's home, the Plaintiff has suffered severe emotional distress, including but not limited to lack of sleep, anxiety, and depression.

106. Plaintiff did not default in the manner stated in the Notice of Default, yet because Defendants' outrageous conduct, Plaintiff have been living under the constant emotional nightmare of losing the Property.

107. As a proximate cause of Defendants' conduct, Plaintiff has experienced many sleepless nights, severe depression, lack of appetite, and loss of productivity at its place of employment.

108. The conduct of Defendants, and each of them, as herein described, was so vile, base, contemptible, miserable, wretched, and loathsome that it would be looked down upon and despised by ordinary people. Plaintiff is therefore entitled to punitive damages in an amount appropriate to punish Defendants and to deter others from engaging in similar conduct.

IX. FIFTH CAUSE OF ACTION:

SLANDER OF TITLE

109. Plaintiff re-alleges and incorporates by reference all preceding paragraphs as though fully set forth herein.

110. Plaintiff incorporates here each allegation set forth above. Defendants, and each of them, disparaged Plaintiff's exclusive valid title by and through the preparing, posting, publishing, and recording of the documents previously described herein, including, but not limited to, the Notice of Default, Notice of trustee's Sale, trustee's Deed, and the documents evidencing the commencement of judicial foreclosure by a party who does not possess that right.

111. Said Defendants knew or should have known that such documents were improper in that at the time of the execution and delivery of said documents, Defendants had no right, title, or interest in the Property. These documents were naturally and commonly to be interpreted as denying, disparaging, and casting doubt upon Plaintiff's legal title to the Property. By posting, publishing, and recording said documents, Defendants' disparagement of Plaintiff's legal title was made to the world at large.

112. As a direct and proximate result of Defendants' conduct in publishing these documents, Plaintiff's title to the Property has been disparaged and slandered, and there is a cloud on Plaintiff's title, and Plaintiff has suffered, and continues to suffer, damages in an amount to be proved at trial.

113. As a further proximate result of Defendants' conduct, Plaintiff has incurred expenses in order to clear title to the Property. Moreover, these expenses are continuing, and Plaintiff will incur additional charges for such purpose until the cloud on Plaintiff's title to the property has been removed. The amounts of future expenses and damages are not ascertainable at this time.

114. As a further direct and proximate result of Defendants' conduct, Plaintiff has suffered humiliation, mental anguish, anxiety, depression, and emotional and physical distress, resulting in the loss of sleep and other injuries to his and her health and well-being, and continues to suffer such injuries on an ongoing basis. The amount of such damages shall be proven at trial.

115. At the time that the false and disparaging documents were created and published by the Defendants, Defendants knew the documents were false and created and published them with the malicious intent to injure Plaintiff and deprive them of their exclusive right, title, and interest in the Property, and to obtain the Property for their own use by unlawful means.

116. The conduct of the Defendants in publishing the documents described above was fraudulent, oppressive, and malicious. Therefore, Plaintiff is entitled to an award of punitive damages in an amount sufficient to punish Defendants for their malicious conduct and deter such misconduct in the future.

X. SIXTH CAUSE OF ACTION:

QUIET TITLE

117. Plaintiff's title to the above-described property is derived as follows: On or about JULY 22, 2005 (hereinafter referred to as "Closing Date") Plaintiff entered into a consumer credit transaction with WORLD SAVINGS by obtaining a $500,000.00 mortgage loan secured by Plaintiff's principal residence, (Subject Property). This note was secured by a First Trust Deed on the Property in favor of WORLD SAVINGS.

118. All Defendants named herein claim an interest and estate in the property adverse to plaintiff in that defendant asserts he is the owner of the note secured by the Mortgage/Deed of Trust to the property the subject of this suit.

119. All Defendants named herein claim an interest and estate in the property adverse to plaintiff in that defendant asserts he is the owner of Mortgage/Deed of Trust securing the note to the property the subject of this suit.

120. The claims of all defendants are without any right whatsoever, and defendants have no right, estate, title, lien or interest in or to the property, or any part of the property.

121. The claim of all defendants herein named, and each of them, claim some estate, right, title, lien or interest in or to the property adverse to plaintiff's title, and these claims constitute a cloud on plaintiff's title to the property.

122. Plaintiff, therefore, alleges, upon information and belief that none of the parties to neither the securitization transaction, nor any of the Defendants in this case, hold a perfected and secured claim in the Property; and that all Defendants are estopped and precluded from asserting an unsecured claim against Plaintiff's estate.

123. Plaintiff requests the decree permanently enjoin defendants, and each of them, and all persons claiming under them, from asserting any adverse claim to plaintiff's title to the property; and

124. Plaintiff requests the court award plaintiff costs of this action, and such other relief as the court may deem proper.

XI. SEVENTH CAUSE OF ACTION:

DECLARATORY RELIEF

125. Plaintiff re-alleges and incorporates by reference all preceding paragraphs as though fully set forth herein.

126. An actual controversy has arisen and now exists between Plaintiff and Defendants concerning their respective rights and duties regarding the Note and Mortgage/Trust Deed.

127. Plaintiff contends that pursuant to the Loans, Defendants do not have authority to foreclose upon and sell the Property.

128. Plaintiff is informed and believes and upon that basis alleges that Defendants dispute Plaintiff's contention and instead contend they may properly foreclose upon the Property.

129. Plaintiff therefore request a judicial determination of the rights, obligations and interest of the parties with regard to the Property, and such determination is necessary and appropriate at this time under the circumstances so that all parties may ascertain and know their rights, obligations and interests with regard to the Property.

130. Plaintiff requests a determination of the validity of the Mortgage/Trust Deeds as of the date the Notes were assigned without a concurrent assignation of the underlying Trust Deeds.

131. Plaintiff requests a determination of the validity of the NOD (Notice Of Default).

132. Plaintiff requests a determination of whether any Defendant has authority to foreclose on the Property.

133. Plaintiff requests all adverse claims to the real property be must determined by a decree of this court.

134. Plaintiff requests the decree declare and adjudge that plaintiff is entitled to the exclusive possession of the property.

135. Plaintiff requests the decree declare and adjudge that plaintiff owns in fee simple and is entitled to the quiet and peaceful possession of the above-described real property.

136. Plaintiff requests the decree declare and adjudge that defendants, and each of them, and all persons claiming under them, have no estate, right, title, lien, or interest in or to the real property or any part of the property.

XII. EIGHTH CAUSE OF ACTION:

Violation of TILA and HOEPA, 15 U.S.C. § 1601, et. seq.

137. Plaintiff re-alleges and incorporates by reference all preceding paragraphs as though fully set forth herein.

138. Plaintiff alleges that the loan that is the subject matter of this complaint was and is a consumer-credit transaction within the meaning of TILA and HOEPA.

139. Defendants violated TILA/HOEPA by failing to provide Plaintiff with accurate material disclosures required under TILA/HOEPA and not taking into account the intent of the State Legislature in approving this statute, which was to fully inform home buyers of the pros and cons of adjustable-rate mortgages in a language (both written and spoken) that they can understand and comprehend; and advise them to compare similar loan products with other lenders. It also requires the lender to offer other loan products that might be more advantageous for the borrower under the same qualifying matrix.

140. Any and all statute[s] of limitations relating to disclosures and notices required pursuant to 15 U.S.C. § 1601, et. seq. were tolled due to Defendants' failure to effectively provide the required disclosures and notices.

141. As a further direct and proximate result of defendants' conduct, Plaintiff lost substantial equity in their home, in that they were unable to refinance when their home had a higher appraisal value.

142. As a direct and proximate result of defendants' conduct, Plaintiff were unable to refinance their home or to obtain any modification of their loan, which has resulted in Plaintiff being permanently burdened by the fraudulent loan made by defendants.

143. An actual controversy now exists between Plaintiff, who contends she has the right to rescind the loan on the Subject Property alleged in this Complaint, and based on information and belief, Defendants deny that right.

144. As a direct and proximate result of Defendants' violations Plaintiff have incurred and continue to incur damages in an amount according to proof but not yet ascertained including without limitation, statutory damages and all amounts paid or to be paid in connection with the transaction.

145. Defendants were unjustly enriched at the expense of Plaintiff who is therefore entitled to equitable restitution and disgorgement of profits obtained by Defendants.

146. Defendants' actions in this matter have been willful, knowing, malicious, fraudulent, and oppressive, entitling Plaintiff to punitive damages in an amount

appropriate to punish Defendants and to deter others from engaging in the same behavior.

XIII. NINTH CAUSE OF ACTION:

Violation of RESPA, 1 U.S.C. § 2601 et. seq.

147. Plaintiff re-alleges and incorporates by reference all preceding paragraphs as though fully set forth herein.

148. The loan to Plaintiff was a federally regulated mortgage loan as defined in RESPA.

149. Housing and Urban Development's (HUD's) 1999 Statement of Policy established a two-part test for determining the legality of lender payments to mortgage brokers for table funded transactions and intermediary transactions under RESPA:

a) Whether goods or facilities were actually furnished, or services were actually performed for the compensation paid and;

b) Whether the payments are reasonably related to the value of the goods or facilities that were actually furnished or services that were actually performed.

150. In applying this test, HUD believes that total compensation should be scrutinized to assure that it is reasonably related to the goods, facilities, or services furnished or performed to determine whether it is legal under RESPA. The interest and income that Defendants have gained is disproportionate to the situation Plaintiff finds themselves in due directly to Defendant's failure to disclose that they will gain a financial benefit while Plaintiff suffer financially as a result of the loan product sold to Plaintiff.

151. No separate fee agreements, regarding the use of WORLD SAVINGS "Cost of Savings" as the Index for the basis of this loan, Disclosures of additional income due to interest rate increases or the proper form and procedure in relation to the Borrower's Rights to Cancel were provided.

152. Defendants violated RESPA because the payments between the Defendants were misleading and designed to create a windfall. These actions were deceptive, fraudulent, and self-serving.

153. As a proximate result of Defendants' actions, Plaintiff has been damaged in an amount not yet ascertained, to be proven at trial.

XIV. TENTH CAUSE OF ACTION:

RESCISSION

154. Plaintiff re-alleges and incorporates by reference all preceding paragraphs as though fully set forth herein.

155. Plaintiff is entitled to rescind the loan and all accompanying loan documents for all of the foregoing reasons: 1) TILA Violations; 2) Failure to provide a Mortgage Loan Origination Agreement; 3) Fraudulent Concealment; 4) Fraudulent Inducement; 5) failure to abide by the PSA; 6) making illegal or fraudulent transfers of the note and Mortgage/Deed of Trust; and 5) Public Policy Grounds, each of which provides independent grounds for relief.

156. The Truth In Lending Act, 15 U.S.C §1601, et. seq. extends Plaintiff's right to rescind a loan to three years from the date of closing if the borrower received false or incomplete disclosures of either the loans terms or Borrower's right to rescind. Here, Defendants have failed to properly disclose the details of the loan. Specifically, the initial disclosures do not initial TILA disclosures, and lack of diligence and collusion on the part of the broker, lender and underwriter to place Plaintiff in a loan she could not afford and would ultimately benefit Defendants following the negative amortization that accrued.

157. The public interest would be prejudiced by permitting the alleged contract to stand; such action would regard an unscrupulous lender.

158. As a proximate result of Defendants' actions, Plaintiff has been damaged in an amount not yet ascertained, to be proven at trial.

WHEREFORE, Plaintiff prays for rescission of the stated loan in its entirety.

PRAYER FOR RELIEF

WHEREFORE Plaintiff, will ask for the following for each Cause of Action to be awarded:

FIRST CAUSE OF ACTION - STANDING

1. For Compensatory Damages in an amount to be determined by proof at trial;

2. For Special Damages in an amount to be determined by proof at trial;

3. For General Damages in an amount to be determined by proof at trial;

4. For Punitive Damages as allowed by law;

5. For Restitution as allowed by law;

6. For Attorney's Fees and Costs of this action;

7. For Declaratory Relief, including but not limited to the following Decrees of this Court that:

    a. Plaintiff, Plaintiff is the prevailing party;

    b. The trustees of the Trusts have no enforceable secured or unsecured claim against the Property;

    c. The Sponsor has no enforceable secured or unsecured claim against the Property;

    d. The Depositor has no enforceable secured or unsecured claim against the Property;

    e. The Mortgage Originator has no enforceable secured or unsecured claim against the Property;

    f. Determines all adverse claims to the real property in this proceeding;

    g. Plaintiff is entitled to the exclusive possession of the property;

    h. Plaintiff owns in fee simple and is entitled to the quiet and peaceful possession of the above-described real property.

    i. Defendants, and each of them, and all persons claiming under them, have no estate, right, title, lien, or interest in or to the real property or any part of the property.

SECOND CAUSE OF ACTION – FRAUD IN THE CONCEALMENT

1. For Compensatory Damages in an amount to be determined by proof at trial;

2. For Special Damages in an amount to be determined by proof at trial;

3. For General Damages in an amount to be determined by proof at trial;

4. For Punitive Damages as allowed by law;

5. For Restitution as allowed by law;

THIRD CAUSE OF ACTION – FRAUD IN THE INDUCEMENT

1. For Compensatory Damages in an amount to be determined by proof at trial;

2. For Special Damages in an amount to be determined by proof at trial;

3. For General Damages in an amount to be determined by proof at trial;

4. For Punitive Damages as allowed by law;

5. For Restitution as allowed by law;

FOURTH CAUSE OF ACTION – I.I.E.D.

1. For Compensatory Damages in an amount to be determined by proof at trial;

2. For Special Damages in an amount to be determined by proof at trial;

3. For General Damages in an amount to be determined by proof at trial;

4. For Punitive Damages as allowed by law;

5. For Restitution as allowed by law;

FIFTH CAUSE OF ACTION – SLANDER OF TITLE

51) For Compensatory Damages in an amount to be determined by proof at trial;

52) For Special Damages in an amount to be determined by proof at trial;

53) For General Damages in an amount to be determined by proof at trial;

54) For Punitive Damages as allowed by law;

55) For Restitution as allowed by law;

56) For Attorney's Fees and Costs of this action;

57) For Declaratory Relief, including but not limited to the following Decrees of this Court that:

    a.   Plaintiff, Plaintiff is the prevailing party;

    b.   The trustees of the Trusts have no enforceable secured or unsecured claim against the Property;

    c.   The Sponsor has no enforceable secured or unsecured claim against the Property;

    d.   The Depositor has no enforceable secured or unsecured claim against the Property;

    e.   The Mortgage Originator has no enforceable secured or unsecured claim against the Property;

    f.   Determines all adverse claims to the real property in this proceeding;

    g.   Plaintiff is entitled to the exclusive possession of the property;

    h.   Plaintiff owns in fee simple and is entitled to the quiet and peaceful possession of the above-described real property.

    i.   Defendants, and each of them, and all persons claiming under them, have no estate, right, title, lien, or interest in or to the real property or any part of the property.

SIXTH CAUSE OF ACTION – QUIET TITLE

1) For Compensatory Damages in an amount to be determined by proof at

trial;

2. For Special Damages in an amount to be determined by proof at trial;

3. For General Damages in an amount to be determined by proof at trial;

4. For Punitive Damages as allowed by law;

5. For Restitution as allowed by law;

6. For Attorney's Fees and Costs of this action;

7. For Declaratory Relief, including but not limited to the following Decrees of this Court that:

    a. Plaintiff, Plaintiff is the prevailing party;

    b. The trustees of the Trusts have no enforceable secured or unsecured claim against the Property;

    c. The Sponsor has no enforceable secured or unsecured claim against the Property;

    d. The Depositor has no enforceable secured or unsecured claim against the Property;

    e. The Mortgage Originator has no enforceable secured or unsecured claim against the Property;

    f. Determines all adverse claims to the real property in this proceeding;

    g. Plaintiff is entitled to the exclusive possession of the property;

    h. Plaintiff owns in fee simple, and is entitled to the quiet and peaceful possession of, the above-described real property.

    i. Defendants, and each of them, and all persons claiming under them, have no estate, right, title, lien, or interest in or to the real property or any part of the property.

SEVENTH CAUSE OF ACTION – DECLARATORY RELIEF

14. For Compensatory Damages in an amount to be determined by proof at

trial;

15. For Special Damages in an amount to be determined by proof at trial;

16. For General Damages in an amount to be determined by proof at trial;

17. For Punitive Damages as allowed by law;

18. For Restitution as allowed by law;

19. For Attorney's Fees and Costs of this action;

20. For Declaratory Relief, including but not limited to the following Decrees of this Court that:

    a. Plaintiff, Plaintiff is the prevailing party;

    b. The trustees of the Trusts have no enforceable secured or unsecured claim against the Property;

    c. The Sponsor has no enforceable secured or unsecured claim against the Property;

    d. The Depositor has no enforceable secured or unsecured claim against the Property;

    e. The Mortgage Originator has no enforceable secured or unsecured claim against the Property;

    f. Determines all adverse claims to the real property in this proceeding;

    g. Plaintiff is entitled to the exclusive possession of the property;

    h. Plaintiff owns in fee simple, and is entitled to the quiet and peaceful possession of, the above-described real property.

    i. Defendants, and each of them, and all persons claiming under them, have no estate, right, title, lien, or interest in or to the real property or any part of the property.

EIGHTH CAUSE OF ACTION – VIOLATION OF T.I.L.A.

1. For Compensatory Damages in an amount to be determined by proof at

trial;

2. For Special Damages in an amount to be determined by proof at trial;

3. For General Damages in an amount to be determined by proof at trial;

4. For Punitive Damages as allowed by law;

5. For Restitution as allowed by law;

6. For Attorney's Fees and Costs of this action;

7. For Declaratory Relief, including but not limited to the following Decrees of this Court that:

    a. Plaintiff, Plaintiff is the prevailing party;

    b. The trustees of the Trusts have no enforceable secured or unsecured claim against the Property;

    c. The Sponsor has no enforceable secured or unsecured claim against the Property;

    d. The Depositor has no enforceable secured or unsecured claim against the Property;

    e. The Mortgage Originator has no enforceable secured or unsecured claim against the Property;

    f. Determines all adverse claims to the real property in this proceeding;

    g. Plaintiff is entitled to the exclusive possession of the property;

    h. Plaintiff owns in fee simple, and is entitled to the quiet and peaceful possession of, the above-described real property.

    i. Defendants, and each of them, and all persons claiming under them, have no estate, right, title, lien, or interest in or to the real property or any part of the property.

NINTH CAUSE OF ACTION – VIOLATION OF R.E.S.P.A.

1. For Compensatory Damages in an amount to be determined by proof at

trial;

2. For Special Damages in an amount to be determined by proof at trial;

3. For General Damages in an amount to be determined by proof at trial;

4. For Punitive Damages as allowed by law;

5. For Restitution as allowed by law;

6. For Attorney's Fees and Costs of this action;

7. For Declaratory Relief, including but not limited to the following Decrees of this Court that:

    a. Plaintiff, Plaintiff is the prevailing party;

    b. The trustees of the Trusts have no enforceable secured or unsecured claim against the Property;

    c. The Sponsor has no enforceable secured or unsecured claim against the Property;

    d. The Depositor has no enforceable secured or unsecured claim against the Property;

    e. The Mortgage Originator has no enforceable secured or unsecured claim against the Property;

    f. Determines all adverse claims to the real property in this proceeding;

    g. Plaintiff is entitled to the exclusive possession of the property;

    h. Plaintiff owns in fee simple, and is entitled to the quiet and peaceful possession of, the above-described real property.

    i. Defendants, and each of them, and all persons claiming under them, have no estate, right, title, lien, or interest in or to the real property or any part of the property.

TENTH CAUSE OF ACTION - RESCISSION

1. For Compensatory Damages in an amount to be determined by proof at

trial;

2. For Special Damages in an amount to be determined by proof at trial;

3. For General Damages in an amount to be determined by proof at trial;

4. For Punitive Damages as allowed by law;

5. For Restitution as allowed by law;

6. For Attorney's Fees and Costs of this action;

7. For Declaratory Relief, including but not limited to the following Decrees of this Court that:

    a. Plaintiff, Plaintiff is the prevailing party;

    b. The trustees of the Trusts have no enforceable secured or unsecured claim against the Property;

    c. The Sponsor has no enforceable secured or unsecured claim against the Property;

    d. The Depositor has no enforceable secured or unsecured claim against the Property;

    e. The Mortgage Originator has no enforceable secured or unsecured claim against the Property;

    f. Determines all adverse claims to the real property in this proceeding;

    g. Plaintiff is entitled to the exclusive possession of the property;

    h. Plaintiff owns in fee simple, and is entitled to the quiet and peaceful possession of, the above-described real property.

    i. Defendants, and each of them, and all persons claiming under them, have no estate, right, title, lien, or interest in or to the real property or any part of the property.

Plaintiffs request from the court leave to amend

Dated:

John Doe 123 Main St

in Pro Per

JOHN DOE AFFIDAVIT OF JOHN Q PUBLIC. AUDITOR

Real Property Located: 123 MAIN STREET.

SAN FRANCISCO, CA 94122

I, John Q Public, declare as follows:

1. I am over the age of 18 years and qualified to make this affidavit. I am a resident of the state of Texas and make this affidavit based on my own personal knowledge. I have no direct or indirect interest in the outcome of this case for which I am offering observations, analysis, opinions and testimony.

2. I am experienced in Securitization Analysis. I research or review the Corporate/Trust Documents, which are officially filed with the Securities and Exchange Commission. I use and review specialty licensed software (Bloomberg L.P.). This permits investors and licensed users to access any "named Trust-Entity". From Bloomberg data, I can see each Note that is held by this named Trust-Entity, and I can see its current status in real time. I have the knowledge and experience to perform these searches and reviews of searches with reliable accuracy. I am available for court appearances, in person or via telephone for further clarification or explanation of the information provided herein, or for cross examination if necessary. I have examined the following documents and Audio Records.

   a. Complaint filed in the District Court of SAN FRANCISCO County, CALIFORNIA, case# _____.

   b. Note of JOHN DOE in the amount of $500,000.00.

   c Recorded Deed of Trust pertaining to the Note of JOHN DOE in the amount of $500,000.00 made payable to WORLD SAVINGS BANK, FSB.

   d. A document purporting to be an "Assignment of Mortgage" recorded JULY 22, 2005.

   e. A complete search of the SAN FRANCISCO County Record pertaining to 123 MAIN STREET SAN FRANCISCO, CA 94122.

3. I have personal knowledge of the audit containing the information retrieved from the terminals and experience to render opinions in the topic areas related the

securitization of mortgage loans, derivative securities, the securities industry, real property law, Uniform Commercial Code practices, predatory lending practices, Truth in Lending Act requirements, loan origination and underwriting, accounting in the context of securitization and pooling and servicing of securitized loans, assignment and assumption of securitized loans, creation of trusts under deeds of trust, pooling and agreements, and issuance of asset backed securities and specifically mortgage-backed securities by special purpose vehicles in which an entity is named as trustee for holders of certificates of mortgage-backed securities, the economics of securitized residential mortgages during the period of 1998-2008, appraisal fraud, and its effect on APR disclosure, usury, exceeding the legal limit for interest charged, foreclosure of securitized, non-securitized residential mortgages.

4. From many hours of study and research and formal training and reviewing thousands of mortgage documents, I learned that one procedure for funding is via mortgage securitization where such pools solicit funds from investors by means of a Pooling and Servicing Agreement (PSA), which was used to explain and govern the Mortgage-Backed Security (MBS). The PSA is the governing document for the MBS pool that was typically established as a Trust. State trust laws uniformly demand that the governing documents of the Trust be strictly adhered to compliance with IRS taxing guidelines.

General Overview of Secured Transactions

5. Ownership of the intangible payment stream collected from a Mortgage Loan can be bought, sold and transferred. This transfer of ownership is evidenced through the sale of a certificate funded by payment stream(s) received from payments made upon what will be defined within this document as the "Obligation". Ownership of the Obligation via buying and selling the certificates (intangible payment stream) is allowable under the governance of UCC Article 9, as a Transferable Record. Transferred ownership can be seen through the financial record of the distributed payment stream. Transfer of ownership through certificates is an actual transfer of a partial ownership of a beneficial interest in the intangible payment stream of the Obligation.

6. The initial and subsequent certificate transactions involving the divided intangible payment stream of the Obligation does not transfer ownership of the Note and the Mortgage to the owners of the intangible payment stream. Transfer of ownership of the Note and the Mortgage would require that partial interest in the tangible instruments, which secure the Obligation (Note and the Mortgage) be transferred/assigned to all and each of the potential multiple owners of the certificates compliant with the local laws of jurisdiction. That described transfer would be impossible. To create the appearance that the transfer of the partial interest of the tangible instruments has been accomplished, the transfer mortgages and deeds of trust are made to a common trustee. Any owner of the security as a transferable record of the payment stream could be in jeopardy of stripping the

security away from the Note unless ownership of the Note is also obtained.

7. In the Commercial Money Ctr., Inc. bankruptcy, the Ninth Circuit Appellate Court had no difficulty concluding that ownership of income streams can be stripped from the records that evidence them.

From Commercial Money Ctr., Inc., 350 B.R. 465, 473-79 (B.A.P. 9th Cir. 2006), rev'g, 56 U.C.C. Rep. Serv. (West) 54 (Bankr. S.D. Cal. Jan. 27, 2005). "This language on its face defines chattel paper to mean the records that "evidence" certain things, including monetary obligations. Payment streams stripped from the underlying leases are not records that evidence monetary obligations they are monetary obligations. Therefore, we agree with NetBank that the payment streams are not chattel paper."

8. Of the three transferable linked parts of every Mortgage Loan, the Obligation, the Note and the Mortgage, two of those transferable parts are tangible instruments, the Note and the Mortgage. The Note is a negotiable instrument that evidences the Obligation. The Mortgage, seen as a Real Property Lien, is a contract listing alternatives for collecting payment due under the Obligation evidenced by the Note.

9. Each Note associated with a Mortgage Loan is created as a negotiable instrument to allow for future sale. When a Note is treated as a negotiable instrument, falling under the governance of UCC Article 3, ownership of the Note shall be transferred by means of special endorsement or by endorsing in blank to create a bearer Note. However, possession of the Note must not be confused with ownership of the Note, where a possessor may not be more than a custodian or agent of an owner. Additionally, a valid subsequent owner, while negotiating ownership of a Note, must exercise care so as to avoid loss of Secured Party status in the negotiation of a Note. (Secured Party status is of serious concern for the Bankruptcy Courts) An alleged subsequent owner of the Note failing to permanently perfect (filing of record as required by law) ownership of the Mortgage (Security) associated with a Note into their name, while negotiating Ownership of a Note, would render a Secured Note being an Unsecured Note. Ownership of Unsecured Note, no longer secured by a mortgage of Deed of Trust, separates the Obligation from the Conditions to enforce the Power of Sale. Where an alleged subsequent owner of a negotiable instrument lacks endorsement for owner/holder status, the UCC allows for such party to obtain endorsements to allow the subsequent party to be entitled to enforcement rights upon the negotiable instrument. However, the UCC has no retroactive means to re-establish an unsecured negotiable instrument back into a secured negotiable Instrument. Secured status and Unsecured status is dependent upon the securing security being in compliance with local laws of jurisdiction. Once the Deed of Trust was separated from the note, the note became unsecured forever under UCC Article 3.

10. A Note transferred in interstate commerce is a negotiable instrument and

therefore falls under the governance of UCC Article 3. Any party who possesses a valid ownership interest in a Note can only transfer that interest by way of negotiation through indorsement. However, because real estate ownership rights are concerned, perfection of transfer of the Mortgage, a contract involving real estate, securing the Note, falls within the governance of Laws of Jurisdiction where the real property resides. Even, within its own language, the Mortgage contains notice that Federal Statutes and/or the Laws of Local Jurisdiction are governing law, therefore attempts to apply UCC Article 9 as governing the transfer of the Mortgage would be misplaced. Subsequently, any party who possesses a valid beneficial interest in a Mortgage can only transfer that interest by way of properly recorded assignment of that interest. Transfer of beneficial interest in a Mortgage, without properly recorded assignment, would place anyone doing so in jeopardy of violating Federal Statutes and/or Local Laws of the applicable Jurisdiction and potentially the common law Statutes of Fraud.

11. A properly recorded assignment of the Mortgage memorializes the Note's negotiation but does not cause the Note's transfer. For a Note to change ownership and remain secured through the Mortgage/Deed of Trust each and every transfer of the Note, by indorsement or negotiation, must be performed with a parallel assignment of the security instrument properly filed in the local County Record. If a Note is endorsed and negotiated to one party while the Mortgage is assigned to another party, a separation between the Ownership of the Note evidencing the Obligation and the Ownership of the Conditions, which secure the Obligation to Real Property occurs.

12. For a Party with ownership of a Note to be a Holder in Due Course with the rights and power of foreclosure, the "Power of Sale", the Note must remain secured to Real Property. When a separation of Ownership of the Obligation and the Ownership of Conditions, which secure the Obligation occurs by failing to follow mandated law, the Mortgage/Deed of Trust (Security) is no longer secured by Real Property. When the Mortgage Loan is no longer secured by Real Property, there can be no Holder in Due Course of a Secured Note. Such Holder of the Note has lost the right to seek alternate payment through the use of a now invalid security instrument. Therefore, any Party seeking to bring a claim, against real estate title in a foreclosure, as Holder in Due Course of a Secured Mortgage Loan, must demonstrate an unbroken chain of properly recorded assignments of the Mortgage and a parallel unbroken chain of completed Note endorsements. Making a claim of beneficial interest in a Mortgage Loan without an unbroken chain of properly recorded assignments of the Mortgage and a parallel unbroken chain of completed Note endorsements would place anyone doing so in jeopardy of violating Federal Statutes and/or Local Laws of Jurisdiction. Where such alternate collection method has been dissolved by failure to follow law, the owner of the Note does (did) have equitable remedy by seeking recovery of the debt by filing suit in a jurisdictional court of equity. The paradox is, where such a holder has pledged a Mortgage Loan (Secured Package) as collateral, knowing that such was not a Secured Package, would present such a pledge with unclean hands.

13. The Mortgage transaction is a contract between the borrower (Payor) and the parties spelled out on the face of the document. A separation between Ownership of the Note and the Ownership of the Mortgage/Deed of Trust would be a violation of the terms of that contract. Under long existing contract law, if the terms of a contract are violated, affecting the conditions under which the Payor is obligated, without the properly evidenced consent of the Payor that contract is void and cannot be returned to without the consent of the Payor.

14. It is an ancient and long held concept within United States Law and CALIFORNIA law that ownership of the Note and ownership of the Mortgage can be separated, however, if ownership is separated, the Mortgage, because it can have no separate existence, cannot survive, and becomes a nullity.

Generally, a transfer by a mortgagee under a deed absolute of his or her interest in the mortgage carries the debt with it. However, where there is no intent to pass the debt, a mortgagee intending to pass the security interest only passes no interest to the grantee. Smith v. J.R. Newberry Co., 21 Cal. App. 432, 131 P. 1055 (2d Dist. 1913). A purported assignment of the security (Deed of Trust or mortgage) is void and ineffective unless accompanied by an assignment of the note, and the purported assignment or delivery of possession of the mortgage or Deed of Trust without a transfer of the obligation secured is both completely ineffective and a legal nullity, or else operates to extinguish the security interest, rendering the note unsecured. Kelley v. Upshaw, 39 Cal. 2d 179, 192, 246 P.2d 23 (1952) (mortgage); Hyde v. Mangan, 88 Cal. 319, 327, 26 P. 180 (1891); Polhemus v. Trainer, 30 Cal. 685, 688, 1866 WL 831 (1866). See Johnson v. Razey, 181 Cal. 342, 344, 184 P. 657 (1919); Restatement (Third) of Property (Mortgages), § 5:4 cmt.e (1997) states: "In general a mortgage is unenforceable if it is held by one who has no right to enforce the secured obligation." Accordingly, [w]hen a note is split from a Deed of Trust, "the note becomes as a practical matter unsecured."

15. Sometimes a Mortgage Loan is sold into MBS Trust. A MBS Trust is governed by a PSA filed with the Securities and Exchange Commission. When a Mortgage Loan is sold into MBS Trust all the well-established Real Estate and Contract Law explained above still applies. For a MBS Trust to be Holder in Due Course of a Secured Mortgage Loan, properly recorded assignments of the Mortgage, as well as completed parallel endorsements of the Note to match, are required not only by well-established Real Estate and Contract Law, but also by the PSA and or REMIC Master Trust Agreement, which governs the MBS Trust in question.

The DOE Mortgage and The DOE Note have been sold by WORLD SAVINGS BANK, FSB on or before JULY 22, 2005.

16. On FEBRUARY 6, 2014, the online Bloomberg database was researched at the request of JOHN DOE whose property address is 123 MAIN STREET SAN

FRANCISCO, CA 94122. JOHN DOE had allegedly signed a Note in favor of WORLD SAVINGS BANK, FSB on JUNE 14, 2005 with the loan number #00002960XXXX. This loan was identified in WORLD SAVINGS BANK MORTGAGE PASS-THROUGH CERTIFICATES REMIC 19 TRUST. The loan is being serviced by WORLD SAVINGS BANK, FSB with the clarifying code and, or abbreviation on the Specialty Licensed Terminal of WORLD SAVINGS BANK MORTGAGE PASS-THROUGH CERTIFICATES REMIC 19 TRUST (herein referred to as "REMIC 19 TRUST").

17. Pursuant to a thorough review of an audit, I have found the aforementioned DOE Mortgage Loan number in multiple classes of the REMIC 19 TRUST Trust. The DOE Obligation has been sold to multiple classes of the REMIC 19 TRUST Trust. Where it remains a performing asset as of FEBRUARY 6, 2014.

18. It is impossible to ascertain to who owns what, as the income stream from the DOE Obligation is no longer owned in a unified manner as described by the Prospectus when discussing the Classes within the Trust Pool. Each class of the REMIC 19 TRUST Trust owns a different partial interest in the DOE Obligation. Even though a Trust may show a Class within that Trust as being paid, this is a predetermined action by the Trust. It does not mean that the DOE Obligation has been paid. It is impossible to make that determination as the DOE Obligation no longer exists in its original form. Subsequently, the ownership of partial interest in the DOE Obligation can no longer be determined, nor can it be determined what or which partial interest in DOE Obligation has been paid nor what percentage of that partial interest in the DOE Obligation has been satisfied/settled. Even though there is some division of performance of the loan from class to class. If ownership the DOE Obligation exists in any class as the Transferable Record of the ownership, the DOE Obligation exists in total within the Trust.

19. Securitization is the process of aggregating the Obligations from a large number of mortgage loans, into what is called a mortgage pool and then selling "shares" (called certificates) of ownership of partial interest of the Obligations to investors. The income stream from the Obligation that the DOE mortgage payments produce flows through fractionalized payments into many different classes to many different investors, of the REMIC 19 TRUST Trust depending on which certificates of which class were purchased by which investor. My research shows that ownership of the DOE Obligation does appear in the schedules and agreements. The divided monthly loan payments paid by JOHN DOE to WORLD SAVINGS BANK, FSB most definitely flowed into multiple classes of the WORLD SAVINGS BANK MORTGAGE PASS-THROUGH CERTIFICATES REMIC 19 TRUST.

20. The ownership of the DOE Obligation has been conveyed as a Transferable Record to multiple classes of the REMIC 19 TRUST Trust. For

ownership of the DOE Obligation not to have been stripped away from the ownership of the DOE Note by that conveyance, ownership of the DOE Note must have also been transferred to multiple classes of the REMIC 19 TRUST Trust.

Even though the DOE Obligation is supposedly owned by multiple classes of the REMIC 19 TRUST Trust, it can only be determined if the original DOE Note had been physically delivered to multiple classes of the REMIC 19 TRUST Trust by checking with the custodian of documents. Until then, there is no evidence multiple classes of the REMIC 19 TRUST Trust possessed or owned in any manner the DOE Note or mortgage before the closing date of JULY 22, 2005, as required by its own agreements.

21. The ownership of the DOE Obligation has been conveyed as a Transferable Record to multiple classes of the REMIC 19 TRUST Trust. For the conditions of DOE Mortgage over the DOE Obligation not to have been stripped away by that conveyance, ownership of the DOE Mortgage must have also been transferred to multiple classes of the REMIC 19 TRUST Trust.

22. The beneficial interest (ownership) of the DOE Mortgage has been recorded in the Official records of SAN FRANCISCO County Registry as being in the name of WORLD SAVINGS BANK, FSB of the loan on JUNE 14, 2005. However, it is clear that WORLD SAVINGS BANK, FSB as recorded as the original lender on the DOE Mortgage sold all ownership interest, in the DOE Obligation to multiple classes of the REMIC 19 TRUST Trust on or about JUNE 14, 2005 near the closing date of the REMIC 19 TRUST Trust. Ownership of the DOE Obligation or Note, but not the mortgage security, is held in multiple classes of the REMIC 19 TRUST Trust, and the payments under the DOE Obligation are disbursed to the investors of REMIC 19 TRUST Trust who hold certificates to the investment classes into which payments under the DOE Obligation are scheduled to flow. Therefore, the transfer of beneficial interest in the DOE Mortgage by WORLD SAVINGS BANK, FSB might be accomplished, but that beneficial interest is no longer attached to ownership of the DOE Obligation.

***

As Multiple Classes of the REMIC 19 TRUST Trust Own the DOE Obligation, Multiple Classes of the REMIC 19 TRUST Trust are Required to have Ownership of the DOE Note and the DOE Mortgage or Deed of Trust

By multiple classes of the REMIC 19 TRUST Trust purchasing the DOE Obligation and doing with it whatever was done, multiple classes of the REMIC

19 TRUST Trust were exercising rights of ownership over the DOE Mortgage Loan and payment stream. By exercising rights of ownership over the DOE Mortgage Loan multiple classes of the REMIC 19 TRUST Trust made claims of ownership of all three parts of the DOE Mortgage Loan.

The DOE Obligation only exists through the tangible instruments creating it, the DOE Note and the DOE Mortgage. The sale of the ownership of the DOE Obligation to multiple classes of the REMIC 19 TRUST Trust, without striping away the ownership of the DOE Obligation from the ownership of the DOE Note, could only be accomplished with the accompanying negotiations of the DOE Note and the accompanying assignments of the DOE Mortgage to multiple classes of the REMIC 19 TRUST Trust.

Multiple classes of the REMIC 19 TRUST Trust have made and continue to make claims of ownership of the DOE Obligation and exercise those claims. To exercise claims of ownership of the DOE Obligation, assignments of the DOE Mortgage should have been accomplished. Multiple classes of the REMIC 19 TRUST Trust are acting as if assignments of the DOE Mortgage have been accomplished.

The assignment of the DOE Mortgage is a conveyance of an instrument concerning real property which must be recorded to be acted upon. United States Code considers that anyone certifying that a real estate instrument has been assigned, when in fact it has not, is guilty of a felonious criminal act.

> Title 18 USC Chapter 47 § 1021
>
> > Whoever, being an officer or other person authorized by any law of the United States to record a conveyance of real property or any other instrument which by such law may be recorded, knowingly certifies falsely that such conveyance or instrument has or has not been recorded, shall be fined under this title, or imprisoned not more than five years, or both.

Multiple Classes of the REMIC 19 TRUST Trust cannot Claim Ownership of either the DOE Note or the DOE Mortgage or Deed of Trust.

Multiple classes of the REMIC 19 TRUST Trust own the DOE Obligation. However, the transfers of ownership of either of the two tangible parts of the security instrument that evidence the DOE Obligation from WORLD SAVINGS BANK, FSB to multiple classes of the REMIC 19 TRUST are not memorialized in the SAN FRANCISCO County Record in a manner which observes United States Code.

Under the Consumer Credit Protection Act Title 15 USC Chapter 41 § 1641(g) any transfer of the DOE Mortgage to multiple classes of the REMIC 19 TRUST would be in violation of Federal Statute, if those transfers had not been recorded SAN FRANCISCO County Record within 30 days along with notification of JOHN DOE that the transfers had occurred. As there are no recorded assignments of the DOE Mortgage from WORLD SAVINGS BANK, FSB to multiple classes of the REMIC 19 TRUST, within 30 days of the of JULY 22, 2005, closing date of the REMIC 19 TRUST, either there has been a violation of Federal Law or multiple classes of the REMIC 19 TRUST, who are the owners of the DOE Obligation, are not the owners of the either the DOE Note or the DOE Mortgage. The assignment of mortgage to the REMIC 19 TRUST was not made until JULY 22, 2005, document number #2005-975XXX of the SAN FRANCISCO County Records.

Title 15 USC Chapter 41 § 1641(g)

(g) Notice of new creditor

(1) In general

In addition to other disclosures required by this subchapter, not later than 30 days after the date on which a mortgage loan is sold or otherwise transferred or assigned to a third party, the creditor that is the new owner or assignee of the debt shall notify the borrower in writing of such transfer, including—

(A) the identity, address, telephone number of the new creditor;

(B) the date of transfer;

(C) how to reach an agent or party having authority to act on behalf of the new creditor;

(D) the location of the place where transfer of ownership of the debt is recorded; and

(E) any other relevant information regarding the new creditor.

23. Multiple classes of the REMIC 19 TRUST are the owners of the DOE Obligation, however, according to CALIFORNIA State Law, multiple classes of the REMIC 19 TRUST can only be entitled to enforce the DOE Mortgage if multiple classes of the REMIC 19 TRUST were transferred ownership of the DOE Mortgage by way of assignments pursuant to

> Cal. Civ. Stat. § 1213 provides: No assignment of a mortgage on real property or of any interest therein, is good or effectual in law or equity, against creditors or subsequent purchasers, for a valuable consideration, and without notice, unless the assignment is contained in a document which, in its title, indicates an assignment of mortgage and is recorded according to law.

> Cal. Civ. Stat. § 2934 provides: Any assignment of a mortgage and any assignment of the beneficial interest under a Deed of Trust may be recorded, and from the time the same is filed for record operates as constructive notice of the contents thereof to all persons; and any instrument by which any mortgage or Deed of Trust of, lien upon or interest in real property, (or by which any mortgage of, lien upon or interest in personal property a document evidencing or creating which is required or permitted by law to be recorded), is subordinated or waived as to priority may be recorded, and from the time the same is filed for record operates as constructive notice of the contents thereof, to all persons.

The DOE Mortgage/Deed of Trust must have been duly assigned to multiple classes of the REMIC 19 TRUST for multiple classes of the REMIC 19 TRUST to be entitled to enforce the DOE Mortgage.

As explained previously in ¶5 thru ¶12 assignments of the DOE Mortgage must be accompanied by parallel endorsements of the DOE Note for the DOE Mortgage Loan to remain secured by the DOE Property. Because indorsements are very often undated and because a plaintiff must prove that it had standing at the inception of a case, Calvo v. HSBC Bank USA, N.A., 199 Cal. App. 4th 118, 125, 130 Cal. Rptr. 3d

815 (2d Dist. 2011), the assignment will be determinative of, or at least evidence that would support or contradict a plaintiff's claim of standing.

Importantly, mere presentment of the DOE Note (even if shown to be the original) is not in itself proof of an equitable transfer of the DOE Note. This demonstration of possession may be sufficient to enforce the DOE Note, but carries no indicia of ownership or intent to transfer. The UCC consecrated a preference in commercial transactions for simple possession of indorsed instruments over proof of actual ownership, an exception in the law that was intended to foster free trade of commercial paper.

The concept that a Note holder, even one who is not legitimate, may nevertheless bring an action on the DOE Note is entrenched in commercial law and commonly summarized by the axiom "even a thief may enforce a note." However, the taking of the DOE Home by foreclosure is an equitable remedy and equity does not allow a "thief" to use a stolen DOE Note to foreclose through the DOE Mortgage lien or Deed of Trust.

For all three parts of the DOE Loan as a whole to have been transferred into the REMIC 19 TRUST there is a chain of entities through which the DOE Mortgage must be assigned, and the DOE Note endorsed. This chain of transfer as required in the REMIC 19 TRUST PSA (Pooling and Servicing Agreement) is to have begun with a recorded assignment of the DOE Mortgage and an indorsement of the DOE Note from the Lender (WORLD SAVINGS BANK, FSB) to the Sponsor (WORLD SAVINGS BANK, FSB). Once the Sponsor (WORLD SAVINGS BANK, FSB) had taken complete ownership, then a recorded assignment of the DOE Mortgage and an indorsement of the DOE Note from the Sponsor (WORLD SAVINGS BANK, FSB) to the Depositor was to have occurred. After the Depositor had taken complete ownership, a recorded assignment of the DOE Mortgage and an endorsement of the DOE Note from the Depositor (to the trustee (THE BANK OF NEW YORK) was next to have occurred. Finally, once the trustee (THE BANK OF NEW YORK) had taken complete ownership, a recorded assignment of the DOE Mortgage and an endorsement of the DOE Note from the trustee (THE BANK OF NEW YORK) to the REMIC 19 TRUST.

Moreover, these assignments were to all be recorded in the Official records of SAN FRANCISCO County Registry as per the PSA for the REMIC 19 TRUST. To explain further with a simple example, Party A must contract and assign to Party B, and Party B must contract and assign to Party C, and Party C must contract and assign to Party D and so on. So a contract and an assignment from Party A to Party D is not allowable.

Of course, all of these dealings must be recorded within the Official records of SAN FRANCISCO County Registry which date stamps each recording so as to prevent any "backdating."

As explained previously, any electronic transfers of the DOE Mortgage that may have been executed without recording within the Official records of SAN FRANCISCO County Registry are void under Uniform Electronic Transactions Act (UETA) USC § 15-96-1-7003.

USC § 15-96-1-7003

(a) Excepted requirements

The provisions of section 7001 of this title shall not apply to a contract or other record to the extent it is governed by—

(3) the Uniform Commercial Code, as in effect in any State, other than sections 1-107 and 1-206 and Articles 2 and 2A

The DOE Note specifically states that it is secured by a Mortgage, dated the same day, and the DOE Mortgage refers to the DOE Note, and incorporates the DOE Note into its terms and conditions.

The written agreement that created the REMIC 19 TRUST is a PSA, and is a matter of public record, available on the website of the Securities Exchange Commission. The REMIC 19 TRUST is also described in a "Prospectus Supplement," also available on the SEC website. The REMIC 19 TRUST by its terms set a "CLOSING DATE" of on or about JULY 22, 2005. The DOE Note in this case did not become REMIC 19 TRUST property in compliance with the requirement set forth in the PSA. The REMIC 19 TRUST agreement is filed under oath with the Securities and Exchange Commission. The acquisition of the assets of the REMIC 19 TRUST and PSA are governed under the laws of New York.

The PSA is the document that governs this trust. The REMIC 19 TRUST operates in the state of New York, and New York law requires strict compliance and adherence to the REMIC 19 TRUST documents. Any action by the REMIC 19 TRUST in contravention to the REMIC 19 TRUST PSA is void under New York Trust Law.

REMIC 19 TRUST PSA substantially states:

This Agreement shall be construed in accordance with the laws of the state of New York, and the obligations, rights and remedies of the parties hereunder shall be determined in accordance with such laws (without regard to principles of conflicts of law other than Section 5-1401 of the

New York General Obligations Law which shall govern). With respect to any claim arising out of this Agreement, each party irrevocably submits to the exclusive jurisdiction of the courts of the state of New York and the United States District Court located in the Borough of Manhattan in The City of New York, and each party irrevocably waives any objection which it may have at any time to the laying of venue of any suit, action or proceeding arising out of or relating hereto brought in any such courts, irrevocably waives any claim that any such suit, action or proceeding brought in any such court has been brought in any inconvenient forum and further irrevocably waives the right to object, with respect to such claim, suit, action or proceeding brought in any such court that such court does not have jurisdiction over such party, provided that service of process has been made by any lawful means.(emphasis added) New York Trust Law Chapter 17- B ¶ 7-2.4 Act of trustee in contravention of trust If the trust is expressed in the instrument creating the estate of the trustee, every sale, conveyance or the act of the trustee in contravention of the trust, except as authorized by this article and by any other provision of law, is void.

Ownership or possession by the WORLD SAVINGS BANK, FSB or its agents, of a Note evidencing an Obligation sold to REMIC 19 TRUST is a violation of the PSA. Additionally, if the DOE Mortgage was transferred to the REMIC 19 TRUST as required by the PSA, then there is no way that WORLD SAVINGS BANK, FSB or its Agents can claim any beneficial interest in the DOE Mortgage to assign.

According to the PSA for the REMIC 19 TRUST, the transfer and sale of all Beneficial Interest of the DOE Mortgage to REMIC 19 TRUST should have been done on or before the closing date of the REMIC 19 TRUST which was JULY 22, 2005. These requirements from the PSA also mean the REMIC 19 TRUST is unable to have any other assets put into the REMIC 19 TRUST after the closing date.

The PSA for the REMIC 19 TRUST holds any conveyance of instrument into the REMIC 19 TRUST subject to the specific procedures explained above and in further paragraphs. Therefore, the conveyance of the DOE Note and Mortgage into the REMIC 19 TRUST, cannot be true unless compliance with the PSA specific procedures of conveyance is also proved to be true. The conveyance of the DOE Note and Mortgage into the REMIC 19 TRUST lacks proof of execution of these specific procedures. Then, as proof of PSA compliant conveyance of the DOE Note and Mortgage into the REMIC 19 TRUST is lacking, and cannot now be made to exist, REMIC 19 TRUST, cannot claim have taken the DOE Note and Mortgage as a secured instrument into its collateral pool.

The DOE Mortgage contains notice to the Borrowers that the DOE Note or a partial interest in the DOE Note may be sold; however, a sale of a "partial interest" in the DOE Note strips ownership of the DOE Obligation from ownership of the DOE Note, leaving the DOE Note without an obligation to evidence and the DOE Mortgage without an obligation to hold conditions over.

The DOE Mortgage documents substantially state:

The Note or a partial interest in the Note (together with this Security Instrument) can be sold one or more times without prior notice to Borrower. A sale might result in a change in the entity (known as the "Servicer") that collects Periodic Payments due under the Note and this Security Instrument and performs other mortgage loan servicing obligations under the Note, this Security Instrument, and Applicable Law...."

The Document Purporting to be an "Assignment Name" is Invalid as an Assignment Name

Black's Law Dictionary defines the term valid as "having legal strength or force, executed with proper formalities, incapable of being rightfully overthrown or sent aside... Founded on trust of fact; capable of being justified; supported, or defended; not weak or defective... of binding force; legally sufficient or efficacious; authorized by law... as distinguished from that which exists or took place in fact or appearance, but has not the requisites to enable it to be recognized and enforced by law." (See *Black's Law Dictionary, Sixth Edition, 1990*, page 1550)

There is a document purporting to be an "Assignment of Mortgage" dated JULY 22, 2005 and recorded JUNE 21, 2005 SAN FRANCISCO County, CALIFORNIA No. #2005- DOE with an assignor MERS with an assignee THE BANK OF NEW YORK as trustee for the REMIC 19 TRUST.

First and most importantly the original lender, WORLD SAVINGS BANK, FSB gave up all ownership of the DOE Obligation on or before JUNE 14, 2005 to multiple classes of the REMIC 19 TRUST. Once WORLD SAVINGS BANK, FSB had given up the ownership of the DOE Obligation, the ownership of the DOE Obligation was stripped away from the ownership of the DOE Note and the ownership of the DOE Mortgage. WORLD SAVINGS BANK, FSB could transfer beneficial interest in the DOE Note or Mortgage; however, that beneficial interest would not include ownership of the DOE Obligation.

The consequences of the ownership of the DOE Obligation being stripped away from the beneficial interests of the DOE Note and Mortgage means the DOE Note is without an Obligation to evidence and the DOE Mortgage is without an Obligation to enforce conditions against.

WORLD SAVINGS BANK, FSB can assign beneficial interest in the DOE Mortgage, albeit with no ownership of the DOE Obligation, to whomever they please. In order for this document purporting to be an "Assignment of Mortgage" to be valid as an actual assignment however, it would have to determine if a transfer could be made to the assignee. I will explain how transfer to the assignee named could not have been accomplished by this document purporting to be an Assignment of Mortgage.

The assignee named by the document purporting to be an "Assignment of Mortgage" is THE BANK OF NEW YORK as trustee for the REMIC 19 TRUST. In order to exist the REMIC 19 TRUST agreed to operate under the REMIC 19 TRUST PSA and all applicable Law. As previously explained in ¶35 in order for the DOE Mortgage Loan to be transferred to the REMIC 19 TRUST a chain of negotiations needed to occur. A direct transfer from the original lender to THE BANK OF NEW YORK violates the terms and conditions under the REMIC 19 TRUST PSA, under New York Trust Law governing the REMIC 19 TRUST, and is void.

Further this document purporting to be an "Assignment of Mortgage" is not timely to properly transfer the DOE Note and Mortgage to the REMIC 19 TRUST where it has been shown to be a performing asset.

From the Prospectus for the REMIC 19 TRUST:

The closing date for the REMIC 19 TRUST was JULY 22, 2005. What this means is that the REMIC 19 TRUST is unable to have any other assets put into the REMIC 19 TRUST after that closing date.

In view of the foregoing, all assignments executed after the REMIC 19 TRUST Trust's closing date are void for the reason that all assignments into the Trust after JULY 22, 2005 violate the express terms of the REMIC 19 TRUST PSA. All assignments of Mortgages/Deeds of Trust and or endorsements of notes executed after the REMIC 19 TRUST closing date are void.

The Prospectus Supplement for the REMIC 19 TRUST provides that any attempted or purported transfer in violation of these transfer restrictions will be null and void and will vest no rights in any purported transferee. Any transferor or agent to whom the trustee provides information as to any applicable tax imposed on such transferor or agent may be required to bear the cost of computing or providing such information.

There are enormous tax consequences, if the document purporting to be an "Assignment Name" filed in the Official Records of SAN FRANCISCO County would be authentic, in that this trust has elected to be a REMIC Trust. According to the Prospectus, under the heading "Federal Income Tax Consequences." Multiple classes of the REMIC 19 TRUST that the DOE Obligation is owned by, elected to be treated as a REMIC, which provides for pass-through tax treatment of the income generated by the Trust assets.

Internal Revenue Code Section 860 regulates the activities and requirements of a REMIC Trust like REMIC 19 TRUST:

According to 26 CFR§ 1.860D-1(c) (2):

Identification of assets. The formation of the REMIC does not occur until (i) The sponsor identifies the assets of the REMIC, such as through execution an indenture with respect to the asset; and (ii) The REMIC issues the regular and residual interests in the REMIC.

In other words, the REMIC is not officially formed until the Credit-Based Asset Servicing and Securitization LLC, the seller/sponsor of the MBS Trust Name Trust identifies and transfers all the specific assets (the specific loans) of the REMIC.

The PSA for the REMIC 19 TRUST specifically identifies a closing date which is the last day that an asset (loan) can be "identified for inclusion" in the Trust/REMIC. The closing date also serves as the Startup Day for the REMIC. According to Internal Revenue code Section, "All of a REMIC's loans must be acquired on the startup day of the REMIC or within three months thereafter".

REMIC 19 TRUST Prospectus:

WORLD SAVINGS BANK, FSB Has No Claim to Ownership of the DOE Note

The DOE Note has been endorsed by WORLD SAVINGS BANK, FSB the original lender. The endorsement states "Pay to the Order of without Recourse". This constitutes a negotiation under UCC Article 3 concerning negotiable instruments. Although no payee is yet named, clearly WORLD SAVINGS BANK, FSB has released all interest in the DOE Note.

UCC 7-501 Form of negotiation and requirements of due negotiation

(a) The following rules apply to a negotiable tangible document of title:

(1) if the document's original terms run to the order of a named person, the document is negotiated by the named person's endorsements and delivery. After the named person's endorsement in blank or to bearer, any person may negotiate the document by delivery alone; (emphasis added).

WORLD SAVINGS BANK, FSB transferred its ownership of the DOE Obligation to multiple classes of the REMIC 19 TRUST and transferred its ownership of the DOE Note. Ownership of the DOE Obligation was transferred to multiple classes of the REMIC 19 TRUST and ownership of the DOE Note traveled on without it.

The Terms of the DOE Mortgage have been Violated and the DOE Mortgage is Unenforceable

WORLD SAVINGS BANK, FSB has released all interest in the DOE Note to an as yet unnamed payee. The DOE Mortgage as a contract can only enforce its contractual terms against the obligation evidenced by the DOE Note.

The DOE Mortgage is governed by CALIFORNIA Law. CALIFORNIA Law and Federal Law requires proper recordation of assignment to transfer ownership of the DOE Mortgage.

It has been explained earlier, how it is not possible for ownership of the DOE Mortgage to have been assigned to THE BANK OF NEW YORK as trustee for the REMIC 19 TRUST.

There is an assignment of the DOE Mortgage recorded in the SAN FRANCISCO County Record, with DOE releasing ownership of the DOE Mortgage intending that transfer to be to THE BANK OF NEW YORK as trustee for the REMIC 19 TRUST. However, WORLD SAVINGS BANK, FSB released, through indorsement, ownership of the DOE Note, evidencing the obligation, to whoever wishes to fill in the payee line. THE BANK OF NEW YORK as trustee for the REMIC 19 TRUST, may attempt to claim ownership of the DOE Mortgage but that ownership would have nothing to enforce the DOE Mortgage contractual terms against. The DOE Mortgage is such an unenforceable contract.

Ownership of the DOE Mortgage is no longer with WORLD SAVINGS BANK, FSB, yet no one else has any authority to enforce its terms, while the DOE Note is waiting for someone to claim ownership. The DOE Mortgage is an unenforceable contract, no longer being tied to an obligation to enforce its contractual terms over.

Under long existing contract law, if the terms of a contract are violated, affecting the conditions under which the Payor is obligated, without the properly evidenced consent of the Payor that contract is void and cannot be returned to without the consent of the Payor. Even if ownership of the DOE Note and the DOE Mortgage, could be rejoined, the DOE Mortgage, as a now unenforceable contract, no longer being tied to an obligation to enforce its contractual terms over, cannot be returned to being an enforceable contract without the party's consent.

Ownership of the DOE Obligation Can Not be Rejoined to Ownership of the DOE Note or the DOE Mortgage or Deed of Trust

Multiple classes of the REMIC 19 TRUST have ownership of the DOE Obligation. Multiple classes of the REMIC 19 TRUST have yet to all and each be named as payee on the DOE Note and do not now have ownership of the DOE Note. For multiple classes of the REMIC 19 TRUST to gain ownership of the DOE Note, multiple classes of the REMIC 19 TRUST would have to all and each be named payee.

REMIC 19 TRUST its classes, its officers and its agents are prohibited from accepting any assets on behalf of the Trust after JULY 22, 2005. The REMIC 19 TRUST, its classes, its officers and its agents can longer accept ownership of the DOE Note. Ownership of the DOE Note and ownership of the DOE Obligation will remain separate.

Because ownership of the DOE Note was separated from ownership of the DOE Obligation, and will remain separate the DOE Mortgage, is left with no way to enforce its conditions over the obligation which should be evidenced by the DOE Note, making the DOE Mortgage an unenforceable contract.

With Ownership of the DOE Obligation Stripped Away and No Way to Enforce the Conditions Under the DOE Mortgage the DOE Loan is a Nullity

The ownership of DOE Mortgage Lien was separated from the ownership of the DOE Note, leaving the DOE Note no Obligation to evidence and DOE Mortgage no Obligation to enforce conditions over.

The limited beneficial interest WORLD SAVINGS BANK, FSB retained in the DOE Mortgage Loan after selling the DOE Obligation to multiple classes of the REMIC 19 TRUST as of JULY 22, 2005, does not include ownership of the DOE Obligation. No acceptable assignments of the limited beneficial interest in the DOE Mortgage to multiple classes of the REMIC 19 TRUST has been recorded into the SAN FRANCISCO County Recorder's Office, nor should there be, as such a lawful intangible assignment would fall under the governance of UCC 9. There is no evidence of the proper negotiations of the limited beneficial interest in the DOE Note to multiple classes of the REMIC 19 TRUST. With no properly recorded owner of the DOE Mortgage, with corroborating ownership of the DOE Obligation, there is no one to enforce the conditions that would have been over the Obligation that would have been evidenced by the DOE Note. The DOE Obligation is no longer secured by the DOE Property.

With no specific properly secured owner of the limited beneficial interest of the DOE Note there is no way to enforce the stripped away DOE Obligation through the DOE Note.

Signature of Securitization Auditor

It was a balmy Missouri summer day in the Honorable Chief Judge Michael W. Mosman's courtroom. The Status Conference for Case 3:14-cv-01836-MO was held on July 8, 2015 and shows in the District Court Transcript 9th CCA.Dkt. 47, Exh A. p. 16, the judge saying, "Well, if she's in default on a note that's forged, then she's not in default in a way that matters ...right? You must have an authentic reason for her to be in default on it, don't you? Isn't that the foundation of foreclosure?"

What this has shown us throughout this book is that in nearly any instance in a foreclosure procedure there is a substantially high chance that the foreclosing parties have absolutely no right to commence with the foreclosure proceedings. We have proved in so many various points that it would be fair to assume that the foreclosing party has no legal standing to foreclose. If you begin your own foreclosure procedure with this premise in mind, you might be halfway to the end before you begin. However, we have also seen that the wheels of justice are not often fair and impartial.

Another thing we have learned is that there is no independent trustee, so in truth, a deed of trust is bogus and void on its face. It is for this reason that we also learned that over 85% of any deed of trusts recorded have fraudulent documentation in their files. Since there is no independent party to oversee the deed or the title to protect it from fraudulent activity, our system is rampant with fraudulent documents tainting the legitimacy of a title.

What we have also come to understand is if there was a point in any part of the loan that the loan was in fact securitized, there is a good chance that the securitization process was done incorrectly and untimely and the securitization of that note is void. There are SEC rules and regulations that dictate these outcomes for securitization.

After my legal battle closed, and while writing this book, I studied, tested, and became a nationally certified Bloomberg Forensic Loan Analyst through the pre-eminent company on this legal strategy, Certified Forensic Loan Auditors (CFLA). Since then, I have spent thousands of hours combing over reams of loan documents with people from across the country, helping them to understand the illegalities of their loan securitization process.

For a note with a Deed of Trust to be securitized, it must first be bifurcated. If the Deed of Trust has been bifurcated from the note, then the outstanding note no longer has any connection to the property through the Deed of Trust.

If that now bifurcated note did not follow the SEC rules and regulations of bifurcation and fully complied with the rules and dates of the pooling and servicing agreement for the securitization, it is to be considered void.

However, we find time and time again through Bloomberg forensic loan securitization audits, and independent studies such as the ones we have previously discussed, these notes have shown a high propensity for non-compliance. Despite this, there are many loans fraudulently placed in mortgage-backed-securities and sold to be a solid and triple-A rated product. Nothing could be further from the truth.

There is a large portion of mortgage-backed-securities that are holding hundreds and thousands of fraudulent notes in their tranches. There are thousands of tranches containing thousands of notes that, according to the rule of law, are in fact fraudulent and therefore void. This leads me to state that Wall Street and its mortgage-backed-security investments are based on fraud and have no true legal standing to be used as an investment vehicle.

Now, if the note was bifurcated from the Deed of Trust, there is no more contractual collateral for the note attached to the property. The Deed of Trust has been removed from the note and can no longer be used as an encumbrance to the property as it is void. This means that the outstanding balance of the note cannot be collected in a foreclosure proceeding. The balance of the note should then be converted to a personal loan and therefore fall under an entirely different set of rules and codes that apply to the collection of that debt. Despite all rule of law outlining this as the way our justice system should work, it fails to.

Although, in some areas and jurisdictions of our justice system there are changes occurring. Perhaps, there is a quantum of justice that is still reserved out there for a homeowner. Perhaps, we see a new light shining on the corrupt darkness.

New Legal Actions for Standing

There is a new law in the state of New York that has been giving parties to a foreclosure action the right to a key defense. They can assert this at any time during a foreclosure procedure on a home loan. This action can delay the foreclosure procedure against them. This new law provides that a defense for a lack of standing to foreclose is not waived if the defendant fails to raise the defense at the onset of the legal action.

As we have come to understand why, one of the most contested points in mortgage foreclosure litigation that followed the 2008 economic collapse was the point of a party's standing to foreclose. As we began to learn more as more stones of corruption began to be overturned, an increasing number of lawsuits would contest whether the plaintiff had an interest in the claim and was legally able to sue the borrower.

Usually, by law, all that is necessary for a plaintiff to have standing to foreclose is that it be the holder or assignee of the promissory note at the time the foreclosure action began.

Due to the exposure of corruption on Wall Street, based on the fraudulent processes of the securitization of mortgages, law firms would routinely allege a lack of standing to foreclose. This assertion would be based on the irregularities in the note endorsements and the chain of assignments during the securitization process.

The state of New York took this issue to task. In Wells Fargo Bank Minnesota, N.A. v. Mastropaolo, New York's Appellate Division Second Department held that this defense of lack of standing to foreclose was something that could be waived unless it was raised by a defendant. The defendant must have raised the point at the onset of a foreclosure procedure. It had to have been raised in an answer to a complaint or in a pre-answer filing of a motion to dismiss, or it was waived and could no longer be used as a defense. Wells Fargo Bank Minnesota, N.A. v. Mastropaolo, 42 A.D.3d 239, 837 N.Y.S.2d 247 (2d Dep't. 2007).

On December 23, 2019, Governor Andrew Cuomo signed legislation amending New York Real Property Actions and Proceedings Law (RPAPL). The legislation added RPAPL § 1302-a to their code books. This new change in their law became effective immediately upon Cuomo's signature.

> RPAPL § 1302-a states as follows:
>
> Defense of lack of standing; not waived. Notwithstanding the provisions of subdivision (e) of rule thirty-two hundred eleven of the civil practice law and rules, any objection or defense based on the plaintiff's lack of standing in a foreclosure proceeding related to a home loan, as defined in paragraph (a) of subdivision six of section thirteen hundred four of this article, shall not be waived if a defendant fails to raise the objection or defense in a responsive pleading or pre-answer motion to dismiss. A defendant may not raise an objection or defense of lack of standing following a foreclosure sale, however, unless the judgment of foreclosure and sale was issued upon defendant's default.

This new provision only applies to a "home loan". A home loan is defined in RPAPL § 1304(6)(a) as a loan that includes an open-end credit plan. The borrower must be a natural person. The debt is incurred by the borrower primarily for personal, family, or household purposes. The loan must be secured by a mortgage or

Deed of Trust on real estate of a one-to-four-unit dwelling. It pertains to real estate in the state of New York.

Now, it became possible for defendants to assert the defense of lack of standing at any stage in a foreclosure procedure, even if they did not assert this argument at the outset of the litigation. Unless the foreclosure was issued upon a defendant's default, the defendant may raise the objection for the defense of lack of standing following a foreclosure sale at any time.

As we have now come to find, there are many instances where a defense can be argued that there was no actual loan to default on. Or there was no default as the defendant might be current on their mortgage. Or there was no default because the foreclosing party had already paid off the mortgage during the securitization process, and therefore are not in a position of ownership to declare a default.

In a foreclosure proceeding a defendant might fail to answer the complaint or otherwise appear to the action, or perhaps, the defendant was not served, or perhaps, they were not served correctly and found their legal documents in the sewer system on a rainy day, or perhaps, service is not required with a notice of motion for judgment of foreclosure and sale. Under these circumstances, the new law may allow the defaulting defendant to vacate the foreclosure sale and the judgment of foreclosure and sale and then assert the lack of standing to foreclose as a defense or an objection. This action in New York shows us the potential changes that are occurring in the judicial system. At least in New York.

As in the state of California, New York case law provides that a foreclosure and subsequent sale of a defendant's property is final as to all questions at issue between the parties and concludes all matters of defense that were or might have been litigated in the foreclosure action. This is part and parcel of the idea that the non-judicial foreclosure process holds the foreclosing documents to have the presumption of correctness. This is due to the supposed independence of the trustee in the Deed of Trust relationship. However, we have found this idea to be false and fraudulent on its face.

The Final Stand on Standing

While I was writing this book, I came across one other piece of information that I wanted to make sure I didn't forget to include in this book. It pertains to "standing" in a foreclosure proceeding. It pertains to the depths of fraud that fill Wall Street and the securitization of notes. It pertains to fraud at such a high level that it has kept me awake many nights since learning about it. It exemplifies the institutional corruption and fraud that has become such a part of Wall Street, financial institutions, and the real estate industry.

I had never thought about it during my lawsuit against Wells Fargo Bank because I would have never thought it could be true. Probably in the same way as many of the readers of this book have come to find some of the information I have uncovered and included herein.

When we initially filed the lawsuit against Wells Fargo Bank for fraud and breach of contract in the beginning of 2011, the opposing counsel for the defendants World Savings, Wachovia, Wells Fargo Bank, Golden West, NDEx, et al., filed the corporate documents of Wachovia and Wells Fargo Bank to show their standing and position in the lawsuit. This is a standard part of a response to a lawsuit to show a party's standing to participate in the lawsuit that is filed against them. World Savings had become a defunct corporation years prior to this litigation by the takeover of the company by Wachovia. Shortly after this corporate action, Wachovia was then taken over by Wells Fargo Bank.

If you are a company in the business of lending money to borrowers for real estate transactions, it is a rule of law that to contract legally you must be a legal entity. To be a legal entity, a company must set itself up appropriately with the legal authorities of the state in which it is doing business. That legal authority is the Secretary of State.

Every Secretary of State has their own website where you can go to sign up and create a corporate structure for a company to begin doing business. Some of the company structures associated with becoming a corporation are a C-Corp, S-Corp, LLC, Limited Partnership, to name a few. You can set up trusts and other types of entities but let us keep on the train of thought here.

I did my research of this kind of information when I was litigating the unlawful detainer action. During that process, if you remember, I found several shell companies created by the people who purchased my property illegally. I was able to uncover a remarkably interesting shell game of how those investors attempt to shield their identities from the public.

***

Linda Nash lived in Seminole County, Florida. Seminole County is in the middle of the state and home to Orlando and Disneyworld. Its locals are a proud and conservative population with a modest average income of $50,000 per year. The presiding judge laid it all out in the FINAL JUDGEMENT.

On May 24, 2005, Linda borrowed $58,000 from a financial institution that called themselves "America's Wholesale Lender". If you were living in the United States of America in 2005 and watched television at nearly any hour of the day you would have seen a commercial with a tag line of "America's Wholesale Lender". The bank was cited to be a New York Corporation.

On September 15, 2014, Nash appeared in the courtroom of the Circuit Court of the Eighteenth Judicial Circuit, in and for Seminole County, Florida. The attorneys for Bank of America were also present. All parties appeared and announced to the court that they were ready for trial for Case No. 59-2011-CA-004389. The plaintiff, Bank of America, N.A., successor by merger to BAC Home Loans Servicing, LP, FKA Countrywide Home Loans Servicing, LP., presented its case in full. After they had completed the presentation of their case, Linda Nash, the defendant, cross-examined the plaintiff's representative and sole witness, Chad Anderson. Other evidence was submitted to the court by the plaintiff consisting of a) Exhibit 1- the Note, b) Exhibit 2- the mortgage, c) Exhibit 3- Notice of Intent to Accelerate, and d) Exhibit 4- Payment History. The defendant's cross-examined and presented to the court its Exhibit 1- the Assignment of Mortgage. The court then announced that it was prepared to enter a final judgement based upon the evidence presented, without the necessity of the defendant presenting its witness and testimony.

The court found that there was a mortgage dated May 24, 2005, executed by the borrower, Linda Nash. It was payable to the alleged lender, America's Wholesale Lender. The note was in the amount of $58,500.00. The mortgage documents cited that "the note states that the borrower owes the lender $58,500.00. However, the note bears an endorsement-in-blank on page three. It reads "pay to the order of (_____) without recourse", and underneath that statement, the note purported to be endorsed by "Countrywide Home Loans, Inc., a New York corporation doing business as America's Wholesale Lender".

The plaintiff's only witness testified in court that the assignment of the mortgage presented as the defendant's only documentary evidence at the trial was the only document that he was aware of that purported to transfer any interest in the mortgage or the note, except for the blank endorsement on page three of the note. The witness acknowledged that he knew of no other documents purporting to the transfer of ownership or interest in the note or the mortgage, which the plaintiff sought to foreclose on in this action.

On the cross-examination by the defense, the plaintiff's witness confirmed that he knew of no evidence of transfer of the ownership or interest in the note other than the blank endorsement on page three, signed on behalf of Countrywide Home Loans, Inc., DBA America's Wholesale Lender.

The witness went on to testify that he was aware that America's Wholesale Lender was not incorporated in the year 2005 when the note and mortgage were signed, and that no such corporation was subsequently formed by either Countrywide Home Loans, or Bank of America, or any other of their related corporate entities. The witness went on to confirm that he was aware that America's Wholesale Lender did not ever have a lender's license in the state of Florida and did not have the legal authority to do business in the state of Florida as a New York Corporation under the Florida Statute 607.1506.

The witness also went on to state that he had no knowledge of the existence of any document transferring any interest in the note or mortgage from the lender to Fannie Mae, who is alleged in the plaintiff's complaint to have been the owner of the note at the time the mortgage foreclosure complaint was filed.

Based on the documentary evidence and the witness testimony, the court found that America's Wholesale Lender, a New York corporation, the "Lender", specifically named in the mortgage did not file this action, did not appear at trial, and did not assign any of the interest in the mortgage. America's Wholesale Lender could not file the action or appear at the trial or assign any of the interest in the mortgage because they did not exist in the state of Florida.

The note and mortgage were void because the alleged lender, America's Wholesale Lender, that was stated to be a New York corporation, was not in fact incorporated in the year 2005, or subsequently, at any time, by either Countrywide Home Loans, or Bank of America, or any other entity for that matter.

America's Wholesale Lender was not licensed as a mortgage lender in Florida in the year 2006, or anytime thereafter. Therefore, the alleged mortgage loan was deemed invalid and void. The alleged lender did not have any legal authority to do business in Florida under Florida Statute 607.1506 and the alleged mortgage loan was void.

The court went on to state that the plaintiff and its predecessors in interest had no right to receive payment on the mortgage loan because the loan was invalid and therefore void because the "Lender", America's Wholesale Lender named in the note, was non-existent, and no valid mortgage loan was ever held by the plaintiff or its predecessors in interest.

The alleged assignment of mortgage that purported to transfer interest in the mortgage of BAC Home Loans Servicing, LP, FKA Countrywide Home Loans Servicing, LP, as assignee, was in fact invalid because Mortgage Electronic Registrations Systems, Inc. (MERS), as nominee for America's Wholesale Lender, had no authority to assign the ownership interest of the mortgage. MERS was not the owner of the mortgage and was only a nominee for America's Wholesale Lender, which was a non-existent corporation. Based on this, the purported assignment was therefore invalid.

The plaintiff's witness had no knowledge of who or what entity might have instructed MERS as nominee to attempt to assign or transfer any interest in the mortgage. None of which would have mattered anyway since any event would have been invalid because that entity, namely MERS, had no ownership interest in the mortgage and was merely named as a nominee for the non-existent corporation.

Based on this evidence and testimony, the court found that Bank of America, the corporation that brought the action to the court, had no standing. The court found that the plaintiff had no legal right to attempt to claim ownership of the note or mortgage, or any right as servicer for some other unknown entity and was without any legal basis to attempt to foreclose on the defendant's note, or to collect any payments on the mortgage and note, because America's Wholesale Lender did not exist in 2005, and was never formed as a corporation by the plaintiff or any other entity.

The court stated that the collection of mortgage payments by the plaintiff and its predecessors in interest was therefore illegal and they were without any legal right to receive and use or disburse the funds on behalf of any owner of the note and mortgage. Based on this, the defendant was therefore entitled to recover from the plaintiff all the funds reflected on the plaintiff's Exhibit 4, in which their witness testified about the payment history of monies paid by the defendant to the plaintiff. All collection of these payments was therefore illegal, and they were without any legal right to receive because the note and mortgage were invalid because the alleged lender did not exist and did not have the legal right to receive and retain or disburse these funds.

The court also found that the defendant was entitled to recover from the plaintiff all costs and attorney's fees incurred by the defendant in the action pursuant to the terms of Florida Statute 57.105 as the prevailing party in the action.

The order was done and set in the court's chambers at Sanford, Seminole County, Florida on October 16th, 2014.

One would think, simply by common sense, that this would end there. By a rule, to have a legal contract the contracting party must be a legal entity or person. In other words, a minor or someone who is not of legal age cannot enter into a contract. Why? Because the law states that they are not of legal age. Simple.

For a corporation to become a legal entity, they must file myriad documents with the Secretary of State for the state in which they are incorporating. This paperwork and filing is basically giving birth to an entity known as "corporation XYZ". This will also give the public the knowledge that this company "XYZ, Inc." is in fact legally able to do business and participate in contracts with other people and businesses in that state, under their registered corporate entity. If they do not do this action, then the company is not born yet. They are not legally able to do business in the eyes of the law. Just as a minor is not legally able to enter into and sign a contract without a parent or guardian's consent until the minor reaches that state's legal age.

Simple contract law 101. I guess things just aren't that simple in the world of law.

For Linda Nash, this ruling was appealed and reversed citing other issues. Apparently, despite her bank not being a legitimate corporation to do business in her state, thereby making her contract in fact null and void, the judges seemed to be able to find a legal premise that made the legal proceeding move forward. This was true even though the contract that the legal proceeding was dealing with was in fact void, blank paper, a non-existent documentation by law. Following that ruling, she appealed again citing that the judge's ruling against her in her case, Richard Orfinger, Wendy Berger, James Edwards, and Brian Lambert had subsequently violated her civil rights. The circuit judges hearing this appeal action against the previous judges GRANTED the motion for summary affirmance of the district court's order and DENIED her motion to stay the briefing schedule as moot.

So, despite her getting a mortgage from an organization that had no legal authority to contract with her in the first place, which to all intents and purposes means that the contract did not legally exist, she lost. The financial institution, America's Wholesale Lender, who supposedly gave her funds for her home, did so knowing they were not a legitimate business in the state she resided. This is an act of fraud. This lending institution was one of the nation's largest lending organizations at that time.

***

While writing the last chapter of this book, I received a phone call from a real estate investment person I know in the southern California region who has had to fight against three different fraudulent foreclosure actions. She was able to win against the fraud a few times. However, there was one specific judge in one action that was corrupt to the core. She told me she had just filed documents in her action that included World Savings, which she thought would end her nightmare. What she had uncovered was right in front of my eyes throughout my litigation and I never saw it. I just never looked.

Valerie Lopez uncovered the fact that World Savings Bank, the entity that was instrumental in my case because they were the lending entity of the loan that was foreclosed on, was not licensed to do business in the state of California. Let this really sink in for a moment.

Ms. Lopez found that World Savings Bank, the entity that was listed on my loan documents, the entity that gave us a "pick-a-pay" loan, the entity that was touted as one of America's greatest financial institutions of its time, was not licensed to do business in the state of California.

She filed her documents showing the court that World Savings

Bank was in fact not a legitimate organization under the Secretary of State of California. She thought that this, coupled with her argument that due to this information there is no legitimate contract that can be foreclosed on, would cause her fraudulent foreclosure action to be expunged. However, the judge acknowledged the motion documents and the information, admitted it into her case file documents, and let it go. The judge quickly went on to another issue at hand, therein denying her true justice as it is based on the facts.

There was no legal company entity set up by the Secretary of State under that company name that could legally do business as a financial institution. However, World Saving Bank did billions and billions of dollars of business under this business entity for decades.

Now, as a caveat, I must be clear that some corporations create other corporations that operate separately, however, they are in truth part and parcel of the main corporation. The main corporation might have numerous other corporations under its control with names that are similar to the name of their main organization. Sometimes, the main corporation might name a sub-corporation an entirely different sounding name, but the chain of ownership of the sub-corporation still falls under the guise of the main corporation.

Despite this, my Deed of Trust contract stated World Savings Bank was the lender of record to my property. It didn't state World Savings "and Trust" Bank, or World Savings "Association" Bank, or World "Bank of Savings", or anything else. The name that is listed on my Deed of Trust documents as the lender was a corporation that was never listed and licensed legally to do business in the state of California.

Since finding this information out, and in the process of doing securitization audits of some of my clients, I have found this to be the case in many instances. In many cases I have found that there are a number of financial organizations that are lending to millions of borrowers without the license to do business in the state they are doing business in.

By law, this means that all the contracts given by these organizations are in fact void. Not voidable, but void, blank sheets of paper. There is nothing in those contract documents that should be legally held to any account. No words or numbers on the pages should legally be held to any standard. The entire document is created and distributed through fraud.

This means that all the loan securitizations done by Wall Street that are holding these millions of loans originated by these illegal entities are in fact void. This means that all those mortgage-backed-securities and collateralized debt obligations that are using these illegal loans are built on mountain ranges of fraud and corruption. This means that the mortgage-backed-securities holding these void loans and using these void loans as investment instruments for their investors are void. Or at least voidable.

The true financial house of cards of capitalism is based on fraud. We have found that many of the wheels of capitalism are based solely on fraudulent and void documents, which are then used to generate trillions of dollars.

Our judicial system has failed when one party can foreclose on another party despite having absolutely no standing to foreclose. It has failed by not mandating that all parties must show proof of standing to legally foreclose on someone.

Our courts have failed to adjudicate that the California Supreme Court law of the trustee needs to be independent. Instead, they have chosen to adjudicate foreclosure from a change in the civil code. This makes the state complicit in the fraud.

Our courts have also failed to adjudicate the rules of service in a litigation. This rule is the foundation of law itself of being able to be aware of a cause of action against you. How can you answer a cause of action or a complaint against you if you are unaware of that action? If you don't answer that cause or complaint you will be found guilty. The fact that a party can ignore service or leave your court documents to blow in the street or get washed up in the city sewer system during the rain is a travesty of justice.

Our judicial system has failed by permitting judges who may own stock in a financial institution, to litigate cases that, in many cases, might create a favorable outcome for a financial institution due to the judge's own personal interest.

I am hoping that the information provided in this book will help initiate, activate, and facilitate the changes that are necessary to help stop the rampant fraud that has permeated our real estate market across the nation and continues to decimate millions of families in its wake. I am hopeful that there are those in positions to be able to expedite the changes necessary to fix the dire issues laid out in this book. I am grateful for all those foreclosure warriors across the nation who have fought against the corruption, not only for themselves, but in doing so have been able to shed light.

A Call to Action

If you are in the state of California and have a loan that was originated by World Savings Bank, please contact us at:

douglasjboggs@substack.com

It is our intent to bring transparency and justice to the financial industry. Perhaps, we can help end decades of nightmares for families across this country who are being foreclosed illegally. My team is putting together what could become one of the nation's largest class action lawsuits for fraud ever in the United States.

If you have proof that whatever the financial institution you have listed on your mortgage or Deed of Trust documents is in fact not registered with the state you are in prior to the date of your contract agreement with that institution, we would like to hear from you.

Postscript

A friend of mine told me at the onset of my writing this book, "Your challenge to writing this book is to find a way to deliver your information so that people can wrap their minds around the fact that the entire paradigm is a sham. It is your task to let people understand that, from the outset of them trying to create their own little part of their dream, they are but pawns in the large picture they are party to but will never profit from. That the whole American Dream idea is built on fraud and corruption and that we all participate in a kind of blind obedience to a systemic monetary paradigm that is a roll of the dice to whether it will be you or your neighbor who will be caught in the cesspool of pain and destruction that it can create. You must try to help people to open their eyes to something that they know exists but choose to ignore."

None of this nightmare began with one act. There is no overall grand conspiracy but a systemic situation that we all participate in, whether we know it or not. It is what exists. But if it didn't always exist this way, and we grew into and created this, it can be replaced. There are huge players that continue to help to facilitate the system. Former President Donald Trump made millions of dollars throughout his career by purchasing foreclosed properties. Former Treasury Secretary Steven Mnuchin was given over $1.5 Billion dollars by the United States government to purchase thousands upon thousands of foreclosed properties and defaulting corporations. Vice-President Kamala Harris had the opportunity to prosecute Mnuchin while she was the acting Attorney General of California, while he was raping and pillaging the public during the 2008 economic collapse but chose not to. Former Vice-President and now President Joe Biden was party to President Obama's financial rescue plans of trillions of dollars to bailout Wall Street financial corporations, whilst giving little to no restitution to the average American against the gross fraud and negligence of the financial or judicial systems.

It simply leads me to wonder why anyone would think things are going to change in any way. The only way things will change for the average homeowner is when the average homeowner decides to stand up and demand a different result. This should include to stand by their neighbor who is being foreclosed on illegally. If your neighbor is dealing with a foreclosure, there is an extremely high chance that it is filled with fraud and is illegal. This fraud against your neighbor will also hurt your own property value. Make it matter for not only your bottom line but for your neighbor and neighborhood. Make it matter for your local communities and schools who lose out on millions in taxes due to the system. Demand that your local legislators change the local rules that give banks free rein to steal your property from you whenever they choose. Demand by voting for judges in your district that are not emboldened by financial institutions through their retirement holdings. If so, demand that the judges be removed from any foreclosure procedures and then vote them out of their office.

If you recall the ending of the Frank Capra movie, *It's a Wonderful Life,* George Bailey did not work with the banks to help him with his financial problems. The people banded together to rise above the system and helped George. This movie was made in 1946 with a setting during the 1929 economic collapse. That narrative has not changed in a hundred years. The fight continues. But we must all be armed with as much information as we can, so that if this nightmare does come to your doorstep, you have enough information to fight.

Ten years have passed since I have received my first fraudulent documents for the illegal foreclosure against me. It has been nine years since I was forced to move out of my home on my birthday:

the home that I built with my two hands and was illegally sold in front of my own eyes. It has been six years since I began writing this book.

I know I have not covered everything that happens in a foreclosure proceeding, let alone all the illegalities that happen in a fraudulent foreclosure. This book wasn't intended to cover all topics in a way that people would be able to use as a handbook to a successful foreclosure. What I hope I accomplished was that this work created an awareness that this nightmare can happen to anyone, anytime, anywhere. I wanted people to be able to understand that their deed of trust is a void document. Families across America write a check every month to a corporation that has no right to collect that money. I wanted people to understand that this fight is far from over and is only beginning. It is still only beginning because the media machine behind all this continues to spread the narrative that foreclosure is the homeowner's fault for not being able to make their mortgage payment. I am hoping that by now you can see that you can find yourself in foreclosure whether you make your payments or not. Therein lies the problem.

People always ask me, "Well, how do they do that?" The answer is simple, "Fraud." That's it. The financial institutions are in the business of making money. And that is making money for them, not you. These corporations are not in business to help their customers but are in business for profit. Much of this profit comes from fraudulent activity. As a society, this has been exposed to us time and again. And nothing happens, and no one is prosecuted.

The judicial system we have in place is deeply flawed. The system allows for financial institutions to file fraudulent documents throughout the entire process of a mortgage. From initiation to close, to sale to securitization, from Wall Street to investors. The house of cards is on unstable ground from the beginning.

As a builder and real estate developer for much of my adult life, I assure you that to build a strong and stable structure we must begin with the foundations. For the structure or system to stand and be stable, the base must be solid, level, and strong. We are far from this, but a foundation can be repaired or replaced.

It is like a virus. We should all understand that, given how COVID-19 has affected all our lives across the planet. If we don't isolate the virus and its components it will continue to spread into every home, and we cannot allow that to happen.

* * * * * * * * * *

Thank you for taking the time to read through

Quantum of Justice.

I welcome your online reviews, personal reflections, and discussions by joining over 20K subscribers in my ever-growing online community at -

douglasjboggs.substack.com

Exhibits

Recording requested by:
LSI Title Company

When Recorded Mail To:
DEx West, L.L.C.
15000 Surveyor Boulevard, Suite 500
Addison, Texas 75001-9013
APN #: 015-1303-013
Property Address:
1038 57TH ST
OAKLAND, CALIFORNIA 94608

DFF20100015011858
DFF20100015011858

THIS IS TO CERTIFY THAT THIS IS A FULL, TRUE AND CORRECT COPY OF THE ORIGINAL RECORDED IN THE OFFICE OF THE COUNTY
RECORDING FEE: $24.00
RECORDED ON: December 29, 2010
AS DOCUMENT NO: 2010-390870
BY: s/ Andres Cortez
LSI TITLE COMPANY (CA)

Space above this line for Recorder's use only

Trustee Sale No.: 20100015011858   Title Order No.: 100731778

IMPORTANT NOTICE
NOTICE OF DEFAULT AND ELECTION TO SELL UNDER DEED OF TRUST

IF YOUR PROPERTY IS IN FORECLOSURE BECAUSE YOU ARE BEHIND IN YOUR PAYMENTS IT MAY BE SOLD WITHOUT ANY COURT ACTION, and you may have the legal right to bring your account in good standing by paying all of your past due payments plus permitted costs and expenses within the time permitted by law for reinstatement of your account, which is normally five business days prior to the date set for the sale of your property. No sale date may be set until three months from the date this Notice of Default may be recorded (which date of recordation appears on this notice).

This amount is $4,584.53 as of 12/28/2010 and will increase until your account becomes current, plus proof must be provided indicating that the senior lien is current. While your property is in foreclosure, you still must pay other obligations (such as insurance and taxes) required by your note and deed of trust or mortgage. If you fail to make future payments on the loan, pay taxes on the property, provide insurance on the property, or pay other obligations as required in the note and deed of trust or mortgage, the beneficiary or mortgagee may insist that you do so in order to reinstate your account in good standing. In addition, the beneficiary or mortgagee may require as a condition of reinstatement that you provide reliable written evidence that you paid all senior liens, property taxes, and hazard insurance premiums.

Upon your written request, the beneficiary or mortgagee will give you a written itemization of the entire amount you must pay. You may not have to pay the entire unpaid portion of your account, even though full payment was demanded, but you must pay all amounts in default at the time payment is made. However, you and your beneficiary or mortgagee may mutually agree in writing prior to the time the notice of sale is posted (which may not be earlier than the three month period stated above) to, among other things, (1) provide additional time in which to cure the default by transfer of the property or otherwise; or (2) establish a schedule of payments in order to cure your default; or both (1) and (2).

Following the expiration of the time period referred to in the first paragraph of this notice, unless the obligation being foreclosed upon or a separate written agreement between you and your creditor permits a longer period, you have only the legal right to stop the sale of your property by paying the entire amount demanded by your creditor.

Exhibit 1a

IMPORTANT NOTICE
NOTICE OF DEFAULT AND ELECTION TO SELL UNDER DEED OF TRUST
Trustee Sale No. : 20100015011858   Title Order No.: 100731778

To find out the amount you must pay, or to arrange for payment to stop the foreclosure, or if your property is in foreclosure for any other reason, contact:

WELLS FARGO BANK, N.A., A/K/A WACHOVIA MORTGAGE, A DIVISION OF WELLS FARGO BANK, N.A. AND F/K/A WACHOVIA MORTGAGE, FSB
c/o NDEX WEST, LLC
15000 Surveyor Boulevard, Suite 500
Addison, Texas 75001-9013
(866) 795-1852

If you have any questions, you should contact a lawyer or the governmental agency which may have insured your loan. Notwithstanding the fact that your property is in foreclosure, you may offer your property for sale provided the sale is concluded prior to the conclusion of the foreclosure.

REMEMBER, YOU MAY LOSE LEGAL RIGHTS IF YOU DO NOT TAKE PROMPT ACTION.

NOTICE IS HEREBY GIVEN THAT: NDEX WEST, LLC is the original Trustee, duly appointed Substituted Trustee, or acting as Agent for the Trustee or Beneficiary under a Deed of Trust dated **07/05/2007**, executed by **MICHELLE A. MOQUIN AND DOUGLAS J. BOGGS**, as Trustor, to secure obligations in favor of **WORLD SAVINGS BANK, FSB**, as Beneficiary Recorded on 07/11/2007 as Instrument No. 2007255632 of official records in the Office of the Recorder of **ALAMEDA** County, California, as more fully described on said Deed of Trust. Including a Note(s)/ Unconditional Guaranty which had a principal amount of **$100,000.00** that the beneficial interest under said Deed of Trust and the obligations secured thereby are presently held by the Beneficiary; that a breach of, and default in, the obligations for which said Deed of Trust is security has occurred in that the payment has not been made of:

DELINQUENCY DUE ON THE SENIOR LIEN; PLUS THE INSTALLMENT OF PRINCIPAL AND INTEREST WHICH BECAME DUE ON 2/15/2010 AND ALL SUBSEQUENT INSTALLMENTS, TOGETHER WITH LATE CHARGES AS SET ORTH IN SAID NOTE AND DEED OF TRUST, ADVANCES, ASSESSMENTS, FEES, AND/OR TRUSTEE FEES, IF ANY.

NOTHING IN THIS NOTICE SHALL BE CONSTRUED AS A WAIVER OF ANY FEES OWING TO THE BENEFICIARY UNDER THE DEED OF TRUST, PURSUANT TO THE TERMS OF THE LOAN DOCUMENTS.

That by reason thereof, the present beneficiary under such deed of trust, has executed and delivered to said agent, a written Declaration of Default and Demand for same, and has deposited with said agent such deed of trust and all documents evidencing obligations secured thereby, and has declared and does hereby declare all sums secured thereby immediately due and payable and has elected and does hereby elect to cause the trust property to be sold to satisfy the obligations secured thereby.

DATED: 12/28/2010

NDEX WEST, LLC as Agent for Beneficiary
By: LSI Title Company, agent

By: _____
Menghong But

Exhibit 1b

Wachovia Mortgage
P.O. Box 659558
San Antonio, TX 78265-9558

Michelle A Moquin **WACHOVIA**

Declaration of Wells Fargo Bank, N.A.

As required by California Civil Code Section 2923.5, I, Alfonso Ramirez, an officer of Wells Fargo Bank, N.A., declare as follows:

Regarding Michelle A Moquin (hereinafter referred to as "borrower"), Wells Fargo Bank, N.A., has met the requirement of California Civil Code Section 2923.5 as indicated below:

( ) Wells Fargo Bank, N.A., has contacted the borrower as set forth in California Civil Code Section 2923.5(a)(2).

(X) Wells Fargo Bank, N.A., has tried with due diligence, as prescribed by California Civil Code Section 2923.5(g), to contact the borrower.

The undersigned authorizes the trustee, foreclosure agent and/or their authorized agent to sign, on behalf of the beneficiary/authorized agent, the Notice of Default containing the declaration required pursuant to Civil Code 2923.5.

I certify (or declare) under penalty of perjury under the laws of the State of California that the foregoing is true and correct.

11-09-10
Date

By: _____
Title: Vice President Loan Documentation

FF006 012 ALA

Wachovia Mortgage is a division of Wells Fargo Bank, N.A.

Exhibit 1c

RECORDING REQUESTED BY AND MAIL TO

Recording Requested by:
Douglas J Boggs and Michelle A Moquin
AND WHEN RECORDED MAIL TO:
Douglas J Boggs and Michelle A Moquin
1038 57th St
Oakland, CA 94608

2011106397 04/11/2011 03:10 PM
OFFICIAL RECORDS OF ALAMEDA COUNTY
PATRICK O'CONNELL
RECORDING FEE: 21.00
3 PGS

Douglas J Boggs
Michelle A Moquin
1038 57th Street
Oakland, CA 94608
510.428.1236 ph
email dboggs07@yahoo.com
Plaintiff In Pro Per

SUPERIOR COURT OF THE STATE OF CALIFORNIA
FOR THE COUNTY OF ALAMEDA

Douglas J Boggs, Michelle A Moquin, Plaintiffs, v. Wells Fargo Bank, N.A.; Wachovia Mortgage; World Savings Bank; NDEx West, L.L.C.; Golden West Savings Assoc. Services Co.; and DOES 1 through 50 Defendants.	Case No. RG11570208 **NOTICE OF PENDING ACTION** **CCP § 409** **Lis Pendens**

NOTICE IS HEREBY GIVEN that the above-entitled action concerning and affecting real property as described herein, was commenced on April 8, 2011 in the above-named Court by the Plaintiffs (Pltfs)

Exhibit 2a

1 Douglas J Boggs and Michelle A Moquin, herein, against the Defendants Wells Fargo Bank, Wachovia
2 Mortgage, World Savings Bank, NDEX West, LLC, Golden West Savings Assoc. Service Co.; and Does
3 1 to 50, inclusive. The action is now pending in the Alameda County Superior Court, State of
4 California.
5   The action affects title to real property situated in Alameda County, State of California and is
6 legally described in Exhibit "1" attached hereto and incorporated herein by this reference.
7   The object of the Plaintiff's action is to enjoin the Defendants' Trustee sale dated April 19, 2011
8 since we cannot presently act on our Foreclosure Notice because on the documentation: **(1)** The
9 documents did not disclose which one, out of two loans, is being foreclosed on. **(2)** The Trustee,
10 Golden West Savings Association Service Co., is **not** the person named on the foreclosure Notice.
11 Therefore, the non-judicial foreclosure procedures are improper.
12
13 DATED: April 8, 2011
14
15   Respectfully submitted
16
17
18
19
20   Plaintiff In Pro Per
21
22
23
24
25
26 Approved by Court per CCP 405.21b   Plaintiff In Pro Per
27   DATE: 4/11/11
28 JUDGE of The Superior Court, Alameda County
        JON R. ROLEFSON

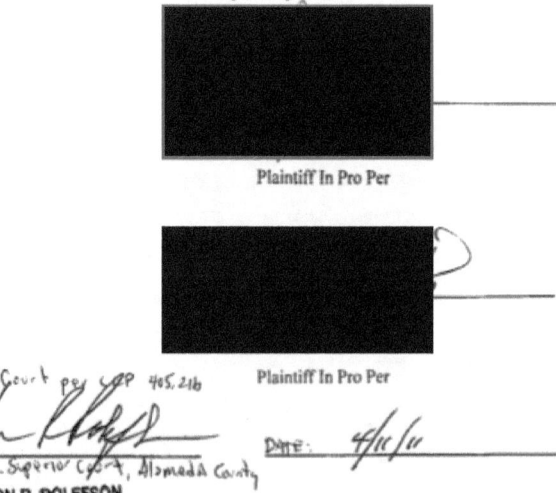

Exhibit 2b

Exhibit 1

PROPERTY DESCRIPTION;

1038 57th Street oakland CA. 94608
APN 15-1303-13
Tracer No. 038412

Lot 26, Block "G" of the Golden Gate Tract, filed April 28, 1890 Map Book 10, Page 66 Alameda County Records

Exhibit 2c

Recording requested by:
LSI Title Company

When Recorded Mail To:
NDEx West, L.L.C.
15000 Surveyor Boulevard, Suite 500
Addison, Texas 75001-9013

APN #: 015-1303-013
Property Address:
1038 57TH ST
OAKLAND, CALIFORNIA 94608

SUB20100015011858

THIS IS TO CERTIFY THAT THIS IS A FULL, TRUE AND CORRECT COPY OF THE ORIGINAL RECORDED IN THE OFFICE OF THE COUNTY
RECORDING FEE: $21.00
RECORDED ON: February 18, 2011
AS DOCUMENT NO: 2011061424
BY: s/ Jon Fischer
LSI TITLE COMPANY (CA)

Trustee Sale No.: 20100015011858 Title Order No.: 100731778

SUBSTITUTION OF TRUSTEE

WHEREAS, MICHELLE A. MOQUIN AND DOUGLAS J. BOGGS was the original Trustor, GOLDEN WEST SAVINGS ASSOCIATION SERVICE CO. was the original Trustee, and WORLD SAVINGS BANK, FSB was the original Beneficiary Recorded on 07/11/2007 as Instrument No. 2007255632 of official records in the Office of the Recorder of Alameda County, California, as more fully described on said Deed of Trust.; and WHEREAS, the undersigned is the present Beneficiary under said Deed of Trust, and WHEREAS, the undersigned desires to substitute a new Trustee under said Deed of Trust in place and instead of said prior Trustee.

NOW, THEREFORE, the undersigned hereby substitutes, NDEx West, L.L.C., WHOSE ADDRESS IS: 15000 Surveyor Boulevard, Suite 500, Addison, Texas 75001-9013, as Trustee under said Deed of Trust.

Whenever the context hereof so requires, the masculine gender includes the feminine and/or neuter, and the singular number includes the plural.

Dated: FEB 0 8 2011

WELLS FARGO BANK, NA SUCCESSOR BY MERGER TO WELLS FARGO BANK SOUTHWEST, NA F/K/A WACHOVIA MORTGAGE FSB F/K/A WORLD SAVINGS BANK, FSB

By NDEx West, LLC
It's Attorney in Fact

Ric Juarez, Assistant Vice President - Foreclosure Operations Manager

State of TEXAS }
County of DALLAS }

On FEB 0 8 2011 before me, **Josie R. Molina**, Notary Public, personally appeared Ric Juarez who is known to me to be the person(s) whose name(s) is/are subscribed to the within instrument and acknowledged to me that he/she/they executed the same in his/her/their authorized capacity(ies), and that by his/her/their signature(s) on the instrument the person(s), or the entity upon behalf of which the person(s) acted, executed the instrument.

WITNESS my hand and official seal.

Signature _____ (Seal)

My commission expires: _____

JOSIE R. MOLINA
Notary Public
State of Texas
My Comm. Exp. 11-14-2011

Exhibit 3

Recording requested by:
LSI Title Company

When Recorded Mail To:
NDEx West, L.L.C.
15000 Surveyor Boulevard, Suite 500
Addison, Texas 75001-9013
(866) 795-1852

APN #: 015-1303-013
Property Address:
1038 57TH ST
OAKLAND, CALIFORNIA 94608

NTSP20100015011858

Exh. C
Case # 115'2028

Space above this line for Recorder's use only

Trustee Sale No.: 20100015011858   Title Order No.: 100731778   FHA/VA/PMI No.:

NOTICE OF TRUSTEE'S SALE

YOU ARE IN DEFAULT UNDER A DEED OF TRUST, DATED 07/05/2007. UNLESS YOU TAKE ACTION TO PROTECT YOUR PROPERTY, IT MAY BE SOLD AT A PUBLIC SALE. IF YOU NEED AN EXPLANATION OF THE NATURE OF THE PROCEEDING AGAINST YOU, YOU SHOULD CONTACT A LAWYER.

NDEX WEST, LLC, as duly appointed Trustee under and pursuant to Deed of Trust Recorded on 07/11/2007 as Instrument No. 2007255632 of official records in the office of the County Recorder of ALAMEDA County, State of CALIFORNIA.

EXECUTED BY: MICHELLE A. MOQUIN AND DOUGLAS J. BOGGS,
WILL SELL AT PUBLIC AUCTION TO HIGHEST BIDDER FOR CASH, CASHIER'S CHECK/CASH EQUIVALENT or other form of payment authorized by 2924h(b), (payable at time of sale in lawful money of the United States).
DATE OF SALE: 04/19/2011   TIME OF SALE: 12:30 PM
PLACE OF SALE: AT THE FALLON STREET ENTRANCE TO THE COUNTY COURTHOUSE, 1225 FALLON STREET, OAKLAND, CA.
STREET ADDRESS and other common designation, if any, of the real property described above is purported to be:
1038 57TH ST, OAKLAND, CALIFORNIA 94608
APN#: 015-1303-013

The undersigned Trustee disclaims any liability for any incorrectness of the street address and other common designation, if any, shown herein. Said sale will be made, but without covenant or warranty, expressed or implied, regarding title, possession, or encumbrances, to pay the remaining principal sum of the note(s) secured by said Deed of Trust, with interest thereon, as provided in said note(s), advances, under the terms of said Deed of Trust, fees, charges and expenses of the Trustee and of the trusts created by said Deed of Trust. The total amount of the unpaid balance of the obligation secured by the property to be sold and reasonable estimated costs, expenses and advances at the time of the initial publication of the Notice of Sale is $105,767.71. The beneficiary under said Deed of Trust heretofore executed and delivered to the undersigned a written Declaration of Default and Demand for Sale, and a written Notice of Default and Election to Sell. The undersigned caused said Notice of Default and Election to Sell to be recorded in the county where the real property is located.

FOR TRUSTEE SALE INFORMATION PLEASE CALL:
AGENCY SALES & POSTING
3210 EL CAMINO REAL, SUITE 200
IRVINE, CA 92602
714-730-2727
www.lpsasap.com

NDEx West, L.L.C. MAY BE ACTING AS A DEBT COLLECTOR ATTEMPTING TO COLLECT A DEBT. ANY INFORMATION OBTAINED WILL BE USED FOR THAT PURPOSE.

NDEx West, L.L.C. as Trustee

Dated: 03/24/2011

11 of 11

Exhibit 4

2010000150118858 B IC

RECEIVED
MAR 14 2011

Michelle Moquin
Doug Boggs
1038 57th Street
Oakland, CA 94608
510.428.1236

NDEx West, LLC
15000 Surveyor Boulevard
Addison, TX 75001
Phone Number (972)386-5040
Fax Number (972)661-7712
United States

Date   Mar. 10st, 2011

Dear Joyce Copeland,

NOTICE TO AGENT IS NOTICE TO PRINCIPAL.

This is notice to you not to hand over my Deed to anyone but me. I do not believe that you are entitled to be the Trustee of my Deed to the property (APN#015-1303-013) located at 1038 57th St., Oakland, CA 94608

According to the Statute of Frauds, to be the legal Trustee of my deed you must have, in your possession, a document in writing with instructions from me to be the Trustee of my Deed. If you have that document send me a copy of that post haste. Because my house is within the foreclosure time frame to be placed on the market for sale I am requesting that you send this document no later than 5:00pm, Mar. 20th, 2011.

If you do not, this is my request that you return my Deed to me immediately, as you are holding it fraudulently.

I am filing a complaint in the Federal Court of the Northern District of CA alleging the same.

This is a further notice to you that I will take all legal remedies available to me to include suing you for all of financial losses I may incur should you hand my Deed over to another party.

Those losses will include any legal costs that I may incur, get my Deed back, to make me financially whole, and the costs of any emotional distress that I, or any of my family, may incur as a result of this legal process.

Respectfully,

Michelle Moquin
Doug Boggs

cc:
James C Frappier - Registered Agent
Ric Juarez – Asst. VP – Foreclosure Operations Manager
Michael Barrett – Pres. CEO

Exhibit 5a

NDeX
EXPERIENCE | SERVICE | RESULTS

15000 Surveyor Blvd.
Addison, TX 75001
Phone: 866-795-1852
Fax: 972-661-7804

March 15, 2011

Michelle Moquin
Doug Boggs
1038 57th Street
Oakland, CA 94608

Re: Trustee Sale Number: 20100015011858
Property Address: 1038 57th Street
Oakland, CA 94608

Mr. Boggs and Ms. Moquin:

We are in receipt of your letter dated March 10, 2011 in which you inquired about the authority of the lender to substitute our company as trustee without your written consent.

I would like to refer your attention to the terms of your agreement contained in the deed of trust dated July 5, 2007 and recorded July 11, 2007 as instrument # 2007255632 in the Alameda County Recorder's Office, which bears the signatures of both Michelle A Moquin and Douglas J Boggs. Under paragraph 21 of this document, entitled "Substitute Trustee," you will find the relevant terms pertaining to the substitution of trustee, which state:

> "Lender, at lender's option, may from time to time appoint a successor trustee to any Trustee appointed hereunder by an instrument executed and acknowledged by Lender and recorded in the office of the Recorder of the county where the Property is located. The instrument shall contain the name of the original lender, Trustee and Borrower, the book and page where this Instrument is recorded and the name and address of the successor trustee. The successor trustee shall, without conveyance of the Property, succeed to all the title, powers and duties conferred upon the Trustee herein and by applicable law. *This procedure for substitution of trustee shall govern to the exclusion of all other provisions for substitution.*"

Please feel free to contact our office if you have any further questions.

Sincerely,

Gregory Peck
General Counsel

The Fair Debt Collection Act requires that we advise you that NDeX, LLC, may be acting as a debt collector, attempting to collect a debt. Any information obtained will be used for that purpose.

Exhibit 5b

FOR IMMEDIATE RELEASE

Contact: Evan M. Rosen
Law Offices of Evan M. Rosen, P.A.
Phone: 855-55-ROSEN
Email: erosen@evanmrosen.com

What is Wrong with Florida's Third District Court of Appeal?

Statistics from every Florida District Court of Appeal show something is wrong with the Third District's handling of foreclosure cases.

Fort Lauderdale, Florida (February 8, 2018) – Statistics reveal what experienced Florida foreclosure attorneys already know, the Third District Court of Appeal has an issue properly adjudicating foreclosure cases. As detailed in one of the attached spreadsheets, of its sixteen written opinions addressing standing[1] in recent-era foreclosure cases, *the Third District has only ruled for a property owner twice. 66 Team, LLC v. JPMorgan Chase Bank Nat. Ass'n*, 187 So. 3d 929 (Fla. 3d DCA 2016) and *Riocabo v. Fed. Nat'l Mortgage Ass'n*, 230 So. 3d 579 (Fla. 3d DCA 2017). (Consider that in *66 Team*, the bank *did not admit any documents or evidence* at trial to prove its case. And in *Riocabo,* the bank confessed error - admitting that it must lose on appeal.)

Yet, every other district in the state has ruled for property owners in the overwhelming majority of its cases, and have issued far more written opinions. The attached chart tabulates and summarizes every Florida appellate written foreclosure opinion on standing over the course of the "foreclosure crisis."

The neighboring Fourth District has issued 121 written foreclosure opinions on standing, 88 (73%) have been in favor of property owners. On this same issue, the Second District has issued 43 written opinions, 36 (84%) have been for property owners; the First District has ruled for owners 83% of the time; and the Fifth District has found for owners 72% of the time.

But, the Third District has ruled for a property owner only twice (13%). It's also noteworthy that the Third has only issued sixteen written foreclosure opinions on standing – the fewest of any appellate court in the state. *There is apparently no justifiable way to explain this.*

Law Offices of Evan M. Rosen, P.A. is a law firm that helps people defend against foreclosure and fight improper debt collection.

###

If you would like more information about this topic, please call Evan M. Rosen at 855-55-ROSEN, or email erosen@evanmrosen.com.

---

[1] Standing is a legal determination that the party bringing the lawsuit is entitled to do so. In foreclosures, this often hinges on who had possession of the promissory note when suit was filed, and to whom the note was payable. Due to banks frequently transferring loans, this has been a major problem. So much so that our state's legislature and Supreme Court enacted special rules and statutes to address it. *Requiring an entity to prove its case before taking another's property is a constitutional issue.* The statistics from all but the Third District demonstrate the depth of this problem and the seriousness with which the other courts have addressed it.

Exhibit 6a

Tabulation of All Florida Appellate Level Written Opinions Addressing Standing In Modern-Era Foreclosure Cases

	Total	Wins for Owner	Win for Bank	% of Wins for Owner	% of Wins for Bank
1st DCA	18	15	3	83.3%	16.7%
2nd DCA	43	36	7	83.7%	16.3%
3rd DCA	16	2	14	12.5%	87.5%
4th DCA	121	88	33	72.7%	27.3%
5th DCA	39	28	11	71.8%	28.2%

Exhibit 6b

Written Standing Related Appellate Decisions in Favor of Property Owners

DCA	CASE NAME	DISPOSITION	Who Won
1D	Booker v. Sarasota, Inc., 707 So. 2d 886 (Fla. 1st DCA 1998)	SJ for P reversed b/c it failed to prove standing. Note was indorsed to P from an alleged receiver, but there was no endorsement to the receiver	Property Owner
1D	Ham v. Nationstar Mortg., LLC, 164 So. 3d 714 (Fla. 1st DCA 2015)	FJ for P reversed - no standing at inception	Property Owner
1D	Hunter v. Aurora Loan Services, LLC, 137 So. 3d 570 (Fla. 1st DCA 2014)	FJ for P reversed - no evidence that P has possession of Note, purchase or transfer	Property Owner
1D	Kelly v. Bank of New York Mellon, 170 So. 3d 145 (Fla. 1st DCA 2015)	FJ for P reversed - no evidence of indorsement at time of suit - testimony of collateral file not enough - testimony that P was holder not enough	Property Owner
1D	Kiefert v. Nationstar Mortg., LLC, 153 So. 3d 351 (Fla. 1st DCA 2014)	FJ for P reversed - substituted P must demonstrate original P had standing at inception	Property Owner
1D	Kyser v. Bank of Am., N.A., 186 So. 3d 58 (Fla. 1st DCA 2016)	FJ for P reversed - testimony as to merger without acquiring all assets not enough, witness did not know when possessed or when indorsed	Property Owner
1D	Lacombe v. Deutsche Bank Nat. Tr. Co., 149 So. 3d 152 (Fla. 1st DCA 2014)	FJ for P reversed and remand for IVD- failure to prove standing at incept - POA, PSA-special indorse req ind and posses-no auth or biz record foundation by current loan servicer for prior record-no second chances	Property Owner
1D	Lindsey v. Wells Fargo Bank, N.A., 139 So. 3d 903 (Fla. 1st DCA 2013)	SJ for P reversed - AOM not mentioning the note is not enough for SJ where note not endorsed	Property Owner
1D	Mazine v. M & I Bank, 67 So. 3d 1129 (Fla. 1st DCA 2011)	FJ for P reversed - no standing	Property Owner
1D	Morelli v. Chase Home Fin., LLC, 197 So. 3d 651 (Fla. 1st DCA 2016)	FJ for P reversed and remand for IVD - Confession of Error on Standing	Property Owner
1D	Pennington v. Ocwen Loan Servicing, LLC, 151 So. 3d 52 (Fla. 1st DCA 2014)	FJ for P reversed - AOM referencing only the M not enough - must have standing at inception and throughout - specifically indorsed requires indorsement	Property Owner
1D	Poag v. Nationstar Mortg., LLC, 198 So. 3d 1002 (Fla. 1st DCA 2016)	FJ for P reversed - P failed to prove lost note count - Denied req for relief from blown RFAs never cross appealed	Property Owner
1D	Seidler v. Wells Fargo Bank, N.A., 179 So. 3d 416 (Fla. 1st DCA 2015)	FJ for P reversed - must prove up lost note for lost page, non-party servicer in possession useless, AOM with note useless, new P must prove original Ps possession	Property Owner
1D	Walton v. Deutsche Bank Nat. Tr. Co., 201 So. 3d 831 (Fla. 1st DCA 2016)	FJ for P reversed and remand for IVD - testimony of loan analyst not enough - no personal knowledge of possession or endorsement - no evidence	Property Owner
1D	Wells Fargo Bank, N.A. v. Robinson, 168 So. 3d 1279 (Fla. 5th DCA 2015)	IVD affirmed - Lost Note elements - no proof that P was entitled to enforce when lost or got it from someone who was entitled when lost	Property Owner
2D	BAC Funding Consortium Inc. ISAOA/ATIMA v. Jean-Jacques, 28 So. 3d 936 (Fla. 2d DCA 2010)	Note payable to original lender, no indorsement to P or other evidence that P purchased or was entitled to foreclose.	Property Owner
2D	Barry v. Vantium Capital, Inc., 198 So. 3d 43 (Fla. 2d DCA 2015)	FJ for P reversed - P seeking deficiency must prove its standing to do so - i.e. right was transferred from judgment holder	Property Owner
2D	Buckingham v. Bank of Am., N.A., 230 So. 3d 923 (Fla. 2d DCA 2017)	FJ for P reversed, remand for IVD - endorse as per merger is anomalous indorsement - no proof of agency where note indorsed to another party	Property Owner
2D	Caballero v. U.S. Bank Nat. Ass'n ex rel. RASC 2006-EMX7, 189 So. 3d 1044 (Fla. 2d DCA 2016)	SJ for P reversed, allonge at SJ different than attached to complaint - AOM not enough only assigned M	Property Owner
2D	Correa v. U.S. Bank N.A., 118 So. 3d 952 (Fla. 2d DCA 2013)	FJ for P reversed and remanded for IVD - lost note elements not proven	Property Owner
2D	Corrigan v. Bank of Am., N.A., 189 So. 3d 187 (Fla. 2d DCA 2016), reh'g denied (Mar. 22, 2016)	FJ for P reversed - no standing at inception	Property Owner
2D	Creadon v. U.S. Bank N.A., 166 So. 3d 952 (Fla. 2d DCA 2015)	FJ for P reversed - note filed with court prior to sub, thus new P could not have been holder at time of sub	Property Owner

Exhibit 6c

Written Standing Related Appellate Decisions in Favor of Property Owners

DCA	CASE NAME	DISPOSITION	Who Won
2D	Cutler v. U.S. Bank Nat. Ass'n, 109 So. 3d 224 (Fla. 2d DCA 2012)	SJ for P reversed - sj not proper where note later appeared with an undated allonge	Property Owner
2D	Dhanuk v. HSBC Bank USA, Nat. Ass'n, 210 So. 3d 113 (Fla. 2d DCA 2016)	FJ for P reversed and remanded for IVD -copy on complaint had no indorsement - copy at trial had blank - no evidence as to when indorsed	Property Owner
2D	Dickson v. Roseville Properties, LLC, 198 So. 3d 48 (Fla. 2d DCA 2015)	FJ for P reversed and remanded for IVD - no proof by substituted P of original P's standing	Property Owner
2D	DiGiovanni v. Deutsche Bank Nat'l Tr. Co., 226 So. 3d 984 (Fla. 2d DCA 2017), reh'g denied (May 16, 2017)	FJ for P reversed and remanded for IVD - Judge crossed the line by doing his own internet research to show standing in specific endorsement to another entity	Property Owner
2D	Eaddy v. Bank of Am., N.A., 197 So. 3d 1278 (Fla. 2d DCA 2016)	FJ for P reversed - no standing at inception, unendorsed note at suit	Property Owner
2D	Eagles Master Ass'n, Inc. v. Bank of Am., N.A., 198 So. 3d 12 (Fla. 2d DCA 2015)	FJ for P reversed - unendorsed note attached to complaint, post dated AOM with predated effective date nor post filed note with indorsement not enough	Property Owner
2D	Feltus v. U.S. Bank Nat. Ass'n, 80 So. 3d 375 (Fla. 2d DCA 2012)	SJ for P reversed - SJ not proper where lost note and P files original endorsed note without amending the complaint	Property Owner
2D	Geweye v. Ventures Tr. 2013-I-H-R, 189 So. 3d 231 (Fla. 2d DCA 2016), review dismissed, SC16-847, 2016 WL 4494435 (Fla. Aug. 26, 2016)	FJ for P reversed - Creadon fact pattern, no standing to enforce	Property Owner
2D	Gonzalez v. Deutsche Bank Nat. Tr. Co., 95 So. 3d 251 (Fla. 2d DCA 2012)	must show standing at time of action - post filed note no good	Property Owner
2D	Heller v. Bank of Am., NA, 209 So. 3d 641 (Fla. 2d DCA 2017)	FJ for P reversed and remand for new trial - must surrender original note - cannot testify as to standing w-o Biz record in evidence	Property Owner
2D	Houk v. PennyMac Corp., 210 So. 3d 726 (Fla. 2d DCA 2017)	SJ for P reversed - trans not needed, sub order not enough, AOM ref all rights not enough, not sworn, verification not enough, contra affs, servicer alone not enough	Property Owner
2D	J-H Home Mortg. Rescue, LLC v. Fed. Nat. Mortg. Ass'n, 184 So. 3d 1168 (Fla. 2d DCA 2015)	FJ for P reversed - no indorsement, no assignment - screen shot not enough - indorsement stamped void	Property Owner
2D	Johnson v. U.S. Bank Nat'l Ass'n, 222 So. 3d 635 (Fla. 2d DCA 2017)	no evidence of holder of note prior to suit - screenshot did not ref note, no MLS, remedy is remand for IVD	Property Owner
2D	Mathis v. Nationstar Mortgage, LLC, 227 So. 3d 189 (Fla. 2d DCA 2017)	FJ for P reversed and remand for IVD - failure to attach the allonge requires IVD - no evidence to support non-holder in poss entitled to enforce (which was not pleaded anyway)	Property Owner
2D	May v. PHH Mortg. Corp., 150 So. 3d 247 (Fla. 2d DCA 2014)	FJ for P reversed and remand for IVD - unendorsed note with complaint and endorsed note filed 8 months later with no proof of standing at inception not enough - judgment at NJT reversed	Property Owner
2D	McLagan v. Fed. Home Loan Mortg. Corp., 145 So. 3d 943 (Fla. 2d DCA 2014)	SJ for P reversed -standing need not be raised in an AD but must be raised at trial level to be preserved for appeal - SJ improper on back dated AOM	Property Owner
2D	Olivera v. Bank of Am., N.A., 141 So. 3d 770 (Fla. 2d DCA 2014)	SJ for P reversed - SJ denied based on subsequent indorsements and no accel letter in SJ evidence	Property Owner
2D	Peters v. Bank of New York Mellon, 227 So. 3d 175 (Fla. 2d DCA 2017)	FJ for P reversed and remand for IVD - AOM which does not ref the note not enough for lost note - beneficial interest in M not sufficient - unsub testimony about entitled to enforce not enough	Property Owner
2D	Powers v. HSBC Bank USA, N.A., 202 So. 3d 121 (Fla. 2d DCA 2016)	FJ for P reversed - PSA not enough as subject loan not part of it - witness DNK when indorsed	Property Owner
2D	Rosa v. Deutsche Bank Nat. Tr. Co., 191 So. 3d 987 (Fla. 2d DCA 2016)	FJ for P reversed and remand for IVD - WF had note not P trust - no constructive possession as per Phan	Property Owner
2D	Russell v. Aurora Loan Services, LLC, 163 So. 3d 639 (Fla. 2d DCA 2015)	FJ for P reversed and remand for IVD - no standing at incept - not indorsed to another party, POA post dated with no ref to original P and no loan schedule	Property Owner

Exhibit 6d

Written Standing Related Appellate Decisions in Favor of Property Owners

DCA	CASE NAME	DISPOSITION	Who Won
2D	Shaffer v. Deutsche Bank Nat'l Tr. for Am. Home Mortgage Inv. Tr. 2006-1, 42 Fla. L. Weekly D889 (Fla. 2d DCA Apr. 19, 2017)	FJ for P reversed and remand for IVD - post dated LPOA no good, RJN no good for PSA	Property Owner
2D	Sorrell v. U.S. Bank Nat. Ass'n, 198 So. 3d 845 (Fla. 2d DCA 2016), reh'g denied (May 16, 2016)	FJ for P reversed and remand for IVD - no proof of standing at inception - original lost note count, no indorsement	Property Owner
2D	St. Clair v. U.S. Bank Nat. Ass'n, 173 So. 3d 1045 (Fla. 2d DCA 2015)	FJ for P reversed and remand for further proceedings - possession not enough PSA note enough - CT cannot fill in the blanks - standing cannot be presumed b-c of servicing	Property Owner
2D	Stoltz v. Aurora Loan Services, LLC, 194 So. 3d 1097 (Fla. 2d DCA 2016)	FJ for P reversed and remand for IVD - no proof original P possessed note at inception - no note attached to complaint - AOM might have done it but it was never admitted into evidence	Property Owner
2D	Strominger v. Bank of New York, 212 So. 3d 1058, 1059 (Fla. 2d DCA 2016)	FJ for P reversed and remand for IVD - no evidence of possession at inception - neither fraudulent assignment nor bailee which referenced acct number did it	Property Owner
2D	Tomlinson v. GMAC Mortg., 173 So. 3d 1121 (Fla. 2d DCA 2015)	FJ for P reversed and remand for IVD - no note attached, post filed note with blank endorsement no good, no testimony of possession, post dated AOM, judicial notice of filing of docs in CT file - contents still hearsay, service transfer letter is not standing	Property Owner
2D	Verizzo v. Bank of New York Mellon, 220 So. 3d 1262 (Fla. 2d DCA 2017)	standing at inception. Unendorsed note appeared after suit was filed, no other evidence of possession at inception.	Property Owner
2D	Winchel v. PennyMac Corp., 222 So. 3d 639 (Fla. 2d DCA 2017)	FJ for P reversed and remand for FJ for D - no standing at inception	Property Owner
3D	66 Team, LLC v. JPMorgan Chase Bank Nat. Ass'n, 187 So. 3d 929 (Fla. 3d DCA 2016)	FJ for P reversed b/c P did not admit any evidence at trial and did not even file an Answer brief	Property Owner
3D	Riocabo v. Fed. Nat'l Mortgage Ass'n, 230 So. 3d 579 (Fla. 3d DCA 2017)	reverse SJ based on confession of error re original Ps standing	Property Owner
4D	3709 N. Flagler Drive Prodigy Land Tr. v. Bank of Am., N.A., 226 So. 3d 1040 (Fla. 4th DCA 2017)	standing of P - Standing = holder or in possession of note.	Property Owner
4D	Alfonso v. JPMorgan Chase Bank, N.A., 182 So. 3d 930 (Fla. 4th DCA 2016)	FJ for P reversed -successor P failed to prove original P's standing - not indorsed to successor P attached to complaint.pdf	Property Owner
4D	Angelini v. HSBC Bank USA, N.A, 189 So. 3d 202 (Fla. 4th DCA 2016)	FJ for P reversed- failure to prove standing at inception - Ownership irrelevant to holder	Property Owner
4D	Assil v. Aurora Loan Services, LLC, 171 So. 3d 226 (Fla. 4th DCA 2015)	FJ for P reversed - new P must prove standing of prior P not indorsed to owner, not P - need something from owner to P - maybe servicing agreement	Property Owner
4D	Balch v. LaSalle Bank N.A., 171 So. 3d 207 (Fla. 4th DCA 2015)	FJ for P reversed -- 1) no evidence of when note indorsed 2) post dated AOM no good 3) no evidence endorser intend to transfer interest to trustee	Property Owner
4D	Barnett v. U.S. Bank Nat. Ass'n, 186 So. 3d 585 (Fla. 4th DCA 2016)	FJ for P reversed - conflicting evidence as to possession does not get it done	Property Owner
4D	Beacon Place of Coral Springs Condo. Ass'n v. Nationstar Mortg., LLC, 182 So. 3d 834 (Fla. 4th DCA 2016)	FJ for P reversed - PH doesn't prove standing, note indorse to other co and later indorsed in blank not enough, no proof of servicing right	Property Owner
4D	Boyd v. Wells Fargo Bank, N.A., 143 So. 3d 1128 (Fla. 4th DCA 2014)	FJ for P reversed - no standing at inception	Property Owner
4D	Braga v. Fannie Mae, 187 So. 3d 1272 (Fla. 4th DCA 2016), reh'g denied (Apr. 27, 2016)	FJ for P reversed - allonge with indorsement in blank not attached to original complaint later shows up with no testimony	Property Owner
4D	Bristol v. Wells Fargo Bank, Nat. Ass'n, 137 So. 3d 1130 (Fla. 4th DCA 2014)	SJ for P reversed - issue of fact as to whether note indorsed in blank filed 2 years after suit showed standing at inception - note does not follow mortgage	Property Owner

Exhibit 6e

Written Standing Related Appellate Decisions in Favor of Property Owners

DCA	CASE NAME	DISPOSITION	Who Won
4D	Calvo v. U.S. Bank Nat. Ass'n, 181 So. 3d 562 (Fla. 4th DCA 2015)	FJ for P reversed - no evidence of when indorsement placed - copies of notes do not match	Property Owner
4D	Cartwright v. LJL Mortg. Pool, LLC, 185 So. 3d 614 (Fla. 4th DCA 2016)	SJ for P reversed, no proof of possession of blank indorsed note at time of suit, substituted P must prove prior Ps standing	Property Owner
4D	Carty v. Bank of Am., N.A., 212 So. 3d 395 (Fla. 4th DCA 2017)	SJ for P reversed - two different versions of the note - no explanation and no counter to standing AD	Property Owner
4D	Charley v. Green Tree Servicing, LLC, 125 So. 3d 285 (Fla. 4th DCA 2013)	SJ for P reversed - no standing at inception proven	Property Owner
4D	Chery v. Bank of Am., N.A., 183 So. 3d 1253 (Fla. 4th DCA 2016)	FJ for P reversed- no note attached - no evidence of when indorsed or possessed	Property Owner
4D	Craven-Lazarus v. Pennymac Holdings, LLC, 199 So. 3d 1029 (Fla. 4th DCA 2016)	SJ for P reversed - SJ affidavit conflicting with complaint as to who held note requires reversal.	Property Owner
4D	Cromarty v. Wells Fargo Bank, NA, 110 So. 3d 988, 989 (Fla. 4th DCA 2013)	SJ for P reversed - P failed to prove standing at inception.	Property Owner
4D	Cruz v. JPMorgan Chase Bank, Nat. Ass'n, 199 So. 3d 992 (Fla. 4th DCA 2016)	FJ for P reversed - no evidence of possession or indorsement at inception - Purchase and assumption does not do it	Property Owner
4D	Darwiche v. Bank of New York Mellon, 185 So. 3d 1261 (Fla. 4th DCA 2016)	SJ for p reversed - no proof of standing at inception - post dated AOM no good	Property Owner
4D	Deutsche Bank Nat. Tr. Co. v. Boglioli, 154 So. 3d 494 (Fla. 4th DCA 2015)	FJ for D Affirmed - no proof of standing at inception - predated AOM	Property Owner
4D	Deutsche Bank Nat. Tr. Co. v. Huber, 137 So. 3d 562 (Fla. 4th DCA 2014)	MIVD affirmed - no evidence the note was surrendered	Property Owner
4D	Diroberto v. Bayview Loan Services LLC, 199 So. 3d 526 (Fla. 4th DCA 2016)	FJ for P reversed -WAMU Purchase and sale agreement not enough	Property Owner
4D	Dixon v. Express Equity Lending Group, LLLP, 125 So. 3d 965 (Fla. 4th DCA 2013)	FJ for P reversed - note indorsed to someone else	Property Owner
4D	Duke v. HSBC Mortg. Services, LLC, 79 So. 3d 778 (Fla. 4th DCA 2011)	SJ for P reversed - no note and no aom, m shows some other than P	Property Owner
4D	Elman v. U.S. Bank, N.A., 204 So. 3d 452 (Fla. 4th DCA 2016)	FJ for P reversed - lost note count and nothing attached to original complaint, PSA unsigned, ex 3 refuted testimony of possession and indorsement	Property Owner
4D	Elston/Leetsdale, LLC v. CWCapital Asset Mgmt. LLC, 87 So. 3d 14 (Fla. 4th DCA 2012)	Order to show cause reversed where P (servicer) did not prove it was real party in interest	Property Owner
4D	Farkas v. U.S. Bank, Nat. Ass'n, 165 So. 3d 796 (Fla. 4th DCA 2015)	FJ for P reversed - no standing at inception - note attached to complaint had no indorsement - no testimony as to when note was indorsed - AOM post dated suit by one day - note attached with indorsement could only go to time of indorsement not posses	Property Owner
4D	Fiorito v. JP Morgan Chase Bank, Nat. Ass'n, 174 So. 3d 519 (Fla. 4th DCA 2015)	FJ for P reversed and remanded for IVD - no evidence of indorsement before suit - no testimony that chase acquired all of WAMUs assets	Property Owner
4D	Fischer v. U.S. Bank Nat. Ass'n, 152 So. 3d 1289, 1290 (Fla. 4th DCA 2015)	FJ for P reversed - no proof od standing at inception, Witness did not know who held the note at inception	Property Owner
4D	Focht v. Wells Fargo Bank, N.A., 124 So. 3d 308 (Fla. 2d DCA 2013)	inception b/c note attached to complaint was different than not at trial and no other proof of possession at inception	Property Owner
4D	Friedle v. Bank of New York Mellon, 226 So. 3d 976 (Fla. 4th DCA 2017)	condition so no Ortiz inference - PSA not enough without the trustee acknowledgement-interim certification	Property Owner
4D	Friedle v. Bank of New York Mellon, 226 So. 3d 976 (Fla. 4th DCA 2017)	FJ for P reversed, remand for IVD - for tipsy to apply, record must support alt theory, unsigned PSA cannot be authenticated, Auth not eq hearsay, Ortiz applies only if original in SAME condition as copy	Property Owner
4D	Frost v. Christiana Tr., 193 So. 3d 1092 (Fla. 4th DCA 2016)	FJ for P reversed - possession but no proof of when indorsed - WAMU-CHASE-FDIC did not prove standing	Property Owner

Exhibit 6f

Written Standing Related Appellate Decisions in Favor of Property Owners

DCA	CASE NAME	DISPOSITION	Who Won
4D	Gallimore v. Bank of Am., Nat. Ass'n, 184 So. 3d 1242 (Fla. 4th DCA 2016)	FJ for P reversed - must have evidence or circumstantial evidence at least of when note indorsed, proof of possession at inception also a must	Property Owner
4D	Gancue v. HSBC Bank, U.S.A., 97 So. 3d 263 (Fla. 4th DCA 2012)	SJ for P vacated because D showed excusable neglect and P did not prove standing at inception	Property Owner
4D	Guzman v. Deutsche Bank Nat. Tr. Co., 179 So. 3d 543 (Fla. 4th DCA 2015)	FJ for P reversed - no proof of possession or allonge at inception - relation back does not apply to standing at inception	Property Owner
4D	Ha v. BAC Home Loans Servicing, L.P., 184 So. 3d 563 (Fla. 4th DCA 2016)	FJ for P reversed - unendorsed note attached to complaint, then later produced with indorsement not enough	Property Owner
4D	Hall v. REO Asset Acquisitions, LLC, 84 So. 3d 388 (Fla. 4th DCA 2012)	SJ for P reversed - P must show record evidence that P had right to enforce before suit was filed	Property Owner
4D	Harris v. HSBC Bank USA, Nat'l Ass'n, 174 So. 3d 600 (Fla. 4th DCA 2015)	FJ for P reversed - no indorsement on original C, indorsed on note with amended C, predated effective date on AOM no good, no witness testimony of when note assigned	Property Owner
4D	Hepworth v. Wells Fargo Bank, N.A., 180 So. 3d 1170 (Fla. 4th DCA 2015)	FJ for P reversed - PSA doesn't do it, no testimony of when indorse-allonge, loan nos don't match	Property Owner
4D	Jallali v. Christiana Tr., 200 So. 3d 149 (Fla. 4th DCA 2016)	FJ for P reversed - clarified the remedy - must prove possession and indorsement prior to suit - post dated AOM useless	Property Owner
4D	Jarvis v. Deutsche Bank Nat. Tr. Co., 169 So. 3d 194 (Fla. 4th DCA 2015)	FJ for P reversed and remand for IVD - no standing at inception, although there was evidence that the note was physically transferred into a trust prior to the complaint being filed, physical transfer by itself not enough - no indorsements and no assignment.	Property Owner
4D	Jelic v. BAC Home Loans Servicing, LP, 178 So. 3d 523 (Fla. 4th DCA 2015)	FJ for P reversed - can't transfer the note via an AOM, even if it references the note - need proof of time of indorsement if it doesn't match the complaint	Property Owner
4D	Jelic v. LaSalle Bank, Nat. Ass'n, 160 So. 3d 127 (Fla. 4th DCA 2015)	FJ for P reversed and remand for IVD - no note attached - one month later NOF with no indorsement, 2nd AOM after suit, PSA did not define servicing, PSA does not prove intent to transfer	Property Owner
4D	Joseph v. BAC Home Loans Servicing, LP, 155 So. 3d 444 (Fla. 4th DCA 2015)	FJ for P reversed and remand for dismissal of complaint - no proof of standing at inception	Property Owner
4D	Kenney v. HSBC Bank USA, Nat. Ass'n, 175 So. 3d 377 (Fla. 4th DCA 2015)	FJ for P reversed and remand for IVD - no endorsement, then in blank at trial, no testimony of when endorsement was placed, procedures from servicer NO, post dated AOM NO, ambiguous testimony of ownership	Property Owner
4D	LaFrance v. U.S. Bank Nat. Ass'n, 141 So. 3d 754 (Fla. 4th DCA 2014)	SJ for P reversed - unendorsed note and then note indorsed at MSJ without anything else does not prove standing at inception	Property Owner
4D	Lamb v. Nationstar Mortg., LLC, 174 So. 3d 1039 (Fla. 4th DCA 2015)	FJ for P reversed and remand for IVD - AOM of Mortgage only not enough, testimony of purchase of prior co not enough, no standing at time of judgment	Property Owner
4D	Lewis v. U.S. Bank Nat. Ass'n, 188 So. 3d 46 (Fla. 4th DCA 2016)	FJ for P reversed - bank's reliance on a pooling and servicing agreement was insufficient to establish the bank's standing to bring suit at the time the suit was filed	Property Owner
4D	Lloyd v. Bank of New York Mellon, 160 So. 3d 513 (Fla. 4th DCA 2015)	FJ for P reversed - standing at inception not proven with note indorsement on NOF which is different from indorsement on copy of note attached to C-back dated AOM not proof	Property Owner
4D	Luiz v. Lynx Asset Services, LLC, 198 So. 3d 1102 (Fla. 4th DCA 2016)	FJ for P reversed - no evidence from subsequent P of standing at inception by initial P - no note attached to initial complaint - in alt no proof that original lender transferred under sub 2 - applies to holder and lost note theories	Property Owner

Exhibit 6g

Written Standing Related Appellate Decisions in Favor of Property Owners

DCA	CASE NAME	DISPOSITION	Who Won
4D	Magaldi v. Deutsche Bank Nat. Tr. Co., 199 So. 3d 982 (Fla. 4th DCA 2016)	FJ for P reversed - PSA doesn't prove indorsement	Property Owner
4D	Matthews v. Fed. Nat. Mortg. Ass'n, 160 So. 3d 131 (Fla. 4th DCA 2015)	FJ for P reversed - affs on standing only for SJ-FN2 - note with no endorsement on complaint payable to BOA then indorsed on original at time of trial, backdated AOM-no good - PH and POA useless	Property Owner
4D	McLean v. JP Morgan Chase Bank Nat. Ass'n, 79 So. 3d 170 (Fla. 4th DCA 2012)	SJ for P reversed - must prove you had standing at time of filing	Property Owner
4D	Miller v. Wells Fargo Bank, N.A., 193 So. 3d 1108, 1109 (Fla. 4th DCA 2016)	FJ for P reversed and remand for IVD - confession of error - witness testified that someone other than trust held note	Property Owner
4D	Monnot v. U.S. Bank, Nat. Ass'n, 188 So. 3d 896 (Fla. 4th DCA 2016)	FJ for P reversed - collateral file does not automatically mean original note is part of it - possession 3 days after suit not good enough - PSA does not do it - note not indorsed with C and then special indorse at time of trial	Property Owner
4D	Morris v. Deutsche Bank Nat. Tr. Co., 182 So. 3d 680 (Fla. 4th DCA 2015)	SJ for P reversed - AOM not enough, not evidence of time of indorsement	Property Owner
4D	Murray v. HSBC Bank USA, 157 So. 3d 355 (Fla. 4th DCA 2015)	FJ for P reversed - nonholder in poss with rights of holder must prove up every step of the chain - also servicing has nothing to do with standing	Property Owner
4D	PennyMac Corp. v. Frost, 214 So. 3d 686 (Fla. 4th DCA 2017)	IVD Affirmed - endorsement was anomalous therefore P was not holder	Property Owner
4D	Peoples v. Sami II Tr. 2006-AR6, 178 So. 3d 67 (Fla. 4th DCA 2015)	FJ for P reversed - foreclosure 101 - must prove standing at inception - unendorsed note attached, indorsed later filed	Property Owner
4D	Perez v. Deutsche Bank Nat. Tr. Co., 174 So. 3d 489 (Fla. 4th DCA 2015)	FJ for P reversed and remand for IVD - no note attached, copy indorsed in blank later filed, PSA not enough because no evidence indorsee had intent to transfer interest to trustee	Property Owner
4D	Powell v. Wells Fargo Bank, N.A. for Structured Asset Mortgage Investments II Inc., 219 So. 3d 828 (Fla. 4th DCA 2017)	FJ for P reversed and remand for IVD - must prove every step of the way for nonholder in possession - no shelter rule	Property Owner
4D	Reynolds v. Nationstar Loan Services, LLC, 190 So. 3d 219 (Fla. 4th DCA 2016)	FJ for P reversed and remand for IVD - no testimony as to when indorsements placed	Property Owner
4D	Rigby v. Wells Fargo Bank, N.A., 84 So. 3d 1195 (Fla. 4th DCA 2012)	SJ for P reversed - post dated assignment and note indorsed in blank not enough to show standing at time of suit	Property Owner
4D	Robelto v. U.S. Bank Tr., N.A., 194 So. 3d 429 (Fla. 4th DCA 2016)	FJ for P reversed - P did not prove that it obtained note from entity entitled to enforce - allonge by POA after the note was lost was not enough to get it done	Property Owner
4D	Rodriguez v. Wells Fargo Bank, N.A., 178 So. 3d 62 (Fla. 4th DCA 2015)	FJ for P reversed and remand for IVD - unendorsed attached, indorsed later filed, no testimony as to time of indorsement, testimony of presuit possession allowed	Property Owner
4D	Russell v. BAC Home Loans Servicing, LP, 42 Fla. L. Weekly D2496 (Fla. 4th DCA Nov. 29, 2017)	Different endorsement at SJ and in complaint with no explanation in SJ affidavit - reverse SJ	Property Owner
4D	Ryan v. Wells Fargo Bank, N.A., 142 So. 3d 974 (Fla. 4th DCA 2014)	FJ for P reversed - note in record indorsed in blank - not surrendered at trial not indorsed - no evidence of standing at inception at trial	Property Owner
4D	Sabido v. Bank of New York Mellon, 43 Fla. L. Weekly D17 (Fla. 4th DCA Dec. 20, 2017)	FJ for P reversed, remand for IVD - P did not prove elements for lost note	Property Owner
4D	Salmon v. Foreclosed Asset Sales & Transfer P'ship, 162 So. 3d 1142 (Fla. 4th DCA 2015)	SJ for P reversed - question of fact as to standing based on note transferred 20 days before suit to another party	Property Owner
4D	Sanchez v. Suntrust Bank, 179 So. 3d 538 (Fla. 4th DCA 2015)	FJ for P reversed - testimony that subsidiary of parent company (who was the P) had standing not enough to prove standing of P absent evidence of parent-subsidiary relationship	Property Owner
4D	Saver v. JP Morgan Chase Bank, 114 So. 3d 352 (Fla. 4th DCA 2013)	SJ for P reversed - no evidence of standing at inception	Property Owner

Exhibit 6h

Written Standing Related Appellate Decisions in Favor of Property Owners

DCA	CASE NAME	DISPOSITION	Who Won
4D	Saffar v. Residential Credit Sols., Inc., 160 So. 3d 122 (Fla. 4th DCA 2015)	FJ for P reversed - note attached payable to ABN, no indorse-allonge - 9 months post NOF with blank allonge- no proof affixed-no proof of holder or nonholder via AOM- sub 2-need to prove every txfr	Property Owner
4D	Segall v. Wachovia Bank, N.A., 192 So. 3d 1241 (Fla. 4th DCA 2016)	FJ for P reversed and remand for IVD - lay person's testimony of merger not enough - must introduce docs - must also show all assets or the particular subject note	Property Owner
4D	Septimus v. Christiana Tr., 183 So. 3d 471 (Fla. 4th DCA 2016)	FJ for P reversed - P failed to prove original Ps standing	Property Owner
4D	Servedio v. U.S. Bank Nat. Ass'n, 46 So. 3d 1105 (Fla. 4th DCA 2010)	SJ for P reversed - no proof of standing because copy of the note and aff of ownership not part of the record and the note was not surrendered at time of SJ	Property Owner
4D	Snyder v. JP Morgan Chase Bank, Nat. Ass'n, 169 So. 3d 1270 (Fla. 4th DCA 2015)	FJ for P reversed and remand for IVD- WAMU FDIC buyout and conflicting testimony not enough	Property Owner
4D	Sosa v. Bank of New York Mellon, 187 So. 3d 943 (Fla. 4th DCA 2016)	FJ for P reversed and remand for IVD- nonholder in possession - internet search not enough to establish relationship between indorsee and P	Property Owner
4D	Sosa v. U.S. Bank Nat. Ass'n, 153 So. 3d 950 (Fla. 4th DCA 2014)	FJ for P reversed and remand for IVD - p failed to establish when it became owner of note - note was lost at inception and later filed	Property Owner
4D	Supria v. Goshen Mortgage, LLC, 42 Fla. L. Weekly D2572 (Fla. 4th DCA Dec. 6, 2017)	FJ for P reversed, remand for FJ for D - reference to 'moneys now owing' does not transfer an interest in the note - no shelter rule for nonholders	Property Owner
4D	Tilus v. AS Michai LLC, 161 So. 3d 1284 (Fla. 4th DCA 2015)	SJ for P reversed - AOM of M only useless - post filed note with indorsement not enough - no mention of what was attached to complaint - need not be owner and holder	Property Owner
4D	Tremblay v. U.S. Bank, N.A., 164 So. 3d 85 (Fla. 4th DCA 2015)	FJ for P reversed and remand for IVD - Note indorsed in blank-attached to complaint not enough if servicer is in possession at inception - not P-Bank	Property Owner
4D	Venture Holdings & Acquisitions Group, LLC v. A.I.M. Funding Group, LLC, 75 So. 3d 773 (Fla. 4th DCA 2011)	SJ for P reversed - even if you are in default, P must still possess original promissory note - lacked standing a inception	Property Owner
4D	Vidal v. Liquidation Props., Inc., 104 So. 3d 1274 (Fla. 4th DCA 2013)	SJ for P reversed - must be holder prior to lawsuit via dated aom or affidavit	Property Owner
4D	Vogel v. Wells Fargo Bank, N.A., 192 So. 3d 714 (Fla. 4th DCA 2016)	FJ for P reversed and remand for IVD - note with cancelled indorsement and indorsement in blank not enough - World Savings merger not enough as not could have already been with FNMA who owned	Property Owner
4D	Wright v. Deutsche Bank Nat. Tr. Co., 152 So. 3d 1289 (Fla. 4th DCA 2015)	FJ for P reversed - no proof of standing at inception - note attached to complaint different that note surrendered at trial	Property Owner
4D	Wright v. JPMorgan Chase Bank, N.A., 169 So. 3d 251 (Fla. 4th DCA 2015)	FJ for P reversed and remand for IVD - absent agreement parent corp cannot enforce subsidiary's note	Property Owner
4D	Zimmerman v. JPMorgan Chase Bank, Nat., 134 So. 3d 501 (Fla. 4th DCA 2014)	FJ for P reversed and remand for further proceedings - need proof of standing at inception - no proof, case must be dismissed	Property Owner
5D	7825 Myrtle Oak Lane, LLC v. Bank of New York Mellon, 193 So. 3d 1087 (Fla. 5th DCA 2016)	records is not evidence - insufficient to prove standing.pdf	Property Owner
5D	Bank of New York Mellon Tr. Co., N.A. v. Conley, 188 So. 3d 884 (Fla. 4th DCA 2016)	FJ for D Affirmed - nonholder in possession must prove all links - AOM by MERS after loan in trust - INEFFECTIVE	Property Owner
5D	Beaumont v. Bank of New York Mellon, 81 So. 3d 553 (Fla. 5th DCA 2012)	SJ for P reversed -standing not waived as p still must prove its case.. items in record not in evidence unless admitted	Property Owner
5D	Bonafide Properties, LLC v. E-Trade Bank, 208 So. 3d 1279 (Fla. 5th DCA 2017)	FJ for P reversed- remand for IVD - P relied on AOM but was signed by itself to itself - no POA admitted	Property Owner

Exhibit 6i

Written Standing Related Appellate Decisions in Favor of Property Owners

DCA	CASE NAME	DISPOSITION	Who Won
5D	Boumarate v. HSBC Bank USA, N.A., 109 So. 3d 1239 (Fla. 5th DCA 2013)	SJ for P reversed - P pleaded lost note but did not prove it	Property Owner
5D	Boumarate v. HSBC Bank USA, N.A., 172 So. 3d 535 (Fla. 5th DCA 2015)	FJ for P reversed - note made payable to another party and lost - not enough just to show P had possession before it was lost	Property Owner
5D	Delia v. GMAC Mortg. Corp., 161 So. 3d 554 (Fla. 5th DCA 2014)	FJ for P reversed and remanded to find lost note and adequate protection	Property Owner
5D	Devries v. CitiMortgage Inc., 188 So. 3d 909 (Fla. 5th DCA 2016)	FJ for p reversed - no evidence of possession or indorsement prior to suit - post dated AOM not enough	Property Owner
5D	Elsman v. HSBC Bank USA, 182 So. 3d 770 (Fla. 5th DCA 2015)	FJ for P reversed remand for IVD- no evidence of when note indorsed - In txfr history and PSA didn't do it	Property Owner
5D	Figueroa v. Fed. Nat. Mortg. Ass'n, 180 So. 3d 1110 (Fla. 5th DCA 2015)	FJ for P reversed and remanded for IVD - no evidence introduce - IVD proper on lost note, standing, damages and CP	Property Owner
5D	Floyd v. Bank of Am., N.A., 194 So. 3d 1071 (Fla. 5th DCA 2016)	SJ reversed - Standing at inception was an issue of fact	Property Owner
5D	Ford v. JPMorgan Chase Bank, 175 So. 3d 375 (Fla. 5th DCA 2015)	FJ for P reversed - no standing when witness has no connection to subject loan	Property Owner
5D	Gee v. U.S. Bank Nat. Ass'n, 72 So. 3d 211 (Fla. 5th DCA 2011)	SJ for P reversed - no proof of successor in interest, no proof of reformation	Property Owner
5D	Gomes v. SunTrust Mortg., Inc., 200 So. 3d 97 (Fla. 5th DCA 2015)	SJ for P reversed - P did not establish standing at inception	Property Owner
5D	Gonzalez v. BAC Home Loans Servicing, L.P., 180 So. 3d 1106 (Fla. 5th DCA 2015)	FJ for P reversed - testimony of holder at inception not enough - need biz records - PH doesn't prove holder - copy attached no indorse	Property Owner
5D	Gorel v. Bank of New York Mellon, 165 So. 3d 44 (Fla. 5th DCA 2015)	FJ for P reversed - note specifically indorsed to another entity requires possession and indorsement by the entity to P	Property Owner
5D	Green Tree Servicing, LLC v. Atchison, 230 So. 3d 635 (Fla. 5th DCA 2017)	FJ for D affirmed - admissible as verbal act to show standing at time of trial - excluding evidence of lost note not harmful error	Property Owner
5D	Green v. Green Tree Servicing, LLC, 230 So. 3d 989 (Fla. 5th DCA 2017)	FJ for P reversed and remand for IVD - copy did not match, merger b-n differing entities not enough, servicing alone does NOT = standing.	Property Owner
5D	Green v. JPMorgan Chase Bank, N.A., 109 So. 3d 1285 (Fla. 5th DCA 2013)	SJ for P reversed - note indorsed in blank and filed a year later not enough	Property Owner
5D	Home Outlet, LLC v. U.S. Bank Nat. Ass'n, 194 So. 3d 1075 (Fla. 5th DCA 2016)	FJ for P reversed and remand for IVD - lost note insufficient - no PK aff deficient and not admitted - original lender must prove standing	Property Owner
5D	Khan v. Bank of Am., N.A., 58 So. 3d 927 (Fla. 5th DCA 2011)	SJ for P reversed - docs conflict - Note indorsed to someone other than P	Property Owner
5D	Lyttle v. BankUnited, 115 So. 3d 425 (Fla. 5th DCA 2013)	SJ for P reversed - P unable to enforce note not made payable to it, indorsed to it or indorsed in blank	Property Owner
5D	Madl v. Wells Fargo Bank, N.A., 43 Fla. L. Weekly D82 (Fla. 5th DCA Dec. 29, 2017)	establish standing to foreclose mortgage where note attached to complaint was payable to original lender but contained no endorsements	Property Owner
5D	Miller v. Bank of Am., N.A., 201 So. 3d 1286 (Fla. 5th DCA 2016)	FJ for P reversed and remand for new trial - not enough knowledge as to creation, accuracy or trustworthiness of standing screenshot - no proof of standing - reverse and remand for new trial	Property Owner
5D	Richards v. HSBC Bank USA, 91 So. 3d 233 (Fla. 5th DCA 2012)	SJ for P reversed - allonge to note was inconsistent with assignment and contradicted allegations in complaint that plaintiff was holder of note	Property Owner
5D	Schmidt v. Deutsche Bank, 170 So. 3d 938 (Fla. 5th DCA 2015)	FJ for P reversed and remand for IVD - PSA and MLPA not enough, testimony of records showing possession, without admitting records, not enough to get past lost note count	Property Owner

Exhibit 6j

Written Standing Related Appellate Decisions in Favor of Property Owners

DCA	CASE NAME	DISPOSITION	Who Won
5D	*Walsh v. Bank of New York Mellon Tr.*, 219 So. 3d 929 (Fla. 5th DCA 2017)	FJ for P reversed and remand for IVD - later filed note indorsed in blank not enough - testimony based on records not in evidence is hearsay	Property Owner
5D	*Walters v. Nationstar Mortg., LLC*, 180 So. 3d 236 (Fla. 5th DCA 2015)	FJ for P reversed and remand for IVD - subsequent P did not prove prior Ps standing at inception	Property Owner

Exhibit 6k

Written Standing Related Appellate Decisions in Favor of Banks

DCA	CASE NAME	DISPOSITION	Who Won
1D	Clay County Land Tr. No. 08-04-25-0078-014-27, Orange Park Tr. Services, LLC v. JPMorgan Chase Bank, Nat. Ass'n, 152 So. 3d 83 (Fla. 1st DCA 2014)	SJ for P affirmed as to judgment - reversed as to amount - P has standing because copy of note with blank endorsement attached to complaint was enough	Bank
1D	Snowden v. Wells Fargo Bank, 172 So. 3d 506 (Fla. 1st DCA 2015)	trial, the court must presume the trial courts findings were based on sufficient evidence presented (by the witness)	Bank
1D	Wells Fargo Bank, N.A. v. Ousley, 212 So. 3d 1056 (Fla. 1st DCA 2016)	IVD reversed - matching copy of note is good enough - mortgage is a public record and a record re interest in property	Bank
2D	Am. Home Mortg. Servicing, Inc. v. Bednarek, 132 So. 3d 1222 (Fla. 2d DCA 2014)	IVD reversed - P had possession of note endorsed in blank which was enough	Bank
2D	AS Lily LLC v. Morgan, 164 So. 3d 124 (Fla. 2d DCA 2015)	FJ for D reversed - substituted P establishing standing at time of sub is enough	Bank
2D	One W. Bank, F.S.B. v. Bauer, 159 So. 3d 843 (Fla. 2d DCA 2014)	ownership irrelevant, P was in possession and that's all that matters	Bank
2D	OneWest Bank, FSB v. Cummings, 175 So. 3d 827 (Fla. 2d DCA 2015)	IVD reversed and remand for further proceedings - testimony based on out of court records of possession is enough	Bank
2D	Stone v. BankUnited, 115 So. 3d 411 (Fla. 2d DCA 2013)	standing demonstrated by BankUnited under FDIC sale through testimony of acquiring all assets	Bank
2D	Taylor v. Bayview Loan Servicing, LLC, 74 So. 3d 1115 (Fla. 2d DCA 2011)	SJ for P reversed on other issues BUT Ct held that P has standing to foreclose	Bank
2D	Wells Fargo Delaware Tr. Co., N.A. for Vericrest Opportunity Loan Tr. 201-NPL1 v. Petrov, 230 So. 3d 575 (Fla. 2d DCA 2017)	IVD reversed - Do not need to offer evidence to prove reverse elston - servicer can show up and testify for P w-o POA	Bank
3D	Bank of New York Mellon v. Beaufort, 42 Fla. L. Weekly D2596 (Fla. 3d DCA Dec. 13, 2017)	IVD reversed, remand for FJ for P - P proved standing with complaint allegations and cert. of possession	Bank
3D	Bank of New York Tr. Co., N.A. v. Rodgers, 79 So. 3d 108 (Fla. 3d DCA 2012)	MIVD reversed because D never objected in any way to P's Motion to be substituted the "real party in interest" AND even if D has not waived standing, P did prove entitlement to enforce lost note in at least 3 ways	Bank
3D	Cabrillo Dev., LLC v. Bayview Loan Servicing, LLC, 193 So. 3d 4 (Fla. 3d DCA 2015)	FJ for P Affirmed - P proved it had standing as holder in due course	Bank
3D	Calixte v. Fed. Nat'l Mortgage Ass'n, 211 So. 3d 1084 (Fla. 3d DCA 2017)	FJ for P upheld. Case remanded only for Ct to find adequate protection	Bank
3D	Citibank, N.A. v. Olsak, 208 So. 3d 227 (Fla. 3d DCA 2016), reh'g denied (Dec. 21, 2016), review denied, SC17-10, 2017 WL 2590706 (Fla. June 15, 2017)	IVD reversed - expert can't testify as to legal conclusions - standing in the 3rd - possession, if you are not the Orig lender - D can't use the PSA	Bank
3D	Deutsche Bank Nat'l Tr. Co. v. Mobley, 212 So. 3d 511 (Fla. 3d DCA 2017), review denied, SC17-648, 2017 WL 2945846 (Fla. July 11, 2017)	IVD reversed and remand for further proceedings- Copy indorsed in blank attached, then with spec ind at trial, coupled with testimony of possession by P at inception was enough - citation to Phan even if serv had poss	Bank
3D	Fed. Nat. Mortg. Ass'n v. McFadyen, 194 So. 3d 418 (Fla. 3d DCA 2016), reh'g denied (May 31, 2016)	FJ for D reversed and remand for FJ for P - judgment for P on a lost note using constructive possession - affidavit attached to biz records cert allowed to be used as evidence	Bank
3D	Guerrero v. Chase Home Fin., LLC, 83 So. 3d 970 (Fla. 3d DCA 2012)	FJ for P reversed BUT remanded for reestablishment of lost note and mortgage count - must surrender note but can amend if note lost before trial but must prove up prongs of lost note	Bank
3D	Mortgage Elec. Registration Sys., Inc. v. Revoredo, 955 So. 2d 33 (Fla. 3d DCA 2007)	IVD reversed and remand for further proceedings - MERS can have standing	Bank
3D	Nationstar Mortg., LLC v. Marquez, 180 So. 3d 219 (Fla. 3d DCA 2015)	IVD reversed and remand for entry of FJ for P -chibnik testified to lost note prongs - dismissal reversed	Bank
3D	PNC Bank, N.A. v. Clark, 211 So. 3d 265 (Fla. 3d DCA 2017), reh'g denied (Mar. 6, 2017), review denied, SC17-603, 2017 WL 2950864 (Fla. July 11, 2017)	IVD reversed and remand to enter FJ for P and findings of fact re damages- as long as P attaches a copy with blank endorsement to complaint, enough for standing	Bank

Exhibit 61

Written Standing Related Appellate Decisions in Favor of Banks

DCA	CASE NAME	DISPOSITION	Who Won
3D	*Rincon v. Bank of Am., N.A.*, 206 So. 3d 793 (Fla. 3d DCA 2016)	Denial of MTV FJ for P Affirmed - note indorsed in blank good enough	Bank
3D	*Wells Fargo Bank, N.A. v. Russell*, 194 So. 3d 1094 (Fla. 3d DCA 2016)	SJ for D reversed - b-c statute requires presuit possession, that proves P had possession	Bank
4D	*ALS-RVC, LLC v. Garvin*, 201 So. 3d 687 (Fla. 4th DCA 2016)	IVD reversed - P has standing because note attached to complaint matched the one at trial, even though there was evidence that the note and mortgage was assigned to another party	Bank
4D	*Bank of New York Mellon on Behalf of Registered Holders of Alternative Loan Tr. 2007-OA7 v. Heath*, 219 So. 3d 104 (Fla. 4th DCA 2017)	IVD reversed and remand for new trial - note indorsed in blank attached to complaint and same version introduced at trial	Bank
4D	*Bank of New York Mellon v. Milford*, 206 So. 3d 137 (Fla. 4th DCA 2016)	IVD reversed and remand to enter FJ for P - copy attached creates inference - references ortiz but inference never stated there	Bank
4D	*Bennett v. Deutsche Bank Nat. Tr. Co.*, 124 So. 3d 320 (Fla. 4th DCA 2013)	SJ for P affirmed - no evidence to overcome the presumption that the signature on the allonge were invalid, thus P has standing	Bank
4D	*Bolous v. U.S. Bank Nat. Ass'n*, 210 So. 3d 691 (Fla. 4th DCA 2016)	FJ for P affirmed - PSA was enough to prove standing at inception	Bank
4D	*Brandenburg v. Residential Credit Sols., Inc.*, 137 So. 3d 604 (Fla. 4th DCA 2014)	SJ for P Affirmed - Substituted P had standing or prior P who has possession at inception	Bank
4D	*Caraccia v. U.S. Bank, Nat. Ass'n*, 185 So. 3d 1277 (Fla. 4th DCA 2016)	FJ for P Affirmed - agency is an exception to possession requirement	Bank
4D	*Deutsche Bank Nat'l Tr. Co. for Fremont Home Loan Tr. 2006-3, Asset-Backed Certificates, Series 2006-3 v. Dowd*, 225 So. 3d 229 (Fla. 4th DCA 2017)	IVD reversed - citing to *Bolous* and *Marciano*	Bank
4D	*Deutsche Bank Nat'l Tr. Co. v. Applewhite*, 213 So. 3d 948 (Fla. 4th DCA 2017)	IVD reversed and remand for further proceedings - note endorsed om blank attached to complaint	Bank
4D	*Fed. Nat'l Mortgage Ass'n v. Rafaeli*, 225 So. 3d 264 (Fla. 4th DCA 2017)	testimony of prior servicer having possession enough - copy and orig match	Bank
4D	*GMAC Mortg., LLC v. Choengkroy*, 98 So. 3d 781 (Fla. 4th DCA 2012)	Sua sponte dismissal of P's case reversed - evidence of equitable transfer prior to filing of the complaint prevented dismissal	Bank
4D	*GMAC Mortgage, LLC v. Pisano*, 227 So. 3d 1279 (Fla. 4th DCA 2017)	IVD reversed - testimony of holder based on review of records OK - b-c no evidence of transfer, must conclude that original lender maintained possession until time of suit - the successor P can proceed	Bank
4D	*Green Tree Servicing LLC v. Sanker*, 204 So. 3d 496 (Fla. 4th DCA 2016)	IVD reversed and remand for FJ for P - P presented evidence of standing at inception and inbroken chain of indorsements ending in blank endorsement	Bank
4D	*Harvey v. Deutsche Bank Nat. Tr. Co.*, 69 So. 3d 300 (Fla. 4th DCA 2011)	FJ for P Affirmed - bank has standing with blank endorsement	Bank
4D	*Hovannesian v. PennyMac Corp.*, 190 So. 3d 681 (Fla. 4th DCA 2016)	FJ for P Affirmed in part on standing - no abuse to let in screen shot to prove standing - remand to establish damages in judgment	Bank
4D	*HSBC Bank USA, Nat'l Ass'n for Fremont Home Loan Tr. 2006-C v. Alejandre*, 219 So. 3d 831 (Fla. 4th DCA 2017)	IVD reversed and remand for FJ for P - PSA and note indorsed in blank enough - even conflicting AOM has nothing to do with standing	Bank
4D	*Isaac v. Deutsche Bank Nat. Tr. Co.*, 74 So. 3d 495 (Fla. 4th DCA 2011)	SJ for P Affirmed - P held a blank endorsed note	Bank
4D	*JPMorgan Chase Bank Nat'l Ass'n v. Pierre*, 215 So. 3d 633 (Fla. 4th DCA 2017)	FJ for D reversed - Foreclosure is note dependent, M and ownership are irrelevant - witness allowed to make it up to get in prior servicer letter and fact that letter was sent - Balkissoon	Bank
4D	*Lewis v. J.P. Morgan Chase Bank*, 138 So. 3d 1212 (Fla. 4th DCA 2014)	FJ for P affirmed - standing at inception proved - substituted party need not have standing at inception	Bank
4D	*McConnell v. JPMorgan Chase*, 190 So. 3d 264 (Fla. 4th DCA 2016)	FJ for P affirmed - law firm records (and affidavit w-o objection) proved possession with blank endorsement	Bank

Exhibit 6m

Written Standing Related Appellate Decisions in Favor of Banks

DCA	CASE NAME	DISPOSITION	Who Won
4D	Meilleur v. HSBC Bank USA, N.A., 194 So. 3d 512 (Fla. 4th DCA 2016)	FJ for P Affirmed - original at trial matches copy with note creates inference - inference supported by AOM - no fundamental error as judge did not offer tips, suggestions or recommendations	Bank
4D	Ortiz v. PNC Bank, Nat. Ass'n, 188 So. 3d 923 (Fla. 4th DCA 2016)	FJ for P Affirmed - if copy attaches matches later filed original, possession and standing at inception proved - substantial compliance is the law	Bank
4D	Peuguero v. Bank of Am., N.A., 169 So. 3d 1198 (Fla. 4th DCA 2015)	FJ for P Affirmed but remand to prove interest - standing upheld b/c witness testified that P held the blank note before filing as this was company policy and Pay his showed collection b/f suit filed, and taxes where being paid by P prior to filing	Bank
4D	Philogene v. ABN Amro Mortg. Group Inc., 948 So. 2d 45 (Fla. 4th DCA 2006)	SJ for P Affirmed - P proved it had possession of the note	Bank
4D	Riggs v. Aurora Loan Services, LLC, 36 So. 3d 932 (Fla. 4th DCA 2010)	SJ for P Affirmed - possession of note endorsed in blank enough for standing	Bank
4D	Spicer v. Ocwen Loan Servicing, LLC, 4D16-2335, 2018 WL 354555 (Fla. 4th DCA Jan. 10, 2018)	FJ for P affirmed - substituted P acquires standing of original P even if the Note is with the clerk	Bank
4D	U.S. Bank Nat. Ass'n v. Clarke, 192 So. 3d 620 (Fla. 4th DCA 2016)	FJ for D reversed and remand for entry of FJ for P - copy is enough - do not need POA to testify	Bank
4D	U.S. Bank Nat'l Ass'n v. Becker, 211 So. 3d 142 (Fla. 4th DCA 2017)	CT treats allonge from entity outside chain as anomalous - result is blank indorsed note - IVD reversed	Bank
4D	U.S. Bank, Nat. Ass'n v. Angeloni, 199 So. 3d 492 (Fla. 4th DCA 2016)	IVD reversed and remand for new trial - Lost note terms met by P	Bank
4D	Wachovia Mortg., F.S.B. v. Goodwill, 199 So. 3d 346 (Fla. 4th DCA 2016)	IVD reversed - P proved that original lender merged/was purchased to become current P, this was enough for standing	Bank
4D	Wells Fargo Bank, N.A. v. Ayers, 219 So. 3d 89 (Fla. 4th DCA 2017)	IVD reversed and remand for new trial - lost note elements proved by habit evidence	Bank
4D	Werb v. Green Tree Servicing LLC, 231 So. 3d 483 (Fla. 4th DCA 2017)	possession of the note is key, not servicing - PH admitted but evidence insuff for various elements of damages	Bank
4D	Wilmington Sav. Fund Soc'y, FSB, v. Louissaint, 212 So. 3d 473 (Fla. 5th DCA 2017)	IVD reversed and remand for entry of FJ for P - if lost then later found, as long as copy matches note at trial, that is sufficient for standing at inception	Bank
5D	Bank of Am., N.A. v. Nash, 200 So. 3d 131 (Fla. 5th DCA 2016), review denied, SC16-1255, 2017 WL 6062032 (Fla. Jan. 12, 2017), and cert. denied, 137 S. Ct. 2195 (2017)	FJ for D reversed and remand for FJ for P - witness proved that the loan was never transferred, instead original lender merged with P	Bank
5D	Bank of New York Mellon for Bear Stearns Arm Tr., Mortgage Pass-Through Certificates, Series 2003-7 v. Thompson, 230 So. 3d 638 (Fla. 5th DCA 2017)	IVD reversed - Note matching good enough - lien priority apparently established when proving elements of foreclosure	Bank
5D	Deutsche Bank Nat. Tr. Co. v. Marciano, 190 So. 3d 166 (Fla. 5th DCA 2016)	FJ for D reversed - PSA enough to prove possession of blank indorsed note	Bank
5D	Le v. U.S. Bank, 165 So. 3d 776 (Fla. 5th DCA 2015)	FJ for P Affirmed - P proved endorsement was placed before filing suit	Bank
5D	Nationstar Mortg., LLC v. Kelly, 199 So. 3d 1051 (Fla. 5th DCA 2016), reh'g denied (Sept. 12, 2016)	IVD reversed and remand for new trial - evidence of presuit assignments enough for standing - possession irrelevant where original lender did not indorse the note	Bank
5D	Nationstar Mortgage, LLC v. Bo Chan, 226 So. 3d 330 (Fla. 5th DCA 2017)	Standing at inception establish so long as note filed with blank endorsement matches the copy attached - substituted party's standing at time of trial not addressed	Bank
5D	Nationstar Mortgage, LLC v. Kee Wing, 210 So. 3d 216 (Fla. 5th DCA 2017)	IVD reversed and remand for further proceedings - Lost note aff allowed in over obj and IVD reversed based on that	Bank

Exhibit 6n

Written Standing Related Appellate Decisions in Favor of Banks

DCA	CASE NAME	DISPOSITION	Who Won
5D	Taylor v. Deutsche Bank Nat. Tr. Co., 44 So. 3d 618 (Fla. 5th DCA 2010)	SJ for P Affirmed - held that written assignment of the note and mortgage from nominee of the original lender to bank was sufficient to confer upon bank the authority to foreclose the mortgage.	Bank
5D	US Bank Nat. Ass'n v. Laird, 200 So. 3d 176 (Fla. 5th DCA 2016)	IVD reversed and remand for new trial - copy of note with special endorsement to P was attached to complaint then admitted at trial in same condition, this is enough for standing	Bank
5D	US Bank, NA for Truman 2012 SC2 Title Tr. v. Glicken, 228 So. 3d 1194 (Fla. 5th DCA 2017)	FJ for D reversed, remanded for FJ for P - Note matches is sufficient-AOM not enough-standing is focused on the note	Bank
5D	Wells Fargo Bank, N.A. v. Morcom, 125 So. 3d 320 (Fla. 5th DCA 2013)	SJ for D reversed - holder of a note is enough to foreclose a mortgage	Bank

Exhibit 60

www.ingramcontent.com/pod-product-compliance
Lightning Source LLC
Chambersburg PA
CBHW020859080526
44589CB00011B/360